Al-Qaida's Jihad in Europe

Al-Qaida's Jihad in Europe

The Afghan-Bosnian Network

Evan Kohlmann

Oxford • New York

English edition
First published in 2004 by
Berg
Editorial offices:
1st Floor, Angel Court, 81 St Clements Street, Oxford, OX4 1AW, UK
175 Fifth Avenue, New York, NY 10010, USA

Berg is the imprint of Oxford International Publishers Ltd.

Library of Congress Cataloging-in-Publication Data
A catalogue record for this book is available from the Library of Congress.

British Library Cataloguing-in-Publication Data
A catalogue record for this book is available from the British Library.

ISBN 1 85973 802 8 (hardback)
1 85973 807 9 (paperback)

Typeset by JS Typesetting Ltd, Wellingborough, Northants.
Printed in the United Kingdom by Biddles Ltd, King's Lynn.

www.bergpublishers.com

Contents

List of Illustrations

Acknowledgments

I would like to personally thank a number of individuals for their invaluable assistance in researching and writing this work. First and foremost, a special thanks goes out to the extraordinarily dedicated past and present staff members of the Investigative Project, the Washington DC-based counterterrorism think-tank founded by *American Jihad* author Steven Emerson in 1995. Among them: Tamar Tesler, my long-time travelling colleague and confidant; Matthew Epstein, the source of infinite patience, intelligence, and sound advice; Lorenzo Vidino, a human encyclopedia on Al-Qaida in Europe, not to mention a good friend with whom I am proud to share this field; and executive director Steve Emerson. A hearty thanks also goes to my staunchly supportive family, friends, colleagues, and professors who have always encouraged my efforts, unusual as they may be.

Preface

In the summer of 2002, only months after the United States had been rocked by one of the worst incidences of terrorism in modern history, I found myself outside the Finsbury Park mosque in a low-income area of North London. The neighborhood is unique but unremarkable, with rows of dreary public housing projects, weathered English storefront shops, and an eclectic collection of Islamic bookstores and religious outreach centers. The mosque itself, set just back from the bustle of the main streets, is an imposing sight with its pale grey minaret rising above the adjoining rooftops.

I had come to Finsbury with a long-time colleague in hopes of speaking with the elusive then-Imam (head cleric) of the mosque: the notorious Egyptian dissident and loyal Al-Qaida apologist Abu Hamza al-Masri (also known as Mustafa Kamel). Abu Hamza is a horribly disfigured, menacing, and unapologetic supporter of Islamic militancy. Those immediately unfamiliar with Abu Hamza, aptly nicknamed 'Captain Hook' by various critics, will perhaps recall that his name has emerged in connection with the investigations of an uncoincidental number of international terrorists, including French nationals Zacarias Moussaoui (an alleged attempted 9/11 hijacker) and Djamel Beghal (accused of plotting a suicide bomb on the United States embassy in Paris); Briton Richard Reid (a would-be 'shoe-bomber'); and American Ernest James Ujamaa (who aimed to set up an Al-Qaida training camp in Bly, Oregon).

Outside the gate of Abu Hamza's mosque, a group of stern-looking young thugs were milling about, quite obviously in order to deter unwelcome visitors. Once inside the center, as I ascended the stairwell to the cramped office of the legendary Abu Hamza, I was much better able to assess the threat posed by his supporters. I soon discovered that the cleric was not lying when he described how hundreds of followers gathered at the mosque every Friday to hear his often hateful sermons. Young men, some clothed in military fatigues and Taliban-style dress, paced back and forth between rooms as we patiently waited for our audience with the mysterious Egyptian exile.

I had many, many unanswered questions I wanted to pose to Abu Hamza – there will perhaps never be enough time to ask them all. But once we had settled into a more flowing conversation, I finally approached an unusual subject of much interest to me: the 'prominent' role of the Arab-Afghans and Al-Qaida in military operations during the horrific Bosnian civil war of the mid-1990s. I seemed to have struck a chord: Abu Hamza, usually a somewhat reluctant interviewee, began to pontificate at some length about the Bosnian Muslim dilemma and his own time spent there with the *mujahideen*. He grew curious, perhaps even a bit suspicious, at my particular interest in Bosnia, especially as I asked him more pointed questions about a former Algerian rival in Zenica and the apparent failure of the Islamic revolution in the Balkans. Yet, with the hint of a guarded smirk, he nonetheless continued, evidently unshaken. The cleric had initially told us that our interview would last no more than 30 minutes; by my best count, it ended up running on for almost 2 hours.

During our prolonged discussion of Bosnia, Usama Bin Laden, and 9/11, several young Muslim adherents sat silently on the floor of Abu Hamza's dingy office; it was difficult to tell if they were present for security reasons, or simply out of their devotion to the eccentric cleric. One of the men seated patiently below us – sporting long, flowing blond hair, blue eye, and a scraggly beard – was quite obviously a Muslim convert of Western European, Canadian, or American origin. In studying him, my immediate thought was of Christophe Caze, a French convert to Islam, a Bosnian war veteran, and another former young fanatic admirer of Abu Hamza discussed at length later in this work. I could easily imagine Caze sitting on this same floor at Abu Hamza's side; that is, shortly prior to Caze's forming a suburban terrorist gang in 1996 with other extremist Muslims who had received military training in Bosnia. In fact, this is exactly what Abu Hamza specializes in: exploiting regional conflicts such as the wars in the Balkans and Afghanistan in order to recruit idealistic young men for a life of *jihad* amongst the international legions of Al-Qaida. It was clear, as I walked through the mosque and examined the materials sold in the lobby bookstore, that Abu Hamza's piercing fascination (and sometimes frustration) with Bosnia is shared by many of his contemporaries, supporters, and sympathizers among the global Sunni radical religious trend.

But simply because the militant fundamentalist minority finds the subject noteworthy does not necessarily make it so. This will perhaps raise the basic question that is undoubtedly on the minds of most who will read this work: of all the places that Al-Qaida has extended its influence to, why study Bosnia so critically? The answer to that question is not so simple; it stems from a number of interrelated factors. First, the deployment of Arab fighters in Bosnia who were generally loyal to the *jihadi* leadership in Afghanistan exploded in the mid-1990s into numbers sometimes estimated even to exceed 5,000. Second, this massive and significant migration of Arab-Afghans to Bosnia occurred at an early stage of the Al-Qaida movement, meaning that the experience had long-lasting effects both practically and ideologically on the terrorist group. Third, Bosnia's unique geographic position directly between Western Europe and the Middle East was the ideal jumping-off point for organizational expansion of the movement into Italy, France, Germany, Austria, Canada, and the United Kingdom. It provided an environment where trained foreign Muslim fighters arriving from Afghanistan could mingle with unsophisticated bug eager terrorist recruits from Western Europe, and could form new plans for the future of the *jihad*. No such contact had ever occurred before in the short history of Al-Qaida, and it provided the organization and its radical membership with limitless possibilities for development and growth.

Simply put, after six years of researching Usama Bin Laden and Al-Qaida starting in the mid to late 1990s, I could not help but notice the particularly enduring influence of the legends of *jihad* and martyrdom persisting from, of all places, the Bosnian civil war. Looming larger than the writings of Shaykh Abdullah Azzam, Shaykh Omar Abdel Rahman, or even Usama Bin Laden, the stories of the men who lost their lives fighting in a supposed Muslim 'holy war' against Eastern European 'crusaders' are much more telling of the history and goals of Al-Qaida, not merely to the organization's followers, but moreover, to the world at large. These men epitomized the sacrificial ideology first pioneered by Azzam that would lead them to enthusiastically offer their lives in exchange for paradise, serving as quixotic 'armed humanitarians' and defending the Muslim *ummah* against a host of real and imaginary enemies. Thus, the importance of the conflict in the Balkans has been repeatedly and unfortunately understated. Americans and Europeans often wonder how Al-Qaida has so effectively penetrated Europe and the West, establishing terrorist cells across Italy, France, Denmark, Austria, Germany, Sweden, Spain, the United Kingdom, Canada, and even the United States. Some of the most important answers can be found in Bosnia, where the cream of the Arab-Afghans tested their battle skills in the post-Soviet era and mobilized a new generation of hardened guerrilla zealots with only two unswerving priorities: armed combat and Islamic fundamentalism.

Using a wide range of open sources (from international media to regional and ethnic news) to offer chronological and historical perspective, this is the untold story of a new generation of transnational underground terrorists, as related through declassified intelligence reports and court documents, secret Al-Qaida internal records, discussions with eyewitnesses and government investigators, and Arab-Afghan propaganda materials. Amateur Bosnian fundamentalist videotapes edited and distributed by Al-Qaida representatives in London have been particularly helpful in his research and analysis, offering substantial visual evidence to the legend of the Arab guerrillas in the Balkans. It is my hope that compending this history together in a single volume will offer readers a unique and compelling perspective of the global *jihad* of the Arab-Afghans, led by Usama Bin Laden and the Al-Qaida military federation.

Prologue: 'In the Land of Ice Cream'

Excerpt from an article in *Assirat Al-Mustaqeem* (*The Straight Path*), January 2000, by Abdallah Abd al-Aziz. Translation provided by Betsy Hiel.

Behind a wall of tears, he looks into the wide horizon, and finds nothing but despair. Again and again, he looks, but sees nothing worth seeing. The place is a big prison of high rises, rows upon rows of them. They call it civilization.

Poor fellow, Abu al-Mawt ['Father of Death']. He imagines he was back in Afghanistan. He wants to look and see the horizon. But he realizes that high walls surround him on every side, like a noose. The streets are full of [people acting like] animals, walking in every direction, totally resigned to Satan. Poor fellow, Abu al-Mawt, for he is a strict fundamentalist. He believes that women should not show their thighs in public, for it is a sin.

He looks upon the sky, upon the land, and his eyes come back with a harvest of sorrow. The naked thighs he has to see . . . poor fellow, Abu al-Mawt. He is a fundamentalist and the women here do not respect his fundamentalism. Animals are everywhere. The sound of laughter rings all around. The noise and voices of animals accompany the din of pop and rock music. Smoke rises everywhere. From mouths, cars, trains, a charred life with an overpowering stench, the stench of sex. The stench of hell and its misery. Differences erode. Women are men and men are women, females are males and males are females, wives are mothers and un-married women are mothers too, husbands are fathers and unmarried men are fathers too!

Poor fellow, Abu al-Mawt. This is the land of the infidels. Poor fellow, Abu al-Mawt. He is prisoner of his sorrows, of his tight chest. Abu al-Mawt is a prisoner of civilization. Abu al-Mawt is a prisoner in the land of the infidels. He sits down to have a cup of tea. The coffee shop is beautiful, attractive, relatively respectable. Not much whoring is going on. Michael Jackson is less terrible (on the ears – being male) than Madonna. The half dressed are less sinful than the undressed. Abu al-Mawt decided to pay for his tea. He does not dare to walk around without money in his pocket.

He puts his hand in his pocket to get out the money and he finds a book. He looks at it, it is the Qur`an. Poor fellow, Abu al-Mawt, he is suffering from amnesia. He opens the Qur`an and reads: 'A Gift from Abu Jihad to Abu al-Mawt.' Tears stream down his cheeks – Abu Jihad was his best friend. They were comrades in their love for God, but Allah has favored Abu Jihad with death. Poor fellow, Abu al-Mawt. His sorrow swells and he sobs. He sees the traces of blood on the Qur`an. Abu Jihad was killed with the Qur`an in his hand.

Abu al-Mawt's sorrow soars, his misery is endless. The blood of Abu Jihad is scented, like a perfume. But, Abu al-Mawt is surrounded by the smell of hamburgers. Poor fellow, Abu al-Mawt, he is suffering from amnesia . . . He feels he is a prisoner of his own skin. Poor fellow. Blood boils in his veins. His head is bursting. He feels lonely.

Poor fellow, Abu al-Mawt is lonely, in exile. His home is lost. He sits and remembers and his heart is bursting, he is shaking like a feather. The [guesthouse] is a beehive of action . . . A group is going tomorrow to the *Al-Farooq* training camp . . . The village of Pabi, the gate of al-Tal, the river of Jalalabad, the mountains of Jaji, the desert of Kandahar, the snow of Jerdiz, a mortar shell, the dust of battle, the frontline, the 'Green Brigade.'

Poor fellow, Abu al-Mawt, carries a heavy burden on his shoulders. He dries his tears and chokes up with sobs. His steps are heavy from exhaustion. He moves his lips as if he is saying something. He is perhaps reciting verses of a poem: 'Would it be that after the Prophet has abandoned their land, you would accept to prosper among the infidels? Haven't you found the path of the Prophet, haven't you heard the songs of the caravan [of martyrs]?'

–1–

The Afghan Crucible

'A small group: they are the ones who carry convictions for this religion. An even smaller group from this group are the ones who flee from this worldly life in order to act upon these convictions. And an even smaller group from this elite group, are the ones who sacrifice their souls and their blood in order to bring victory to these convictions and ambitions. So they are the cream of the cream of the cream . . . It is not possible to reach glory except by traversing this Path. It is not possible for the structures of [Islam] to be established, nor for its banner to be raised, nor for its vessel to be launched, except by traversing this Path. This Path is one: the Blessed Path of Jihad . . . Indeed, the manuscripts of history are not inscribed except with the blood of these martyrs, except with the stories of these martyrs, except with the examples of these martyrs.'

> Shaykh Abdullah Azzam, 'Martyrs: The Building Blocks of Nations'

'O! You Muslims, You have slept for a long time, long enough for the tyrants to take control over you. You accepted to live as slaves and submitted to tyrants. Now the time has come to revolt and destroy the shackles of slavery.'

> Shaykh Abdullah Azzam, 'Who is Poor to his Lord'

To fully comprehend the Islamic *jihad* in Bosnia, one must first appreciate the significance of the Soviet-Afghan war of the 1980s through the eyes of the ideological 'godfather' of the contemporary Sunni Islamic revolutionaries, Shaykh Abdullah Yusuf Azzam. In the minds of Azzam and his successors, the *jihad* in Afghanistan is treated as a critical turning point in modern world history and considered a basic blueprint for the larger struggle to ultimately 're-create' an omnipotent theocratic empire, stretching from Morocco to the Philippines. Just as in Bosnia, the young men who came from Saudi Arabia, Egypt, Algeria, Yemen, and elsewhere to sacrifice their blood and souls in the battle to 'save' Afghanistan from the infidel communists are revered to this day as heroes of the highest order. Their faces and their names are legendary, even beyond the traditional Muslim world. These inexperienced but unusually persistent fighters simply referred to themselves as *mujahideen*, or 'Islamic holy warriors.' In the Western discourse, they have become collectively known during the years since as the 'Arab-Afghans.'

At first glance, no one could have imagined the lasting significance of the Soviet invasion of Afghanistan in December 1979. Afghanistan was not an American Cold War ally; in fact, the United States had more or less consciously ignored opportunities during the 1960s and 1970s to draw Afghanistan into the Western fold. With most attention focused on the importance of neighboring Pakistan, Afghanistan was largely left to its own devices. By 1978, it was already in the shadows of Soviet-inspired Marxist rule. However, vicious internal power struggles and public discontent with the communist regime threatened to topple the political status quo that the Soviets had carefully constructed. Fearing the collapse of Marxism in Afghanistan, the Soviets invaded under the pretext of restoring order and replaced the ruling government with one more beholden to the interests of Moscow. The sporadic rebellion in the tribal hinterlands against the reformed Afghan communist regime in early 1979 was not predicted to have much of a future. In the face of thousands of arriving Soviet troops, one former United States Ambassador to Afghanistan even estimated that 'the Russians would wipe out the resistance in months.'[1]

But rather than achieving a quick victory, the Soviets found themselves surrounded by a relentless guerrilla adversary. Countless Afghanis joined the Islamic resistance, which was organized into several native *mujahideen* organizations with headquarters in Peshawar, Pakistan. Though these Afghan parties were theoretically structured along Islamic ideological lines, there is good reason to believe that many local guerrillas who fought in the war against the Soviets had motivations outside of religion, including jealousy and greed. *Mujahideen* units in Afghanistan often switched party allegiances, and even entered into alliances with the supposedly 'infidel' Soviets against their own indigenous Afghan Muslim rivals.

Nevertheless, the flurry of activity in Peshawar caught the imagination of the entire Islamic world, far beyond the borders of battered Afghanistan. Notions of universal Muslim 'brotherhood' were awakened after years of neglect and misuse. A number of Arab and Islamic states rallied to the cause, arranging for vast amounts of money and weapons to be channeled to the *mujahideen* parties in Pakistan. This fundraising and mobilization drive was not restricted to official channels either; many wealthy and pious private citizens of Saudi Arabia and other Gulf states donated massive amounts of money and material to the cause.

In certain fanatic circles, the indignity and injustice of the Soviet invasion had aroused a much more enraged response. One Muslim cleric in particular – Shaykh Abdullah Azzam – had an extraordinary obsession with the issue of Afghanistan (Figure 1). Born in the Palestinian village of Ass-ba'ah Al-Hartiyeh (near Jenin) in 1941, Azzam had become firmly disillusioned with the Arab struggle against Israel by the late 1960s. Although he had initially joined the Palestinian guerrilla forces based in Jordan, Abdullah Azzam regarded the secular nationalist principles championed by fighters that referred to themselves as *mujahideen* as utter hypocrisy.

Figure 1. Shaykh Abdullah Yusuf Azzam, founder of the *Makhtab-e-Khidamat al-Mujahideen* ('Mujahideen Services Office') in Peshawar, Pakistan.

Angry and alienated, he left Jordan to eventually teach at the King Abdelaziz University in Jeddah, Saudi Arabia.[2] While there, Azzam became preoccupied with the idea of *jihad*, or 'Islamic holy struggle.' A student and close friend later explained the realization that Azzam had while teaching in Jeddah:

> Sometimes you are looking for justice in this life or something more to give to the Muslims all over the world and when you see the world slipping [from] the Muslims everywhere, you wake up, the *jihad* wakes up inside of you. You see them in Bosnia,

Sudan, Somalia, Kashmir, Afghanistan, Albania, Egypt, Syria . . . You think about these things and if you don't get together and if you don't hold hands and believe in the same cause, then others will destroy you without you knowing. You have to do something . . . *jihad* is the only savior.[3]

Azzam became utterly convinced that the Islamic world was under siege by its enemies; at any moment, they would spring forth and devour the last remnants of the glorious Muslim *ummah* (community). The struggle to propagate Islam was no longer an evolutionary campaign; either Islam would triumph by the sword over its unjust and disbelieving enemies, or it would be swept into the dustbin of history. Azzam declared his new personal philosophy to be *'jihad* and the rifle alone: no negotiations, no conferences, and no dialogues.'[4]

For Azzam, the invasion of Afghanistan was the fulfillment of divine prophecy. A European people, imbued with the ideas of secularism and modernization, had swept into a Muslim land to conquer, pillage, and wipe the land clean of ancient culture and religion. The scattered Islamic resistance there faced a goliath super-power opponent with a seemingly insurmountable supply of ammunition and men. With his message of apocalyptic religious confrontation, Azzam quickly travelled to Peshawar to offer his services to the *mujahideen*. His organizing abilities and personal charisma were legendary; his followers bragged that 'Sheikh Abdullah is a person who even his enemy respects . . . because he says what he believes.' They often lauded his unparalleled ability to unify and energize disparate Muslim factions: '[Azzam] has no problems with anybody. He always says stop speaking and let's do, let's work, stop fighting, then serve the name of the organization. Serve what the organization comes to serve: the cause. He wanted to get everyone together.'[5] Azzam was unshakably committed to his own ideological principles; either the holy struggle in Afghanistan would succeed, or he would become a *shaheed* (martyr) and die fighting there.

Azzam's fervor about the idea of *jihad* only grew as he witnessed the cruel and bloody warfare waged in the mountains of Afghanistan. He quickly developed his own independent mission in Peshawar. Ultimately, Azzam sought not only to evict the Russian armies from Afghanistan, but moreover, to subsequently remove all 'infidel' regimes and to reestablish the rule of a greater Islamic empire. He planned to use the *jihad* in Afghanistan to recruit and train Muslim guerrilla fighters from across the Middle East and South Asia. The first of these Arab fighters stayed in Azzam's 'guest house' in Peshawar, which by the mid-1980s had become *Makhtab-e-Khidamat Al-Mujahideen* (MAK), the *'Mujahideen* Services Office.' Prior to 1985, there were only about thirty-five steadfast foreign volunteers based in Peshawar. All operations were extremely secret: standing orders were left that 'no Arab brother was to be found in the office.'[6] At that time, the nascent MAK even lacked a dependable system for bringing recruits into Afghanistan and training them in combat tactics. Consequently, during the first 5 years of the war, foreign Islamist leaders like Abdullah Azzam primarily played roles as financiers and facilitators of the *jihad*, not as military commanders.

The major turning point came in early 1985, when Azzam reached an agreement with Abd-i-Rab Rasoul Sayyaf, the chairman of the indigenous fundamentalist guerrilla coalition known as the Islamic Unity of Afghan *Mujahideen*. Sayyaf agreed to allow the use of the *Salman Al-Farisi* training camp (bordering the Kunar province of Afghanistan) to specifically train Arab recruits. By April of that year, twenty-five volunteers were enrolled in the first official 'Arab-Afghan' *jihad* training course. One of these first volunteers was a Saudi Muslim activist and fundraiser living in Tucson, Arizona – Wael Hamza Jalaidan – who quickly became a top aide to Abdullah Azzam and other prominent figures in the Arab-Afghan network. Jalaidan later explained their vision behind the training camps:

> We wished that everyone coming after us should pass through the same method of preparation – by participating and sharing – as we had started with . . . after morning prayers we would get together for Qur'an recitation, while after the afternoon prayer, we would get together to read some *hadith* [religious narratives attributed to the Prophet Mohammed] and benefit from them. After that, if there were any military operations, we would participate in them.[7]

Azzam's plan was not simply to singularly indoctrinate the volunteers in combat tactics; rather, in teaching unity of religion and thought, he sought to create a brotherhood that would obliterate any ethnic or regional distinctions. Into Afghanistan would come a mixed group of Egyptians, Palestinians, Saudis, and Yemenis. But, when they left, only Muslim holy warriors would remain.

The class of would-be guerrillas grew so quickly that Sayyaf was soon forced to cordon off an entire section of the *Al-Sadda* camp specifically for the training of Arab recruits.[8] In 1988, *Al-Sadda* was described in the founding minutes of Al-Qaida as an 'open camp' from which the best 'brothers' would be selected to join the new terrorist organization.[9] Indeed, a corresponding number of *Al-Sadda* graduates have gone on to perform key roles in the international *jihad* movement. A former Al-Qaida member testified in a United States court that Ramzi Yousef (the mastermind behind the 1993 World Trade Center bombing in New York) was himself one of the eager students at *Al-Sadda* during this period: 'near the border between Pakistan and Afghanistan, we got camp over there, and at that time run by Ibrahim al-Rari, and I saw [Ramzi Yousef] over there and he got trained over there.'[10]

Azzam's militancy was a magnet for other would-be revolutionaries – including a young and wealthy student of his, an anonymous upstart from a powerful and well-connected Saudi family who abandoned a middling business career for a life as the primary private financier and organizer of the growing Arab *mujahideen* forces fighting in Afghanistan: Usama Bin Muhammad Bin Laden. What Bin Laden lacked in actual religious knowledge he made up for with a fiery ideological zeal and deep, generous pockets. At his last public press conference, Azzam spoke of the key role Bin Laden was playing in the growing Arab-Afghan movement:

> He came himself, with his wealth, in the way of Allah, and he is paying for [*mujahideen*] tickets and looking after their families, paying for their rent and their transport, and their sustenance inside Afghanistan. He is in the frontline, where the fighting is . . . One hundred Arabs have given their lives for Allah. What have they come for? Someone like Usama Bin Ladin, like Wael Jalaidan, and others from leading families in Saudi Arabia . . . [who] have come in search of paradise. They believe that there is a God and that there is a paradise, and that life is cheap.[11]

Yet, the initial performance of the Arab-Afghans in actual battle was something less than legendary. Many of the new recruits came from upper middle-class families in the Arabian Gulf region; they knew much more about engineering and business than armed combat. These ragtag guerrillas were often a liability to both themselves and any Afghan *mujahideen* unit willing to fight alongside them. The native Afghan 'holy warriors' were typically very suspicious of their new Arab allies, regarding these foreigners as 'Gucci' soldiers who were out of touch with the social and religious fabric of the Afghan people.[12] In fact, a number of heated arguments between the Arabs and the Afghans over money, training, and military strategy largely precluded effective cooperation in battle.

Nevertheless, the limited experience in warfare gained by the Arabs was incalculably important. Blood and sweat bound these soldiers together, each earnestly convinced that death in battle would lead to *shuhadaa* (martyrdom) and eternal paradise. One Arab fighter, after witnessing the near annihilation of his unit by a Russian air attack, commented, 'for me, this battle was really a big boost that motivated me to carry on. It gave us the assurance that no one is hit except if that was destined for him by Allah.'[13] Paradoxically, every foreign guerrilla that the Soviets managed to kill simply encouraged a greater bloodlust; those that remained alive felt 'cheated' and sought ever more desperately to achieve martyrdom in the name of Islam.

In the early months of 1988, Azzam's greatest dream finally reached fruition. The war in Afghanistan appeared to be coming to a close, and against all odds, a diverse, fractious group of Muslim 'holy warriors' had ultimately defeated the mighty Russian bear. Azzam and the foreign legion of mostly Arab *mujahideen* fighters had played at best a minor role in the war, but that victory was considered quite a seminal event. On a fundraising trip to the United States, Azzam proclaimed to his followers, 'Oh brothers, after Afghanistan, nothing in the world is impossible for us anymore. There are no super powers or mini-powers – what matters is the willpower that springs from our religious belief.'[14] This armed fundamentalist movement revolutionized contemporary Islamic politics by offering an unprecedented radical alternative to peace and cooperation with the *kuffar* (non-Islamic 'infidels').

With thousands of Arab recruits arriving regularly in Pakistani north-western border towns to get training to fight the 'enemies of Islam,' Azzam publicly announced the foundation of Al-Qaida, or the 'Solid Foundation.' In his monumental treatise published in *Al-Jihad* magazine (the MAK's official newsletter), he reasoned that every revolutionary ideology needs a rugged, elite cadre to protect it, inspire it, and lead it to ultimate victory. This Leninist-style vanguard, hardened by toil and sacrifice, 'constitutes the solid foundation for the desired society.' According to Azzam, the war in Afghanistan emblemized a divine 'trial by fire' of the vanguard; it was a test of their true commitment to establish Islam at any cost. Only by continued armed struggle would the unified strength of the Muslims be brought to bear on their supposed enemies. In concluding, Azzam issued what he referred to as 'the final call': 'We shall continue the Jihad no matter how long the way is until the last breath and the last beating of the pulse or we see the Islamic state established.'[15] One of Azzam's top lieutenants, Tamim al-Adnani declared to a rapt audience later that year, 'the best thing is [to] continue Jihad. Nothing but Jihad . . . Even after liberation of Afghanistan, even after the Islamic government, [the *mujahideen*] will not stop. They will go up to the Muslim countries of Russia, Islamic republics. They will go down to Palestine, to [Jerusalem].' Moreover, Al-Adnani offered this chilling addendum: '[if] Anybody stops in their way, Oh my God! Smash them! Any ruler, [if] he will not let us go, we will go by force! Jihad!'[16]

But despite its pretences toward strong unity, by 1988, the Arab-Afghan movement was beset by quarrelling among some of its 'founding fathers.' The factioning reached even the highest levels of the *mujahideen* – including between long-time partners Abdullah Azzam and Usama Bin Laden. Bin Laden's fanatic enthusiasm to immediately spread *jihad* worldwide had occasionally clashed with the more patient and long-term strategy of Azzam. While alive, Azzam had pressed for a final, complete victory in Afghanistan and the creation of an Islamic state there before attempting to 'export the revolution' elsewhere. However, the younger, hot-headed Bin Laden had other ideas. Even before Azzam's murder, some of Bin Laden's followers approached him and told him, 'You shouldn't be staying with Abdullah Azzam. He doesn't do anything about the regimes – Saudi, Egyptian, Algerian. He's just talking about Afghanistan.'[17]

Following the legendary battles at Jaji in 1987 and the founding of Al-Qaida, Bin Laden quietly distanced himself from Azzam and turned his attention in new directions. According to Mamdouh Mahmud Salim (also known as Abu Hajer al-Iraqi), one of the original founders of Al-Qaida, Bin Laden 'did not announce his separation publicly because he is averse to disunity.'[18] The problem essentially stemmed from a long-term strategic dispute between Azzam and Bin Laden. Bin Laden was interested in centralization, regimentation, and utmost secrecy. Using the Afghan war as a cover, he wanted to segregate all the foreign *jihadi* recruits together and train them as one body – preparing them as a mobile international Islamist blitzkrieg unit, trained to seize power quickly and violently through the use of terrorism. Azzam was more of a practicalist; by contrast, he was more concerned with forging long-term bonds with Afghani Islamist allies in hopes of establishing a future Islamic state there and consolidating *mujahideen* power. With Afghanistan as the 'solid foundation,' Azzam hoped to then later use a unified Muslim army – comprised of Arab and Afghan alike – to 'liberate' the entire Islamic world.

Shaykh Tamim al-Adnani later attempted to explain the uneasy schism: 'It was as if [Bin Laden] wanted to profit from the jihad rather than the jihad profiting from us, whereas we wanted the jihad to benefit from us rather than us benefiting from the jihad. The conceptual difference is a very minor one since it was jihad in either case.'[19] Enaam Arnaout (also known as Abu Mahmoud al-Suri), director of a purportedly charitable Al-Qaida front group called the Benevolence International Foundation (BIF, also known as Lajnat al-Birr al-Islamiyya), likewise dismissed the squabble as a 'minor' one. At the time, Arnaout took pains to emphasize the strong and enduring relationship between Azzam and Bin Laden, despite the troublesome meddling of some of their associates who Arnaout deemed to be spies for foreign intelligence agencies.[20] Even when Azzam's inner circle openly confronted their revered chief with the problem posed by the rising star of Bin Laden, he calmly insisted to them that 'if there ever was a representative of Allah on earth, it would most likely be Usama bin Laden.'[21]

Though a number of Azzam's closest followers were reluctant to trust him, the apparent vast majority of the Arab-Afghan movement (including its most radical elements) greatly admired the awkward but subtly charismatic figure of Bin Laden. Moreover, a new wave of arriving *jihadi* recruits, mostly 'young Muslim kids, without passports, running away from who knows what,' idolized the unassuming Saudi cast-out – he represented the embodiment of their own distant dreams for personal redemption and glory.[22] Among these radical youth, talk of overthrowing hated Middle Eastern governments in a suicidal wave of terror resonated much more clearly than manning an artillery post during a cold night in a desolate corner of Afghanistan. In a crude attempt to mimic the early struggles of the Prophet Mohammed, these ragtag soldiers intended to use the time spent in exile to strengthen their ranks and prepare for a promised apocalyptic holy war against the excommunicated 'infidel regimes,' Jews, Hindus, and anyone else who stood in the way of creating a global Islamic empire – a philosophy known in Arabic as *Takfir waal Hijra*.

By 1990, the Arab-Afghan movement had certainly come full circle: a small group of motivated fundamentalists, upset by the degraded state of the Muslim world, had been transformed in five short years into an influential transnational terrorist army backed by the fabulous wealth of Usama Bin Laden, the more-or-less undisputed 'prince' of the movement following the mysterious assassination of Abdullah Azzam in 1989. Suspicion in the murder of Azzam now centers largely around Egyptian Muslim radicals who had fought long battles with the hardline Palestinian cleric over money and control of the Arab-Afghan movement. The Egyptians craved Bin Laden's riches and saw him as more sympathetic to their grand schemes. Meanwhile, according to former Saudi Arab-Afghan Hassan abd-Rabbuh al-Surayhi, in the aftermath of Azzam's assassination and the Soviet withdrawal from Afghanistan, a mass of predominantly Egyptian *mujahideen* began to congregate at the residence of Usama Bin Laden in Peshawar.[23]

The Egyptians were eager to win the young Saudi's attention and support, and invited a number of journalists and representatives of 'relief agencies' with them to 'put him in the spotlight.' Asked whether this was done deliberately to win Bin Laden's financial backing, al-Surayhi replied, 'Bin-Ladin's finances were not a secret to anyone and I think the Egyptians wanted to exploit this angle.' They cozied up to the ambitious Saudi expatriate and convinced him to wage an expansive global *jihad* against the international enemies of Al-Qaida. Surayhi further ventured that '[p]erhaps [Bin Laden] accepted the idea in order to become an amir so that all the Islamic jihad groups would be under his control, especially those that are in Egypt which are famous and well known.'[24] In the end, irrespective of the reason, with Bin Laden's eager blessings, the Arab-Afghans were free to turn their attention to new targets outside of the borders of Afghanistan.

Soon their gaze, along with much of the rest of the world, became locked on the horrific plight of Bosnian Muslims caught in the worst armed conflict in Europe since 1945. The story of the Arab-Afghan *mujahideen* struggle in Bosnia is long, complicated, and often understated in its importance. Under the destabilizing influence of a cadre of Al-Qaida disciples, a string of towns in central Bosnia developed into the new frontier posts of Islamic *jihad* in a post-Cold War world. The cream of the militant Islamist crop gathered there to train and test a new generation of idealistic holy warriors bent on offering their lives as sacrifice towards the creation of an imagined Muslim empire. The interactions that took place during the war were monumental in their importance: hundreds of Arab *mujahideen* veterans caught in the civil turmoil in Afghanistan and with nowhere else to go found asylum in Bosnia. This new refuge, close to both the heart of Europe and the Middle East, provided an excellent tactical base for espionage, fundraising, and terrorist activities by Al-Qaida.

Moreover, the influence of European culture and technology also gave the Arab-Afghan movement a big boost: according to representatives of the *mujahideen*, the influx of Westernized European Muslims to the fundamentalist movement

> . . . was instrumental to, not just the jihad in Bosnia, but the world-wide jihad, for what they managed to achieve. And you think this is an exaggeration, but by the hands of the brothers they did many things that you wouldn't believe. Books were translated and produced, in the front-lines, because you had the English brothers that could speak English and the Arab brothers that could speak Arabic and a bit of English, and they go together and translated books about Jihad. Now, these books are guiding other brothers back to the Jihad again. They've computerized whole computer networks because of their computer knowledge.[25]

Perhaps what is most striking about the story of the *jihad* in Bosnia is that, unlike Afghanistan, it did not take place in a region far from the reach of American influence; rather, quite to the contrary, these *mujahideen* were able to organize and prosper right under the nose of United States and United Nations troops in the midst of an abortive international peacekeeping mission.

Notes

1. Eliot, Theodore L., Jr. *Gorbachev's Afghan Gambit*. Institute for Foreign Policy Analysis: Cambridge MA, 1988, p. 1.
2. 'Sheikh Abdullah Azzam.' Azzam Publications: London UK. http://www.azzam.com/html/storiesabdullahazzam.htm.
3. Emerson, Steven and Khalid Duran. 'Interview with Abu Iman.' 4 November 1993.
4. 'Sheikh Abdullah Azzam.' Op. cit.
5. Emerson, Steven and Khalid Duran. Op. cit.
6. Muhammad, Basil, *Al-Ansaru l'Arab fi Afghanistan*. Committee for Islamic Benevolence Publications.
7. Ibid., p. 112.
8. Ibid., p. 183.
9. Government's Response to Defendant's Position Paper as to Sentencing Factors.' *United States of America v. Enaam M. Arnaout*. United States District Court Northern District of Illinois Eastern Division. Case #: 02 CR 892, p. 38.
10. *United States v. Usama bin Laden, et al.* S(7) 98 Cr. 1023 (LBS). United States District Court, Southern District of New York. Trial Transcript, 20 February 2001, p. 28.

11. Videotape of the last press conference of Shaykh Abdallah Azzam.

12. Kabbani, Shaykh Muhammad Hisham and Matten Siddiqui. 'Usama Bin Laden: The Complete File.' *The Muslim Magazine*, October 1898, pp. 20, 23, 62, 67.

13. Muhammad, Basil. Op. cit., p. 187.

14. Emerson, Steven. *Jihad in America*. SAE Productions (for PBS): Washington DC. Originally aired 21 November 1994. Running time: 1 hour.

15. Azzam, Dr Abdallah. 'Al-Qa`ida.' *Al-Jihad*, 1988, 41, April, p. 46.

16. Emerson, Op. cit.

17. Engelberg, Stephen. 'One Man and a Global Web of Violence.' *The New York Times*, 14 January 2001, http://www.nytimes.com/2001/01/14/world/14JIHA.html.

18. Muhammad, Basil. Op. cit., p. 200.

19. Muhammad, Basil. Op. cit., p. 201.

20. Muhammad, Basil. Op. cit., p. 226.

21. Muhammad, Basil. Op. cit., p. 226.

22. Miller, Judith. 'A Witness Against Al Qaeda Says the US Let Him Down.' The New York Times, 3 June 2000.

23. Al-Banyan, Hasin. 'Saudi "Afghan" Talks About Involvement With al-Qa`ida, Bin-Ladin, Related Topics.' *Al-Sharq al-Awsat*, 25 November 2001.

24. Ibid.

25. Azzam Publications. 'In the Hearts of Green Birds.' Audiocassette tape transliterated by Salman Dhia Al-Deen, http://www.azzam.com.

–2–

Jihad Comes to Bosnia

The Charter of Islamic Struggle: We as Muslims have been given the task to realize the supremacy of the law of God on earth and of not allowing that any group on earth govern without the law of God. We fight whoever refuses that and refuses obedience [to God] . . . The fight is imposed on us to remove the apostate ruler from the land of Islam, to fight those who support them and their laws, to impose the caliphate, to revenge Palestine, Spain, the Balkans, the Islamic Republics in Russia and to free the Muslim prisoners. Our enemies are: Christians, Jews, apostates, those who adore the cow and fire, our secular rulers that replace the laws of Islam and the hypocrites . . . Jihad has been introduced to spread God's religion and to destroy any ruler that is not subject to the adoration of God . . . Fighting the infidels has the purpose of exalting the revelation of God.

Document found by Italian police at the Islamic Cultural Institute (ICI) in Milan

The civil conflict in the former Yugoslavia first erupted in June 1991 after Slovenia and Croatia declared their respective independence from Serbia. At first, the war was relatively subdued: Slovenia's war with the Serbs ended in less than a month with under seventy dead. However, the other states of the former Yugoslavia did not win peace so easily. Croatia's war of secession against local Serb rebels backed by the Yugoslav army lasted six months and killed an estimated 10,000 people. A tenuous ceasefire finally took hold there in January 1992. Unfortunately, while bringing relative peace to Croatia, that ceasefire also opened up the possibility of renewed civil conflict in other newly independent provinces. Of the various parts of the former Yugoslavia, Bosnia-Herzegovina was a particularly troubled region: divided into a fractious, multi-ethnic patchwork since the days of the Ottoman Empire, it had a long history of religious and political tensions. Not surprisingly, ethnic Serbs rebelled against Bosnia's self-declared independent government in April 1992.

When the carnage of the war began unfolding that spring, the Muslim-led Bosnian government was outgunned, outmanned, and almost entirely on the defensive. Western diplomatic condemnation of ethnic Serb offences was met with deaf ears, and the embattled Muslims struggled to hold out against a superior military force. This grave predicament captured the attention of sympathetic Muslims elsewhere in the world, and particularly in the Middle East. During the war, thousands of young men driven by a warped sense of religious chivalry travelled to Bosnia ostensibly in the hopes of defending the ancient and threatened Muslim community in the Balkans. The first of these volunteers to arrive were full of enthusiasm, but were without widespread military experience or any significant organized leadership. A glaring lack of organization naturally also entailed a regular shortage of basic military equipment and supplies. These early 'mujahideen' typically joined Bosnian civil defence forces, which by their own estimates 'proved largely ineffective.'[1] Not surprisingly, these foreign soldiers were disappointed at the little impact their efforts were making.

It would not be long before a much more serious effort was made by distant Islamic extremists to aid the suffering Bosnian Muslims. These young men, galvanized by hateful religious and political ideologies, were determined to turn the global tide against the 'infidel' regimes, even those outside the traditional boundaries of the Middle East. 'At the forefront' of the movement of Arab volunteer soldiers to Bosnia were the *mujahideen* veterans of the anti-Soviet *jihad* in Afghanistan, which had served as 'an institute for the teaching of jihad' and was the birthplace of Al-Qaida.[2]

The Bosnian war happened to occur at a propitious time for the Arab-Afghans. In January 1993, the Pakistani government, eager to put the Afghan *jihad* in the past, ordered the closure of Arab *mujahideen* offices in the country and threatened any illegal foreign fighters who attempted to remain in Pakistan with official deportation. A month later, the FBI secretly recorded a senior Egyptian *jihad* leader offering over the telephone to send new volunteers to the Arab-Afghan training camps in Pakistan. He was told, 'all of them [are] closed, Sheik, nothing is left open . . . even the Base [*Al-Qaida*] is closed completely and they all departed from here . . . except for special situations.'[3] These displaced men faced a serious problem, because return to their countries of origin meant certain arrest, torture, and likely death. At the time, a Saudi spokesman for the Arab-Afghans in Jeddah explained in the media, 'the Algerians cannot go to Algeria, the Syrians cannot go to Syria or the Iraqis to Iraq. Some will opt to go to Bosnia, the others will have to go into Afghanistan permanently.'[4] His assessments were predictably accurate and a number of prominent Arab guerrillas left South Asia destined for a new life of asylum and 'holy war' amidst the brutal civil conflict in the Balkans.

Among these men, Shaykh Abu Abdel Aziz 'Barbaros' (literally meaning 'the red bearded,' also known as Abdelrahman al-Dosari) was to be particularly feared (Figure 2). Born in Saudi Arabia in 1942, al-Dosari was originally of Indian-Hyderabadi ethnic descent, and sported a characteristic thick reddish-orange-colored beard. He had started his career as a simple and unassuming administrator in a personnel office with Saudi Airlines, married with a wife and nine children.[5] Yet, al-Dosari was also known as a widely respected Islamic lecturer in the Arabian Gulf who had no hesitation in urging confrontation with the corrupt Saudi regime.[6]

Figure 2. The foreign *mujahideen* in Bosnia, December 1992; Abu Abdel Aziz 'Barbaros' at far right.

When the Soviet invasion of Afghanistan intensified in the early 1980s, he abandoned the tedium of the lecture circuit and family life to join in the new international Islamic crusade. 'Shaykh Abu Abdel Aziz,' as he was now known, volunteered and took part in extensive *jihad* operations in Africa, Kashmir, the Philippines, and Afghanistan.[7] In his own words, he later explained what had happened:

> Now, concerning the beginning of Jihad in my case, I was one of those who heard about Jihad in Afghanistan when it started . . . One of those who came to our land [Saudi Arabia] was Sheikh Dr Abdullah Azzam – may his soul rest in peace – I heard him rallying the youth to come forth and [join him] to go to Afghanistan. This was in 1984 – I think. I decided to go and check the matter for myself. This was, and all praise be to Allah, the beginning [of my journey with] Jihad. I am still following this same path.[8]

During the first Afghan war, Shaykh Abu Abdel Aziz gained the nickname 'Hown' for his particular combat proficiency with Russian-made 'Hound' artillery rockets. United States counter-terrorism officials also believe that the tenacious 'Hown' was inducted early on into the nascent Al-Qaida military group led by Abdullah Azzam and Usama Bin Laden. Abu Abdel Aziz never addressed the subject of Al-Qaida or Bin Laden publicly, but spoke at great length about his combat tours with them: 'The Jihad in Afghanistan was a great experience. Whoever was involved in this experience had the great desire that Allah would keep them engaged in Jihad until their death and that Allah would give them their death in the battlefield of Jihad. And this is also our desire that we are killed in the way of Jihad.'[9]

Shaykh Abu Abdel Aziz possessed a strong personal charisma, in the style of Abdullah Azzam, that proved vital in the recruitment of untold numbers of suicidal *mujahideen* volunteers from Europe, the Middle East, and Central Asia. These idealistic young men listened obediently as the Saudi militant ordered them in his lectures:

> Fight for the sake of Allah – not fighting by shouting, not fighting by burning tires by the road . . . no, this is not the Muslim way . . . [It is] the fight . . . killing the enemy, and to be killed. And this [duty] is not new for Muslims, not new for Islam . . . It is required from every Prophet to perform Jihad . . . If you are not going to go for jihad, if you are not going to leave your business, not going to leave your family, not leaving this earth, and fighting in the sake of Allah, Allah (SWT) is going to punish you . . . Go alone, without any arms, without any weapons, without anything, you go. It is your duty. And Allah is responsible about your food and about your weapons and about everything . . . we will give you direction.[10]

Following the *mujahideen* conquest of Kabul in April 1992, Shaykh Abu Abdel Aziz had travelled with four other unidentified veteran Arab-Afghan commanders to Bosnia-Herzegovina to 'check out the landscape' and determine if the Balkans would serve as fertile ground for the displaced Arab-Afghan movement, which was no longer officially welcomed in Pakistan.[11] However, unlike other remote stops in his worldwide tour of Muslim 'hot spots,' Bosnia was truly a foreign land to the Islamic extremists of the Middle East. Prior to the Western media coverage of the expanding civil war there, many had admittedly never even heard of the place. In an interview with *Al-Daawah* magazine, Abu Abdel Aziz confessed that, at this point, 'we were unable to understand where Bosnia was, was it in America or in the southern hemisphere or in Asia? We had no idea where it was. When we found out that it is a part of Yugoslavia in Eastern Europe, we still had no idea how many Muslims were there and we had no idea as to how and when Islam reached there.'[12]

But after witnessing the injustice of the bloody conflict, the Saudi *jihadi* swiftly concluded that this was indeed a legitimate holy war. 'All Muslims should participate,' he suggested, 'either by contributing money, caring for orphans and widows, taking in refugees or fighting in the jihad.'[13] Abu Abdel Aziz had no illusions about his mission in Bosnia. Though he spent part of his time encouraging *da`wa* (Islamic missionary work), he cautioned 'we are not here to bring supplies like food and medicine . . . There are a lot of organizations that can do that. We bring men.'[14] Upon his arrival, the *mujahideen* leadership in Bosnia and Afghanistan designated Shaykh Abu Abdel Aziz as the first *Amir*, or commander-in-chief, of the Bosnian Arab-Afghans. The new *Amir* quickly established his first headquarters at the Mehurici training camp, near the central-Bosnian town of Travnik.

In the fall of 1992, Usama Bin Laden personally ordered a former key Sudanese member of Al-Qaida – later turned government informant – Jamal Ahmed al-Fadl, to travel to nearby Zagreb, Croatia for consultations with key Arab-Afghan leaders operating as Al-Qaida emissaries in Bosnia, including: *Amir* Shaykh Abu Abdel Aziz, Enaam Arnaout (also known as Abu Mahmoud al-Suri), and Abu Zubair al-Madani, a cousin of Bin Laden's discussed in Chapter 4 of this work. Uncoincidentally, the meeting was held at the local offices of Arnaout's Benevolence International Foundation (BIF) in Zagreb.[15] Discussions centered largely around Al-Qaida's growing interest in acquiring Bosnian businesses and forging relationships with local banking networks to hide terrorist financing activity.[16] As per briefs published by the United States Attorney's office in Chicago, during that conference, Abu Abdel Aziz (identified in these documents by his alias Abdulrahman Al-Dosari) advised Jamal al-Fadl that 'al Qaeda was seeking to establish training camps in Bosnia, forge relations with relief agencies in Bosnia and establish businesses to support al Qaeda economically.'[17] He also discussed the purchase of weapons from Germany destined for the *mujahideen* in the Balkans, and stressed the need for a *fatwah* (religious edict) permitting Al-Qaida members to dress and act as Westerners while in Bosnia in order to conceal their presence and 'blend in.'[18]

Once these housekeeping issues had been taken care of, Abu Abdel Aziz proceeded to elaborate further on Usama Bin Laden's master plan for Bosnia. He told al-Fadl without hesitation that Al-Qaida's primary goal in Bosnia 'was to establish a base for operations in Europe against al Qaeda's true enemy, the United States.' Not long afterward, Abu Hajer al-Iraqi (Mamdouh Mahmud Salim, one of the original founders of Al-Qaida in Afghanistan) confirmed to al-Fadl that Abu Abdel Aziz had spoken the truth, and Usama Bin Laden's interest in Bosnia was largely as a staging area from which to strike at America.[19] Consequently, Enaam Arnaout personally arranged for nine elite instructors from the *Al-Sadda* terrorist training camp in Afghanistan to be immediately imported into central Bosnia (Figure 3).[20]

For Bin Laden's strategy to succeed, other intelligent and experienced Arab Afghan commanders were desperately needed on the ground in the Balkan region to coordinate overall operations. During the opening months of the war in the spring of 1992, the militant Egyptian Shaykh Anwar Shaaban fashioned an epic role for himself (reminiscent of the style of Abdullah Azzam) as the political leader and chief spokesman for the foreign *jihadis* based in Bosnia (Figure 4).[21] Shaaban was a well-known veteran of the Afghan *jihad* who later became the *Imam* (head Muslim cleric) of the Islamic Cultural Institute of Milan, Italy. Shaaban sought to convince his followers that death while engaged in the struggle to defend Islam was a noble and honorable fate. In one instance, he lectured to his supporters:

> The person with the sound [religious] belief is the one who is aware that he may die at any instant, wherever he may be . . . for he knows, that if Allah wills for a shell to hit us now, we would all be killed and if Allah wills for a shell to hit us on the frontline then

Figure 3. Al-Hajj Boudella, an Algerian combat instructor transferred in 1992 from the *Al-Sadda* training camp in Afghanistan to central Bosnia.

we would be killed there, and if Allah wills for us to be killed in our homes, in our bedrooms, then we would die there. So the Mujahid [holy warrior] . . . knows that his death can come at any moment when Allah wills, so he is not afraid of death.[22]

While still a student studying Islam in Egypt, Shaaban had loudly protested against the secular government of Anwar Sadat and Hosni Mubarak in Cairo. His calls for an Islamic revolution were taken very seriously by Egyptian authorities, and Shaaban soon thereafter sought asylum in Afghanistan and several other 'Muslim countries.' But like many other Arab-Afghans, by 1991, Shaaban no longer felt safe in Afghanistan as it collapsed into civil turmoil. He sought and obtained political asylum in Italy, and was disappointed by what he found: 'the Muslim community in Italy was just the same as elsewhere in Europe: asleep and busy in

Figure 4. Shaykh Anwar Shaaban, a senior lieutenant in *Al-Gama`at Al-Islamiyya* and overall leader of the foreign *mujahideen* fighting in the Balkans until his death in 1995.

the worldly affairs.' Aided by a collection of Afghan war veterans and Italian fundamentalist sympathizers (especially among disenfranchised North African immigrants), Anwar Shaaban opened a major new Islamic center in a converted garage in Milan. Knowledgeable Al-Qaida sources have praised Shaaban's efforts in Milan, and noted that Islamic Cultural Institute was 'the center of much activity and it gained much popularity amongst the local Muslims.'[23]

Similarly, L'Houssaine Kherchtou, a former Al-Qaida member, testified during the recent trials of four Bin Laden followers convicted in the 1998 East Africa Embassy bombings that Shaaban used the Islamic Cultural Institute as a critical Arab-Afghan recruiting center for young, disaffected Muslims living in Europe. According to Kherchtou, 'Sheik Anwar Shaban was managing the Islamic Cultural Institute, so I used to go there every weekend.' Kherchtou also testified that Shaaban had personally helped arrange Pakistani visas for him and three other *jihadi* recruits who then went on to a Bin Laden-affiliated camp in eastern Afghanistan for training in weapons and explosives.[24] Evidence accumulated by United States and Italian authorities indicates that these four were not alone, and that Shaaban was personally responsible for arranging the training of hundreds (potentially thousands) of Al-Qaida recruits from Europe.[25]

The center quickly developed under Shaaban's leadership into the major hub in the network of Arab-Afghan activity in all of southern Europe, including the

Balkans. French counterterrorism officials later concurred that the ICI in Milan, under the lead of Shaaban, had served an 'essential role' as a command center for groups including Al-Gama`at Al-Islamiyya, the Tunisian An-Nahda ('Islamic Revival'), and the GIA.[26] The ICI had generated a mini-Islamic underworld in Italy, with operators working for the center collecting up to a 30 per cent surcharge from fearful local Muslim businessmen in Italy in order to support the 'Islamic cause.' Shaaban and his aides at ICI then allegedly used the *jihad* funds to, among other things, underwrite extensive arms trafficking and provide 'logistical support' to Arab mercenaries destined for Bosnia.[27]

In the summer of 1992, Shaykh Anwar Shaaban led the first quasi-official Arab-Afghan delegation to arrive in Bosnia, accompanied by a number of his Italian cohorts. Shaaban subsequently served for over three years as the spiritual and political Shaykh of the foreign *mujahideen* in the Balkans. But, as the fighters themselves have testified, 'Sheik Anwar was not a textbook scholar: he was a scholar who practised what he preached and fought oppression at every level, just like the companions and the early generations of Muslims . . . with books in his hands and military uniform on his body. Not only did he teach but he fought as well.' Indeed, with such words of praise, one cannot help but point out the significant parallels between the roles of the Palestinian Abdullah Azzam in Afghanistan and the Egyptian Anwar Shaaban in Bosnia. Al-Qaida sources seem to endorse that characterization; in one audiotape, *mujahideen* representatives attempt to unravel the mysterious life of Shaaban and note that 'in the footsteps of Sheik Abdullah Azzam, Sheik Anwar Shaaban carried the responsibilities of the Mujahideen regiment in Bosnia . . . teaching, encouraging, and inspiring the fighters, laying the same foundation in Bosnia that Shaykh Abdullah Azzam laid in Afghanistan.'[28]

Shaaban shuttled back and forth from his Peshawar-style headquarters in Milan, bringing with him to Bosnia a host of Al-Qaida veteran fighters and new recruits, including his wife, daughter, and five sons. In a fax from Shaaban in Milan to a potential Muslim donor in Qatar, he spoke of how he was personally 'convinced that the Islamic projects in Europe must have absolute priority, considering how making these places stable bases for Muslims can be useful for Muslims all over the world.'[29] Undoubtedly, Shaaban hoped to use the Bosnian war to as a means to create a headquarters and a network for Al-Qaida (and particularly its North African adherents) in Europe. Not surprisingly, many of those that Shaaban introduced to Bosnia in 1992 became 'the commanders and trainers, the cream of the Mujahideen.'[30]

Shaaban's influence also extended to a number of other Italian fundamentalist clerics, such as Mohamed Ben Brahim Saidani, a Tunisian volunteer fighter in Bosnia and Imam of a mosque on Massarenti Street in Bologna, Italy. Saidani had been one of a number of participants in a guerrilla training course held in Afghanistan in 1993. Upon his return to Italy, he quickly convinced thirty of his local followers to enlist in the foreign *mujahideen* brigade active in Bosnia. He founded a front company in Italy that provided seemingly legitimate work authorization permits to *jihadi* volunteers and veterans, allowing them to travel without hindrance to different parts of the world, including Bosnia.[31] In witness testimony in the trial of conspirators convicted of involvement in the 1998 East Africa embassy bombings, Al-Qaida lieutenant Jamal al-Fadl discussed his trip to Zagreb in mid-1992, specifically how he had been instructed to meet with Mohamed Saidani so he could get 'information about what's going on in Bosnia' and bring this intelligence back directly to Usama Bin Laden.[32]

Religious and political leadership figures were critical at this stage – but so were experienced military advisors and commanders. With proper guidance, the early rookie mistakes made in combat in Afghanistan could perhaps be leapfrogged in Bosnia. Enaam Arnaout had provided some of the muscle straight from Al-Qaida's training camps in Afghanistan – and these men were not alone. In the weeks following the initial ethnic Serb rebellion in April 1992, Anwar Shaaban had met with a group of 'leading [military] personalities from the Afghan jihad' and agreed on the necessity of establishing a significant *mujahideen* presence in Bosnia. These 'leading personalities' were primarily Shaykh Abu Abdel Aziz, Wahiudeen al-Masri, Moataz Billah, and Husaamudeen al-Masri.[33]

Wahiudeen al-Masri, another Arab legend of the Bosnian war, was born in southern Egypt. As he grew older, Wahiudeen became 'heavily involved' in the Muslim Brotherhood, the comparatively mainstream Islamist opposition party in Egypt. However, like many radical Egyptian fundamentalists, he grew tired of the mostly non-violent approach of the Brotherhood, and Wahiudeen instead chose to join the anti-Soviet *jihad* in Afghanistan seeking to help establish a new Islamic empire. He enlisted in a *mujahideen* training camp, and grew to be an unusually proficient guerrilla soldier. His teacher at the camp 'took notice of Wahiudeen's quick learning of the arts of war' and assigned him to train new recruits as they arrived at the camp. When the Afghan civil war degenerated into intra-*mujahideen* factional fighting, he left Afghanistan and arrived in Bosnia in the summer of 1992. Arab-Afghan sources lionized Wahiudeen as a 'very professional soldier and military-minded, although . . . very pious and very humble.'[34]

Moataz Billah and Husaamudeen were also both Egyptian veterans of the Afghan *jihad* and suspected followers of Shaykh Omar Abdel Rahman. (The Arabic pseudonym 'Husaamudeen' translates roughly as 'Sword of the Faith.') Even before Afghanistan, in Egypt, Moataz Billah was a well-known student activist in the Islamist movement. His courage was the subject of hallowed (often far-fetched) legend; one story recounted how, in a bid to escape Egyptian authorities, he had jumped off a five-storey building and somehow miraculously escaped bodily harm. In any event, he was an ideal candidate to join the militant Arab exiles in Afghanistan, and developed into a professional and charismatic guerrilla fighter after spending years there engaged in the *jihad*. By the start of the Bosnian war in 1992, Moataz Billah (in his mid-twenties) had gained impressive 'military experience to complement his intensive mind.' At that point, he gained the dubious honor of personally overseeing combat training at the newly established Al-Qaida camps in central Bosnia. Billah taught his recruits, both Arab and Bosnian, with 'military and combat experience unmatched by any of the world's special forces . . . Unlike them, Muataz's experience was not gained in a classroom but it was gained in the dusty mountains of Afghanistan against the world's largest superpower at the time.' Virtually all of the early volunteers among the foreign *mujahideen* based in Bosnia were personally trained by Billah. He also participated directly in combat operations, and was wounded several times.[35]

In May 1992, the Arab-Afghan *mujahideen* commanders arrived and, under the leadership of Shaykh Anwar Shaaban and *Amir* Abu Abdel Aziz Barbaros, formed *jihad* camps in two main locations: at an abandoned retirement home in Zenica, in central Bosnia, and (20 miles away) in Mehurici, six miles outside of Travnik and at the foot of a cliff, 'in what usually serves as a cattle market.'[36] There were also smaller pockets of foreign *mujahideen* based on Mt Igman, south of Sarajevo (under the overall guidance of 'General' Abu Ayman al-Masri); and in Turbe, Radina, and elsewhere in the Lasava Valley in central Bosnia.[37] The commanders built the camps exactly along the Afghan model: intense, aggressive recruitment and training in both military tactics and the violent, confrontational form of Islamic fundamentalism borrowed from the Al-Qaida training camps in the Hindu Kush. Propaganda videos of the military training in the Bosnian camps reflect strong similarities to those of Al-Qaida in Afghanistan: demanding calisthenic exercises, daunting obstacle courses, basic weapons and explosives, and legions of black-clad, bearded guerrillas chanting the *shahada*: '*la ilaha il-Allah, Muhammedurasool Allah!*' ('There is no God but *Allah*, and Muhammed is his messenger!').[38] By late August, Shaykh Abu Abdel Aziz told a British journalist, 'Now we have quite good numbers and every day it is more. Most fought in Afghanistan, but for some this is the first time they have been involved in jihad.'[39]

It was immediately clear that the senior leadership would need to organize to acquire weapons and other necessary military supplies. In light of these concerns, Shaykh Abu Abdel Aziz began a major fundraising and recruitment drive to help support the *jihad*. He spread news of the Bosnian *mujahideen* to a number of fundamentalist Muslims clerics throughout the Middle East who were sympathetic to and often joined the ranks of the Arab-Afghans. These radical clerics, mobilized by seemingly endless scenes of civilian bloodshed in Bosnia, castigated their followers that they were cowards and 'disbelievers' if they did not help the *mujahideen* defeat the 'Crucifixers' in the Balkans. Like Anwar Shaaban, many were also willing and eager to transform Bosnia into the next Afghanistan. According to Al-Qaida propaganda videos, the most important religious leaders to offer their support to the Arab-Afghan *jihad* in Bosnia were: Shaykh Salman al-Awdah (Saudi Arabia), Shaykh Omar Abdel Rahman (Egypt), Shaykh Abu Talal al-Qasimy (Egypt), Shaykh Abdul-Majid az-Zindani (Yemen), and Shaykh Omar bin Ahmad Saif (Yemen).[40] These men are all constants in the world of religiously-motivated terrorism who have directly inspired many acts of violence perpetrated by the international Al-Qaida network.

Shaykh Salman al-Awdah is one of the most notorious and controversial Islamist clerics in Saudi Arabia. During the mid-1990s, he was formally detained by Saudi authorities for 5 years stemming from his extremist rhetoric and calls for military confrontation with the West – only to be inexplicably released from custody by the Saudis in 1999. Usama Bin Laden has referred to al-Awdah as a personal hero, and in an interview with journalist Peter Arnett, cited him as a direct inspiration for taking up 'my duty of enjoining what is right and forbidding what is wrong.'[41] Conversely, according to at least one Al-Qaida online magazine published in Saudi Arabia, al-Awdah has told other terrorist leaders based in Saudi Arabia that he is 'proud to be one of the soldiers of Abu Abdallah [Bin Laden].'[42]

Al-Awdah was particularly sensitive when it came to hardships that plagued various foreign minority Muslim communities. In 1995, al-Awdah released a short manifesto entitled 'From Behind Bars.' Drawing attention to the situation of Muslims particularly in Bosnia, Somalia, Tajikistan, Egypt, Syria, and Palestine, Awdah warned that 'it is a betrayal on our part to neglect our fellow Muslims and leave them as easy targets for their enemies.'[43] Very specifically, on the issue of the Bosnian war itself, Shaykh Salman al-Awdah has admonished his followers:

> The scholars of history have said, 'the most distinguished of wars throughout history are those based on belief,' because a man who fights for his creed, believes that when he dies, he dies as a martyr . . . What occurred in Bosnia Herzegovina was not merely a war between the Muslims and the Serbs, but it was a war between Islam and Christianity. And this is how we must understand it. It was a war carried out by the entire West against the Islamic world.

Indeed, al-Awdah blamed Europe and the United States not merely for ignoring the humanitarian crisis and the terrible suffering of the Bosnians, but, moreover, for being the prime orchestrators behind an international conspiracy to suppress Islam. In taped lectures, he angrily attacked the UN weapons embargo as inequitable and deliberately biased against the Muslims: by purposefully preventing the Bosnians from arming themselves in self-defence, al-Awdah charged that the United States and UN had quietly 'resolved that the Muslims would be killed through the Serbian attacks, in a clever, well-thought-out manner.'[44]

The second of this group of influential clerics, Shaykh Omar Abdel Rahman, is the quite infamous jailed spiritual leader of both major Egyptian Islamist terrorist groups, Al-Gama`at Al-Islamiyya and Al-Jihad. The blind Shaykh is said to have been quite close to Usama Bin Laden from the days of the Afghan *jihad*, and allegedly was among the group of Egyptians who first persuaded Bin Laden to 'have a clear idea to use [the Arab recruits] after Afghanistan for other wars.'[45] In an Arabic-language radio broadcast in 1993, Shaykh Omar condemned the United States, explaining, 'Americans are descendants of apes and pigs who have been feeding from the dining tables of the Zionists, Communism, and colonialism.'[46] The cleric's zealous hatred for non-Muslim 'infidels' reflected the dark and ultra-fanatical direction that the Arab-Afghan movement had taken in the years since Bin Laden and his henchmen had seized the reins of power.

Usama Bin Laden and his cohorts did not take the subsequent arrest and federal conviction of Shaykh Omar in the United States lightly. Following the detention of the blind Shaykh in wake of the 1993 World Trade Center bombing, Al-Qaida turncoat Jamal al-Fadl attended leadership meetings in Khartoum, Sudan with other senior Bin Laden aides. According to al-Fadl, Al-Qaida regarded Shaykh Omar's arrest as 'very sad and . . . very bad . . . and we have to do something . . . They talk about what we have to do against America.'[47] Shortly thereafter, in December 1994, a group of Algerian Islamic militants seized control of an Air France jetliner in Algiers in a unsuccessful, premature bid to suicide-crash it into the Eiffel Tower on Christmas Day. After securing the plane, the would-be hijackers demanded (in exchange for passengers held hostage), 'the release of Dr. Omar Abdel Rahman and [Shaykh] Salman al-Awdah.'[48] Likewise, in September 2000, a new videotape mysteriously surfaced of Bin Laden and other terrorist leaders meeting in Afghanistan. Bin Laden addressed the camera and promised 'to work with all our power to free our brother, Sheikh Omar Abdel Rahman, and all our prisoners in America, Egypt, and Riyadh.'[49] Also in attendance at the meeting was Shaykh Omar's son Asadullah, who vigorously applauded Bin Laden's words and urged Muslims to 'move forward and shed blood.'[50]

Shaykh Abu Talal al-Qasimy (also known as Talaat Fouad Qassem), third in the group of clerics involved in the Bosnian *jihad*, was born in Egypt in June 1957. He first acted as the representative of Al-Gama`at Al-Islamiyya in the Engineering faculty of Al-Minya University in Egypt, and then eventually became the overall *Amir* of Al-Gama`at at Al-Minya between 1979 to 1981. He was imprisoned several times by the Egyptian government both before and following the assassination of the late President Anwar Sadat. Shortly thereafter, al-Qasimy was able to use fake travel documents to escape Egypt and join the growing number of militant Muslim exiles in Afghanistan. While there, he 'made an appointment with Jihad in the path of Allah, and . . . embraced the rifle.'[51]

Working closely with another famous Al-Gama`at commander and senior aide to Usama Bin Laden, Abu Hazim al-Masri (a.k.a. Mustafa Hamzah),[52] al-Qasimy also made vigorous efforts to organize Egyptian Arab-Afghan *jihadis* together into a unified military and ideological force to one day overthrow the secular and pro-Western Egyptian regime of Hosni Mubarak.[53] In Afghanistan, he established Al-Gama`at's official magazine, *Al-Murabeton*, and wrote most of the early issues. When the Afghan civil war degenerated into hazardous factional fighting, al-Qasimy found political asylum in Denmark, where he continued to spread his radical message as an editor at the foreign office of *Al-Murabeton* in Copenhagen.[54] One of the other four editors working in Copenhagen was Dr Ayman al-Zawahiri, a founding member and second-in-command of Al-Qaida.[55] Al-Qasimy was also a close friend of the *Amir* of the Bosnian *mujahideen*, Anwar Shaaban, and took an aggressive, committed, and hands-on role in the Bosnian *jihad*.

But staunch support for the Arab *mujahideen* in Bosnia came from other sources than merely Saudi Arabia and Egypt. Shaykh Abdul-Majid az-Zindani is the longtime ideological leader of the Yemeni *Al-Islah* opposition party and a celebrated and veteran Arab *mujahideen* commander. From 1984 until the end of the decade, Zindani brought between 5,000 and 7,000 Arabs, including many Yemenis, to Al-Qaida camps in Afghanistan for military training and religious teaching under his personal guidance. He was an integral part of the Arab-Afghan movement. In the aftermath of the Soviet-Afghan *jihad*, Zindani encouraged refugee Arab-Afghan fighters to resettle and continue their training in the mountainous, tribal regions of Yemen.[56] He started his own religious university there, the very same institution where the future American Taliban John Walker Lindh studied before travelling on to Pakistan. According to a Jordanian criminal indictment, Shaykh az-Zindani gave $10,000 on behalf of Usama Bin Laden to help finance a radical Islamic terrorist cell in Jordan that committed several fatal bombings in 1994.[57] Cassette tapes of Zindani's fiery sermons in the wake of 11 September 2001, allege, among other things, that President George Bush conspired with the Jews to destroy the World Trade Center and then blame it on Muslims.[58] With Zindani's active encouragement, Yemen developed into a major preliminary gathering point for would-be volunteers for the *jihad* in Bosnia.

As a further example, in three days alone, between 31 August and 2 September 1992, as many as 250 would-be *mujahideen* fighters reportedly arrived from the Middle East in the Zenica area.[59] When I spoke to Al-Qaida sympathizer Abu Hamza al-Masri in London, he tried to explain to me the mindset of the volunteers who came to Bosnia at the start of the war: 'People are dedicated to the [religion] . . . They went to Afghanistan to defend their brothers and sisters. So, they find Afghanistan now, the destruction of war and Muslims fighting against each other.' As a result, in the aftermath of the Afghan *jihadi* debacle, 'they want to [struggle against] something that is indisputable, which is non-Muslims raping, killing, and maiming Muslims.'[60]

Simply put, the Afghan war had devolved in the early 1990s from a legendary struggle of Muslim 'heroes' battling the 'godless' infidels into an endless parade of selfish internal squabbles that were progressively annihilating any remnants left of Afghan civil society. On the other hand, in Bosnia, the divergence between good and evil was much more clear for those with carelessly idealistic views of political Islam. For the extremists, the conflict in the Balkans could be easily framed in terms of an apocalyptic, one-dimensional religious confrontation between Muslims and non-Muslims. This was really the only type of environment in which an outlandish fundamentalist ideology like that of Al-Qaida could potentially prosper.

The first major concentrations of *mujahideen* to fight in the Bosnian war took part in combat operations during the summer of 1992 in a region of north-central Bosnia adjacent to the cities of Tesanj (often transliterated in Arab sources as 'Tishin'), Doboj, and Teslic. During that summer, ethnic Serb forces mobilized and initiated a significant offensive against Muslims forces in the region. At first, the armed clashes were predominantly short, guerrilla-style assaults between Muslim and Serb forces, often on the heights of Mount Bandera overlooking Tesanj. Mount Bandera was an important objective, strategically placed between the Serb, Croat and Muslim frontlines, and offering easy control of the entire surrounding region. The very first Arab-Afghan *jihadi* to be 'martyred' in Bosnia, Abu Ali al-Makki Hassan al-Quraishi (a 21-year old Saudi), was killed by a hand grenade while on Mount Bandera in the early phases of military action in June.[61] During the same battle, another Saudi from Mecca, Abu el-Baraa al-Makki Hussaam el-Deen, was also wounded. At the time, it was unclear whether the two men had independently joined the Bosnian war, or whether they were part of a 'more co-ordinated move' to bring full units of Arab *mujahideen* to the Balkans.[62]

In August and early September 1992, a group of 43 mostly Saudi *mujahideen* initiated combat operations in the area between Tesanj and Teslic.[63] These foreign volunteers had crossed the Austrian-Slovenian border at the beginning of August, and soon made their way to Croatia. The Arab fighters were given an official certificate enabling them to enter Bosnia through Kamensko, it being claimed that the foreigners 'had been dispatched to [Bosnia] to investigate the possibilities for delivering humanitarian aid.'[64] UN investigators later identified the *Amir* of this group as Abu Ishaq al-Makki (also known as 'Abu Ishak'), a prominent Saudi born in Mecca. Abu Ishaq, 'famous for heroic feats in Afghanistan,' later fled to Yemen after playing a significant role in the *jihad* in the Balkans. According to *mujahideen* sources, he was shortly thereafter apprehended by Saudi authorities and personally taken home by Saudi Interior Minister Prince Nayef bin Abdel Aziz to face punishment for allegedly participating in terrorist activities.[65]

Aiding Abu Ishaq in Bosnia were a number of other Saudi veterans of Afghanistan: the notorious Shaykh Abu Abdel Aziz, Abu Suhayb al-Makki (deputy commander), Shaykh Abu Sulaiman al-Makki (the spiritual guide of the unit), Abu Saleh al-Jiddawi (a senior military adviser of the unit), Abu Zubair al-Haili (artillery supervisor), and Abu Musaid al-Makki (chief navigator and topographer).[66]

Other than Shaykh Abu Abdel Aziz, Abu Sulaiman al-Makki (also known as Shaykh Khalid Harbi, Khalid al-Saif) was perhaps the most celebrated of these men. Born in Saudi Arabia in 1966 and a teacher at the holy mosque of Mecca, he was also a veteran fighter of the Afghan *jihad* formerly in 'the company of [the Martyr] Sheikh Abdullah Azzam.'[67] In December 2001, United States investigators were shocked to discover the re-appearance of Abu Sulaiman in a videotape produced by Usama Bin Laden in which the latter took credit for organizing and financing the September 11 suicide hijackings.[68] The two men, sitting on the floor together in a plain white room, discussed the intricate details of the 9/11 plot. After a grinning Bin Laden explained how he had schemed to crash commercial airliners into the World Trade Center, Abu Sulaiman chimed in and spoke of his joyous reaction when he heard 'the news':

> That day the congratulations were coming on the phone non-stop . . . No doubt it is a clear victory . . . Thank Allah America came out of its caves. We hit her the first hit and the next one will hit her with the hands of the believers, the good believers, the strong believers. By Allah it is a great work. Allah prepares for you a great reward for this work . . . I live in happiness, happiness, I have not experienced, or felt, in a long time . . . In these days, in our times, that it will be the greatest jihad in the history of Islam.[69]

Like Abu Sulaiman, Abu Zubair al-Haili (also known as 'The Bear,' a 300-pound monster of a man) had also first gained a reputation as a fearless and calculating military commander in Afghanistan before serving as an artillery expert with the Arab *mujahideen* in Bosnia. Until recently, Abu Zubair was a resident of Tooting, south London, where he regularly sent young recruits from the West to Taliban and Al-Qaida training camps in Central Asia. He came from the same area of Saudi Arabia as Bin Laden, and had first fought alongside the infamous Al-Qaida chief during the Soviet-Afghan war.[70] Two years ago, 'the Bear' even reportedly helped coordinate the escape of Usama Bin Laden from the collapsing Tora Bora cave complex. Abu Zubair was finally detained while in Morocco, in the midst of plotting to send an explosives-laden dingy in a suicide mission against United States and British vessels in the Straits of Gibraltar. His capture was hailed by one United States official, cited in an interview with *The Washington Times*, as quite significant: 'Al-Haili is of interest to us and there is reason to believe that he has information that could be helpful in the prevention of any future terrorist attacks.'[71] During his long career with Al-Qaida, Abu Zubair had served as a senior deputy to both Afghano-Bosniak Abu Ishaq al-Makki and also Abu Zubaydah, (also known as Mohammed Hussein Zein-al-Abideen) – Zubaydah, the better known of the two, is a ruthless Palestinian Al-Qaida terrorist training camp manager, a rumored veteran of the Bosnian war, and a Bosnian passport holder.[72]

Although there were no initial reports of any major battles involving Abu Ishaq al-Makki's unit in central Bosnia, in one particular instance, several of his *mujahideen* allegedly killed three Serbian Territorial Defence members and placed their heads on poles in a rather gruesome display of their poignant resolve.[73] Simultaneously, in late August and early September, an American surgeon from California spent two weeks performing remedial surgery on Bosnian war victims. To his horror, the doctor reportedly found that irregular Muslim soldiers, including *mujahideen* 'some from Afghanistan and Saudi Arabia,' had 'routinely performed crude, disfiguring, non-medical circumcisions on Bosnian Serb soldiers,' including one 18-year old Serb soldier 'who was so brutally circumcised that eventually the entire organ required amputation.'[74] In 1992, Dejan Jozic, a 13-year old Croatian was stopped on his way home from school one day in Zenica by three foreign *mujahideen*: 'They asked, "Why doesn't your family leave Zenica?" I didn't know what to say.' The three men pushed Jozic to the ground and, without any further explanation, cut off the ring finger of the boy's right hand. Jozic's terrified family took the message to heart and fled their home.[75]

This fact was no coincidence and by the early fall of 1992, a new base for *jihad* was quickly growing in the Balkans. With the help of influential clerics and *Al-Qaida* military commanders, the foreign Bosniak brigade was coalescing together various disparate elements in the international Arab-Afghan network. The *mujahideen* war machine so familiar in Afghanistan had been successfully revived many hundreds of miles westward in the heart of Europe. But even Usama Bin Laden could not personally bankroll the *jihad* in Bosnia; its future would depend entirely on whether Abu Abdel Aziz, Anwar Shaaban, and their various aides would be able to marshal the same underground pipeline of money and weapons as was first developed in Afghanistan in order to outfit their new European Islamist army.

Notes

1. 'The Martyrs of Bosnia: Part I.' Videotape. Azzam Publications: London, 2000.
2. Ibid.
3. FBI Transcript of conversation involving Omar Ahmad Ali Abdel Rahman, 'Muhammad' LNU, and two unidentified males, 20 March 1993. *United States v. Omar Ahmad Ali Abdel Rahman et al.* S3 93 Cr. 181(MBM). Government Exhibit 7057, p. 11.
4. Evans, Kathy. 'Pakistan clamps down on Afghan Mojahedin and Orders Expulsion of Arab Jihad Supporters.' *Guardian (London)*, January 1993.
5. 'Hafiz Mohammed Saeed: Pakistan's heart of terror.' *Kashmir Herald*. Vol. 2, No. 2, July 2002.

6. 'What is a Salafy or Wahabi and their affiliation with the Saudi Government.' http://www.ummah.net/alsalafyoon/EnglishPosts/salafy.html. December 2001.
7. Post, Tom with Joel Brand (1992), 'Help from the Holy Warriors.' *Newsweek.* 5 October.
8. Tabib, Tawfig, (1994) 'Interview with Sheikh al-Mujahideen Abu Abdel Aziz.' *Al-Sirat Al-Mustaqeem*, No. 33, August 1994.
9. 'The Jihad in Bosnia.' *Al-Daawah* (Islamabad), Waseem, Ahmed: Islamabad, January 1993.
10. Shaykh Abu Abdel Aziz. 'Jihad and the Revival.' Islamic Assembly of North America (IANA) 1993 Conference, Chicago, IL. IANA Tape #3352.
11. Tabib, Tawfig. Op. cit.
12. 'The Jihad in Bosnia.'
13. Sudetic, Chuck. 'Muslims heed call to arms.' *The New York Times,* November 1992, Issue 104, section 1, p. 5.
14. Post, Tom with Joel Brand. 'Help from the Holy Warriors.' *Newsweek*, 5 October 5 1992.
15. 'Bill of Particulars.' *United States of America v. Enaam M. Arnaout.* United States District Court Northern District of Illinois Eastern Division. Case #: 02 CR 892. 3 February 2003, p. 5.
16. Ibid.
17. 'Government's Evidentiary Proffer Supporting the Admissibility of Co-Conspirator Statements.' *United States of America v. Enaam M. Arnaout.* United States District Court Northern District of Illinois, Eastern Division. Case #: 02 CR 892. 31 January 2003, pp. 24–5.
18. 'Bill of Particulars.' Op. cit.
19. 'Government's Evidentiary Proffer Supporting the Admissibility of Co-Conspirator Statements." Op. cit.
20. 'Government's Response to Defendant's Position Paper as to Sentencing Factors.' *United States of America v. Enaam M. Arnaout.* United States District Court Northern District of Illinois Eastern Division. Case #: 02 CR 892, p. 38.
21. 'The Martyrs of Bosnia: Part I.' Op. cit.
22. 'The Martyrs of Bosnia: Part I.' Op. cit.
23. 'Under the Shades of Swords.' Audiocassette sequel to 'In the Hearts of Green Birds.' Azzam Recordings; London, 1997.
24. *United States v. Usama bin Laden, et al.* S(7) 98 Cr. 1023 (LBS). United States District Court, Southern District of New York. Trial Transcript, 21 February 2001, pp. 1106–7.
25. Ibid., pp. 1108–9.
26. Jean-Louis Bruguiere and Jean-Francois Ricard. *Requisitoire Definitifaux aux Fins de Non-Lieu. De Non-Lieu partiel. De Requalification. De Renvoi devant le Tribunal Correctionnel, de mantien sous Controle Judiciaiare et de maintien*

en Detention. Cour D'Appel de Paris; Tribunal de Grande Instance de Paris. No. Parquet: P96 253 3901.2, 2001, p. 99.

27. Willan, Philip. 'Italians arrest suspected Islamic militants.' *United Press International,* 26 June 1995.

28. 'Under the Shades of Swords.' Audiocassette sequel to 'In the Hearts of Green Birds.' November 1997. Azzam Recordings: London.

29. Italian Division of General Investigations and Special Operations (DIGOS) Anti-Terrorism Report. 'Searches at the Islamic Cultural Center, Viale Jenner 50, Milano, 6/26/1995.' Dated 15 September 1997.

30. 'Under the Shades of Swords.' Op. cit.

31. Jean-Louis Bruguiere and Jean-Francois Ricard. Op. cit., p. 97.

32. *United States v. Usama bin Laden, et al.* Op. cit., 20 February p. 97.

33. 'The Martyrs of Bosnia: Part I.' Op. cit.

34. 'In the Hearts of Green Birds.' Audiocassette transliterated by Salman Dhia Al Deen. Azzam Recordings: London.

35. 'Under the Shades of Swords.' Op. cit.

36. Eykyn, George. '"Mujahidin" rush to join Islamic fundamentalists in war.' *The Times* (London), 23 September 1992.

37. 'The Martyrs of Bosnia: Part I.' Op. cit.

38. 'The Martyrs of Bosnia: Part I.' Op. cit.

39. Hogg, Andrew. 'Arabs join in Bosnia war.' *The Sunday Times* (London), 30 August 1992.

40. 'The Martyrs of Bosnia: Part I.' Op. cit.

41. 'CNN/Time Impact: Holy Terror?' Transcript of Osama Bin Ladin interview with Peter Arnett. CNN. March 1997.

42. 'Voice of Jihad: Issue #1.' http://www.cybcity.com/suondmag/index.htm. October 2003.

43. Al-Awdah, Shaykh Salman. 'From Behind Bars,' 1995, p. 13.

44. 'The Martyrs of Bosnia: Part I.' Op. cit.

45. Engelberg, Stephen. 'One Man and a Global Web of Violence.' *The New York Times,* 14 January 2001.

46. Friedman, Robert I. 'The CIA and the Sheik.' *The Village Voice,* 30 March 1993.

47. *United States v. Usama bin Laden, et al.* S(7) 98 Cr. 1023 (LBS). Op. cit., 6 February 2001, p. 296.

48. American Islamic Group (AIG). 'Urgent–Air France Real Story – Part II (What Really Happened) [*Malhamat Al-Shahadah*]. *Islam Report,* 31 December 1994.

49. 'Bin Laden vows to free Islamist sheikh jailed in US.' Agence France Presse. 22 September 2000.

50. Cooley, John K. 'We Will Free Our Brothers.' ABC News, 25 September 2000.

51. Sheikh Abu Ithar. 'Sheikh Abu Talal Al-Qasimy, Infatuated With the Pen and the Spear.' *Al-Nida`ul Islam*. 21, December–January 1997–8, http://www.islam.org.au.

52. Abu Hazim (a.k.a. Mustafa Hamza) is discussed in Egyptian court testimony as having 'close ties' to Al-Qasimy, including having gone "through the [Afghan] experience with [Al-Qasimy]." By 1999, both Swiss and Egyptian authorities concluded that Abu Hazim had "ordered directly or indirectly" the infamous November 1997 terrorist attack in Luxor, Egypt, that killed 58 European tourists. Egyptian officials added that following the attack, Abu Hazim fled his temporary residence in the Sudan for the safety of Bin Laden's camps in Afghanistan. Hauser, Christine. 'Bin Laden "behind Luxor Strive."' *Middle East Times*, 23 May 1999.

53. Sharaf-al-Din, Khalid. 'Fundamentalists' Leaders Formed Bogus Organizations To Confuse the Security Organs.' *Al-Sharq al-Awsat*, 7 March 1999, p. 6. See also: Hauser, Christine. 'Bin Laden "behind Luxor strike."' *Middle East Times*, 23 May 1999.

54. Sheikh Abu Ithar. Op. cit.

55. 'MSANews Egypt Update: 27 June 1995: Zawahiri, Kassim, Ben Laden and the gang . . . and a brotherly gesture from Russia (fwd).' *MSANews*, 27 June 1995.

56. Bruce, James. 'Arab Veterans of the Afghan War.' *Jane's Intelligence Review*, 1 April 1997; Vol. 7, No. 4, p. 175.

57. 'Prosecutor Issues "Explosions" Case Indictment.' *Al-Dustur* (Amman), 8 July 1994.

58. Kristof, Nicholas D. 'The True Arab Leaders.' *The Washington Post*, 29 March 2002.

59. McLeod, Charles. ECMM, Report on Inter-Ethnic Violence in Vitez, Buscovaca and Zenica, April 1993, IHRLI Doc. No. 29043–29131, at 29064; Plavsic, Biljana, Republic of Serbia Presidency, To Serbs All Over the World, 30 September 1992, IHRLI Doc. No. 48072–48093, at 48081.

60. Interview with Shaykh Abu Hamza al-Masri at the Finsbury Park Mosque. 28 June 2002.

61. 'Battle of Tishin, North Bosnia, October 1992: 25 Mujahideen defeat 200 Serb Special Forces.' http://www.azzam.com.

62. Darwish, Adel. 'Saudi killed in Bosnia.' *The Independent* (London), 19 August 1992, p. 6. This incident was first reported by *Asharq al-Awsat* (London) on 18 August.

63. Though these fighters were primarily Saudi, the group also included Sudanese, Egyptians, Algerians, Palestinians, and other Muslim recruits from throughout the Arabian Gulf. The forty-three *mujahideen* reportedly included Abu Abdullah al-Jiddawi (killed only weeks later during the 'Battle of Tishin'),

Abu Asim al-Makki (also known as Muhammad Hamdi al-Ahdal, Abu Hajer al-Makki (fatally wounded during the 'Battle of Tishin'), Abu Talib al-Makki.

64. 'Right of peoples to self-determination: Use of mercenaries as a means of violating human rights and impeding the exercise of the right of peoples to self-determination.' United Nations General Assembly Item 106, Provisional Agenda, 29 August 1995. http://www.unhchr.ch. See also: Toholj, Miroslav [former Minister of Information of the Serb Republic]. 'Mujaheddins in Bosnia and Herzegovina,' http://www.karadzic.org/rat/svedok_mudza hedini_e.html.

65. 'Saudi tortures rape mujahideen during interrogation.' February 1999. http://www.azzam.com.

66. 'Right of peoples to self-determination: Use of mercenaries as a means of violating human rights and impeding the exercise of the right of peoples to self-determination.' United Nations General Assembly Item 106, Provisional Agenda. August 29, 1995. http://www.unhchr.ch. See also: Toholj, Miroslav (former Minister of Information of the Serb Republic). 'Mujaheddins in Bosnia and Herzegovina.' http://www.karadzic.org/rat/svedok_mudza hedini_e.html.

67. 'Battle of Tishin, North Bosnia, October 1992: 25 Mujahideen defeat 200 Serb Special Forces,' http://www.azzam.com.

68. 'Government's Response to Defendant's Position Paper as to Sentencing Factors.' Op. cit., pp. 36–7.

69. Transcript of confiscated Usama Bin Laden videotape, December 2001. Transcript commissioned by the United States Department of Defense. Transcript and annotations independently prepared by George Michael, translator, Diplomatic Language Services and Dr. Kassem M. Wahba, Arabic language program coordinator, School of Advanced International Studies, Johns Hopkins University. Released on http://www.cnn.com, 31 December 2001.

70. Burke, Jason. 'The Great Disappearing Act.' *The Observer* (London), 1 August 2002.

71. Seper, Jerry. 'Morocco shares information on senior al Qaeda official.' *The Washington Times*, 20 June 2002.

72. Purvis, Andrew. 'Targeting "Eagle Base."' *Time*, 5 November 2001, p. 36.

73. Federal Republic of Yugoslavia, Second Report Submitted to the Commission of Experts, 1993, IHRLI Doc. No. 28401–29019, at 28533.

74. 'Fourth Report on War Crimes in the Former Yugoslavia.' Department of State Dispatch; United States Department of State. Vol. 3, No. 52, 28 December 1992.

75. Cardinale, Anthony. 'Croat Teen Flees Terror of Bosnia.' *The Buffalo News*, 17 July 1995, p. 1B.

The Role of the Islamic Charities

The jihad by one's wealth is obligatory if the mujahideen are in need of it . . . Ibn Taymiyya was [once] asked the question: 'We have only sufficient money to feed the starving, or to fund the jihad, which would otherwise suffer?' He answered, 'We give priority to the jihad, even if the starving must lose their lives.' As in the case of the human shield, in which they are inadvertently killed by our hands, here they die by Allah's action . . . I say, if the rich were to direct what they waste in one day to the Afghani mujahideen, their money, by the permission of Allah, would help to cause a great leap forwards towards victory.

Fatwah released by Shaykh Abdullah Azzam

Allah is the one who gives you the money. He will ask you for this money as a loan . . .when you give this money to those who are fighting for the sake of Allah . . . Allah will multiply it manyfold before returning it . . . Give it to the fighters, Allah will return it to you as a good loan. Why don't you hurry to this magnificent reward?

Speech by Shaykh Omar Abdel Rahman

The roots of the modern Al-Qaida financial network that has emerged in Bosnia and other conflict zones across the Muslim world can be traced directly to early lessons learned during the chaotic days of the first Soviet-Afghan *jihad*. As the 1980s drew to a close, thousands of Islamic fundamentalists arrived in Central Asia seeking heroic adventures amid 'holy war,' often with no local guide or accommodation. At the time, several wealthy Arabian Gulf charitable organizations, typically under the guise of aiding Afghan and Pakistani refugees, stepped forward to help channel the fanatical recruits where they were most needed. These wealthy organizations, sponsored by prominent Gulf businessmen, provided weapons, guest houses, and travel papers to needy members of the quickly coalescing Al-Qaida movement. Medical ambulances belonging to the Saudi Red Crescent and other fundamentalist-run relief groups were even diverted to bring Arab fighters back and forth from combat operations.[1] By clothing their militant activity with charitable ideals, Arab-Afghan leaders discovered that they were able to slip below the radar of many international intelligence agencies – but not all of them. In 1996, a recently declassified United States government report – attributed by the *Wall Street Journal* to the Central Intelligence Agency (CIA) – alleged that a number of these

Islamic NGOs support terrorist groups or employ individuals who are suspected of having terrorist connections.'[2] The efficiency and success of the Afghan *jihad* financing model was quite an accomplishment for Usama Bin Laden and his international allies – so much so that operations continued even after the end of the Soviet-Afghan war and the expulsion of Bin Laden from the region.

In September 1992, evidence emerged that this prolific terrorist financial and recruitment network was rapidly expanding to southern Europe, including Bosnia. The 1996 American intelligence report concluded that 'nearly one third of the Islamic NGOs in the Balkans have facilitated the activities of Islamic groups that engage in terrorism, including the Egyptian Al-Gama`at Al-Islamiyya, Palestinian Hamas, and Lebanese Hizballah.' The report added that 'some of the terrorist groups, such as Al-Gama`at, have access to credentials for the UN High Commission for Refugees and other UN staffs in the former Yugoslavia.'[3] One radical Bosnian Muslim convert in Travnik revealed his naively romantic view of the use of charitable and humanitarian groups as a cover for *jihad*: '[s]ome of the Arabs who came here cried when they saw our plight – and when it was time for them to go home, they asked to stay . . . We could not say "no" to them. We could not send them away. So they stayed to help.'[4] This recurring phenomenon was self-evident to almost any experienced observer in the region. Early in the war, one British reporter confronted a group of Arabs she found wearing *kaffiyyehs* (traditional Arab headdress) in Travnik.

> 'Where are you from?' we asked. He laughed: 'All that matters is that we're here now.' He admitted that he and his colleagues were fighting the Serbs, but moments later said that they were 'humanitarian aid workers, here to help the children and provide medicine.' The Toyota then left at speed with its camera-shy militiamen still covering their faces.[5]

Such incidents were occurring on a alarmingly frequent basis. On 17 September, 44-year-old British aid volunteer Gulam Jilani Soobiah was killed in an artillery attack near Mostar that caused six other casualties. At the time of his death, Soobiah was purportedly on a humanitarian mission carrying medicine, blankets and food. However, the only survivor of Soobiah's group, a Turkish Kurd, claimed that, in fact, Soobiah and himself were part of a convoy of twelve foreign *mujahideen* that were travelling in a British-registered Land Rover. Rather than transporting medicine and charitable goods, they were actually smuggling rifles, grenades, and other more serious weapons to Muslim military forces. Investigators found documents inside the charred Land Rover linking it to a Leicester-based charity that subsequently disavowed any affiliation with Mr. Soobiah.[6]

Despite these vigorous denials, the *jihadis* quickly learned to rely on the crucial assistance and complicity of a variety of international Islamic charitable organizations working in the region. Groups were predominantly based in the Arabian Gulf,

Western Europe, and North America. From these sources, Arab fighters were often similarly able to obtain documentation allowing them to travel freely throughout the region apparently disguised as 'humanitarian relief workers.' Though the Muslim NGOs flatly rejected regular allegations aid was being given the *mujahideen*, a mountain of evidence tells a quite different story.

In late 1993, Usama Bin Laden notified his senior lieutenants that one of these organizations, the Saudi-based Lajnat al-Birr al-Dawaliyya (also known as Lajnat al-Birr al-Islamiyya, the Committee for Islamic Benevolence, Benevolence International Foundation or BIF), was being used 'to move funds to areas where *al Qaeda* was carrying out operations.' That same year, Saudi Arabia allegedly detained a BIF employee when a embarrassing 'link' was discovered between BIF and Usama Bin Laden. Yet in a perplexing display of duplicity, the Saudis went to great lengths to hide what they had found, and kept the vital intelligence on Bin Laden's financial network secret from the United States. In the words of one federal court brief filed in the case, 'the problem had been handled.'[7]

But it was hardly a closely guarded secret that BIF was involved in more than just charitable activities. The entity openly advertised itself in its Arabic-language fundraising appeals as a 'trustworthy hand for the support of [both] the mujahideen and refugees' in Bosnia.[8] Similarly, documents taken from BIF's United States-based offices in December 2001 included handwritten Arabic notations explaining that its headquarters in Croatia was established 'for relief operations and support of jihad in Bosnia-Herzegovina . . . Contribute with your mujahideen brothers to repel the Crusader-Zionist attack on Muslim lands.'[9] Another handwritten note found in Illinois by investigators revealed BIF's supreme 'unwritten law': 'no matter how poor/sick – first priority is for mujahideen.'[10]

The raid of BIF's Illinois office also turned up a number of other documents directly related to the war in Bosnia: a receipt dated 21 July 1994, from the 'Black Swans' Bosnian Muslim commando brigade for 300 blankets and 200 pairs of boots obtained from BIF; a receipt from the BiH army dated 3 June 1994, for 2,000 uniforms, 2,000 pairs of shoes, and ten 'mass communication stations' donated by BIF to 'this military unit'; a request dated 31 December 1994, from the Bosnian army for a combat ambulance (later delivered as promised in January 1995); and, a memorandum to BIF director Enaam Arnaout dated 17 November 1995 describing the recent contribution of 200 tents to the Muslim army.[11]

The BIF was represented in New York by a senior Bosnian diplomat and 'Minister Counsellor' at the Bosnian Mission to United Nations: Saffet Abid Catovic. Since 1993, Catovic has been a prominent charitable fundraiser for the Balkans and an outspoken voice at the UN mission on Islamic religious and political issues.[12] He has had a close relationship with the Kingdom of Saudi Arabia and, in interviews in 1994, he publicly thanked the Saudis for their generous financial assistance to Bosnian religious projects.[13]

In the lectures that he gave at Islamic conferences across the northeastern United States, however, it seems that Catovic was also advocating physical confrontation against the opponents of radical Islam in Bosnia and elsewhere. In a videotaped lecture published by an Islamic media outlet in New Jersey, Saffet Catovic introduced Shaykh Omar Abdel Rahman's lieutenant Siddig Ali (later convicted of a central role in a fundamentalist conspiracy to bomb New York landmarks – see Chapter 5) to speak on the subject of 'Jihad: The Forgotten Duty.' Catovic offered heartfelt praise of Siddig, and told his camera audience that they should feel 'honored to have our dear brother from Sudan, a land which is participating in the Jihad in the struggle itself, and by the mercy of Allah, has almost succeeded in gaining that victory totally and completely.' Not known to disappoint, Siddig Ali ordered his fellow fundamentalist sympathizers:

> If the Da`wa [Islamic Call] is confronted, anybody, anywhere, by any power, then the sword is to be absolutely used and implemented . . . Brother Saffet just showed us today a video of what is going on today in Muslim Bosnia. What happened to our involvement as Muslims, to attack the core of this disease? . . . Allah (SWT) warned us in the Qur`an when he said, 'O you who believe, what is the matter with you, that when it is time that you are asked to go forth to fight in the cause of Allah, you cling heavily to the earth? . . . As if we came back from our respective countries with the same defeatist mentality, that we cannot announce and pronounce these ayat [verses] of Jihad . . . because we are still afraid that the CIA or the FBI or the authorities or countries are going to be behind us . . . [and we do not] confront the kuffar [infidels] who has taken our own sisters, our brothers, as slaves in Bosnia.[14]

It is fundamentally significant that a ranking official at BIF, an organization now officially recognized by the United States government as an Al-Qaida terrorist front group, had such a close relationship with Siddig Ali, arguably one of the lead conspirators in the abortive 1995 New York terror plots case. Likewise, when police seized the personal affairs of the Egyptian El-Sayyid Nosair – later convicted for his role in the 1993 World Trade Center bombing – they discovered the business card of Saffet Catovic.

Yet, in an even more curious twist, in the wake of the conviction of Ali, Nosair, and others for plotting acts of mass murder, Catovic seems to have appropriated the responsibility of promoting *jihad* in the New York area. On 24 November 2000, the Dorral Forrestal Conference Center in Princeton, New Jersey hosted a three day local Muslim 'spiritual retreat.' One of the speakers at the event was Saffet Catovic, whose lecture was titled 'Political and Social Jihad.' In an article about the retreat, the author explained, 'Brother Saffet Catovic has been active in the Bosnian Jihad for many years.'[15] Between 20 and 26 August 2001, Catovic was a featured invitee and speaker at a 'Jihad Camp' organized for Muslim men between the ages of 14 and 25, sponsored by the northeast regional branch of the 'Young Muslims of

North America.' Though there was no explicit mention of any martial purpose, the flyer was printed in camouflage colours and the text was in military-style block print.[16] The conference registration form began with a quote from the Qur`an: 'Jihad is ordained for you (Muslims) though you dislike it, and it may be that you dislike something which is good for you and that you like something which is bad for you. Allah knows but you do not know.'[17]

Bosnian law enforcement authorities raided several locations tied to Saffet Catovic's employer BIF in March 2002, including its local headquarters in Sarajevo. They discovered three firearms, a ski mask, numerous military manuals on topics including small arms and explosives, fraudulent passport materials, and photographs of Usama Bin Laden.[18] Also found were transcripts of communications between BIF management and senior commanders of Al-Qaida based in Afghanistan. In the aftermath of the September 11 terrorist attacks, the United States government froze the assets of BIF and commenced legal action against one of its principal directors and founders, Enaam Arnaout. An FBI affidavit in the case confirmed, 'BIF was used in the early 1990s by Usama Bin Laden as a means to transfer money to bank accounts, generally held by purported relief organizations, in countries where al Qaeda members or associates were conducting operations.'[19] Nevertheless, in a sadly ironic footnote, the BIF posted a letter of recommendation on their Web site dated 15 October 2001, from the Director of the Newark Police Department, Joseph J. Santiago. Santiago had written to Saffet Catovic to 'personally thank you and your organization "Benevolence International Foundation" . . . for your ongoing and continuing efforts in demonstrating to the community that you are an organization of concern and compassion . . . Your organization exemplifies the true spirit of what America is all about.'[20]

The BIF was far from alone in its efforts to support the international *jihadi* network based in Bosnia. Not long after the assassination of Shaykh Abdullah Azzam in 1989, the notorious Shaykh Omar Abdel Rahman and his followers had violently seized control of the major Arab-Afghan fundraising and recruitment outlet based in America: the *Al-Kifah* Refugee Center, with domestic offices in Tucson, Arizona; Boston, Massachusetts; and Brooklyn, New York. In 1993, the Boston *Al-Kifah* office, also known as 'Care International,' issued a flyer to local Muslims titled, 'A Call to Jihad in Bosnia' (Figure 5). After discussing the human tragedy in Bosnia, the flyer followed: 'Ask yourself what you are doing for these Muslims. Ask Muslim governments what they are doing for these Muslims and their freedom. If you Desire to provide the Emerging Jihad Movement in Bosnia with more than Food and Shelter, Please send your [religious donations] to [*Al-Kifah*].'[21]

Al-Kifah's English-language newsletter *Al-Hussam* (*The Sword*) also began publishing regular updates on *jihad* action in Bosnia alongside its traditional column on *mujahideen* news from Afghanistan. Under the control of the minions of Shaykh Omar Abdel Rahman, the newsletter aggressively incited sympathetic

A Call For Jihad In

Bosnia

ICNA Reports:

• More than a hundred thousand killed

• 3 Million Homeless

• Thousands of Muslim girls and women have been kidnapped and kept in Yugoslav army camps for sex . Old men and children are kept in Nazi style concentration camps

• Tens of Thousands Missing and Wounded

• $150 Billion in Property Damage

Ask yourself what you are doing for these Muslims.
Ask Muslim governments what they are doing for these Muslims and their freedom.

If you Desire to provide the Emerging Jihad Movement in Bosnia with more than Food and Shelter, Please send your Sadaka to:

Bosnia Fund
c/o Alkifah Refugee Center
1085 Commonwealth Avenue
Suite 124
Boston, MA 02215

Muslims helping Muslims
since we are one

Figure 5. A pamphlet printed by the *Al-Kifah* Refugee Center advertising the *jihad* in Bosnia.

Muslims to join the *jihad* in Bosnia and Afghanistan themselves. The April 1993 edition of *Al-Hussam* carried an indignant, rambling front-page editorial about Serb atrocities against Bosnian Muslims and the appropriate Islamic response. Relating his reaction to a photo of an elderly Muslim woman being severely beaten by three Serb soldiers, the anonymous author wrote:

> I almost cried for a second time, but then I heard another voice, yelling inside of me: 'cry
> . . . like a woman,' the blood started running through my veins . . . through my head,
> through my face. No, I will not cry like a woman! *This is the time for action, not for tears*
> . . . They killed her, they killed her husband and her children . . . All are guilty . . . I
> almost gave up if it weren't for a verse in the book of Allah that sounded in my ears:
> '*Fight them, and Allah will punish them by your hands, and disgrace them and help you
> (to victory) over them, and sooth the hearts of the believers.*' . . . As for you (Serbian
> soldier) . . . you Pagan devil . . . we shall meet soon.[22]

The *Al-Kifah* Bosnian branch office in Zagreb, Croatia, housed in a modern, two-story building, was evidently in close communication with the organizational headquarters in New York. The deputy director of the Zagreb office, Hassan Hakim, admitted to receiving all orders and funding directly from the main United States office of *Al-Kifah* on Atlantic Avenue controlled by Shaykh Omar Abdel Rahman.[23] Corroborating this, several documents originating from the Zagreb bureau were found in Brooklyn in the wake of the February 1993 World Trade Center bombing. In one letter dated 11 July 1993, Hassan Hakim, on behalf of the Zagreb office, begged administrators in New York to arrange for the purchase of an ambulance from Germany. He suggested that the vehicle would initially be taken on a goodwill tour of Bosnian refugee camps and makeshift civilian hospitals 'with the help of doctors volunteering from Boston,' at least 'until we get an opportunity to hand it over to the *mujahideen* in the field.'[24] This was a tactic adopted directly from Afghanistan, where ambulances belonging to the Saudi Red Crescent and other fundamentalist-run relief groups were routinely diverted to bring Arab fighters back and forth from combat operations.[25]

Founded in 1978, the International Islamic Relief Organization (Hay'at al-Ighatha al-Islamiyya al-'Alamiyya or IIRO), based in Jeddah, Saudi Arabia, was also used by the *mujahideen* as a major conduit for sending money, men, and weapons to and from the Balkans. According to IIRO's former 'general supervisor,' 'IIRO was the first relief organization to enter Bosnia-Herzegovina and the Balkan region. From the very beginning of the Bosnia war, we were there to help.'[26]

However, IIRO had a much larger agenda in the Balkans than its supervisor was willing to discuss. In September 1992, a number of documents were found on the bodies of dead foreign guerrillas loyal to the Saudi Afghano-Bosniak commander

Abu Ishaq al-Makki near Tesanj. Among these papers was an official humanitarian aid worker identification card for 'Khalil Abdel Aziz,' a teacher from Saudi Arabia. Intriguingly, the card was printed by the Peshawar, Pakistan office of the International Islamic Relief Organization (IIRO, often referred to as 'IGASA' or 'Igasse' in the local Bosnian press – this seems to be a reference to *Ighatha*, part of IIRO's name in Arabic). The discovery of the identification card in Bosnia was certainly no coincidence: until he moved to Europe in the early 1990s, the Egyptian Islamic radical Abu Talal al-Qasimy had personally been in charge of the very same IIRO issuing office in Peshawar.[27]

The Canadian government, among others, has classified IIRO itself as 'secretly fund[ing] terrorism,' branding it a terrorist charity.[28] Much of Canada's expertise on IIRO was developed during the investigation of Mahmoud Jaballah, a suspected Egyptian Al-Jihad member jailed in Canada and accused of having contact with agents of Al-Qaida. According to Canadian officials, Jaballah spent at least 3 years working for IIRO in North America.[29] Indian intelligence has likewise reported that IIRO in Pakistan specifically financed a military training camp in Kunduz, Afghanistan for would-be fundamentalist 'holy warriors' preparing for combat in Bosnia, Chechnya, and Kashmir.[30] Even Fayez Ahmed al-Shehri, a September 11 suicide hijacker, told his father that he was preparing to do international charitable work on behalf of IIRO just prior to leaving home and committing one of the worst single acts of terrorism in modern history.[31]

Since 1994, IIRO has become quite infamous for its often direct and inexplicable links to Usama Bin Laden. Following the 1998 Embassy bombings in East Africa, the group's chapter in Nairobi was deregistered by the government of Kenya for its alleged connection to the terrorists responsible for the devastating blasts. In the wake of the American retaliation for the suicide bombings, Indian police arrested a number of suspects charged in a successive attempted attack on the United States consulates in Madras and Calcutta. This terrorist cell was led by a Bangladeshi national, Sayed Abu Nasir, acting on orders from, among others, the director of IIRO operations in Asia.[32]

IIRO is a major financial sub-branch of the Muslim World League (MWL), a Saudi 'evangelical charity' and yet another humanitarian organization accused of fundraising for militant causes in Bosnia and elsewhere.[33] According to credible *mujahideen* sources, it was none other than Shaykh Abdullah Azzam himself who had secured the approval of the MWL to open and head a branch office in Peshawar, Pakistan, in order to aid arriving Arab-Afghan volunteer fighters beginning in the early 1980s. The Peshawar office was initially financed by Usama Bin Laden, and later was subsidized by large donations from the Kingdom of Saudi Arabia.[34]

More recently, the Peshawar MWL branch office was taken over for a time by Wael Hamza Jalaidan (Figure 6), an old friend of Usama Bin Laden and Abdullah

Figure 6. Wael Hamza Jalaidan (also known as Abu al-Hassan al-Madani).

Azzam.[35] In the spring of 2000, United States officials sent a confidential memorandum to UN police forces in southeastern Europe titled 'Secret: US office onlyRelease to UNMIK [the UN administration in Kosovo].' The document named MWL representative Wael Jalaidan as an associate of Usama Bin Laden and stated that Jalaidan had directly assisted Bin Laden to 'move money and men to and from the Balkans.'[36] Indeed, in a 1999 interview with Qatar-based Al-Jazeera television, Bin Laden had discussed the assassination of Abdullah Azzam and the founding of Al-Qaida. He recalled, 'We were all in one boat, as is known to you, including our brother, Wa`el Jalaidan.'[37] United States authorities have also alleged contacts between Jalaidan and senior military lieutenants of Bin Laden, including Dr Ayman al-Zawahiri and captured terrorist mastermind Abu Zubaydah. As a result, on 6 September 2002, the United States and Saudi governments announced an unprecedented joint action to freeze Jalaidan's assets and to specially designate him as a supporter of international terrorism.[38]

The Saudi-based Al-Muwafaq Foundation, headed by businessman and philanthropist Yasin Abdullah al-Qadi, was another notable, well-funded, and influential NGO charged by the United States government with providing aid to the Arab mujahideen – allegations strongly denied by al-Qadi. In an interview with *As-Sharq al-Awsat*, al-Qadi explained that *Al-Muwafaq* was originally conceived by a collection of wealthy Saudis who wanted to aid 'disaster-stricken Muslim brothers in several areas of conflict.' Subsequently, the foundation opened a regional bureau in Bosnia in the early 1990s affiliated with the 'Croatian Islamic Center.'[39]

Qadi and the other leaders of Al-Muwafaq then needed to fill the vacancy at the head of that office left when the old director, a local Bosnian, was fired. Wael Jalaidan, Bin Laden's old friend from Afghanistan, nominated Chafiq bin Muhammad Ayadi, a veteran Tunisian Arab-Afghan activist for the post.[40] On 12 October 2002, the United States Treasury Department officially named both Yasin al-Qadi and Chafiq Ayadi as Specially Designated Global Terrorists (SDGT), and ordered that their personal assets be frozen.[41] According to a Treasury Department press release, al-Qadi 'heads the Saudi-based Muwafaq Foundation. Muwafaq is an al-Qaeda front that receives funding from wealthy Saudi businessmen . . . Saudi businessmen have been transferring millions of dollars to Bin Laden through [Al-Muwafaq].'[42] The report further indicated that Chafiq Ayadi 'is connected to the bin Laden financial network through the Mouwafaq Foundation in Munich, Germany.'[43]

Wael Jalaidan had first met Ayadi in Pakistan, shortly after Ayadi was treated in Saudi Arabia for combat wounds suffered in Afghanistan. Upon his return to the region, Ayadi began working for the Muslim World League under the direct tutelage of Jalaidan. In 1993, Ayadi suddenly asked his boss to help him find a new job in the European offices of any amenable Islamic charitable group. Jalaidan, aware of the vacancy at the Al-Muwafaq office, asked al-Qadi (a close family friend) to hire Ayadi. According to al-Qadi:

> Julaydan's nomination of Ayadi was not wrong . . . I can say that he is one of the best people I have worked with in charitable activities. During his work, he managed to provide great services to Bosnian Muslims. In addition, he won the confidence of government officials, led by the then Bosnian President Alija Izetbegovic and members of his government. On many occasions, Ayadi was the main link between the Saudi Standing Committee for the Collection of Donations for Bosnia-Herzegovina and needy people there.[44]

The Third World Relief Agency (TWRA), founded in 1987 in Vienna, Austria (with additional offices in Sarajevo, Budapest, Moscow and Istanbul) quickly became notorious for allegedly serving as a financier of – and arms broker for – irregular Muslim soldiers and *mujahideen* in Bosnia, in direct violation of an international arms embargo. The purported mission of the agency was to stimulate the spread of Islam throughout Eastern Europe and the former Soviet Union in the aftermath of the end of the Cold War. However, according to Western intelligence officials, at least half of the $350 million collected by TWRA was used primarily to purchase and transport illegal weapons on behalf of the Bosnian government and allied Muslim militants loyal to Usama Bin Laden. Quite frequently, these funds were covertly laundered through anonymous European bank accounts in Liechtenstein and Monaco.[45]

The relief agency was founded and managed primarily by Mohammed el-Fatih Hassanein, a devout Muslim and prominent member of the Sudanese National Islamic Front (NIF) party. The NIF, under the leadership of fundamentalist icon Hassan al-Turabi, opened the door to Bin Laden and his corps of followers in 1991, and gave crucial shelter and assistance for almost five years to Al-Qaida as it plotted a global war of terror against the United States and its allies. Not altogether surprisingly, Sudan (at the time home to both Hassanein and Bin Laden) also served as a major transit point and source for illegal arms shipments to Bosnia.[46] As Sudanese cultural attaché in Vienna starting in March 1992, Hassanein was unofficially responsible for supervising NIF foreign policy in Eastern Europe. He explained in 1994 magazine interview that the Bosnian civil war was not just about bringing peace or repelling a hostile invader; rather, he argued, 'Bosnia, at the end, must be Muslim Bosnia.' If not, 'everything has lost its sense and this war was for nothing.'[47]

The 1996 United States intelligence report on Islamic charities stated that Hassanein, considered 'the most influential NGO official in Bosnia,' also 'supports US Muslim extremists in Bosnia.'[48] During the 1995 trial of conspirators charged with involvement in a terrorist plot to attack landmarks in New York, Clement Rodney Hampton-el, an American Muslim who trained in the Afghan camps run by Al-Qaida, confirmed that he had been smuggling money into the United States obtained from the Third World Relief Agency for the purpose of financing the military training in New York, Connecticut, and Pennsylvania of Arab-Afghan *mujahideen* destined for Bosnia.[49] Several graduates of these makeshift camps helped organize and carry out the 1993 bombing of the World Trade Center.

Hassanein assembled a like-minded group of radical supporters and sympathizers to help manage and support the TWRA. In April 1995, when Croatian authorities arrested and searched an Algerian envoy of the *Al-Kifah* Refugee Center, they discovered 'passports of Arab individuals in Bosnia, including an employee of the Third World Relief Agency.'[50] Similarly, when Croat gunmen shot and killed five foreign *mujahideen* (including wanted members of Al-Gama`at Al-Islamiyya) outside of the town of Zepce on 14 December 1995, one of the slain suspects was carrying a Third World Relief Agency identification card.[51]

Usama Bin Laden, himself, is suspected to have donated large sums of money to the TWRA to finance the purchase of weapons and aid Muslim radicals within the Bosnian government.[52] Towards that end, investigators have also alleged a direct connection between the imprisoned Shaykh Omar Abdel Rahman and the TWRA. In secret recordings of conversations between Rahman and Third World Relief Agency's office in Vienna, the relief agency volunteered to spread the message of Al-Gama`at Al-Islamiyya, and sell the Shaykh's militant videotapes and sermons in mosques throughout Europe.[53] Faxes from the TWRA under the name of the Austrian Office 'General Director,' Mohammed el-Fatih Hassanein, were found during the Italian investigation of Shaykh Anwar Shaaban's Islamic Cultural Institute in Milan.[54] According to the CIA, even after the end of the Bosnian war, TWRA director Hassanein had intended 'to resume funding Al-Gama`at [al-Islamiyya] and other extremists in Milan and Rome [once] the network was rebuilt.'[55]

The TWRA was also involved in the procurement and transportation of weapons primarily from Sudan and the former Soviet Union directly to the Bosnian frontline. In September 1992, Western intelligence officials learned of a major ongoing project of the relief agency to ship 120 tons of Soviet-made assault rifles, mortars, mines, and ammunition via Sudan and Slovenia to Muslim forces in Bosnia. After Soviet-built transport planes deposited the arms in a Slovenian warehouse leased by the TWRA, chartered helicopters provided by a joint Russian-American venture shuttled the weapons from the warehouse through Croatia directly to Tuzla and Zenica. It was in September that Croatia suddenly decided to halt the helicopter flights through its territory. After a year-long investigation, Slovenian officials finally raided the dormant warehouse, discovering 10,000 assault rifles, 750,000 rounds of ammunition, and various rockets and explosives valued at about a total of $10 million.[56] In 1993, German police uncovered another arms smuggling operation worth $15 million financed by the TWRA. As part of that operation, Malaysian and Turkish soldiers participating in the UN peace-keeping mission in Bosnia, particularly sympathetic to the desperate plight of their local co-religionists, were instrumental in bringing the weapons into the country from Croatia.[57]

However, what is most disturbing about the illicit activities of the TWRA is that the American government allegedly had full knowledge of them. In 1996, a senior Western diplomat in Europe accused the Clinton administration of deliberately ignoring the TWRA's blatant violations of the international arms embargo. According to him, in 1993, 'We were told [by Washington] to watch them but not interfere . . . Bosnia was trying to get weapons from anybody, and we weren't helping much.

The least we could do is back off. So we backed off.'[58] As one senior Western intelligence source explained to a *Washington Post* reporter, 'The men who worked for TWRA formed a cell that is dedicated to pushing Bosnia toward the more radical movements of the Middle East. We do not believe that all of Bosnia's Muslims want that. But TWRA gave these men money, influence and power. It brought them and their ideas a long, long way.'[59]

Paradoxically, much of this 'blood money' was not even coming from Usama Bin Laden, but rather, supposed United States allies in the Muslim world. In fact, quite embarrassingly, the government of Saudi Arabia was the single largest donor to TWRA. In October 1992, in one instance alone, a Saudi royal emissary arrived suddenly at the relief agency's bank in Vienna clutching two large suitcases filled with $5 million in cash. The Saudi government has never attempted to excuse or explain its deep financial involvement with the undeniably disreputable relief agency.[60] One well-informed Saudi figure casually bragged about the efficiency of the secretive radical Islamic financing network anchored in the Arabian peninsula: 'No one can control the flow of money from Saudi Arabia . . . It is not one person – it is a thousand. We are here. Money comes to us from inside Saudi Arabia. We have private talks with businessmen. Sometimes directly, sometimes indirectly. But it comes.'[61] As is discussed later in this work, that militant alliance extended even to the highest levels of the Saudi High Commission for Relief, a quasi-official charitable group active in Bosnia with extremely close ties to the Saudi regime.

It is important to note that these predominantly Saudi-funded organizations are merely examples of a larger phenomenon and were by no means isolated cases of wrongdoing: numerous other Muslim 'humanitarian' organizations directly aided the flow of men and arms to the Arab-Afghan *mujahideen* and allied Bosnian forces in the Balkans.[62] Fundraising videotapes produced by the Egyptian Human Relief Agency (EHRA) in 1993 conveyed in Arabic that the group provided support to refugees, orphans, and 'the families of the *shuhadaa* [martyred guerrillas].' Later in these tapes, a young Bosnian woman in hijab bitterly vowed, 'we will continue to fight as *mujahids* to remain in our land and to uphold the flag of Islam. Allah promises us victory, and this is enough for us.'[63] The forty Egyptians employed by the notorious charity in Bosnia flaunted their status as wanted terror suspects. Ayman el-Hamalaway, a member of the EHRA staff, declared, 'We are all code red . . . If we ever go back to Egypt, which we will not, our names come up bright red on a computer so the police know we should be immediately arrested.'[64] Other non-Arab sources also lined up to sponsor the Bosnian *jihad*: in one incident in early September, UN and Croatian authorities turned back an Iran Air jet that landed at Zagreb, because its purported cargo of 'humanitarian aid' happened to include 4,000 assault rifles.[65]

Thus, within only a few months of the start of the Bosnian civil war, the Arab-Afghan *mujahideen* had already established an impressive local infrastructure in the region, replete with substantial financial resources, indigenous fundamentalist allies, and prolific arms smuggling operations. The true extent of the strategic underground support network remains to yet be fully revealed; however, a number of recent intelligence discoveries suggests that this network was much more expansive and complex than many had ever imagined. Millions of dollars in cash and material, crudely disguised as humanitarian relief, were collected, transferred, and disbursed to various foreign *mujahideen* combat units.

Some of these resources never even reached a conflict region; instead, they were quietly siphoned off to underwrite Al-Qaida's international network of terrorist sleeper cells. The scenes of a disturbing number of terror attacks around the world bear the distinctive footprint of the radical religious charities; notably including the 1993 World Trade Center bombing, the 1995 Bojinka plot in the Philippines, the 1995 Paris Metro bombings, the 1998 East Africa embassy bombings, the failed Algerian Millennium terror conspiracy, and the September 11 suicide hijackings. Only in recent months have Saudi authorities finally agreed to investigate and carefully regulate the activities of some of the most notorious of these alleged Al-Qaida front groups, including those active in the Balkans. It remains to be seen whether they will indeed follow up on this much-delayed promise.

Meanwhile, in 1992, as equipment and new recruits continued to arrive in Zenica and Travnik on a daily basis, the foreign *mujahideen* were about to jump headlong into meaningful armed combat against their enemies in the Balkans. For this purpose, frontline base camps had been constructed in what were once cow pastures, and local schoolhouses were likewise converted into guerrilla field hospitals. The time for boastful rhetoric was at an end, and the Arab-Afghans now stood poised to attempt to prove their much vaunted military mettle. However, it was their remarkable fanaticism and blind cruelty that quickly distinguished them in an already bloody civil war in Bosnia; one that would come to define the opening years of the 'New World Order.'

Notes

1. Muhammad, Basil *Al-Ansaru l'Arab fi Afghanistan*. The Committee for Islamic Benevolence Publications, p. 187.
2. January 1996 CIA report on 'International Islamic NGOs' and links to terrorism, p. 1. See also: Affidavit by Senior Special Agent David Kane (Bureau of Immigration and Customs Enforcement, Department of Homeland Security). *United States of America v. Soliman S. Biheiri*. United States District Court for

the Eastern District of Virginia, Alexandria Division. Case #: 03-365-A. 14 August 2003, p. 2.

3. Ibid.

4. Fisk, Robert. '"Arab brothers" come to aid of Bosnian forces.' *Independent* (London). 4 December 1992, p. 11.

5. Eykyn, George. '"Mujahidin' rush to join Islamic fundamentalists in war.' *The Times* (London). 23 September 1992.

6. 'Mujahideen riddle over Briton killed in Bosnia.' *Daily Mail* (London). 22 September 1992, p. 10.

7. 'Bill of Particulars' *United States of America v. Enaam M. Arnaout*. United States District Court Northern District of Illinois Eastern Division. Case #: 02 CR 892. 3 February 2003, p. 2.

8. Institute for Study and Documentation. 'The Balkan War.' Video produced by the Committee for Islamic Benevolence, Saudi Arabia (Lajnat al-Birr al-Islamiyya).

9. Sworn affidavit of FBI Special Agent Robert Walker. United States of America v. Benevolence International Foundation, Inc. 29 April 2002. District of Illinois, Eastern Division. Case number: 02CR0414, p. 29.

10. 'Government's Evidentiary Proffer Supporting the Admissibility of Co-Conspirator Statements.' *United States of America v. Enaam M. Arnaout*. United States District Court Northern District of Illinois, Eastern Division. Case #: 02 CR 892. 31 January 2003, p. 57.

11. Ibid., pp. 67–9.

12. Mehdi, Anisa. 'Catch the Spirit: Program #93-23 (Bosnia).' 1.5 hour VHS videocassette produced by the United Methodist Church featuring Saffet Abid Catovic, Rev. Samuel B. Phillips, Stephen W. Walker, and Kathleen M. Pratt, 1993.

13. Shaikh, Habib. 'U.N. subject to whims of "Big Five": Catovic.' *Arab News*, 17 July 1994.

14. 'Jihad: The Forgotten Duty, by Br. Siddig Ali, and Jihad in Kashmir and Bosnia.' Islamic Educational Video Series from The International Institute of Islamic Research: Burlington NJ.

15. Iqbal, Sameera. 'Seeking the Love of Allah.' *Al-Nasihah*. Newsletter of the Islamic Society of Rutgers University, Vol. 1, Issue 4, November/December 2000, p. 12.

16. http://www.ymusa.org/northeast/JihadCamp1.jpg. 3 August 2001.

17. http://ymusa.org/northeast/. 3 August 2001.

18. Sworn affidavit of FBI Special Agent Robert Walker. *United States of America v. Benevolence International Foundation, Inc.* 29 April 2002. District of Illinois, Eastern Division. Case number: 02CR0414, p. 10.

19. Ibid., p. 6.

20. Santiago, Joseph J., Police Director, Newark Department of Police. Letter dated 15 October 2001, addressed to Saffet Abid Catovic, Director of Public Relations. PO Box 548, Worth IL 60482.
21. The *Al Kifah* Refugee Center. 'A Call to Jihad in Bosnia.' Flyer found amongst material found at the former headquarters of the *Al-Kifah* Refugee Center in Brooklyn NY.
22. Care International. 'Soon . . . We Shall Meet!' *Al-Hussam*, Vol. 1, No. 7., 16 April 1993, pp. 1–2.
23. Coll, Steve and Steve LeVine. 'Global Network Provides Money, Haven.' *The Washington Post*, 3 August 1993, p. A1.
24. Letter from 'Hassan' at the Al-Kifah Zagreb office to the Al-Kifah Refugee Center, 552 Atlantic Avenue, Brooklyn NY. Dated 11 July 1993.
25. Muhammad, Basil. Op. cit.
26. 'IIRO saves forty thousand Bosnians from starvation.' *Moneyclips*, 4 July 1993.
27. *Compass Newswire*. 1 November 1995. See also: Emerson, Steven. 'An Investigation into the Modus Operandi of Terrorist Networks in the United States: The Structure of Osama Bin Laden, Al-Qaeda, Hamas and other Jihadist Organizations in the United States.' Testimony given before the House Subcommittee on National Security, Veterans Affairs and International Relations of the House Committee on Government Reform, 11 October 2001.
28. Evidence introduced by the Canadian government in the Trial of Mahmoud Es-sayy Jaballah
29. McCoy, Kevin and Dennis Cauchon. 'The Business Side of Terror.' *USA Today*, 16 October 2001.
30. Ba-Isa, Molouk Y. and Saud Al-Towaim. 'Another Saudi "hijacker" turns up in Tunis.' *Middle East Newsfile*. 18 September 2001.
31. Ba-Isa, Molouk Y. and Saud Al-Towaim. 'Another Saudi "hijacker" turns up in Tunis.' *Middle East Newsfile*, 18 September 2001.
32. Dugger, Celia W. 'Anti-US Plot in India Is Foiled; Militant Islamist Intended to Bomb 2 Consulates, Police Say.' *The New York Times*, 21 January 1999, p. 4.
33. Tanjug News Agency (Serbia), http://www.truthinmedia.org/images/muja82-3.jpg. April 2002. *Note:* Peshawar is the infamous town in the North-West Frontier Province (NWFP) of Pakistan known widely to be the 'gateway to jihad' in Afghanistan, especially for Arab volunteers of Al-Qaida.
34. Muhammad, Basil. Op. cit., p. 193.
35. Sharaf-ad-din, Nabil. 'Usama BinLaden – A Millionair [sic] Finances Extremism in Egypt and Saudi Arabia.' *Rose Al-Yusif*. No. 3388, 17 May 1993. See also: Muhammad, Basil. Op. cit., p. 26.
36. Cited in BBC news report, 3 April 2000.

37. Office of Public Affairs, United States Treasury Department. 'Treasury Department Statement on the Designation of Wa'el Hamza Julidan.' 6 September 2002. Document #PO-3397.
38. Ibid.
39. 'Saudi Businessman Al-Qadi Rules Out Suspect Ayadi's Link to al-Qa`ida.' *Al-Sharq al-Awsat* (London). 23 October 2001, p. 6.
40. Ibid.
41. The Office of Public Affairs, US Department of Treasury. 'Treasury Department Releases List of 39 Additional Specially Designated Global Terrorists.' Press release dated 12 October 2001.
42. The Office of Public Affairs, US Department of Treasury. 'Entities.' Press release dated 12 October 2001.
43. Ibid.
44. 'Saudi Businessman Al-Qadi Rules Out Suspect Ayadi's Link to al-Qa`ida.' Op. cit., p. 6.
45. Pomfret, John. 'How Bosnia's Muslims Dodged Arms Embargo: Relief Agency Brokered Aid From Nations, Radical Groups.' *The Washington Post*. 22 September, p. A01.
46. Ibid.
47. Ibid.
48. January 1996 CIA Report on 'International Islamic NGOs' and links to terrorism. p. 13. See also: Affidavit by Senior Special Agent David Kane (Bureau of Immigration and Customs Enforcement, Department of Homeland Security). *United States of America v. Soliman S. Biheiri.* United States District Court for the Eastern District of Virginia, Alexandria Division. Case #: 03-365-A. 14 August 2003, p. 2.
49. Sworn affidavit of FBI Special Agent Robert Walker. Op. cit., p. 6.
50. January 1996 CIA Report on 'International Islamic NGOs' and links to terrorism, p. 10. See also: Affidavit by Senior Special Agent David Kane (Bureau of Immigration and Customs Enforcement, Department of Homeland Security). *United States of America v. Soliman S. Biheiri.* United States District Court for the Eastern District of Virginia, Alexandria Division. Case #: 03-365-A. 14 August 2003, p. 2.
51. Pomfret, John. 'Bosnian Officials Involved in Arms Trade Tied to Radical States.' *The Washington Post*, 22 September 1996, p. A26. For more on this incident and the mysterious death of Anwar Shaaban, see Chapter 8.
52. Pomfret, John. 'Bosnian Officials Involved in Arms Trade Tied to Radical States.' Op. cit., p. A26.
53. Pomfret, John. 'Bosnian Officials Involved in Arms Trade Tied to Radical States.' Op. cit., p. A26.

54. Italian Division of General Investigations and Special Operations (DIGOS) Anti-Terrorism Report. 'Searches at the Islamic Cultural Center, Viale Jenner 50, Milano, 6/26/1995.' Dated 15 September 1997.

55. January 1996 CIA Report on 'International Islamic NGOs' and links to terrorism, p. 13. See also: Affidavit by Senior Special Agent David Kane (Bureau of Immigration and Customs Enforcement, Department of Homeland Security). Op. cit.

56. Pomfret, John. 'How Bosnia's Muslims Dodged Arms Embargo: Relief Agency Brokered Aid From Nations, Radical Groups.' Op. cit., p. A01.

57. Pomfret, John. 'How Bosnia's Muslims Dodged Arms Embargo: Relief Agency Brokered Aid From Nations, Radical Groups.' Op. cit., p. A01.

58. Pomfret, John. 'How Bosnia's Muslims Dodged Arms Embargo: Relief Agency Brokered Aid From Nations, Radical Groups.' Op. cit., p. A01.

59. Pomfret, John. 'Bosnian Officials Involved in Arms Trade Tied to Radical States.' Op. cit., p. A26.

60. Pomfret, John. 'How Bosnia's Muslims Dodged Arms Embargo: Relief Agency Brokered Aid From Nations, Radical Groups.' Op. cit., p. A01.

61. Coll, Steve and Steve LeVine, (1993), A1 'Global Network Provides Money, Haven.' *The Washington Post*. 3 August, p. A1.

62. Rogosic, Zeljko. 'Vast investigation in Bosnia Herzegovina.' *Nacional* (Bosnia), issue 306; 27 September 2001.

63. Egyptian Humanitarian Relief Organization ('Human Relief Agency'), The Bosnian Holocausts.' Videocasette. Egyptian Humanitarian Relief Organization: Zagreb, Croatia, 1993.

64. Hedges, Chris. 'Foreign Islamic Fighters in Bosnia Pose a Potential Threat for G.I.s.' *The New York Times*, 3 December 1995, section 1, p. 1.

65. Vigodda, Jon. 'Allah's Army Goes West.' *The Jerusalem Report*.

–4–

The Battle Begins

Pledge, O Sister:
> To the sister believer whose clothes the criminals have stripped off;
> To the sister believer whose hair the oppressors have shaved;
> To the sister believer whose body has been abused by the human dogs.

Pledge, O Sister:
> Covenant, O Sister . . . to make their women widows and their children orphans;
> Covenant, O Sister . . . to make them desire death and hate appointments and prestige;
> Covenant, O Sister . . . to slaughter them like lambs and let the Nile, al-Asi, and Euphrates rivers flow with their blood;
> Covenant, O Sister . . . to be a pick of destruction for every godless and apostate regime;
> Covenant, O Sister . . . to retaliate for you against every dog who touches you even with a bad word.

From an Al-Qaida training manual exhibited during the trial of conspirators from the 1998 East Africa Embassy Bombings

The Arab-Afghans and their disciples saw themselves as magnificent, divine warriors who could, even in small numbers, change the ultimate course of a larger battle. The radical Islamic units trained at the Al-Qaida camps were instructed to serve as a hardened spearhead inspiring and leading larger forces of less-experienced local Muslim recruits. Instead of 'liberating' one Islamic country at a time (as per the strategy of Abdullah Azzam), the new generation of Arab-Afghans would secretly float around the world planting seeds of anger and revolt. The *mujahideen* had arrived in Europe with ghastly enthusiasm, fully intending to turn the Balkans into the new training ground for their next generation of suicidal holy warriors. To prove their fatal resolve, the foreign fighters traded gruesome 'martyrdom' songs glorifying the young Arab men who had fought the Soviets in Afghanistan and been killed during battle. In the midst of such horrific excess, both the adversaries of the *mujahideen* and often even their allies had cause to respect and fear them. The infamous reputation soon proved to be well-deserved and Al-Qaida's decision to take up arms in the Bosnian civil war contributed in turning much of central Bosnia into a humanitarian nightmare.

At about the same time as the Third World Relief Agency was busy smuggling weapons to Bosnia from the Sudan in September 1992, the first 'official' offensive by the Arab *mujahideen* took place in the environs of central Bosnia. According to Shaykh Abu Abdel Aziz, the plan was to 'attack[] Sarajevo from Yesiko[sic] . . . whatever happens we wanted to open a route into Sarajevo so that aid could get inside.' The fifty-five-man unit responsible for this operation was under the lead of Abu Muhammad al-Faatih al-Bahraini (a prince in the Bahraini royal family, also known as Shaykh Hamid al-Khalifa, Abu al-Khawla al-Bahraini), with Anwar Shaaban as his vice-commander.[1] Deeply respected by his peers, al-Faatih had relinquished his former life of wealth and privilege in the Arabian Gulf and instead chose to fight in the Afghan *jihad*, where he gained 'a high level of military experience.'[2]

According to the guerrillas who fought under Abu Muhammad al-Faatih during the battle, this first *mujahideen* assault was relatively effective and managed to disrupt the Serb frontlines. However, lacking heavy weapons of any sort, they were forced to withdraw when the Serb forces counterattacked with a barrage of artillery. But no matter what their propaganda claimed, the guerrillas could not deny the embarrassing combat casualties they suffered as a result. Al-Faatih had instructed that, should he be killed, Abu Anas al-Jiddawi, and then subsequently Abu Shareef al-Masri should take over tactical command of the unit. Both Abu Anas and Abu Shareef were experienced, well-trained fighters; yet, the operation entirely unravelled when al-Faatih was shot and killed by a Serb sniper and, thus, became the second 'official' Arab fighter to achieve *shuhada*, or 'martyrdom,' in Bosnia. Within minutes, Abu Anas and Abu Shareef teamed up to provide machine-gun cover to other guerrillas attempting to rescue al-Faatih's dead body. As they labored to rescue their fallen leader, a mortar shell hit their position, killing both Anas and Shareef simultaneously. Before the remainder of the unit retreated, five other foreign *mujahideen* were killed, including Umar al-Tahawi, a veteran Egyptian Arab-Afghan fighter.[3]

In September, Arab fighters trained in Afghanistan were also battling enemy forces in Gorazde and near the strategic central Bosnian town of Travnik. In Gorazde, a combined force of *mujahideen* and Bosnian Islamists initiated a campaign of harassment and violence against local Christian civilians in order to 'cleanse' the area. The guerrillas were organized into units of between fifteen and twenty seasoned fighters each, and repeatedly ambushed victims on the routes between Sarajevo and Serb-controlled regions, including near Gorazde.[4]

The *mujahideen* suffered numerous casualties near Travnik, including 29-year-old, Saudi-born Hussam al-Deen al-Sadat. Al-Sadat had grown up in a Western society, far away from the political and religious conflicts of Bosnia and the Middle East. He attended a prestigious private school in Boston, living the life of a modern American. However, al-Sadat's life took a dramatic turn in his freshman year at

Pima College in Tucson, Arizona. At that time, Tucson had become a major center of Islamic fundamentalism and Arab-Afghans had established the first offices of the *Al-Kifah* Refugee Center there. In this ideological environment, it is not entirely surprising that the young al-Sadat was successfully recruited into a life of terror and violence.

The Saudi student suddenly abandoned his college career in 1987 and left with a small group of Muslims (including at least one other American) to join in the Soviet-Afghan *jihad*. After spending two tours of duty in Afghanistan, Hussam al-Deen developed into a battle-hardened guerrilla platoon leader. His life had so dramatically changed that an existence outside of war was no longer a tolerable possibility. He again returned to the combat zone in July 1992, this time in Bosnia. A little over two months later, an official claiming to be from the 'Islamic Relief Organization' notified Hussam al-Deen's parents of his death. Later, the relief agency forwarded his personal effects to them, including a letter he wrote as he died and a bloodstained Bosnian Army uniform patch. His mother told the *New York Times*, 'He said he wanted to be a martyr, and he asked me to pray for this.'[5]

The next significant military encounter of the *mujahideen* proved no more encouraging than the initial debacle at Tesanj. By October, the ongoing clashes between the various armed forces surrounding Tesanj reached their peak, and a major confrontation took place between Arab *mujahideen* and Serbian soldiers on Mount Bandera. At first, the military manoeuvre referred to by the *jihadis* as the 'Battle of Tishin' seemed to be going well. In the weeks leading up to the conflict, Bosnian Army soldiers had formed frontline combat positions at the peak of Mount Bandera with the assistance of twenty-five experienced Arab guerrillas, most of whom were Saudi veterans of the Soviet-Afghan *jihad* (including several who had previously fought with Abu Ishaq). This time, these men were under the general command of Shaykh Abu Sulaiman al-Makki, who had also helped lead the early *mujahideen* operations near Tesanj. Under interrogation by United States authorities, Enaam Arnaout (Abu Mahmoud al-Suri) has admitted that a number of these fighters were sponsored by his organization BIF, were met at the airport and taken to a BIF guesthouse in Zagreb, and later were given temporary barracks at a BIF 'schoolhouse' in Tesanj.[6]

At the start of hostilities on Mount Bandera, the Arab-Afghans claimed to have swiftly killed a number of Serb soldiers, taking no casualties of their own.[7] However, the optimistic mood of the battle suddenly changed when the Serbs initiated a massive counterattack. Bosnian and Arab-Afghan frontline positions were pounded for three days by Serbian artillery. According to *mujahideen* sources, they 'were in their bunkers and they could hear nothing but the sounds of the shells exploding around them.' Unbeknownst to the *jihadi* guerrillas, the frightened Bosnian Army soldiers had quietly withdrawn without mentioning anything to their Muslim comrades. Unaware that their reinforcements had vanished, the Arab fighters set out once again and brazenly raided a Serb supply line, unwittingly revealing their positions to a much larger enemy force. The Serbs counterattacked from three sides causing heavy casualties, with six dead and two critically injured out of the original twenty-five-strong *mujahideen* unit.

In the initial chaotic minutes of the Serb counterattack, the Muslim soldiers suddenly found themselves within mere feet of their enemy, and shrapnel rained down on their positions. Abu Umar at-Tayyib (22 years old, from Medina, Saudi Arabia), a veteran of the Soviet-Afghan *jihad*, leapt from the safety of his trench and fired indiscriminately with his PK machine-gun at Serb positions until he was cut down in a hail of gunfire. Abu Hajer al-Makki (24 years old, from Mecca, Saudi Arabia) attempted to cross the combat zone to retrieve Abu Umar's body. Facing stiff resistance, Abu Hajer was severely wounded and quickly died of his injuries.[8] Shortly thereafter, three other Afghan *jihad* veterans were killed by falling grenades and gunfire: Abu Abdullah al-Jiddawi (24 years old from Jeddah, Saudi Arabia), Abu Shaheed ash-Sharqi (18 years old from eastern Saudi Arabia), and Abu Abdullah al-Falastini, a 25-year-old Palestinian who was a respected and experienced military trainer at the notorious *Al-Sadda* guerrilla training camp in Afghanistan.[9] According to Al-Qaida sources, '[m]any Mujahideen received military training through [Abu Abdullah's] hands.'[10] His death, though celebrated as a shining example of 'martyrdom,' was clearly a blow to the overall cause of the Arab-Afghans. By the beginning of October, Shaykh Abu Abdel Aziz was publicly admitting that at least seventeen of his foreign fighters had been killed in battle since the start of the conflict in April.[11]

Once again during this battle, the senior unit commander was among the casualties of failed attempts to rescue the bodies of dead *mujahideen*. Shaykh Abu Sulaiman al-Makki was 'sprayed' by automatic weapons fire as he dashed across the no-man's land between opposing military trenches to retrieve the body of Abu Khaleel al-Makki, another Saudi volunteer 'martyred' during the battle. Though he was seriously injured and was near death, Abu Sulaiman was at last recovered by other Arab guerrillas and carried to safety. A few days afterwards, though he ultimately survived his injuries, Shaykh Abu Sulaiman lost feeling and movement in his legs and was permanently paralysed from the waist down.[12]

Muhammad Hamdi al-Ahdal (also known as Abu Asim al-Makki, Muhammad al-Hamati) was also among the wounded from the battle. Al-Ahdal was a resident of Saudi Arabia, previously of Yemeni origin. He trained and joined the Arab guerrillas in Afghanistan during the late 1980s, and reportedly fought heroically in the opening stages of the Bosnian campaign. Despite the impressive networking connections he made, Abu Asim paid a terrible price for his involvement in the *jihad* there: during the Battle of 'Tishin,' he had a near encounter with a hand grenade, losing one leg entirely and remaining paralysed in one arm ever since.[13] He soon left the Balkans and returned to the Arabian peninsula. The personal sacrifice Abu Asim made in Bosnia only encouraged him further along the path of violence in the name of radical Islam. In Yemen, he became one of the owners of honey-production companies accused by United States federal authorities[14] of being prominent Middle Eastern financial conduits of Al-Qaida.[15]

Facing heavy casualties and disorder in their ranks, the Arab *mujahideen* at last withdrew to a nearby Bosnian Muslim village to rally their remaining troops and treat the wounded. Several hours later, ten foreign fighters with only 'lighter injuries' returned to Mount Bandera alongside fifteen Bosnian soldiers. Arab sources claimed that this mixed military force was able to eventually dislodge the Serbs, pushing them back to distant defensive positions. Overall, the *mujahideen* generally claimed the October battle on Mount Bandera as a glorious victory for their cause, ignoring the heavy human price that had been paid for such a question-able triumph. They lauded 'Tishin' as a 'turning point' in the war because the local Bosnian Muslim populace, who had been quite sceptical at first, admired the brave efforts of the Arab fighters in battle: 'the Bosnians changed their opinions about the Mujahideen and began to respect them as sincere, brave fighters, who came to fight not for fame or money, but for the defence of their religion and honour of their people and to please Allah the Almighty.'[16] But even some Arab-Afghan sources publicly admitted that the operation 'did not go perfectly: many mujahideen were frustrated by how easily Bosnian army units retreated and withdr[e]w under Serb attack.'[17] Anger at the cowardice of the Bosnian military and the resulting debacle on Mt. Bandera convinced at least several disillusioned, would-be members of the *mujahideen* to abandon the *jihad* in Bosnia and dejectedly return to their respective homelands.

Despite the, albeit, serious tactical errors made during the Tesanj campaign, the Arab-Afghan struggle in Bosnia was still far from over. At the same time as the Battle of Tishin on Mount Bandera, *jihadi* units in another nearby combat zone turned their attention to more sensational targets. For months, the ethnic Serb army had seized various strategic positions in the mountains surrounding Sarajevo, leading to the virtual strangulation of the city. Dramatic camera footage was played on television stations around the world of civilians in Sarajevo caught in the bloody crossfire of mortars, artillery, and Serb snipers. A thin layer of UN international peacekeepers had neither the military capability nor the mandate necessary to take firm action to protect the embattled residents of the city. In October 1992, another group of seven Arab *mujahideen* based on Mt. Igman teamed up with local Bos-nian army soldiers in a bold operation to 'liberate' the international airport in the suburb of Butmir and surrounding environs south of Sarajevo from the tenacious grip of nearby Serb troops and armor.[18]

Butmir was a Bosnian army-held outpost and an absolutely crucial link in a supply chain between military camps on Mt. Igman and Sarajevo proper. The October battle, though debatably successful, developed into quite a legendary tale.

Figure 7. Abu Zubair al-Madani (also known as Mohammed al-Habashi), a cousin of Usama Bin Laden fighting in Sarajevo.

It was memorialized and made relatively famous in a widespread propaganda and fundraising video distributed by the Saudi headquarters of Lajnat al-Birr al-Dawaliyya (Benevolence International Foundation, BIF). The video documented dramatic scenes of frontline combat and interviews with Arab survivors who discussed the events that took place near Sarajevo.

The seven *mujahideen*, led by Abul-Abbas al-Madani, included Abu Zubair al-Madani (also known as Mohammed al-Habashi), 'Abu Iyas,' and 'Abu Marwan.' Abu Zubair, a 24-year-old Saudi and cousin to Usama Bin Laden, was born and raised in the city of Medina. In 1985, at the age of 17, he travelled to Afghanistan and joined the Arab-Afghan volunteer corps, spending most of the war in the vincinity of Khost.[19] Towards the end of the conflict, he personally participated in the *mujahideen* battles for Jaji, Jalalabad, and Kabul. Abu Zubair (Figure 7) was one of the most famous of a group of 'notable Mujahideen personalities' to participate in these celebrated combat operations – that select group also included, to name a few, Shaykh Abdullah Azzam and Bin Laden himself.[20] However, Abu Zubair was much more modest about his exploits; in one amateur videotape interview shot in Bosnia, he explained, 'we were there in Afghanistan, but our participation was not real serious action like here now because the Afghans took us to be guests. So they didn't want us to be too exposed or for us to die there.'[21]

After the fall of Kabul in the spring of 1992, he returned to Saudi Arabia and spent several months at home in Medina. Abu Zubair was 'blessed with a beautiful voice' and, while in Medina, recorded a renowned audiocassette entitled *Qawaafil-us-Shuhadaa* (*Caravans of the Martyrs*). That tape, which became a classic in the annals of the *mujahideen*, related the inspirational tales of the fallen Arab-Afghan 'martyrs' of the first Soviet-Afghan *jihad*. Indeed, according to those who fought alongside Abu Zubair, he had an extraordinary obsession with the concept of martyrdom in the name of Islam. His *mujahideen* eulogy recounted: 'Once [Abu Zubair] was asked, 'Why do you hurry for Martyrdom, whereas you have not yet done much for Islam?' And he replied, 'What did my brothers give for Islam, who were killed before me. Our souls are the most valuable things that we can give.'[22]

Accompanied by his close friend from Medina Abul-Abbas al-Madani, Abu Zubair resolved to travel to Bosnia in the summer of 1992 and again participate in the *jihad*. The Saudis arrived and joined their Arab-Afghan brethren in August, eventually being deployed to the training camp at the summit of Mount Igman, towering over 8,000 feet above Sarajevo. Less than two months later, they mobilized and prepared for the battle to 'liberate' Butmir.[23]

The two travellers from Medina and five other Arab companions were fighting alongside a much larger Bosnian army force led by a famous commander named 'Zulfikar.'[24] With over 2,000 men at his command, the 30-year old Zulfikar had organized 'Operation Labyrinth': an intricate military operation designed to pull together disparate bands of Muslim troops (including the *mujahideen*) in a 'final offensive' to free Sarajevo. Zulfikar was a self-styled Muslim guerrilla, and his loyal troops on Mount Igman enthusiastically chanted 'the war cry of the Islamic *jihad*: "In the name of Allah!"' 'Zuka,' as he preferred to be called, frankly told British reporters shortly before 'Operation Labyrinth,' '[i]f we lose 10,000 men in the battle for Sarajevo – and we might – there will still be another 10,000 to break the siege and free our capital. You only live once and our lives are as nothing compared with our cause.' Despite his vocal bravado, Zulfikar was not really a hardcore fundamentalist. However, with little other choice, he openly embraced his Islamist allies, hoping to tip the delicate balance in the see-saw battle for Sarajevo.

The situation in Butmir by this time was extremely tense: not only had Serbian forces surrounded the area with troops and tanks but there was a major United Nations base at the airport. The strip at Butmir served as the primary landing point for the convoy of Western humanitarian and peacekeeping flights providing crucial aid to the beleagured city of Sarajevo. On 4 September, unknown assailants fired a surface-to-air missile at an Italian transport plane landing at Butmir, destroying the aircraft and killing the four-man crew.[25] Four days later, a French UN convoy from the 403rd Logistics Support Battalion came under fire south of the airport. The incident resulted in five casualties, including two dead French soldiers.[26] On 10 October two Egyptian UN soldiers were injured by a falling mortar round in their emplacements surrounding Butmir. Throughout this time, the airport and base controlled by the UN had come under sporadic shelling.[27] A tense crisis developed in mid-October when Bosnian military forces, alleging that Serbian tanks were infiltrating the area, blockaded the access road between Butmir and the city of Sarajevo. The two warring sides were about to face off directly in the midst of the stranded international peacekeeping mission.

At approximately 6 p.m., after an intense artillery bombardment, the battle finally began. According to one Arab *mujahid*, 'may God bless them, Abu Iyas and Abul-Abbas and Abu Marwan, they advanced to the enemy's location . . . only a street separated us . . . and they saw with their own eyes that [the Serbs] were running away.' As the foreign *jihadis* engaged the Serbs, the fighting grew fierce and a number of Muslim soldiers were injured, including 'Abu Iyas.' The group of Arab-Afghans mostly departed to seek urgent medical care, while Zulfikar and the Bosnians pressed on against the Serbs: 'we withdrew to the rear, to the nearest point, therefore we did not have any news about the brothers.'[28]

Abu Zubair and Abul-Abbas had both suffered fatal injuries during their participation in the battle. Abu Zubair was wounded by shrapnel in his throat but did not immediately appear close to death; Abul-Abbas was apparently struck seriously in the chest and the leg by splinters from a tank round. Underestimating the seriousness of their injuries, the Arab companions attempted to transfer Abu Zubair and Abul-Abbas 'in big cars' from a regrouping point in Hrasnica to the Arab-Afghan headquarters in Zenica. As a *mujahideen* witness noted, Abu Zubair's condition 'was very bad . . . it seems that he bled to death.' The harrowing eight-hour journey proved ultimately fruitless: even in Zenica, there were no provisions for the degree of medical attention they both required.[29] The deaths of the two men did little to faze the enthusiasm of their Al-Qaida companions, who considered them as divine 'martyrs.' Abu Zubair's father, interviewed later, proclaimed:

> Praise be to Allah, and we offer thanks to Allah. We kneel before Allah, out of gratefulness for this martyrdom because he did not want anything else. I would have been sad if they had come to me and told me [my son] has been made a prisoner. So, I prayed for his martyrdom, and thanks be to Allah, his wish has been fulfilled . . . Our history is glorious and our religion is mighty. Our religion is Islam.[30]

Abul-Abbas' father offered similar thoughts:

> This martyr is a source of pride to me, it is my son Fadil . . . Praise be to God, thank God. I have been blessed with children and I thank God that they have followed the way of the Prophets and the Companions . . . tell me, how can I sleep, how can I sit, how can I enjoy my rest while our Muslim brothers are slaughtered by the infidels . . . how can I not be a fundamentalist? By Allah, I would sleep on reeds.[31]

However, as later accounts of the battle proved, Abu Zubair and Abul-Abbas were not in fact killed by their hated Serbian enemy. Rather, apparently in the midst of the exchange, nearby 'infidel UN forces' – among them Egyptian soldiers – intervened and attempted to disrupt the battle. Abu Zubair and Abul-Abbas engaged them in a shootout and were both killed by these Egyptian troops. According to *mujahideen* sources, French UN soldiers also killed another *jihadi* en route to the battle, a British Muslim named Abu Ibrahim al-Turki. Moreover, it was further alleged that, as part of the same operation, UN personnel 'killed a Syrian and an Algerian student in Sarajevo.'[32]

The Islamists loudly proclaimed that this was all the evidence they needed: 'it became apparent the cunning role that the international forces were playing. They always protected the Christians and hunted the Muslims because all [infidels] only stay loyal to each other. It is not possible for the problems of the Muslims to be resolved at the conference tables of the [infidels].'[33] Henceforth, for the *mujahideen*, the UN would be treated as just another 'infidel' warring faction in the Bosnian civil war, and could be targeted with equal moral justification as attacking the Serbs. Though the Bosnian army usually did its best to keep peacekeepers from Western nations away from strongholds of foreign fighters, often (such as in this case), confrontation was inevitable.

For their part, the UN troops in question apparently acted in self-defence. On 16 October, at about the same time as the 'Battle of Butmir,' UN peacekeepers reported coming under significant fire near the airport. It was not immediately known who shot at the peacekeepers, but some Bosnian troops had earlier pledged to deal with UN forces exactly as their Serb enemies if the international peace-keepers tried to forcibly open the road to the airport.[34] The following day, the UN formally accused Bosnian government soldiers of firing at UN personnel.[35] Available evidence suggests that, rather than Bosnian military troops, it may have been, in fact, primarily Arab fighters who were to blame for the unprovoked attack. Thus, the resulting death of the venerated Abu Zubair al-Madani took on an even greater propaganda significance: he had had been 'martyred' in a distant Muslim frontier land while battling the international 'enemies of Islam.' Despite the disappointing losses the Arab unit had suffered, the foreign *mujahideen* nevertheless celebrated when they heard that the Bosnian army had made significant progress in Butmir under the stirring command of Zulfikar. In fact, Muslim forces had advanced even to within sight of the airport. The victory emboldened the *jihadis* and one Arab survivor predicted, as a result, 'hopefully, we will take Sarajevo and free the Muslims there. The news was good so far.'[36]

At the beginning of November, a new group of *mujahideen* was dispatched to the heights of Mt. Bjelasnica, another mountainous approach to Sarajevo only 20 minutes south-west of the city. In peacetime, Bjelasnica was known as a popular spa and alpine skiing resort, drawing tourists from across the world and hosting several parts of the 1984 Winter Olympic Games. However, during the war, the imposing mountain (at 2,067 m) was used by Serb forces as a highly defensible artillery post. From their positions, the Serbs incessantly shelled the surrounding area, including Sarajevo. All fourteen Muslim villages that dotted the mountain itself were destroyed, and their inhabitants exiled to remote parts of Bosnia and German refugee camps. On 7 November the *mujahideen* attacked Serb positions on Bjelasnica and claimed to make significant progress, even capturing the peak of the mountain.[37] However, irrespective of these supposed Muslim military victories, de facto fighting continued there until August. Serb forces ultimately withdrew not because of the military prowess of their *mujahideen* enemies, but because of threats issued by NATO of armed reprisals for the continuing disastrous siege of Sarajevo.

The Arab-Afghans continued undaunted in their efforts to help lift the siege of Sarajevo through the end of 1992. In late December, Abu Talha al-Masri organized a group of *mujahideen* from the Mehurici training camp to aid outnumbered Bosnian army forces in the surburbs of Sarajevo. Abu Talha was originally from Egypt and, like many of the Bosnian *jihadis*, had studied abroad at the Islamic University of Medina, in Saudi Arabia. Abu Talha was assisted in this operation by Abu el-Ma`ali (also known as Abdelkader Mokhtari, 'The Gendarme'), a young commander from the Algerian Armed Islamic Group (Al-Jama'ah al-Islamiyya al-Musallah, or GIA), who had arrived in Bosnia soon after the war had begun in hopes of supporting the growing *mujahideen* base there.[38] At least two other Algerian fundamentalists, Abu Muhajir al-Djazairi and Abu Sabir al-Djazairi, also joined Abu Talha's unit for this operation.[39]

In the early 1990s, returning Algerian Arab-Afghan veterans were largely responsible for founding the GIA, an organization that championed a particularly ruthless philosophy of murdering anyone who stood in the way of a fundamentalist regime, including competing Muslim clerics, politicians, foreigners, journalists, teachers, women, children, and other such 'enemies of Allah.' The GIA was so brutal and feared by even those in the Arab world that Bin Laden himself allegedly urged its leadership to rename and reform themselves in order to present a 'better image of the Jihad.'[40]

However, the nefarious group found many eager recruits from the downtrodden North African urban ghettos throughout Western Europe. With soaring unemployment and systematic racial intolerance against Arabs, French slums and jails particularly provided ideal breeding grounds for youths to be brainwashed in radical Islam. One Parisian of Algerian descent explained: 'There are millions of us who feel excluded and unwanted . . . A lot of us think since we have nothing to lose, we might as well turn to violence to get some respect. There is so much disgust around here that one day the authorities will wake up and find they are fighting a civil war.' Another unemployed north African immigrant in Paris chimed in: 'I think you have to be a little soft in the head to follow these Islamic radicals, but I understand why there is so much frustration. When you can't get a job and you get checked five times by the police even when you are well dressed, you begin to think that society has declared you an enemy. So you want to fight back.'[41]

The extremism of the Algerian Islamists extended far beyond the borders of North Africa, including to the Balkans. The Algerian *mujahideen* volunteers saw many parallels between their own struggle and that of the embattled Bosnians. 'I hate the French,' an Algerian Arab-Afghan in Sarajevo bitterly noted, 'hate them – more than I do other countries, because of what they did in Algeria. We drove them out of my country and we will also win in Bosnia.'[42]

Abu el-Ma`ali was no exception among his fanatic North African comrades: he has since been aptly described by United States officials as a 'junior Osama bin Laden.'[43] In reflection, Abu Hamza al-Masri, an Egyptian Islamist militant based in London who has known Abu el-Ma`ali since the early days of the Bosnian *jihad*, mused 'I think he's a good person, a good-hearted person. Hard working. He was a leader . . . hard worker, a lion in fighting . . . a good brother – but he's too young and he's too naive.'[44] Nevertheless, the fearless Algerian would soon become a sacred legend among the Arabs fighting in Bosnia. Little is known of his background, and the Arab-Afghans have gone to extraordinary efforts to protect his identity. Videos taken of him leading combat operations in the Balkans have been deliberately edited to distort and conceal his appearance. This offers, perhaps, only a small inkling of how important Abu el-Ma`ali has been to the overall international *jihad* of Al-Qaida and its various affiliate organizations.

After departing from the Mehurici camp, Abu Talha, Abu el-Ma`ali, and the rest of the men travelled from the frontline near Travnik into the mountains south-west of Visoko, less than 10 km away from Sarajevo. On 29 December, the unit moved forward alongside a large contingent of allied Bosnian army soldiers in what the Arabs later termed 'Operation Ilijas' or, alternatively, 'the second Visoko operation.' The advance appeared to be going well, and made significant progress until patrolling Serb helicopters and accompanying troops discovered the Muslim force near the village of Ilijas and attacked it. Similar to the previous debacle at 'Tishin,' facing a heavy firefight, the Bosnian soldiers quickly withdrew, thereby cutting off the communication lines of the *mujahideen*. Abu Talha, the commander, was shot in the leg by a sniper, and was among a large number of Muslim wounded.

Abu el-Ma`ali dragged Abu Talha, bleeding profusely, to a nearby house where they sought shelter from a Serb artillery barrage. Leaving Abu Talha behind, Abu el-Ma`ali crawled through the snow to safety, eventually reaching friendly frontline positions. Rather than going himself, he ordered three Bosnian volunteers attached to the *mujahideen* unit to go back and retrieve Abu Talha. The rescue mission came to an abrupt end when all three were killed by Serb shelling before they even reached Abu Talha. Abu Talha, abandoned by his Arab and Bosnian companions alike, eventually bled to death where he lay. Though the *mujahideen* had come tantalizingly close to Ilidza, 'lacking sufficient troops to occupy the territory' they had managed to conquer, once again, the Arabs retreated to more defensible positions closer to Visoko. Overall, the combined Serb air and ground counterattack had caused heavy casualties: seven foreign fighters were killed as well as 'a large number' of allied Bosnian soldiers. The seven *jihadi* 'martyrs' included the commander Abu Talha, Abu Muhammad al-Falastini, Abu Maryam al-Afghani, Abu Hudaifah al-Afghani, Abul-Harith al-Bahraini, Imraan al-Turki, and Saeed al-Turki.[45] Other accounts of these battles indicated that seven Arabs from Saudi Arabia, Egypt, Morocco, Algeria, Tunisia and Bahrain were also wounded in the fighting near Travnik.[46]

Abu Muhammad al-Falastini (also known as Abu Mahmud al-Falastini) was a Palestinian medical student studying in France. While there, he befriended a French Muslim named Abul-Waleed. The two shared similar enthusiasm for radical Islam, and they both travelled together to Bosnia in hopes of joining the *mujahideen*. They were trained at the camps near Zenica, run by *Amir* Abu Abdel Aziz Barbaros. By December, Abu Muhammad was preparing to return to France after his 'tour of duty' when he learned of the planned operation near Ilijas. He forewent his chance to return home, and instead, enlisted with Abu Talha's unit. In the midst of attacking a Serb bunker alongside Abu Hamza al-Suri and Abu Sabir al-Djazairi, he was shot and killed by an enemy sniper.[47]

Abu Maryam al-Afghani was an Afghan veteran of the anti-Soviet *jihad*. Before travelling to Bosnia, Abu Maryam spent several years living in Germany, where settled, married, and became 'extensively' involved in Islamic activism there. With the blessing of his supportive wife, he again sought the join in the *jihad*, this time in Bosnia. With his best friend Abu Hudaifa al-Afghani, he travelled to the Balkans to help the *mujahideen*. During the Ilijas operation, Abu Maryam and Abu Hudaifa were both killed within minutes of each other.[48]

Imraan al-Turki was originally from Turkey, but had moved to the United States and adopted American citizenship. He arrived in Bosnia in the fall of 1992. There, he became the *Amir* of the Turkish recruits, who were sufficient in number to be sequestered in their own separate living quarters in Zenica, away from the Arab volunteers. Imraan would reportedly translate the fundamentalist religious and political lectures given to the Arabs during training, and attempt to deliver them to his largely secular Turkish-speaking brethren. After two months of combat, Imraan was finally preparing to return to his home in the United States. While staying with Abu Muhammad al-Falastini, he learned of Abu Talha's planned operation and, on his last bid for martyrdom, finally met with success after being fatally shot in the stomach.[49]

Abul-Harith al-Bahraini was another volunteer soldier who had given up a life of fame and fortune for a chance to struggle 'in pursuit of Allah's pleasure.' In Bahrain, he was a talented and renowned soccer player. However, for one engaged in such trivial pursuits, he had unusually strong Islamist religio-political ideals. Leaving a lucrative sports career behind, Abul-Harith first went to Afghanistan in the mid-1980s and fought with the Arab *mujahideen* there. According to those who were with him, he 'devoted his heart and his soul to the worship of Allah,' often consulting the Qur`an while he stood guard at his post. At 23 years of age, he again abandoned his comfortable lifestyle in Bahrain to fight in Bosnia. During the battle of Ilijas, Abul-Harith discovered Abu Maryam's lifeless body. As he crawled forward past Abu Maryam, he too was struck down by a sniper's bullet. With fierce gunfire all around, his Arab comrades-in-arms gave up their attempts to bury him, and instead, placed his body in the trunk of a nearby tree.[50]

Back in the town of Travnik, a Moroccan *jihadi* volunteer calling himself 'Ali' consented to be interviewed by a freelance Western journalist in early November 1992. Wearing unmarked military fatigues and brandishing a Chinese-made AK-47 assault rifle, he first explained that he had come to Bosnia to help combat 'Western aggression against the Muslim peoples.' According to Ali, by the twilight of 1992, the corps of foreign fighters in the Balkans had grown to over 700 men drawn from Iran, Turkey, north Africa, Afghanistan, and Palestine. Many of the guerrillas had trained in Afghanistan, and some had additionally visited the Hizballah-run terrorist camps located in the lawless Lebanese Beqaa valley. Ali identified the principal goal of the *mujahideen* as winning the struggle to 'reclaim the Muslim lands of Europe.'[51] The interview with the Moroccan guerrilla volunteer also brought home another significant point: there were now more than just Saudis involved in Bosnia. Indeed, even as early as September, a leader of the Egyptian Al-Gama`at Al-Islamiyya, admitted, 'We have fighters in Bosnia. I can't say how many they are . . . that's a strategic secret.'[52]

There were also even a surprising number of Muslims from Western countries like the Unite States who had joined the conflict. In Zenica, one journalist encountered a 'beefy man' from Detroit in a black uniform and a prominent *kafiyyeh*. The man fingered his automatic weapon and clarified, 'I'm an American Muslim.'[53] On 23 December, Shoaib Saljuki, a 29-year old Afghan-American and devout son of an 'Islamic scholar,' was killed in combat in Bosnia. Years earlier, he had protested in a 1979 anti-communist uprising near Kabul and 'spoke frequently of dying as an Islamic martyr.' Instead, on his parents' advice, he left for Germany seeking a Western education. However, after witnessing the civil war in Bosnia, Shoaib suddenly left Germany in October 1992 alongside a number of Algerians and other Arabs in order to fight with the *mujahideen*. While shaken and grieving, Shoaib's father was remarkably unperturbed by the violent circumstances of his son's death. He commented, '[f]or Muslims, this is not strange to go and die in other people's homelands.'[54]

Los Angeles Times reporter Kim Murphy was travelling abroad in Riyadh, Saudi Arabia in December 1992, when she met a number of Arab-Afghans who were already weathered veterans of the 8-month old Bosnian civil war. A 28-year-old Saudi civil servant and veteran of the Soviet-Afghan *jihad* known by the pseudonym 'Abu Ali' claimed to be about to take his third combat tour in Bosnia. Before first joining the *mujahideen* in Afghanistan, Abu Ali had lived for a substantial period of time in the now distant city of Pittsburgh, Pennsylvania. He explained to

Murphy, 'I and many young people like myself – our great hope is to die as martyrs, in defense of our religion and righteousness, regardless of where and how we face this destiny.' Among this group of men, there was also a strong undercurrent of hatred and resentment of the Unite States, Europe, and the United Nations. One Saudi veteran of the siege of Sarajevo bitterly threatened, 'Every person, Muslim, Christian or Jewish, who watches that suffering in Bosnia and does nothing about it will pay . . . Sooner or later, they will pay. The Muslims are keeping the accounts, and you can give that message to President Bush.'[55]

Overall, the year 1992 had proven costly for the Arabs and other foreign extremists who had dared to pioneer *jihad* in Bosnia. Out of an initial volunteer corps of perhaps no more than 300 total fighters, various reports indicate that at least twenty-two Saudi nationals had been killed in combat by the end of December and there were even rumors of secret corpse-smuggling flights between Bosnia and Alexandria containing at least 12 additional Egyptian 'martyrs.'[56] In Travnik, in the twilight of 1992, the bodies of 53 fallen Muslim soldiers dotted local public parks.[57] 'Bruno,' a five-year veteran paratrooper in the Belgian army who fought as a mercenary alongside a group of Arab *mujahideen* through 10 months of combat, was thoroughly impressed – and frightened – by what he had seen in Bosnia. 'It's not like what you see on television, or in basic training,' he explained in an interview. 'I was scared – I'm still scared.'[58]

Thus, despite a series of near catastrophic human setbacks, the *mujahideen* had nevertheless established themselves as a viable and respected fighting force by the end of 1992. While relatively small in number, they had proven on occasion to be more courageous and capable in the heat of battle than their Bosnian counterparts. Their reputation grew in importance despite the fact that they had achieved no clear victories against the Serb enemy. Meanwhile, the stories of dramatic 'martyrdom' emerging from the Balkans were generating tremendous interest in the larger international Islamic community. Spreading word of the sacrifices made by these early 'martyrs' was a compelling tool to lure future would-be *jihadis*. A broad collection of young men from across the Muslim, dreaming of similar glory, would seek to emulate this example, even if it meant certain death – and with the Arab foreign legion in Bosnia gaining recognition from the highest circles, these militants saw a bright future for themselves on the horizon. However, the year 1993 would be much more of a challenge for the holy warriors in Bosnia. It was then that the lone and critical ally of the Bosnian Muslims, the Croats, changed their wartime allegiances and dramatically upset the regional balance of power.

Notes

1. 'The Jihad in Bosnia.' *Al-Daawah* (Islamabad). Waseem Ahmed: Islamabad, January 1993.
2. 'The Martyrs of Bosnia: Part I.' Videotape. Azzam Publications: London, 2000.
3. 'The Martyrs of Bosnia: Part I.' Op. cit.
4. 'How Gorazde Was Sacrificed to Help Bring The US Into the Bosnian War.' *Defense and Foreign Affairs' Strategic Policy*, 31 May 1994, p. 6.
5. Hedges, Chris. 'Saudi Fighter in Afghanistan Becomes "Martyr" in Bosnia.' *The New York Times*, 5 December 1992, section 1, p. 6.
6. Government's Response to Defendant's Position Paper as to Sentencing Factors.' *United States of America v. Enaam M. Arnaout.* United States District Court Northern District of Illinois Eastern Division. Case #: 02 CR 892, p. 36.
7. 'Battle of Tishin, North Bosnia, October 1992: 25 Mujahideen defeat 200 Serb Special Forces,' http://www.azzam.com.
8. 'Battle of Tishin, North Bosnia, October 1992: 25 Mujahideen defeat 200 Serb Special Forces.' Op. cit.
9. 'Government's Response to Defendant's Position Paper as to Sentencing Factors.' Op. cit.
10. 'Battle of Tishin, North Bosnia, October 1992: 25 Mujahideen defeat 200 Serb Special Forces.' Op. cit., p. 38.
11. Post, Tom with Joel Brand. 'Help from the Holy Warriors.' *Newsweek*. 5 October 1992.
12. 'Battle of Tishin, North Bosnia, October 1992: 25 Mujahideen defeat 200 Serb Special Forces.' Op. cit.
13. 'Saudi tortures rape mujahideen during interrogation.' February 1999. http://www.azzam.com.
14. 'Appendix A to 31 CFR Chapter V.' Office of Foreign Asset Control (OFAC), United States Treasury Department. 26 October 2001, http://www.access.gpo.gov/su_docs/aces/fr-cont.html. See also: Miller, Judith, (2001), 'Honey Trade Said to Provide Funds and Cover to bin Laden.' The New York Times, 11 October 2001. Sec. A, Page 1.
15. In 1998, Abu Asim was allegedly arrested by Saudi authorities on suspicion of being involved in international terrorism, and was taken to the Ar-Ruwais Intelligence Centre. In one letter published by a *mujahideen* information outlet on the Internet, an Islamic militant claiming to be a former fellow prisoner at Ar-Ruwais described how he witnessed Abu Asim being subjected to relentless interrogation by Saudi prison officials. According to the anonymous author, Abu Asim's grim face reflected 'severe physical and mental torture.' But, despite this rough treatment, inexplicably, after a year of detention, Saudi

authorities abruptly released and deported Abu Asim. Shortly thereafter, he disappeared in the remote tribal regions of Yemen. Within a year, he was already wanted by the US government for his involvement in the terrorist attack on the USS Cole in the Yemeni port of Aden in October 2000, which killed 17 United States sailors. Abu Asim's name has also surfaced in the investigation of the parallel October 2002 suicide bombing of the French supertanker *Limburg* off the coast of Yemen. See: Azzam Publications. 'Saudi tortures rape mujahideen during interrogation.' February 1999. http://www. azzam.com; Al-Haj, Ahmed. 'Dead al-Qaida suspect related to Sept. 11 hijacker.' Associated Press, 14 February 2002; Smith, Craig S. 'Al Qaeda Member Arrested in Kuwait.' The New York Times, 16 November 2002.

16. 'Battle of Tishin, North Bosnia, October 1992: 25 Mujahideen defeat 200 Serb Special Forces.' http://www.azzam.com.
17. 'The Martyrs of Bosnia: Part I.' Op. cit.
18. Op. cit. 'The Martyrs of Bosnia: Part I.' Op. cit.
19. 'In the Hearts of Green Birds.' Audiocassette transliterated by Salman Dhia Al Deen. See also: Institute for Study and Documentation. 'The Balkan War.' Video produced by the Committee for Islamic Benevolence, Saudi Arabia (Lajnat al-Birr al-Islamiyya).
20. 'Saudi tortures rape mujahideen during interrogation." Op. cit.
21. 'The Balkan War.' Op. cit.
22. 'Abu Zubair al-Madani.' http://www.azzam.com.
23. Ibid.
24. 'Zulfikar' himself was, in fact, not technically a Bosnian, but from Sanjak, a predominantly Muslim Balkan region situated between Bosnia and Kosovo.
25. Burns, John F. 'US Plane Lands in Sarajevo to Resume Airlift of Aid to Bosnia War Victims.' The New York Times, 4 October 1992, section 1, p. 12.
26. Hardy, Sgt. Kerensa. 'Troops gather for opening of Butmir memorial.' *SFOR Informer*, No. 114, 30 May 2001.
27. 'Serbs in Armor attack Sarajevo.' *St. Louis Post-Dispatch*, 10 October 1992, p. 7A.
28. Op. cit.
29. Op. cit.
30. Op. cit.
31. Op. cit.
32. 'The Martyrs of Bosnia: Part I.' Op. cit.
33. 'The Martyrs of Bosnia: Part I.' Op. cit.
34. 'UN-peacekeeping forces come under fire at airport.' *Associated Press*, 16 October 1992.
35. Knoy, Laura. 'Weekend Edition.' *National Public Radio*. 17 October 1992.
36. 'The Balkan War.' Op. cit.

37. 'The Martyrs of Bosnia: Part I.' Op. cit.
38. 'The Martyrs of Bosnia: Part I.' Op. cit.
39. 'The Martyrs of Bosnia: Part I.' Op. cit.
40. 'Bin Laden held to be behind an armed Algerian Islamic movement.' *Agence France Press (AFP)*, 15 February 1999 11:39GMT.
41. Drozdiak, William. 'France's "Unwanted"; Alienated Arab Youths Turning to Violence.' *The Washington Post*, 14 November 1995, p. A14.
42. Fisk, Robert. 'An alien "brother" fights for Muslims.' *The Independent* (London), 14 July 1993, p. 9.
43. Pyes, Craig with Josh Meyers and William Rempel. 'Bosnia Seen as Hospitable Base and Sanctuary for Terrorists.' *Los Angeles Times*, 7 October 2001.
44. Interview with Shaykh Abu Hamza al-Masri at the Finsbury Park Mosque. 28 June 2002.
45. 'The Martyrs of Bosnia: Part I.' Op. cit.
46. Sachs, Susan. 'Muslims for Bosnia; Islamic envoys call for action against Serbs.' *Newsday*, 3 December 1992, p. 117.
47. 'The Martyrs of Bosnia: Part I.' Op. cit.
48. 'In the Hearts of Green Birds.' Op. cit.
49. 'In the Hearts of Green Birds.' Op. cit.
50. 'Abul-Harith al-Bahraini.' http://www.azzam.com.
51. Vigodda, Jon 'Allah's Army Goes West.' *The Jerusalem Report*, 5 November 1992, p. 22.
52. Sammakia, Nejla (1992), 'Government Uneasy As Fundamentalists Rally To Cause of Bosnian Brethren.' The Associated Press. 26 September 1992.
53. Vulliamy, Ed. 'Town feels Winter and War Tightening their Noose.' *Guardian* (London), 15 September 1992, p. 8.
54. Strobel, Warren. 'Area Muslims lose son in defense of Sarajevo.' *The Washington Times*, 24 January 1993, p. A1.
55. Murphy, Kim. 'Islamic Volunteers Rallying to Killing Fields of Bosnia.' *Los Angeles Times*, 14 December. Part A, p. 1.
56. Murphy, Kim. Op. cit., Part A, p. 1.
57. Fisk, Robert. Op. cit., p. 11.
58. Crary, David. 'After 10 Months In Bosnia, A Soldier of Fortune Calls It Quits.' The Associated Press. 28 July 1993.

–5–

Confrontation with the Croats (1993–4)

Oh you who believe! Take not the Jews and the Christians as your allies – they are but friends to one another. And if any amongst you takes them as friends, then surely he is one of them . . . Verily, Allah does not guide the wrongful oppressors who disobey Allah.

Qur`an, Sura 5: 51

Oh Allah, grant us success. Oh Allah, make us shoot with accuracy. Oh Allah make us firm on your religion. Oh Allah make us firm upon your appointment (with the enemy).

Mujahid prayer from Bosnia

By the start of 1993, the Arab-Afghans had been fighting in Bosnia for nearly a year – and were growing steadily in power and numbers. The *mujahideen* volunteer unit was becoming more than just a curious combat accessory to the Bosnian army; instead, it had developed into a mysterious international political phenomenon. In line with the stated long-term policy of Usama Bin Laden and Abu Abdel Aziz, the commanders of the Afghano-Bosniak *mujahideen* sought to channel their success in Afghanistan and the Balkans toward the primary goal of attacking the global 'infidel' regimes. With a secure military base in Bosnia, the Arab-Afghans would be in an unprecedented position to strike at will at the underbelly of Western Europe and the United States.

This cunning strategy echoed in the events of 26 February 1993, when disciples of the Arab-Afghan movement executed their first successful terrorist strike on the American homeland. A rental truck packed with powerful explosives detonated in an underground parking lot below the World Trade Center, killing six bystanders and causing havoc in downtown Manhattan. The chief bombmaker – later determined to be Ramzi Yousef – born in Kuwait but of Pakistani descent – was an ambitious graduate of Al-Qaida's *Al-Sadda* training camp, not to mention the nephew of senior Al-Qaida terrorist mastermind Khalid Shaykh Mohammed, who '[t]hrough additional intelligence and investigative efforts in 1995 – was also connected to the first World Trade Center bombing.'[1] Under interrogation, Ramzi Yousef admitted having fled Kuwait following the 1990 Iraqi invasion and enrolling in a six-month comprehensive training course (among a class of fifty-five other *jihadi* recruits) at various *mujahideen* camps in Afghanistan, learning 'explosives, defensive tactics, weapons use, etc.'[2] Several Arabic bomb-making manuals destined for Yousef were discovered inside an envelope marked with the letterhead of Lajnat Al-Birr Al-Islamiyya (the Benevolence International Foundation), the now designated Al-Qaida financial front group.[3] Likewise, other co-conspirators in the terror attack were avid followers of the blind Shaykh Omar Abdel Rahman (not to mention, graduates of Al-Qaida-affiliated militant camps in Afghanistan).

Following his later capture in Pakistan, Yousef told FBI agents that

> he wished . . . to cause the tower to fall . . . [h]e indicated that, had he been able to obtain additional financing, he would have been able to construct the device in such a way as to focus more of the blast horizontally, against the 'beam' of the World Trade Center tower, and would have been able to topple one tower into the other.[4]

Yousef envisioned the flaming wreckage of the twin structures crashing down upon the Wall Street district, crippling the economic heart of America and killing perhaps as many as 250,000 innocent people. When an FBI agent pointed out the still-standing Trade Center to Yousef on his way to trial in 1995, he thought for a moment and replied, 'Next time, if I have more money . . . I'll knock it down.'[5] At the time, Yousef also acknowledged to the FBI that 'he was familiar with the name Usama Bin Laden' but refused to elaborate further.[6]

After months of investigation, the FBI and United States Justice Department announced the discovery of an alleged *jihad* cell based in the New York metropolitan area. Several members of the cell were responsible for aiding Ramzi Yousef in the February bombing – others were planning successive dramatic acts of terrorism against New York landmarks, including the headquarters of the FBI in New York, the United Nations building, and the Holland and Lincoln tunnels. Government agents listened in on wiretaps as conspirators joked how 'the economy will come to a standstill' and 'everything will be broken into smithereens, everything.'[7]

Two of the key players in the latter set of plots were Siddig Ibrahim Siddig Ali, a senior assistant to Shaykh Omar Abdel Rahman; and Clement Rodney Hampton-el (also known as Dr Abdul Rashid Mujahid), an American Muslim convert who had fought with the Arab-Afghan *mujahideen* against the Soviet army. On 16 January 1993, only weeks prior to the first explosion in Manhattan, Siddig Ali had organized a charitable fundraising lecture given by Omar Abdel Rahman at Public School 179 in Brooklyn.[8] As part of a 'Conference on Solidarity with Bosnia/Herzogovina,' the blind Shaykh addressed his audience and demanded:

Who is the one who is fighting the Muslims? And, who is the one who wants to destroy them? There are two main enemies. The enemy who is at the foremost of the work against Islam are America and the Allies. Who is assisting the Serbs? And who is providing them with weapons and food? Europe, and behind it is America.[9]

Furthermore, according to Shaykh Omar, because the United States and Great Britain seek to 'exterminate the Muslims [in Bosnia] . . . then, we must be terrorists and we must terrorize the enemies of Islam and to frighten them and to disturb them and to shake the earth under their feet.' He concluded by directing listeners to 'ready your strength to the utmost of your power, including steeds of war, with which you frighten the enemies of Allah, your enemies.'[10] At that one event, Siddig Ali reportedly collected more than $4,000 for 'our Muslim brothers and sisters' in Bosnia. Ali did not offer specifics as to the actual recipient of the money; '[h]e would only say that it was going to fund the jihad.'[11] According to his wife (who was interviewed later by *Al-Hayat*), Siddig and his accomplices 'were intending to go to Bosnia to help the Muslims there . . . A lot of the brothers are thinking of going . . . to help Muslims there.'[12]

In fact, some of the funds collected by Siddig Ali and Hampton-el ostensibly to help the suffering Bosnian Muslims were actually being diverted to finance the costs of a much grander *jihad*, with targets that included the World Trade Center in New York. At the time, the two men were seeking to bankroll clandestine Arab *mujahideen* training camps setup inside the United States. The recruits consisted primarily of Muslim-American volunteers from the north-east (including relatives and accomplices of the future World Trade Center bombers). In a wiretapped conversation with an FBI informant, Siddig explained: 'Our goal is that these people get extensive and very, very, very good training, so that we can get started at anyplace where Jihad is needed . . . And after they receive their training, they go to Bosnia, I mean, they depart . . . And whoever survives, I mean, could come and . . . [instruct] somewhere else, or Egypt, or any other place, etc.'[13]

Hampton-el's search for a *jihad* sponsor soon led him to influential Muslim activists and political leaders in the Kingdom of Saudi Arabia. In federal court, he later testified to visiting the Saudi embassy in Washington DC in December 1992 at the invitation of Saudi Prince Faisal in order to make the pitch for 'Project Bosnia.' Out of respect for Hampton-el's 'Afghan exploits,' Faisal agreed to provide $150,000 for the project, of which approximately $48,000 was given directly to Hampton-el.[14] According to Siddig Ali:

The money donors were Arabs from the Gulf, Saudi Arabia. They donate in the millions, my brother, yes, by God . . . For what purpose? For the purpose of Jihad . . . So the brothers over here, we told them, 'Brothers, they want to establish a camp here' . . . Dollars, many dollars, I mean, a lot of money . . . They collected the money . . . and nominated [Hampton-el] to be the camp's supervisor . . . to help the brothers in Bosnia. He left just like that. He went to Bosnia.[15]

Between December 1992 and January 1993, Siddig Ali, Clement Rodney Hampton-el, and their would-be squad of 'ten or twelve' American *mujahideen* retreated a makeshift camp in rural New Bloomfield, Pennsylvania, where they were educated in the 'firing of semi-automatic assault rifles, commando style shooting exercises, intense physical fitness training, hand-to-hand combat techniques, martial arts instruction, pepper mace training, and mock nighttime assaults on a nearby electric power substation.' The men, predominantly of Egyptian and Sudanese origin, were protected and armed by a sympathetic US Fish and Wildlife Services Officer – a Muslim convert himself – who was told that 'they wanted the paramilitary training so they could fight as mercenaries in Bosnia.'[16]

Abu Ubaidah Yahya served as the chief instructor of the eager but immature New Bloomfield recruits, and was later named by US Attorney Mary Jo White as a possible unindicted co-conspirator in the New York terror plots case. According to Siddig Ali, the mysterious Abu Ubaidah was a former US Marine who 'had two tours' in Vietnam. This experience greatly impressed Siddig: 'One tour represented hell . . . and this guy served two tours. Thus, he's decorated and has a lot of medals . . . and also, may bless, he was, I mean, a great trainer . . . [k]nowledgeable who communicates with precision.'[17] Siddig elaborated on what had transpired during the months spent with Abu Ubaidah in New Bloomfield:

> So the people were dropping out. I mean, the people that were out of shape. He was a strict instructor, brother. He applies, he applies, he applies the doctrine, which is the Marines' program on these people . . . [b]ut what a team, oh my God . . . [t]hey become one of the best brothers.[18]

Shortly after completion of the Pennsylvania camp, Hampton-el moved 'Project Bosnia' into its second phase: preparing additional *mujahideen* volunteers at the frontline in the Balkans. Siddig Ali explained in a wiretapped conversation: '[w]hen we went there . . . we are supposed to train people – training, train/people . . . troops. And we lead them in missions and sorties . . . That's how it is supposed to be.'[19] Local eyewitnesses offered insight into the identity and mission of those who participated in Project Bosnia. A Bosnian *mujahid* interviewed years later by an Associated Press reporter discussed how 'a mosque in Newark, New Jersey' had sponsored an undertaking by fourteen Americans claiming to be veterans of United States special forces to help train Arab and Bosnian fighters near the town of Tuzla. This foreign mercenary team was led by 'Abu Abdullah,' purportedly a former colonel in the United States military. Within two months during the winter of 1993, the group of United States nationals had trained twenty-five more *mujahideen*, including at least eight Sudanese Islamic militants, in 'insurgency warfare.'[20] Despite their professed mission as 'armed humanitarians' protecting innocent Bosnians, twelve of the American instructors and all of the Sudanese fighters inexplicably departed the combat zone following completion of the brief guerrilla warfare course.

Thus, only months after the commencement of hostilities in the Balkans, the Arab-Afghan notion of heroically saving Bosnia's threatened Muslim population was already taking a backseat to the primary goal of using Bosnia as the spring-board for a greater and more expansive international 'holy struggle.' Even as fierce battles continued between the Serbs and Muslims for control of Sarajevo, Shaykh Abu Abdel Aziz Barbaros left the region on a major fundraising jaunt across the Middle East. Barbaros sought to collect large sums of money (especially from wealthy Arabian Gulf donors), spread word of the *jihad* in Bosnia, and 'explain the situation to the scholars.'[21] Interviewed in the Arab press, Abu Abdel Aziz explained what his message to the clerics and their followers would be:

I have come out of Bosnia only to tell the Muslims that at this time this offers us a great opportunity . . . Allah has opened the way of jihad, we should not waste it . . . This is a great opportunity now to make Islam enter Europe via jihad. This can only be accomplished through jihad. If we stop the jihad now we will have lost this opportunity.'[22]

Abu Abdel Aziz began an unofficial tour of Turkey, Jordan, Bahrain, Kuwait, and Pakistan in late December 1992. During a series of public speeches and radio appearances in Kuwait, he called upon Kuwaitis to support the *jihad* in Bosnia. He also held private conferences with a number of prominent Kuwaiti 'fundamentalist groups' and wealthy merchants known for their strong Islamist political leanings. According to those he met with in Kuwait, his message was simply, '[w]e don't need money, we need weapons.' A number of Kuwaiti charities stepped forward to answer the pleas of Shaykh Abu Abdel Aziz.[23]

Crucial meetings were also taking place elsewhere in the world, as North African and Middle Eastern militants were adapting and converging to establish a pan-European terrorist super-structure anchored in Bosnia. According to documents found in the Islamic Cultural Institute in Milan, on 24 April 1993, Abu Talal al-Qasimy convened the first meeting of the 'Shura Council of the European Union' in Copenhagen. The other participants, a group of senior Egyptian *jihadis*, included Shaykh Anwar Shaaban and Abu el-Fadhl Mahmoud Taha – a 'known terrorist' working for Al-Gama`at Al-Islamiyya in Egypt. Abu Talal had a number of objectives to cover during the meeting with his comrades-in-arms. First on the agenda, he advised that they develop the Shura Council in Europe as an independent command organism to 'coordinate and make decisions.' Second, he wanted to discuss stepping up efforts to provide aid to allied militant Islamic guerrilla groups across North Africa. Third, Abu Talal had new ideas on ways to manipulate humanitarian organizations and charities 'for the cause of the organization.'[24]

The presence of Egyptian radicals based in Austria at the meeting was no coincidence. At this time, Vienna was a key hub in the European Arab-Afghan network. By media accounts, the Bosnian embassy in Vienna had issued a passport in 1993 in the name of Usama Bin Laden himself.[25] But, particularly for Zawahiri and the Egyptian Jihad group, Austria was popular safe haven. A ranking member of Al-Jihad's Shura Council, was a known resident of the suburbs of Vienna.[26] Prior to 11 September 2001, the Austrian government took surprisingly little action to quash the violent dissidents. However, less than a month after the terror attacks in New York and Washington, Austrian police finally arrested Muhammad Abd Rahman Bilasi-Ashri, an Egyptian asylum seeker sentenced *in absentia* to 15 years in prison for supporting Zawahiri's Al-Jihad terrorist faction.[27]

Three months after the first meeting of Abu Talal al-Qasimy and Anwar Shaaban's European Shura council, Italian law enforcement and intelligence officials grew concerned after intercepting a letter from a fundamentalist militant imprisoned in southern Italy in July 1993 discussing potential terror attacks on American and French targets in the region. The seized letter appears to be one penned by Mondhèr Ben Mohsen Baazaoui (also known as 'Hamza the Tunisian'), an activist in the An-Nahda ('Islamic Revival') movement and, according to an Italian police statement, 'a fighter for a mujahideen unit during the ethnic conflict in Bosnia . . . believed to be in the front row of fundamentalist, Islamic terrorist networks.'[28] Baazaoui wrote to Mohamed Saidani (the Imam in Bologna who was on close terms with both Anwar Shaaban and Usama Bin Laden) to tell him that if his prison hunger strike did not secure his immediate release, Baazaoui would commit a 'homicide operation . . . [to] die gloriously.'[29]

He then pleaded with Saidani to avenge his death with a spectacular eulogy of terror:

> All I can suggest to you is the French: leave not a child nor an adult [alive]. Work for them, they are very numerous in Italy, especially in the Tourist areas. Do what you will to them using armed robbery and murder. The important thing is that you succeed at sparking the flames that burn inside me against them, and this is to be a promise between you and me.[30]

These threats came already in the wake of stark warnings of an August 1992 An-Nahda terrorist plot to kill the President of Tunisia with either a suicide commando team or else a United States-built Stinger shoulder-fired surface-to-air missile smuggled in from Afghanistan.[31]

The heightened level of foreign guerrilla activity across southeastern Europe had attracted much attention from Bosnia's neighbors, both near and far. The former director of the Algerian Judiciary Police revealed to a Spanish journalist that his country had witnessed 'illuminating cooperation' with United States authorities in counterterrorism efforts after the first attack on the World Trade Center.[32] Suspicious about the true motives of the foreign *mujahideen*, these states feared becoming potential targets for stranded Middle Eastern terrorists gathering just beyond their own porous borders. This sentiment particularly applied to the weaker European post-communist states that lay in close proximity to the foreign fighters in Bosnia. During the *jihad* in Afghanistan in the 1980s, Arab militants had a relatively easy time finding safe havens and supply routes adjacent to the combat zone. However, the situation 10 years later in Bosnia was an utter contrast. In south-eastern Europe, with the exception of Albania and tiny Kosovo, central Bosnia stood out as a besieged island of Islam amid a vast sea of neighboring Christian, mostly Slavic, regions. Thus, there would understandably be few local sympathizers along access routes to Bosnia for a Muslim fundamentalist movement seeking to establish a base in the Balkans.

These simple realities aside, Croatia, narrowly separating Bosnia from the Adriatic Sea, provided a natural choice as a gateway to central Bosnia. For much of 1992, Bosnian Croats were more or less allied with Bosnian government forces against the Serb onslaught. Thus, foreign Muslim fighters were usually able to cross Croatia and transport weapons *en route* to Bosnia without incident. However, early in the first fall of the war, the Croats became increasingly restrictive about the flow of men and arms through their territory. Usama Bin Laden himself complained in a 1993 interview that although he had the same vision for Bosnia as he did previously for Afghanistan, the situation in the Balkans did 'not provide the same opportunities as Afghanistan. A small number of mujahedin have gone to fight in Bosnia-Herzegovina but the Croats won't allow the mujahedin in through Croatia as the Pakistanis did with Afghanistan.'[33]

The Croatian policy shift was most likely in preparation for the ultimate severing of the alliance between the Croats and the Muslims. Like the Muslim-led government, Bosnian Croat nationalists also had dreams of their own independent autonomous ethnic region, or perhaps even unification with greater Croatia. Soon, they would abandon previous friendly arrangements with the Muslims and, instead, tacitly cooperate with rebel Serb forces to drive Muslims from central Bosnia in hopes of independently striking a better ultimate deal for themselves.

An early indication of that change occurred in September 1992 when Croatia suddenly cracked down on arms smuggling routes through its territory. Though the change occurred over time, the *mujahideen* certainly were aware of the debilitating new restrictions. For instance, the temporary weapons pipeline setup by the Third World Relief Agency through Croatian seaports came to a near complete halt.[34] But despite these humiliating setbacks, remaining Croatian supply routes were still vital to the *jihad*, and the Arab fighters could not afford a larger confrontation with the

Croats. They attempted to ignore the treachery of their erstwhile ally and kept the relative peace.

However, by November, the Croats took clear and unmistakable steps to switch sides. Jajce, a major Muslim town in northwest-central Bosnia, was forced to surrender to a conquering Serb army after a severe round of shelling. From the viewpoint of the *mujahideen*, the seizure of Jajce was only made possible by a 'clear betrayal' by the Croats, and a sudden refusal to interfere with Serbian military operations against Muslim strongholds.[35] One Bosnian Muslim soldier in Travnik angrily (and in retrospective, prophetically) told journalists, '[y]ou can see who the Croats believe in. They're fighting the Serbs alongside us for now, but things may change. We may end up having to fight both the Croats and the Chetniks when they try to divide up Bosnia between themselves.'[36]

The friction between the Roman Catholics and the Muslims was strengthened because both sides maintained their own command structures, communications, and supply routes. Each side accused the other of cowardice and duplicity in battle against the Serbs. The presence of the *mujahideen* and their emphasis on religious-based military conflict predictably only worsened affairs. Svebor Kranjc, a Croat militiaman, commented, 'I feel there is an "us versus them" atmosphere when it should be us versus the Chetniks (the Serbs).'[37]

Croatian authorities began to harass foreign fighters travelling through areas under their control, and stole money and weapons from them. Abu Alala, a 34-year-old Saudi oil worker and Arab-Afghan veteran, wanted to join the *jihadis* in Bosnia, but never made it farther than Zagreb. 'I am going back to Jidda . . . to go back to collect money for these people.' He was deterred from trying to travel through Croatia by numerous reports of severe punishment meted out to arriving *mujahideen* by hostile local authorities.[38] When Croat and Serb military forces discovered that Arab fighters were attempting to evade their blockade by assuming the cover of Islamic relief workers, they widened their searches and detentions of foreigners working for Middle Eastern charitable groups, too. Jusuf Khan, a program coordinator for the London-based charitable group Islamic Relief World-wide (IRW), sharply denied any implications of illegal conduct on behalf of IRW: 'We really try to avoid going through [Serb and Croat] territory . . . They treat us like we are thieves or something.'[39] Still, though bitter and angered, perhaps in hopes of riding out the storm, the Arab guerrillas did not attempt to respond or retaliate. The crisis would finally come to a head at the beginning of 1993.

When *Amir* Shaykh Abu Abdel Aziz temporarily departed from Bosnia in December 1992, the Egyptian Wahiudeen al-Masri consequently took over official military command of the Bosnian *mujahideen*.[40] Wahiudeen had little time to settle into his new leadership position before the ongoing Croatian 'situation' degene-rated into a full-blown crisis. Perhaps sensing weakness in the absence of Shaykh Abu Abdel Aziz, the Croats harshly cracked down on the foreign guerrillas. In

January and February, Croatian supply routes were either totally cut off, or would thereafter require prohibitively expensive bribes and payoffs to be available to the Muslim fighters. Then, the Croatians made an attempt to disable the movement entirely by arresting and imprisoning its membership. In the late winter, a small delegation of Arab-Afghan *mujahideen* (including Abu Ali al-Kuwaiti, Abdul-Wahid al-Qahtani, Abu Muaz al-Qatari, and Abu Sahar al-Haili) passing through Srebnic (near Travnik) faced a pitched battle during a confrontation with the Croats.

Abu Ali al-Kuwaiti was a first lieutenant in the Kuwaiti Air Force.[41] As part of his official military duties, he was sent to France to receive lessons in advanced artillery training. However, while in Europe, Abu Ali learned of the *jihad* in Bosnia and was especially captivated by the accounts of struggle and combat offered by Shaykh Abdel Aziz Barbaros. When the Kuwaiti Air Force discovered that Abu Ali had unexpectedly abandoned his French training course, they contacted him 'several times,' warning that he would be discharged if he did not immediately return to his post. However, Abu Ali refused to listen to his military superiors; as one *mujahideen* source explained, 'How could he return once he tasted the pleasure of jihad and the defense of the front lines?'[42] He became well-known for carrying a loudspeaker with him and dispensing motivational Islamic slogans with it in the midst of intense combat.[43]

Abdul-Wahid al-Qahtani was from the Eastern Province of Saudi Arabia. He first decided to join the *jihad* in 1989, when he travelled to Afghanistan to train with the *mujahideen* and help fight the Afghan communist government. He was among the first Arab-Afghan guerrillas to arrive in Bosnia in 1992, and fought in difficult battles with both Serb and Croat forces. Abdul-Wahid had a remarkable talent for survival and was a weathered veteran of no less than six different *jihad* conflicts – including tours of Afghanistan, Bosnia, Israel, Chechnya, and Kosovo. By the time of the September 11 terrorist attacks, he had returned to Afghanistan and was manning guard posts on the Taliban frontlines north of Kabul. Finally, on 19 November 2001, he was among a group of Arab fighters killed when the building they had sought shelter in was hit by a devastating blast of American airborne ordinance. Abdul-Wahid's belated death was the subject of significant discussion in *mujahideen* news reports: 'His martyrdom, after 11 years in Jihad, proves that martyrdom is not easy, but something special that is endowed by Allah to those who are patient and who remain firm on the path of Jihad, despite difficulties and hardships, even when others have lost their patience in Jihad.'[44]

After making a wrong turn near Travnik, these *jihadis* were stopped unexpectedly at a Croatian roadblock in Srebnic and held at gunpoint. At first, the men were unsure of what to make of this troubling development. Abu Muaz and Abu Ali seem to have been in favor of quietly surrendering to the Croats in hopes of being released later after proper negotiations. However, Abu Sahar[45] had other ideas; he wanted the group to stubbornly (and suicidally) attempt to battle their way out of enemy custody. When the Croats saw Abu Sahar raise his loaded Kalashnikov, they shot him five times and killed him.[46] They immediately disarmed and arrested the other members of the group and detained them for interrogation. According to the survivors, the Croats relentless pressed their foreign prisoners for useful intelligence information, including through the use of torture.[47]

When the *mujahideen* found Abu Sahar's body dumped on the side of the road, they could no longer contain their fury. While the fanatic young Algerian Abu el-Ma`ali gradually assumed control of the *jihadi* forces based in Zenica, Dr Abul-Harith al-Liby, a Libyan Arab-Afghan, was appointed to replace Wahiudeen as the third *Amir* of the Bosnian *mujahideen*. The selection of Dr Abul-Harith was a deliberate move designed to ensure a mature, stabilizing influence in the absence of other senior authority figures. In his late 30s, Abul-Harith had worked as a doctor in Austria for many years prior to the Bosnian war. Convinced that he had a duty to help his fellow Muslims, he travelled to Bosnia in the summer of 1992 to join the foreign *mujahideen*. His medical skills and sharp mind were invaluable assets to the group of impulsive and trigger-happy guerrillas, and he soon became for Bosnia what Bin Laden advisor Ayman al-Zawahiri was to be for Afghanistan. Al-Qaida sources have since written of Dr Abul-Harith:

> With a Kalashnikov rifle in one hand and a medical kit in the other, he accompanied the mujahideen in all of their operations. Fighting in the front line one minute and attending to the injured in the second line in the next minute, Abul-Harith used the medical knowledge that Allah had given him, and became the doctor in charge of the mujahideen . . . His wisdom, intelligence, and strong character made him a senior figure amongst the foreign fighters. While some of the younger brothers would urge irrational actions at some incidents, Abul-Harith would take things more easy and not make haphazard decisions based on panic and emotion. He would encourage the brothers to avoid talking much but to concentrate their energies into positive action.[48]

Dr Abul-Harith was a zealous Islamic militant who harboured no fear of armed combat. With his blessing, under the influence of a new and younger cluster of ultra-radical fundamentalists, the foreign guerrillas began to prepare an elaborate revenge operation against the Croats. Appeals to both the allied Bosnian Muslim army and even the United Nations to mediate in the crisis met with little response. Neither one was interested in involving themselves in a risky and politically unattractive operation aimed at rescuing rogue Arab-Afghan adventurers held by the Croats. A collective decision was made by the senior leaders of the *mujahideen* (including Dr Abul-Harith, Moataz Billah, and Abu el-Ma`ali) to adopt sweeping changes in combat tactics in order to face the new Croatian threat. The fighters split themselves into three main groups: the Mehurici corps near Travnik, a second group based in Bjala-Bucha near Travnik, and the units in Zenica. The guerrillas from Mehurici were tasked with adopting ambush and espionage tactics against enemy Croatian forces. Those in Bjala-Bucha and Zenica were charged with the responsibility of 'special operations,' primarily the kidnapping and assassination of Croatian 'leadership figures.'

Moataz Billah, in the absence of Wahiudeen perhaps the most senior Egyptian left amongst the *mujahideen*, urged his comrades that the only solution was to kidnap and hold hostage the leader of the local Croatian military forces. The other commanders ultimately agreed on his plan, and recruited sympathetic local Bosnian Muslims from Travnik to join the Arabs in this operation. Moataz Billah then selected a 'core group' of the men assembled at the training camps near Zenica and Travnik for a crash-course in advanced combat tactics.[49] Veteran Arab-Afghan fighters taught these zealous trainees lessons in urban warfare, guerrilla operations, covert reconnaissance, explosives, landmines, heavy weapons (mortars and RPGs), sniper skills, and subjected them to intense fundamentalist indoctrination.[50] These were the very same courses simultaneously being taught by Usama Bin Laden and his lieutenants to terrorist recruits in the Sudan and southern Afghanistan.

This new style of training caused a number of disturbing and ominous regional developments. Within weeks, one group of these elite 'special forces' *mujahideen* kidnapped four suspected Croatian intelligence officers in Travnik. Another unit followed this feat with the dramatic abduction of the vice commander of Croatian military forces active in Bosnia and six accompanying enemy soldiers. Attempts by the UN to seize the foreign kidnappers at hastily arranged roadblocks failed when the *mujahideen* retreated into the wilderness to safeguard their hostages and plan new operations. On 16 April 1993, Croatian military sources reported that Arab guerrillas had attacked their positions in Vitez and seized ten more Croat soldiers in hopes of exchanging them for their imprisoned brethren.[51]

Meanwhile, mirroring the Arab-Afghan descent into violence, the local political and civil situation deteriorated rapidly. Croatian sources alleged that, by late spring, as many as 20,000 Croat civilians had fled the unending internecine warfare.[52] The UN warned that 'increasing clashes' between Croats and Muslims reflected the 'Lebanization' of the Bosnian war.[53] By May 1993, Western journalists were describing most of central Bosnia along the Lasava River Valley as a scene of 'lawlessness' and 'murderous chaos': 'Armed gangs of Muslims and Croats roam the forested hills and valleys, attacking villages and torching houses. Road blocks and front lines become even more intimate, often pitting one village against each other, and sniper fire is ever present.'[54]

These tit-for-tat ambushes eventually led to a full-blown crisis on 15 April 1993, when Arab *mujahideen* organized a surprise attack on a vehicle transporting Zivko Totic, the commander of the Croatian Defense Council (HVO) in Zenica.[55] According to Al-Qaida sources, this terrorist ambush 'was one of the most spectacular operations undertaken by the Mujahideen in Bosnia.'[56] As early as August 1992, Totic had made himself a public enemy of the *jihadis* by openly criticizing the presence of foreign fighters in Bosnia: 'Croats here have bitter feelings about all this. We are able to defend ourselves. We don't want Arab soldiers here who, when the war is over, would like to create a fundamentalist country.'[57] Totic was not aware that sympathizers of the Arab fighters had infiltrated his staff and obtained copies of his officers' personal papers and diaries. Those documents had given the Muslim militants a precise guide to his comings and goings of Totic, as well as those of his senior aides.[58] Meanwhile, the Croatians remained ignorant of the perilous threat they were facing.

Early in the morning of 15 April Totic was travelling by car through Zenica protected by four bodyguards. Suddenly, a car and a van driven by foreign guerrillas boxed in and trapped Totic's vehicle at a predetermined location. A group of *mujahideen* jumped out of the van and raked the Croatian entourage with gunfire.[59] The bloody kidnapping attempt (which happened right at the entrance to the Zenica HVO headquarters) left everyone in the car but Totic dead, and spurred a series of 'fierce clashes' between Muslim guerrillas and Croatian troops. Nevertheless, for radical *mujahideen* leaders like Moataz Billah and Abu el-Ma`ali, this operation was a tremendous success because now the Muslims could deal with the Croats on terms that would reflect the true strength of the *jihadi* fighters.

On 17 May, a negotiated compromise was finally reached between the senior Arab *mujahideen* leadership in Bosnia, the Croats, and UN representatives for a major prisoner swap in Zenica (Figure 8).[60] In the outdoor parking lot of a hotel, and as a host of UN soldiers and curious onlookers watched, Arab fighters assembled to await the freeing of their jailed brethren. A Western reporter on hand for the exchange described the dramatic events he witnessed:

> Ringing the car park are dozens of armed men in camouflage fatigues, Kalashnikovs and rocket launchers balanced provocatively on hips, faces masked by green balaclavas. They are led by a group of sober young Arabs, three in combat jackets, and one, tall with a wispy black beard in flowing brown robes, who chatters in Arabic into a hand held radio. As negotiations drag on with the Croats, huddled in back of a British Warrior armored personnel carrier, the gunmen tell a lone TV [cameraman] to leave or be shot.[61]

The lead Arab 'in brown robes' talking into the radio described by the journalist was Abu el-Ma`ali, who was personally on hand to oversee the operation. A video taken by the *mujahideen* of the exchange depicted a group of confident, heavily armed, and clearly well-trained guerrillas who were taking no risks of a UN or Croatian double-cross. However, once a compromise agreement was finally reached, and the Arab detainees emerged from the darkness of a UN transport vehicle, pandemonium broke loose.

Suddenly, the intricate commando operation envisioned by Moataz Billah and Abu el-Ma`ali devolved into an amateurish and peculiar sort of victory

Figure 8. The UN-supervised Prisoner Exchange Operation in May 1993.

celebration. Various *jihadis* leapt forward to embrace their newly released comrades, crying *Allahu Akhbar*! and cheering wildly. One *mujahid*, closely resembling Abu Ali al-Kuwaiti, dropped to his knees and kissed the ground immediately following his liberation. The UN arbitrator on hand was pleased to reach a successful resolution to the tense standoff and, subsequently, asked Wahiudeen al-Masri, present at the scene, to shake his hand as a demonstration of good faith. But, Wahiudeen sternly and insultingly refused the request, quipping, 'I do not shake hands with the infidels.'[62]

However, for the most part, the men simply could not contain their surging exhilaration. The sight of so many heavily armed, strangely dressed men madly dancing and celebrating created a bizarre, circus-like atmosphere. At last, the Arabs departed in a convoy of vehicles like a parade of conquering heroes. The guerrillas enthusiastically attempted to rally the crowd in support while firing their weapons indiscriminately into the air. But, though many of the countless Bosnians who witnessed the prisoner swap seemed amused by the frantic revelry of the *mujahideen*, few visibly responded to their rallying cries for holy war.

Two days later, the Kuwaiti Society for the Revival of Islamic Heritage reported that Shaykh Kulaib al-Mutairi, a Kuwaiti Muslim cleric and official emissary of their organization, had been discharged from Croatian custody at the same time as the UN-supervised *mujahideen* prisoner release. According to Tareq al-Issa, a representative of the Society, al-Mutairi, who had arrived in Bosnia in December 1992, was 'not in a good condition' after his ordeal. Allegedly, both his Croat jailers and fellow prisoners who were ethnic-Serbs brutally tortured him while in custody. Many Kuwaitis had first become aware of al-Mutairi's plight after viewing a news agency photograph released to the public of foreign detainees (including him) held by Croats.[63] In a subsequent report issued by the Society for the Revival of Islamic Heritage offering news of recently 'martyred' *mujahideen* in Bosnia, an 'official source' noted that, despite his *de jure* release from confinement, Shaykh al-Mutairi was subsequently nevertheless 'trapped' by heavy fighting in Zenica with three other Kuwaitis and a Saudi citizen.[64] There was no explanation offered as to why al-Mutairi had been arrested and held by the Croats amongst a group of foreign guerrillas, rather than fellow humanitarian workers.

In the wake of the embarrassing ordeal of the prisoner exchange in May 1993, the Croatian HVO initiated a campaign of 'open war' on all Muslim forces, particularly against the Arab volunteer army. Much in the same way that the Serbs had done to Sarajevo, the Croats now hoped that by seizing the mountains surrounding Travnik and the Mehurici camp, and by blockading the access route between *mujahideen* bases in the Travnik area and Zenica, they would quickly asphyxiate local Muslim forces. This theory was not entirely incorrect: Arab-Afghan reports, reflecting on the situation, confessed that '[t]his was one of the most difficult periods for the mujahideen.'[65]

Desperate to break out of the elaborate Croatian trap, Bosnian forces openly battled the Croats across the Lasava river valley region. Playing a 'key role' in this massive Muslim counterattack, the *mujahideen* focused their efforts on opening a new unobstructed transit route between Travnik and Zenica.[66] According to witnesses, the foreign soldiers fought alongside the Sixth Bosnian Muslim Brigade from Zenica and the Bosnian Krajiska Brigade from Travnik. Units of *mujahideen* were seen frequently operating in small patrols ahead of the approaching BiH troops.[67] They eventually met with military success during combat operations in the Croatian town of Milasic (near Mehurici). In Milasic, the *mujahideen* themselves admitted to 'killing all the fighters and taking the women and children as prisoners.'[68]

This marauding spirit was even more evident from eyewitness accounts and actual videotape taken of the next conquest of the Arab *jihadis*: the predominantly Croat town of Guca Gora, northeast of Travnik. On 8 June, a combination of Bosnian Muslim troops and Arab *mujahideen* were able to assault and capture Guca Gora, thus reopening a route to Zenica; they also seized two 120 mm mortars and a large ammunition cache.[69] Croatian survivors later recounted to the American media, '[m]ost of the houses have been set alight, plundered and burned. We've heard that the women and children . . . have been released and are up in the village.'[70] According to British UN spokesman James Myles, international monitors reported 'civilians running away from the Bosnian (Muslim) militia under machinegun fire. There is strong evidence of atrocities . . . We have no witnesses of a massacre, but we have found a large number of civilian dead.' Meanwhile, UN peacekeepers overseeing the situation in Guca Gora were forced to return to their local base and assume defensive positions after being repeatedly fired on, apparently intentionally, by Muslim forces.[71]

All this was mere prelude to what happened once the *mujahideen* discovered the 800-year-old Church and monastery of St Francis located in the town. As many as 200 Croatian civilians had sought shelter in the church, and were fortunately eventually escorted to relative safety by British UN troops.[72] The UN peacekeepers, forced to evacuate the civilians in armored personnel carriers, fired 'hundreds of rounds' from a 30 mm rapidfire mobile cannon to counter a constant salvo of Muslim sniper fire.[73] By the morning of 9 June, the church was finally emptied of the Croatian refugees and the relentless Arab-Afghan besiegers moved in for a closer look at their new conquest. The scene there was essentially reminiscent of the atmosphere during the May prisoner swap in Zenica. A group of approximately thirty Arab guerrillas rampaged through the church with their weapons held in the air, shouting *Allahu Akhbar!*[74] They knocked over pews and other sacred symbols of the ancient church, vandalized the historic and irreplaceable mural above the main altar, and finally scraped off the faces of Jesus and the Virgin Mary on another painting near the altar.[75] This action was taken for much the same reason that the Taliban obliterated the Bamiyan Buddhas in Afghanistan in the spring of 2001: the paintings were considered to be heretical depictions of infidel religious symbols. In that respect, the *mujahideen* seemed to derive a profound and starkly perverse joy in desecrating the icons of their enemy's faith. The wide grins and looks of amazement of the Arab fighters as they toured the empty church betrayed the impression that, for them, the conquest and domination of a revered Croatian church was just as significant as any military victory against Croatian soldiers. Simply put, all infidels would be regarded as the enemy, regardless of their combatant status.

Then, in their fanatic excitement, the Arabs placed packs of dynamite around the monastery and prepared to raze it completely to the ground. After a number of tense moments, Bosnian army soldiers finally arrived on the scene and eventually persuaded the foreign guerrillas to remove the explosives. However, this did not end the marauding victory celebration of the *mujahideen*. In late June, the Arab extremists marched from Guca Gora to a school in the neighboring town of Metrovici containing 231 Croat civilian refugees. Without provocation, the *jihadis* suddenly took the refugees hostage and threatened to slaughter them *en masse*. In the end, local Bosnian army guards forcibly ejected the Arabs from the Metrovici and eventually negotiated an acceptable compromise with them by agreeing to move all the Croats out of Muslim territory.[76]

The Arabs, however, were not always so easily dissuaded from acts of violence. On 30 April, *en route* to Guca Gora, the *mujahideen* advanced forward to the tiny mountain village of Miletici, 12 miles northwest of Zenica. They faced scattered resistance and, according to a spokesman for the United Nations High

Commissioner for Refugees, lost only one fighter in a brief battle. However, upon their arrival, the *jihadis* abruptly announced that one of their lives was worth five Croats.[77] One survivor, 83-year-old Croatian civilian Marko Pavolic explained, 'We knew they were foreigners because we could not understand their language.' These mysterious foreigners collected everyone in the village and forced them at gunpoint into a local house. Eventually, four younger men were brought outside, brutally tortured, and had their throats summarily cut. With bizarre cruelty, Pavolic recalled, as 'their blood gushed out, it was collected in a bowl and ladled back over their heads as they died.'[78] Margaret Green, a representative of the UN High Commissioner for Refugees (UNHCR), saw the bodies, and called them 'gruesome.' Ms. Green added:

> One man's face had been sliced off. Another's head was almost severed. Two others had had their throats cut. I saw the house where the men must have been killed. There were pools of congealed blood and bits of bone and tissue covering the living room floor. A trail of dried blood led from the doorway, down the steps, to the centre of the village.[79]

This unyielding philosophy of violence applied not only to the Croatians, but moreover, to all 'infidel' forces active in Bosnia, including British UN soldiers and civilian volunteers. During two weeks in February, between six and ten British nationals (including several military advisors attached to the Bosnian army) were mysteriously abducted and murdered. Among this number were Ted Skinner and Derek Arnold, two Britons who were training local Bosnian army units in tactical and paramedic skills. Without warning, the two were kidnapped and taken from Travnik to Turbe. They were later found tied up and shot through the head, with definite signs of torture and mutilation. United Nations investigators and British officials alleged that foreign Muslim extremists (specifically referred to as *mujahideen*) were responsible for the crimes. Apparently, the murders had a larger political motive. Responding to puzzled questions concerning the uncertain number of victims, a spokesman for British military forces in Bosnia commented that some of the corpses 'may never be found. We only found the others because we were told about them, and if we were told about them it was because the opposition wants others to know as a warning.'[80] The murders may have even involved possible espionage; some reports indicated that Skinner and Arnold were actively providing British forces with intelligence on Muslim military operations, 'something to which Mujahedin mercenaries fighting alongside them might have taken exception.'[81] In any event, the message to Westerners was clear and unambiguous: stay away, or be targeted for terror.

Later, in June, one Croat militiaman returning from the frontlines offered an ominous and prophetic warning to British reporters covering the bloodshed in Travnik and Guca Gora: 'the Muslims believe if they die in battle they will go straight to paradise. It makes them fearless. They will be here soon and you British will be caught in the middle.'[82] Indeed, as promised, the confrontation between the *mujahideen* and British UN troops attempting to protect civilians along the Zenica-Travnik access routes grew more serious on 13 June, when an armored car carrying visiting journalists and UK army escorts was forced to return to the UN base in Vitez after coming under heavy automatic weapons fire. Later in the same day, a British patrol of four APC's was stopped at an Arab-Afghan roadblock near Guca Gora.[83] A group of approximately fifty *mujahideen* fighters, who 'looked north African or Middle Eastern,' had assembled there to intercept mobile enemy troops. The frightened British soldiers told journalists later that the foreigners had long, wispy beards, Afghan-style caps, and uniforms unlike anything worn by local Bosnian guerrillas.[84]

Though the *jihadis* instantly trained their rocket propelled grenade launchers and rifles at the UN vehicles, the *mujahideen* commander on scene, an unidentified man of British origin wearing an Afghan hat and a blue scarf over his face, addressed the British officer in charge of the patrol, Major Vaughan Kent-Payne, in perfect English and coldly reassured him 'be cool, these people won't fire until I give them the order.'[85] After approximately a half-hour of tense negotiation, the *mujahideen* lowered their weapons and grudgingly released the British soldiers. However, when Major Kent-Payne approached one of the Arab fighters he had settled terms with and attempted to shake his hand the unidentified guerrilla refused, saying (according to a British interpreter), that 'he would not touch the flesh of an infidel,' in the same spirit as Wahiudeen al-Masri.[86] As part of the compromise, only Kent-Payne and one other British soldier were permitted to continue on to the village of Maljine, where the Croats had reported the mass execution of forty Croatian militiamen committed by unspecified radical fundamentalists. Once there, Kent-Payne discovered widespread Muslim graffiti and hastily scrawled religious slogans throughout the town, that (despite widespread starvation) all the local pigs had been mysteriously slaughtered, and that the local children had been instructed to repeatedly chant *Allahu Akhbar!*[87] Later, the Croats would claim that the *mujahideen* had also transported an unspecified number of Croatian women and children as hostages back to the training center at Mehurici.[88]

The intimidation of international peacekeepers in Bosnia increased as the *jihadi* commanders realized that the UN forces would inevitably back down in any confrontation, no matter how unprovoked. On 11 July, two British army Warrior fighting vehicles were on patrol near their Vitez base. They were stopped by two lone Arab *mujahideen* in a black jeep, who 'politely but firmly' told them to leave at once. At that moment, between twenty-five and forty more 'Afghan'-style guerrillas suddenly arrived in trucks. The foreign fighters swarmed around the British APCs, yelling slogans and acting as threatening as possible. One of the

British soldiers in the Warriors recalled, '[t]hey were chanting "Allahu Akbar"' . . . It was quite deafening if you've got 40 guys doing it.' He commented further, '[t]hey were very organized . . . [t]hey had the heavy weapons at the back. There were Kalashnikovs, heavy machine guns, Russian 66s and two types of Russian made anti-tank rockets, like bazookas.'[89] Thoroughly alarmed, the British troops quickly withdrew from their patrol in order to avoid any bloodshed.

Then, on 12 July 1993, the United States State Department took the unprecedented step of issuing a warning of potentially serious threats to American citizens in Bosnia. According to spokesman Michael McCurry, though there were 'no specifics as to timing or targets,' a 'credible source' indicated that *mujahideen* units comprised of Iranian terrorist operatives were preparing acts of violence against Westerners throughout the former Yugoslavia. The notion that such a terror conspiracy was hatched by Iranian agents is not so far-fetched; this warning came directly in the wake of a number of international bombings allegedly carried out by Iranian-inspired Hizballah operatives. According to McCurry, 'We recently received indications of threatening activity and we thought it would be prudent to release a warning in light of those reports.'[90]

However, although this may have been mere coincidence, the character and timing of this alleged plot seem to match perfectly with the, at that time, ongoing fundamentalist Sunni Arab campaign in central Bosnia. As the fighting intensified in June and July, the militant Afghan-trained corps certainly aimed at sending the message that any United States, European, or UN military intervention in the Balkans would end in a disaster comparable to that of the bungled American encounter with radical Shi'ite movements in Lebanon in the early 1980s. United States policymakers, rigidly adhering to theories of 'state-sponsored terrorism,' often had arguable difficulty determining whether it was the revolutionary regime in Iran or the scattered, but well-funded Islamic exiles trained in Afghanistan who presented the most serious international geopolitical problem. As Balkan expert Stephen Schwartz writes in his recent book *The Two Faces of Islam*, 'the Saudis had sold the West a false depiction of Shi'as everywhere as wild-eyed fanatics and of Wahhabis as trustworthy defenders of the traditional Islamic order.'[91] The radical Sunnis were quite amused by the amateurish intelligence gathering of their enemies. Suleman Ahmer, former operations manager for the United States branch of Benevolence International (BIF), scoffed in a videotaped lecture, 'I was there for 9 months and never met a single Iranian.'[92]

In retrospect, it seems that it was certainly the disciples of Arabia who had the most reaching and enduring military influence in the Balkans region. Interviewed recently, Richard Holbrooke, the lead United States peace negotiator in the Balkans, blamed imprecise and 'sloppy intelligence' for the mistaken focus on the supposed but untimately uncredible Iranian threat lurking in Bosnia.[93] It is not unreasonable to conclude that this fundamental intelligence confusion may have effectively prevented Western policymakers from making accurate judgments as to emerging security threats in Bosnia. Meanwhile, in late June amidst a Western foreign policy paralysis, a Bosnian guerrilla warned journalist Robert Adams: 'In a few months there will be babies and women bleeding to death on the streets of Paris and London . . . You will be angry with us, but there is nothing that you can do to Bosnia which will be worse than what you have already done to us.'[94]

Flushed with these victories over both the Croats and the monolithic 'Westerners,' the Arab guerrillas continued to advance past Guca Gora under the leadership of the Egyptian Arab-Afghan veteran Hussaamudeen into the daunting surrounding mountain range. On 25 June 1993, the hodgepodge of Muslim troops ran into heavy enemy fire and took several casualties, including Jamaludeen al-Yemeni and Muhammad al-Turki.[95] Jamaludeen was another young veteran of the Soviet-Afghan *jihad* who had arrived in Bosnia early in 1992 at roughly the age of 20 years to serve with the *mujahideen*.[96] Jamaludeen and Muhammad al-Turki were assigned to a heavy 12.7 mm DShK machine gun post, and reportedly fought bravely. However, as the Muslims advanced on their enemy's positions, the Croats unleashed a rain of mortar shells on their opponent. One shell landed next to Jamaludeen and Muhammad, killing both of them and ripping Jamaludeen's body apart. When the *mujahideen* returned later to recover the bodies of their fallen comrades, they discovered that Jamaludeen was missing. For several days, the *jihadis* mourned him, believing that his body had been taken and mutilated by the vengeful Croats.[97] Another Arab participant in the battle, recounted the last thoughts of Jamaludeen:

> Jamaludeen, hours before his death said to me: 'Oh Abu Uthman, maybe we will meet again in Paradise.' I replied, 'I don't think so!' He replied, 'I have a feeling that Allah will choose me from the martyrs.' So we headed towards the battlefield, joking and laughing as we went . . . I expected to be in Jamaludeen's group, but I wasn't . . . so news of his death reached me, and I was extremely saddened, more for myself than for him because I was not from amongst those chosen by Allah for martyrdom.[98]

Even afterwards, the *mujahideen* never reported finding Jamaludeen's body. His death left a bitter taste in the mouths and embittered the minds of his many friends among the Arab corps.

Not long afterwards, the *mujahideen* again found themselves on the defensive when Croatian and Serbian forces jointly attacked the Muslim town of Bjala-Bucha, near Travnik. In the midst of Muslim attempts to repel their attackers, a number of Arab fighters were 'martyred,' including Abu Saif Ash-Shahrani, Abu Hamad al-Otaibi, Abu Khaled al-Tunisi, and Abu Hanzala al-Masri.[99] Abu Saif and Abu Hamad were both Saudis in their early twenties. Abu Saif, formerly a professional soldier in the Saudi Arabian Army, witnessed the destruction in Bosnia on television and was reportedly urged by his mother, 'Look what they are doing, they are raping our sisters and killing our brothers. My son, get [up] and go and I don't want to see you again!' Abu Saif then travelled to Riyadh where he joined a fellow would-be *mujahid*, Abu Hamad al-Otaibi. Abu Hamad was eager to find martyrdom in combat, despite a severe medical condition that kept him in fairly constant and intense pain. Together, the two made the now hazardous and difficult journey to the Mehurici militant training camp in Bosnia near Travnik. By the time they finished their training, the two had become close friends and were immediately dispatched together to the Muslim frontlines in the village of Bjala-Bucha.[100]

One evening shortly after Abu Saif and Abu Hamad arrived in the village, the Serbs suddenly attacked their positions and repelled an attempted Muslim counter-attack with a wave of artillery. Abu Hamad, in the rear of the unit, was hit by a 120 mm shell, and his head was blown half off. The other guerrillas agreed to conceal the news of Abu Hamad's death from his good friend Abu Saif until at least after the battle. Abu Saif, unaware of what had happened, enthusiastically advanced towards the Serbs carrying a PK machine gun. Not long afterwards, Abu Saif was also struck down by three enemy bullets. The *jihadis* buried the two Saudis together in one grave: 'They loved each other in this world and they shall love each other in the Next.'[101]

By the summer of 1993, the reckless behaviour of the *mujahideen* was even bringing them into conflict with their own Bosnian allies. While the Bosnian army soldiers were trying to keep the looting and scapegoating to a minimum, the Arabs were exacerbating the problem and precluding the possibility of any future peaceful co-existence between Muslims and their Croat and Serb neighbors. Colonel Stjepan Siber, deputy commander of the Bosnian army and its operations chief in central Bosnia, boldly argued in the Western press:

> It was a mistake to let [the Arab guerillas] in here. No one asked them to come. They commit most of the atrocities and work against the interests of the Muslim people. They have been killing, looting and stealing. They are not under the control of the Bosnian army and they must go. We hope that in the next few days President Izetbegovic will order them out.[102]

Rasim Delic, the then-commander of the Bosnian Muslim army, admitted that the foreigners were 'perpetrating senseless massacres, like their enemies . . . They are kamikaze, desperate people.'[103] Even the mayor of Zenica, Besim Spahic, could not help but disavow any relationship with the foreigners: 'They operate independently. They are no force in a military sense. But they already have done us huge damage.'[104] The most frank explanation came from Emirza Hajric, spokesman for the Bosnian Information Centre in London. Hajric complained:

We need Muslim UN soldiers to control the foreign Mujaheddin who have taken up positions in Bosnia. Our soldiers find it hard to control these foreigners, and they will not listen to orders from soldiers from Britain or France who they consider to be infidels . . . These guys come from Algeria, from Pakistan, from Afghanistan, from God knows where. They are of no use to us, all they do is make great propaganda for our enemies . . . They come here full of ideals about dying in battle and going to paradise. Bosnians are not so stupid. We want to live for Islam, not die for Islam.[105]

The unofficial and extralegal status of the *mujahideen* naturally caused significant friction with local civil authorities. In one instance, the *jihadis* threatened to kill a Muslim judge presiding over a case involving a truck carrying Islamic soldiers accused of colliding with a UN vehicle.[106] Then, the Arab fighters entered and temporarily occupied the European Community's (EC) local offices at gunpoint and surrounded the Hotel International in Zenica with a virtual bazaar of heavy weapons.[107] There was a litany of stories and local media reports of *mujahideen* fighters vandalizing bars in Travnik, slaughtering pigs in rural villages, even kidnapping a nun and four other Croats and holding them hostage to obtain the freedom of a captured Arab held in Vitez.[108] The foreigners were less and less an integrated part of the Bosnian armed forces, and instead, increasingly, a thuggish guerrilla band with an independent religio-political agenda.

Concurrently, the Arab fighters also began to increasingly criticize the combat performance of their more-or-less secular Bosnian allies. The mistakes and failures made in the war against the Serbs and Croats were largely blamed on the inexperience and unreliability of the Bosnian soldiers. An Algerian fighter with 9 months of combat experience had few words of praise for the Bosnian army:

You know, when we stage an attack, the Bosnians come with us but they don't want to die. They go forward and then they turn back again. Several times, I have been out in front, up in the hills above the city, and we have broken through the Serbs. But just when they are winning, the Bosnians want to go back home. They want to live.[109]

Moreover, in the opinion of the Arab leadership, the lack of a central Islamic command authority made it difficult to mount coordinated assaults and easy for traitors to infiltrate the ranks of the Bosnian army. As a result, during the summer, the main *shura* (advice) council of the *mujahideen* approved an official request to the Bosnian government to recognize the foreign fighters as an independent, self-controlled battalion within the general boundaries of the Bosnian army. Unified together in one body, the Arabs would no longer have to fear potentially fatal acts of treachery or cowardice by their fellow fighters. Eager to please their sole remaining ally, the Bosnian government agreed to this simple request.

On 13 August, the government officially mobilized the Kateebat al-Mujahideen ('Battalion of the Holy Warriors') on the personal orders of Bosnian president Alija

Izetbegovic, to whom the unit was directly responsible.[110] The battalion was formally under the command of the Seventh Muslim Liberation Brigade (Sedmi Korpus) of the Bosnian Third Army Corps.[111] Its headquarters was in Zenica, where 200–300 Arab fighters were based.[112] Dr Abul-Harith al-Liby remained the overall *Amir* of the group (perhaps in reflection of how much had been accomplished under his temporary control), and Wahiudeen al-Masri now served again in his most effective role as the unit's senior military commander. Abu el-Ma`ali took over gradual responsibility for running *jihadi* operations in the Zenica region and increased his already formidable reputation.

The camp in Mehurici was established as a principal training center, and 'hundreds' of additional local fundamentalist Bosnian Muslims were recruited to be indoctrinated and join the *mujahideen*.[113] These men were not only schooled in the arts of war, but moreover received intensive indoctrination on the subjects of Islam, *jihad*, and 'holy martyrdom.' They grew long beards and soon followed the same ardent Wahhabi-style Islamic faith as the Arab *mujahideen*. At the camp in Mehurici, British reporters secretly videotaped a group of thirty Bosnian Muslims receiving firearms training and target practice from clearly experienced foreign instructors, described simply as 'Islamic fundamentalists' by local representatives at the camp.[114] At a youth camp in South Florida in July 1996, Suleman Ahmer, BIF operations manager, described the struggle by the Arab émigrés to indoctrinate native followers: '. . . the Bosnians were well away from Islam . . . They couldn't even say the word "jihad." They used to call "*mujahideen*," "*muhajideen*." It took them many months to learn the right word.' But, Ahmer insisted that the effort was not made in vain; after witnessing the fearlessness of the foreign battalion, the Bosnians responded, 'if this really, if this is what Islam teaches you, we are fools if we don't practice Islam.'[115]

Added to these men was a small but dedicated cadre of long-time Bosnian Islamic radicals who had fought in the Soviet-Afghan war of the 1980s; a Bosnian Muslim officer explained to journalist Robert Fisk, 'Afghanistan was our school . . . [i]nstead of fighting the Communist Russians outside Kabul, we are now fighting the Communist Chetniks Serbs outside Travnik. Even their tanks are the same. In Afghanistan, we hit the T-55s in the mountains. Here, we hit T-55s in the mountains.'[116] But, even those Bosnians who had not experienced the first *jihad* against the Soviets could not help but draw inevitable parallels to Afghanistan. One Bosnian commander in the *mujahideen* (somewhat egotistically) compared himself to Gulbuddin Hekmatyar,[117] the legendary and quite infamous *jihadi* guerrilla leader from Afghanistan.[118] Clearly, there were at least some Bosnians who were entranced by Al-Qaida's notions of suicidal sacrifice in the name of religion. During a 1993 media interview, several local fundamentalist Bosnian fighters in Travnik had been particularly interested in discussing with journalist Robert Fisk a shadowy and charismatic young Saudi exile in the Sudan known as Usama Bin Laden.[119]

Though they did not necessarily always share their religious zeal, the Bosnian native troops clearly did respect the combat experience of the Arabs: one Bosnian Muslim soldier observed, '[t]hey are good fighters . . . They are not afraid to move forward even when our men hold back.'[120] High-placed Muslim officials aided the foreign fighters, and attempted to legitimize their presence in Bosnia.[121] The Bosnians now had an estranged but useful ally: the Arab brigade, though the source of much controversy and chaos, was combat trained and motivated by a willingness to carry out missions that meant even certain death. Their infamous reputation struck fear into the hearts of the enemies of Bosnia's Muslims, and thus the legend of the foreign fighters served as a useful propaganda tool.

Despite these striking accounts, obviously not everyone in the Balkans had a positive impression of the *mujahideen* or their fanatic adherence to 'holy' warfare. One Bosnian officer aptly summed up these widespread criticisms of the Arab-Afghan religio-political ideology in Bosnia: '[t]he idea that we are going to build a Muslim state here like Libya is ridiculous . . . I would fight against such a state.'[122] Lieutenant Nadja Ridjic agreed; he explained: 'If I thought this was going to lead to some Muslim republic, then I would not be involved.'[123] 'Zafir,' a 27-year-old Muslim from Travnik observed: 'If [the Arabs] want to offer the people religion, culture and language, that's good . . . But if they insist on it, that's not good.' 'Bektas,' a local army platoon leader in Travnik, was more measured in his response: 'It's good for us that they are here. But after the war, who knows?'[124] Another local, 'Emir,' casually joked that the Arabs 'ask us to pray five times a day, but we prefer to have five drinks a day.'[125]

Many Bosnian Muslims were incredulous that the foreign fundamentalists absolutely abstained from both pork and alcohol, both longtime parts of Bosnian culture and cuisine. This dogmatic form of Islam was entirely alien to the moderate and European Muslim society that had thrived in the Balkans for so long. Thus, the motivation for many Bosnians to join alongside the Arabs came not from choice, but necessity. 'Faruk,' a Muslim refugee in Slovenia, indignantly declared: 'I am not a fundamentalist, but I will take a gun from the fundamentalists and thank them for it.'[126]

As the number of Arab recruits grew, the domain of the *mujahideen* spread quickly in central Bosnia, often in a wave of intimidation and terror. In Konjic, Arab-Afghan guerrillas were part of a 100-man Bosnian government force stationed at Liscioi since February 1993.[127] Reportedly, the volunteers arrived in Konjic in small groups, claiming to be students from Afghanistan. They were armed with H&K automatic weapons and former Yugoslav army equipment.[128] According to Croatian sources, these *jihadis* killed and expelled civilian villagers, and looted and vandalized houses across the Jablanica and Konjic regions.[129] Units of foreign fighters had also been present further south in Mostar since early June 1993. They were reportedly stationed in the Santica neighborhood on the Croat/

Muslim frontlines, where typically in groups of six or seven, they manned bunkers and were armed with semi-automatic weapons, machine-guns, and even anti-tank weapons. Many of these men eventually left the Mostar area by mid-August 1993.[130]

The *mujahideen* would take additional casualties before the summer of 1993 ended, including several British Muslims and Islamic converts who had eagerly joined the Bosnian *jihad* movement. The Bosnian war caused a strong backlash in the prominent and outspoken British Muslim community, particularly among enraged college students. These educated and idealistic youths angrily protested against the persecution of fellow Muslims in Bosnia. One student, a classmate of several men who had left to seek training in Afghanistan and Bosnia, saw nothing wrong with taking up arms against the 'enemies of Islam': 'You cannot turn a blind eye when Muslims are being massacred, because what will you do when it is happening on your doorstep?'[131] In Bosnia, amateur *mujahideen* cameramen interviewed several British volunteers, including a masked man who identified himself as 'Abu Ibrahim,' a 21-year-old third-year medical student at Birmingham University living in Golders Green, London. Abu Ibrahim criticized the hypocrites among his peers in the UK who swore revenge on the Serbs and Croats, yet were too afraid to join the *jihad* in Bosnia:

> . . . what we lack here is Muslims that are prepared to suffer and sacrifice. There in Britain, I see Muslims, every medical student is saying that my third year is for Islam, my third year is for the Muslims. They get their job, they get their surgery. 50, 60, £70,000 a year they're earning. And then, no struggle, no sacrifice.

Abu Ibrahim spoke of the intense sense of satisfaction he felt fighting in the Bosnian war, as compared to the apathy of the secular Muslims who remained in London. In Britain:

> I watch the TV and tears roll down my face when I see the Muslims in Bosnia, Muslims in Palestine, Muslims in Kashmir. And then I come [to Bosnia] and you feel a sense of satisfaction. You feel that you are fulfilling your duty. You feel that you are doing what the Prophet and his companions done [sic] 1400 years ago.[132]

Abu Muslim al-Turki, of an older generation, was originally of Turkish descent but had lived most of his life in Britain as a secular Muslim. Until he was in his late forties he was not an avid follower of Islam and was in fact married to a non-Muslim. However, after witnessing the dramatic Muslim-Serb struggle in Bosnia, Abu Muslim experienced a reawakening of religious idealism. One of the very eldest of the *mujahideen*, Abu Muslim first arrived in Bosnia in the fall of 1992, and had trained at the Mehurici camp. During the physical endurance part of the training, special amenities were in place for him 'due to his old age and the difficulties he would have.' However, firmly set on the path of *jihad*, Abu Muslim survived and eagerly battled first the Serbs and, later, the Croats. Reportedly, he had to plead his case every time with the military commanders to allow him to join the fighters. Hesitant about Abu Muslim's advancing age and wounded state, Dr Abul-Harith reluctantly agreed to put him in battle, at least in the back of the guerrilla unit. However, during the combat that subsequently followed, the group of *mujahideen* were encircled by the Croats, and the rear of the unit exposed to a direct attack – it was not long before Abu Muslim was cut down by enemy gunfire.[133]

Apparently as either the result of the same battle or one following soon thereafter, another British Muslim was also 'martyred,' this time a convert named David Sinclair. Sinclair (also known as Dawood al-Brittani) was a 29-year-old employee of a computer company in the UK. After suddenly converting to Islam and adopting traditional Muslim dress, Sinclair ran into problems with senior management at his company. Within a week of wearing his new clothes to work, he was reportedly terminated. He thereupon decided to travel to Bosnia and to join the Islamic military organization based there. In the midst of his training, he generously gave away his two British passports to Arab-Afghan 'brothers in need.' Dawood refused to return to the UK evidently out of a determination to avoid living the life of a *kafir* (infidel). During combat with the Croats, he was shot and killed near an enemy bunker. The Croats eventually returned the bodies of Abu Muslim al-Turki and David Sinclair together to the *mujahideen* three months later.[134]

On 5 September 1993, Wahiudeen al-Masri organized another fierce assault, labelled the '1st Vitez Operation,' on the Croatian suburbs of Travnik, this time in the mountains near the town of Novni-Travnik. The Arab fighters admitted that the battle was fought equally against Croatian soldiers and also civilians, and further claimed that roughly forty Croats were killed in total. During the advance, Abu Ali al-Kuwaiti (who had only been freed from Croatian custody a few months before) and 'Hamdu' (a local Bosnian *mujahid* volunteer) were both killed.

Abu Hamza al-Urdani, Abu Ali's roommate at the time, explained that Abu Ali had been put in charge of a mortar position, when he abandoned his post to help another Arab brother, Abu Minna, fix his jammed Metroleoze machine gun. After the *jihadi* unit captured the area and again moved forward, a number of fighters heard a large explosion. Abu Mustafa al-Falastini investigated the noise and discovered Abu Ali trapped in a minefield. Abu Ali had inadvertently wandered into the danger zone and had paid dearly for his mistake when one leg was blown straight out from underneath his body.[135] Dr Abul-Harith al-Liby attempted to use his medical skills to save Abu Ali, but it was far too late, and the Kuwaiti volunteer soldier died where he lay, mortally wounded, on the battlefield.[136] According to Abu Sa'd al-Busnawi, 'Hamdu,' the other combat casualty, 'was one of the first Bosnians to join the Foreign Mujahideen forces.'[137]

Undeterred, on 18 September 1993, Wahiudeen led yet another attack on the Croatians, codenamed the '2nd Vitez Operation' or 'Operation Kruscica.' At the frontlines near Kruscica (in the vicinity of an explosives factory), the *mujahideen* confronted a group of Croatian militiamen and forced them to retreat. However, the battle proved ultimately disappointing: first, Hussaamudeen al-Masri, the veteran Egyptian Arab-Afghan commander, suffered a 'critical injury'; and, secondly, the guerrillas were forced to withdraw due to the alleged but unspecific 'weaknesses of the Bosnian army.'[138] The following day, the fundamentalist guerrillas attempted to recapture the positions they had momentarily seized during the previous battle. It appears that, this time, the Croats were better prepared for such an attack, and repulsed the *mujahideen* offensive, killing one foreign recruit, Abu Musab al-Swedani.

According to his friend and *jihad* companion Abu Hudhaifa al-Afghani, Abu Musab was born in Sweden to a Swedish mother and an Algerian father. He grew up in Scandanavia, but at the age of 20 years suddenly developed an intense interest in studying Islam. He travelled to Saudi Arabia on a personal pilgrimage to learn Arabic and study the Islamic *Shariah* (religious law). During the nearly two years he spent on the Arabian Peninsula, he became a devout fundamentalist who, upon his return to Sweden, began actively proselytizing his religion to others around him, including his family and relatives.[139]

The *jihad* in Afghanistan was making major international headlines during this period of the 1980s, catching the avid attention of the pro-Islamist community in the West. Abu Musab 'began to follow the news of the Muslims around the world and in particular the killing of the Muslims and their expulsion from their homes. He then understood that there is no dignity for the Muslims except through Jihad.' Abu Musab travelled to Peshawar, the 'gateway to *jihad*,' with another young, radical Muslim who was already a member of the *mujahideen*. Abu Musab was, at first, mostly interested in proselytizing Islam to non-Muslims. However, after spending time with his inspiring, if militant, companion, he soon ventured forth into Afghanistan to seek combat training and to fight on behalf of the Islamic revolution. Upon returning to Sweden and marrying a Muslim woman, he decided to, once again, make a *jihadi* pilgrimage – this time in Bosnia. He arrived in the region and joined up with the extremists based in the camp on Mount Igman, under the lead of 'General' Abu Ayman al-Masri. In this camp, there were a number of Western and European guerrilla recruits, including at least one red-bearded, caucasian American known as 'Abu Umar.'[140] After fighting in Bosnia for some time, Abu Musab attempted to leave the war zone and return home to Sweden. *En route*, he was captured by the Croats and was detained for almost 2 months. It is unclear if he was freed during the infamous April UN-supervised prisoner exchange, however, it was indeed about this time that he was released from captivity and rejoined the foreign guerrilla corps. Only a few months later, in this battle near Vitez, Abu Musab was finally struck down by a sniper's bullet.[141]

Despite these setbacks, the *mujahideen* continued to infiltrate Croatian frontline towns and villages, and moved back and forth between areas under their control. These operations were extremely hazardous because the foreign fighters did not know the area well, and were operating precariously close to heavily armed Croat militiamen. This lesson was demonstrated clearly when a group of five Arab-Afghans led by Wahiudeen al-Masri ran into trouble while driving near Mount Scit south of Kruscica. The unit became disoriented and accidentally ventured 7 km inside Croat-controlled territory. According to the *mujahideen*, Croatian militiamen promptly sideswiped the vehicle with a volley of fire from an anti-aircraft weapon. Several of the fighters apparently survived the initial ambush and attempted to fend off the Croats with their light arms, predictably, to no avail.[142] Four of the men inside the car perished, including Wahiudeen, Abu Khalid al-Qatari, Abu Abdurrahman al-Masri, and Abu Hamza al-Suri.

Another former sports star, Abu Khalid al-Qatari was a well-known player on Qatar's national handball team, and was quite recognizable in his homeland due to his being 'of black descent.' In the twilight of his teenage years, Abu Khalid witnessed the events taking place in Afghanistan during the 1980s, and had wanted to travel and join the *jihad* there. However, according to accounts of his friends amongst the *mujahideen*, his mother had put her foot down and absolutely forbid him to go. Disappointed at not being able to join the Islamic guerrillas in Afghanistan, he jumped at the chance to travel to Bosnia at the end of 1992. He told the men he fought with in the Balkans: 'Back in Qatar, I bought some fighting clothes to go and fight in Afghanistan, but my mother prevented me from going. But, [God-willing], this time, with these same clothes, I will be killed in Bosnia.' Abu Khalid's wish was fulfilled in less than a year of combat; and evidently, according to those who had recovered his body, he was so badly burned that the skin on his face and hands had turned a grisly white.[143]

Yet another casualty of this confrontation, Abu Abdulrahman al-Masri was a thirty-something Arab fighter, distinguishing him from amongst the comparatively mostly younger members of Kateebat al-Mujahideen. A former student at the Islamic University in Madina in Saudi Arabia, he had been one of the first Arab fighters to arrive in Bosnia. Among his more notable accomplishments, Abu Abdurrahman fought with Abu Ishaq al-Makki's unit and later in the mid-October 1992 battle near Tesanj (later memorialized as the 'Operation of Muhammad al-Faatih' in honour of the slain *Amir*). He was also involved in the '1st Vitez Operation,' and was among the group of elite 'Muslim special forces' who had specifically trained in the spring of 1993 to terrorize and spread fear among the Croats – including being a member of the actual *jihadi* unit subsequently responsible for the kidnapping of Croatian HVO chief Zivko Totic.[144]

In addition to the continuing sporadic battles with the Croats and Serbs, the Arab-Afghans continued to escalate their confrontations with international United

Nations forces attempted to keep the warring sides apart from one another. A number of *jihadi* dispatches speak of one particular incident that occurred in either late 1993 or early 1994 involving four Muslim fighters: Abu Muaz al-Qatari, Abu Salih al-Qatari, Abu Abdullah al-Qatari, and Abdullah Afendi al-Busnawi. Abu Muaz, 21 years old, was considered to be an Islamic scholar (a *Hafiz* of the Qur`an, to be precise), a trained military commander who had fought in Afghanistan, and the son of a wealthy Qatari businessman. He had already survived a close encounter with the enemy, when his unit was captured by the Croats in Srebnic and held hostage until the infamous May prisoner exchange. Abu Muaz and his fellow Qataris Abu Salih and Abu Abdullah decided to journey to Sarajevo and join military operations near the capital. *En route*, the group of Arabs spent two days at the home of a sympathetic Bosnian Muslim, Abdullah Afendi. After hearing their inspiring tales of brotherhood and *jihad*, Afendi agreed to accompany the Arabs to Sarajevo and help out as he could. However, back on the road to Sarajevo, they ran into several UN vehicles manned by 'Russian' soldiers. Although it is unclear how the confrontation began, both sides fired at each other repeatedly until all four *jihadis* were shot dead.[145]

The year 1993 had not turned out as badly as it could have for the *mujahideen* in Bosnia. Despite the obvious setback in relations with the Croats, the Arab-Afghans and their new disciples were continuing to grow more powerful as a political, religious, and military force to be duly respected. Al-Qaida's projected base in the Balkans – once a fantasy in the minds of men like Anwar Shaaban and Abu Abdel Aziz – was now firmly established and cemented with the recruitment of hundreds of local Bosnian volunteers for the *jihadi* brigade. Matar al-Walid, a former *mujahid*, told a Kuwaiti newspaper that when he had initially arrived in Bosnia in December 1992, there was only one larger formation of Islamic fundamentalist volunteer soldiers. Nine months later, in October 1993, al-Walid claimed 'now there are at least 12 formations.'[146]

With a network of local supporters and sympathizers, the Arab-Afghan émigrés could travel freely throughout large swaths of central Bosnia. While the arms and supply routes through Croatia were effectively cut, new opportunities were emerging, including receiving direct aid from powerful sponsors like the Sudan, Iran, and Usama Bin Laden. Furthermore, despite the significant casualties taken (including the mourned military commander Wahiudeen), the new generation of senior commanders like Dr Abul-Harith, Moataz Billah, and Abu el-Ma`ali had trained the Arab-Afghan corps in advanced combat and terror tactics, enabling them to deal debilitating blows to their enemies.

Notes

1. 'Report of the Joint Inquiry into the Terrorist Attacks of September 11, 2001.' House Permanent Select Committee on Intelligence/Senate Select Committee on Intelligence. Senate Report No. 107-351/House Report No. 107-792. 107th Congress, 2nd Session; December 2002, p. 32.
2. FBI Transcript of interview of Ramzi Ahmed Yousef. 7 February 1995, p. 3.
3. Government Exhibit 2800-A. *United States of America v. Mohammed Salameh.* United States District Court for the Southern District of New York. Case #: S5 93 CR 180.
4. FBI Transcript of interview of Abdul Basit Mahmoud Abdul Karim (also known as Ramzi Ahmed Yousef). 14 February 1995, p. 2.
5. Waller, Douglas. 'Inside The Hunt For Osama.' *Time*, 21 December 1998, p. 32.
6. FBI Transcript of interview of Abdul Basit Mahmoud Abdul Karim: 'Aircraft in Flight.' 28 February 1995, p. 19.
7. FBI Transcript of conversation involving Siddig Ibrahim Siddig Ali. 19 June 1993. *United States v. Omar Ahmad Ali Abdel Rahman et al.* S3 93 Cr. 181(MBM). Government Exhibit 352-T, p. 10.
8. Sennott, Charles M. 'Terror Report: Mastermind held public benefits.' *The New York Daily News*, 26 June 1993.
9. Shaykh Omar Abdel Rahman. 'The Inevitability of Jihad for the Solution of our Problems and for the Frightening of the Enemies of God.' Speech given at the Conference on Solidarity with Bosnia/Herzogovina. 16 January 1993.
10. Ibid.
11. Sennott, Charles M. Op. cit.
12. 'Suspect's Wife: We Were Bosnia-Bound.' *Newsday*, 14 July 1993, p. 89.
13. FBI Transcript of conversation between Emad Salem and Siddig Ibrahim Siddig Ali. *United States v. Omar Ahmad Ali Abdel Rahman et al.* S3 93 Cr. 181(MBM). Government Exhibit 641-1T, pp. 19–21.
14. Trial Transcript from *United States v. Omar Ahmad Ali Abdel Rahman et al.* S3 93 Cr. 181(MBM), pp. 15629–30, 15634–5, 15654, 15667–8, 15671, 15763.
15. FBI Transcript of conversation between Emad Salem and Siddig Ibrahim Siddig Ali. Op. cit., 19, 28–9.
16. 'Press Release.' Statement by United States Attorney David M. Barasch on the conditional plea of Kelvin E. Smith. U.S. Department of Justice; Office of the United States Attorney for the Middle District of Pennsylvania, 30 September 1998.
17. FBI Transcript of conversation between Emad Salem and Siddig Ibrahim Siddig Ali. Op. cit., p. 19.

18. FBI Transcript of conversation between Emad Salem and Siddig Ibrahim Siddig Ali. Op. cit., pp. 19–21.

19. FBI Transcript of conversation between Emad Salem and Siddig Ibrahim Siddig Ali. Op. cit., pp. 13–14.

20. Brumley, Bryan. 'Bosnian Mujahedeen Will Welcome, Not Threaten, US Soldiers.' Associated Press. 4 December 1995.

21. 'The Martyrs of Bosnia: Part I.' Videotape. Azzam Publications.

22. 'The Jihad in Bosnia.' *Al-Daawah* (Islamabad), January 1993.

23. Berger, Carol. 'Bosnian Muslims Turn to Kuwait for Money, Arms.' *The Christian Science Monitor*, 28 January 1993, p. 6.

24. Italian Division of General Investigations and Special Operations (DIGOS) Anti-Terrorism Report. 'Searches at the Islamic Cultural Center, Viale Jenner 50, Milano, 6/26/1995. Dated 15 September 1997.

25. Kurop, Marcia Christoff. 'European Jihads: Al Qaeda's Balkan Links.' *The Wall Street Journal Europe*, 1 November 2001.

26. 'Egyptian Jihad's Organizational Chart.' *Indigo Publications Intelligence Newsletter*, No. 353, 25 February 1999.

27. Finn, Peter. 'Europe renders dissidents and terrorist suspects to Egypt.' *The Washington Post*, 29 January 2002, p. A01.

28. Jean-Louis Bruguiere and Jean-Francois Ricard. 'Requisitoire Definitifaux aux Fins de Non-Lieu. De Non-Lieu partiel. De Requalification. De Renvoi devant le Tribunal Correctionnel, de mantien sous Controle Judiciaiare et de maintien en Detention.' Cour D'Appel de Paris; Tribunal de Grande Instance de Paris. No. Parquet: P96 253 3901.2, p. 94. See also: 'Italian police arrest alleged Tunisian militant.' Reuters. 29 September 2002.

29. Jean-Louis Bruguiere and Jean-Francois Ricard. Op. cit., p. 96.

30. Jean-Louis Bruguiere and Jean-Francois Ricard. Op. cit., p. 96.

31. Lemyre, Normand (lawyer on behalf of Canadian Ministry of Justice) (1996). 'Avis du Ministre en Vertu du Sous-Alinéa 69.1(5)(a)(ii) de la Loi sur L'Immigration et du Paragraphe 9(1) des Règles de la Section du Statut de Réfugié.' Commission de l'Immigration et du Statut de Réfugié; Section du Statut de Réfugié. Case #: M92-10133. 25 April 1996, p. 3.

32. Manresa, Andreu. 'Algiers accuses the Saudi millionaire Bin-Ladin of paying the GIA terrorists.' *El Pais* (Madrid), 8 October 1998.

33. Fisk, Robert. 'Anti-Soviet warrior puts his army on the road to peace.' *The Independent* (London), 6 December 1993, p. 10.

34. Pomfret, John. 'How Bosnia's Muslims Dodged Arms Embargo: Relief Agency Brokered Aid From Nations, Radical Groups.' *The Washington Post*, 22 September 1996, p. A01.

35. 'The Martyrs of Bosnia: Part I.' Op. cit.

36. Vigodda, Jon. 'Allah's Army Goes West.' *The Jerusalem Report*, 5 November 1992, p. 22.
37. Vigodda, Jon. Ibid.
38. Sudetic, Chuck. 'Muslims heed call to arms.' *The New York Times*, 14 November 1992, section 1, p. 5.
39. Rohde, David. "Islamic Money Helps Muslims in Bosnia, but Not Enough to Win." *The Christian Science Monitor*, 26 January 1995, p. 1.
40. Azzam Publications. 'The Martyrs of Bosnia: Part I.' PAL/NTSC Format. Length: 150 minutes approximately. ©2000.
41. 'In the Hearts of Green Birds.' Audiocassette transliterated by Salman Dhia Al Deen. Azzam Recordings: London.
42. 'The Martyrs of Bosnia: Part I.' Op. cit.
43. 'In the Hearts of Green Birds.' Op. cit.
44. 'Abdul-Wahid Al-Qahtani Joins the Ranks of the Martyrs.' http://www.azzam.com.
45. Abu Sahar al-Haili was from Hail, in north-central Saudi Arabia. Though *mujahideen* representatives have widely distributed the story of his martyrdom, little was revealed of his shadowy past prior to coming to Bosnia. They referred to him simply as 'a very brave and patient brother.'
46. 'In the Hearts of Green Birds.' Op. cit. See also: 'Abu Sahar al-Hailee.' http://www.azzam.com.
47. 'In the Hearts of Green Birds.' Op. cit.
48. 'Under the Shades of Swords.' Audiocassette sequel to 'In the Hearts of Green Birds.' Azzam Recordings: London, UK.
49. Ibid.
50. 'The Martyrs of Bosnia: Part I.' Op. cit.
51. US Department of State, 1993, IHRLI Doc. No. 62612-62877, at 62629; see also Charles McLeod, ECMM, Report on Inter-Ethnic Violence in Vitez, Busovaca and Zenica, April 1993, IHRLI Doc. No. 29043-29131, at 29072 (attack on Vitez).
52. Njavro, Marko. 'The suffering of Croats in the Lasva Valley!' Newsgroups: soc.culture.croatia. 6 April 1999.
53. 'Conflict in central Bosnia becoming like Lebanon: UN' Agence France Presse. 5 June 1993.
54. Stephen, Chris. 'Bosnia-Hercegovina: Murderous Chaos swirls through the Valleys.' Inter-Press Service. 21 May 1993.
55. Njavro, Marko. Op. cit.
56. 'Under the Shades of Swords.' Op. cit.
57. Hogg, Andrew. 'Arabs join in Bosnia war.' *The Sunday Times*, 30 August 1992.
58. 'Under the Shades of Swords.' Op. cit.

59. 'Under the Shades of Swords.' Op. cit.
60. 'The Martyrs of Bosnia: Part I.' Op. cit.
61. Stephen, Chris. Op. cit.
62. 'In the Hearts of Green Birds.' Op. cit.
63. 'Kuwaitis say Croats tortured Moslem preacher.' Reuters. 19 May 1993.
64. The three Kuwaitis included Muteb Saad al-Walid, Yaqoub al-Qatami, and Mansour al-Najdi. The Saudi, Saad al-Shemmari, was a permanent resident in Kuwait. See: 'Trapped Kuwaitis in good condition.' *Arab Times*, 27 June 1993. Reprinted in *Moneyclips*, 28 June 1993.
65. 'The Martyrs of Bosnia: Part I.' Op. cit.
66. Bishop, Patrick. 'Islamic warriors lead Balkan attack.' *The Daily Telegraph*, 14 June 1993, p. 10.
67. US Department of State, (1993). Op. cit.
68. 'The Martyrs of Bosnia: Part I.' Op. cit.
69. 'The Martyrs of Bosnia: Part I.' Op. cit.
70. 'Bosnian Croats Decry Ethnic Politics.' National Public Radio, 16 June 1993.
71. Frost, Bill. 'As thousands flee, the dead must lie where they fall in the blood fields of Travnik.' *The Times* (London), 9 June 1993.
72. Frost, Bill. Op. cit.
73. 'British Troops dodge bullets to rescue Villagers.' The Press Association Limited. 9 June 1993.
74. 'Serbs step up attacks on Muslim haven.' Reuters. 9 June 1993.
75. Sheehan, David. 'The Road to Guca Gora.' St David's Relief Foundation. http://www.stdavids.org/reports-road.htm. See also: Stephen, Chris. (1993), 'Mujahideen madness imperils dream of multi-ethnic Bosnia.' *The Observer* (London), 27 June 1993, p. 13.
76. Stephen, Chris. 'Mujahideen madness imperils dream of multi-ethnic Bosnia.' *The Observer* (London), 27 June 1993, p. 13.
77. Rodrigue, George. 'Muslim paramilitary units blamed for Bosnian atrocities.' *The Dallas Morning News*, 3 June 1993, p. 1A.
78. Hogg, Andrew. 'Terror trail of the mujaheddin.' *Sunday Times* (London), 27 June 1993.
79. Nevill, Hugh. 'Muslims take revenge on Croat village.' *The Independent* (London), 1 May 1993, p. 10.
80. '10 Britons believed killed in Bosnia.' *Evening Standard* (London), 10 February 1993, p. 6.
81. Boggan, Steve. 'Britons flock to fight in Bosnia.' *The Independent* (London), 10, February 1993, p. 1.
82. Frost, Bill. 'British troops poised to quit Vitez base.' *The Times* (London), 14 June 1993.
83. Ibid.

84. Bishop, Patrick. Op. cit. p. 10. See also: O'Kane, Maggie. 'Mujahedeen fighting in Bosnia, British say.' *The Guardian* (London), 14 June 1993, p. A6.

85. 'Moslem fighters "led by Briton."' *Daily Mail* (London), 29 October 1993, p. 2.

86. O'Kane, Maggie. 'Foreigners spearhead Muslim offensive at Vitez.' *The Guardian* (London), 14 June 1993, p. 6.

87. Ibid.

88. Croatian Information Centre. 'Weekly Bulletin.' No. 1, 9 August 1993.

89. Bellamy, Christopher. 'Mujahedin force in Vitez.' *The Independent* (London), 14 July 1993, p. 9.

90. Balman, Sid jr. 'U.S. warns of Iranian terror in Balkans.' United Press International. 12 July 1993.

91. Schwartz, Steven. *The Two Faces of Islam*, Doubleday: New York, p. 168.

92. 'Jihad, The Misunderstood Word.' Lecture given by Suleman Ahmer at the World Assembly of Muslim Youth (WAMY) Okeechobee Summer Da`wah Camp. 26 July 1996. Videotape obtained from the Meccacentric Da`wah Group.

93. Pyes, Craig, Josh Meyer, William C. Rempel. 'Bosnia Seen as Hospitable Base and Sanctuary for Terrorists.' *The Los Angeles Times*, 7 October 2001, p. A1.

94. Adams, Robert. 'Bosnia-Hercegovina: The Price of Betrayal.' Inter Press Service, 15 July 1993.

95. 'Trapped Kuwaitis in good condition.' *Arab Times*, 27 June 1993. Reprinted in *Moneyclips*, 28 June 1993.

96. 'The Martyrs of Bosnia: Part I.' Op. cit.

97. 'In the Hearts of Green Birds.' Op. cit.

98. 'Jamaludeen al-Yemeni.' http://www.azzam.com.

99. 'Trapped Kuwaitis in good condition.' Op. cit.

100. 'Abu Saif ash-Shahrani and Abu Hamad al-Otaibi.' http://www.azzam.com.

101. Ibid.

102. Hogg, Andrew. 'Terror trail of the mujaheddin.' Op. cit.

103. Bodansky, Yossef. 'Iranian and Bosnian Leaders Embark on a New, Major Escalation of Terrorism Against the West.' *Defense and Foreign Affairs' Strategic Policy*, 31 August 1993, p. 6.

104. Rodrigue, George. Op. cit., p. 1A.

105. Adams, Robert. Op. cit.

106. Hogg, Andrew. 'Terror trail of the mujaheddin.' Op. cit.

107. Rodrigue, George. Op. cit., p. 1A.

108. Eagar, Charlotte. 'Muj more fun if you're a Cool Dude in Bosnia.' *The Observer*, 7 November 1993, p. 19.

109. Fisk, Robert. 'An alien "brother" fights for Muslims.' *The Independent* (London), 14 July 1993, p. 9.

110. Rogosic, Zeljko. 'Vast investigation in Bosnia Herzegovina.' *Nacional* (Bosnia), Issue 306, 27 September 2001.

111. Bodansky, Yossef. *Some Call It Peace: Waiting For War In the Balkans*, International Media Corporation: London, 1996, Part I, Chapter 3.

112. Sadiq, Muhammad. 'Qisa al-afghan al-Su`udiyiin.' *Al-Majalla*, 11 May 1996, p. 19.

113. 'The Martyrs of Bosnia: Part I.' Op. cit.

114. Eykyn, George. '"Mujahidin" rush to join Islamic fundamentalists in war.' *The Times* (London), 23 September 1992.

115. 'Jihad, The Misunderstood Word.' Lecture given by Suleman Ahmer at the World Assembly of Muslim Youth (WAMY) Okeechobee Summer Da`wah Camp, 26 July 1996. Videotape obtained from the Meccacentric Da`wah Group.

116. Fisk, Robert. 'To Sarajevo, by way of Riyadh.' *Independent* (London), 22 December 1992, p. 17.

117. It was Gulbuddin Hekmatyar who ordered his forces to raze Kabul to the ground in an endless blitz of rocket barrages when rival *mujahideen* factions would not immediately comply to his demands. As of the summer of 2002, Hekmatyar became a target of U.S. military forces in Afghanistan after being implicated in a plot to kill Afghan leader Hamid Karzai. At least once, he has already narrowly escaped being targeted by an anti-tank missile fired from a CIA-operated drone.

118. Hogg, Andrew. 'Terror trail of the mujaheddin.' Op. cit.

119. Fisk, Robert. 'Anti-Soviet warrior puts his army on the road to peace.' Op. cit., p. 10.

120. Sudetic, Chuck. Op. cit., section 1, p. 5.

121. BBC World News. 'Supreme Islamic Leader says 140,000 Muslims killed in Bosnia-Hercegovina.' 16 October 1992. Originally reported by the Iranian Revolutionary News Agency (IRNA) on 11 October 1992.

122. Sudetic, Chuck. Op. cit., section 1, p. 5.

123. Vulliamy, Ed. 'Town feels Winter and War Tightening their Noose.' *The Guardian* (London), 15 September 1992, p. 8.

124. Post, Tom with Joel Brand. 'Help from the Holy Warriors.' *Newsweek*, 5 October 1992.

125. Vulliamy, Ed. Op. cit., p. 8.

126. Hogg, Andrew. 'Islamic militants boxed in by reality of Bosnian warfare.' *Sunday Times* (London), 6 September 1992.

127. US Department of State. 1993, IHRLI Doc. No. 62612-62877, at 62756.

128. Ibid., at 62648 and 62756; Croatian Information Centre, Weekly Bulletin, No. 9, 4 October 1993, IHRLI Doc. No. 36434-36438, at 36435.
129. US Department of State. 1993, IHRLI Doc. No. 62612-62877, at 62614.
130. Ibid., at 62742 and 62677.
131. Aydintasbas, Asla. 'Why they can't turn their backs on the veil.' *Independent* (London), 28 April 1994, p. 22.
132. Unidentified video interview of 'Abu Ibrahim.' Originally obtained from the Finsbury Park Mosque, London.
133. 'Abu Muslim al-Turki.' http://www.azzam.com.
134. 'In the Hearts of Green Birds.' Op. cit.
135. 'The Martyrs of Bosnia: Part I.' Op. cit.
136. 'In the Hearts of Green Birds.' Op. cit.
137. 'The Martyrs of Bosnia: Part I.' Op. cit.
138. 'The Martyrs of Bosnia: Part I.' Op. cit.
139. 'The Martyrs of Bosnia: Part I.' Op. cit.
140. 'The Martyrs of Bosnia: Part I.' Op. cit.
141. 'The Martyrs of Bosnia: Part I.' Op. cit.
142. 'Abu Khalid al-Qatari.' http://www.azzam.com.
143. Ibid.
144. 'The Martyrs of Bosnia: Part I.' Op. cit.
145. 'In the Hearts of Green Birds.' Op. cit. Some other *mujahideen* accounts derived later from 'In the Hearts of Green Birds' claim that it was, in fact, vehicles belonging to 'Bosnian Communists' (i.e. Serbs) who attacked Abu Muaz and his friends. 'Abu Muaz al-Qatari,' Op. cit.
146. Delo (Ljubljana). 27 October 1993. Originally reported in Al-Qabas (Kuwait).

–6–

Attention Turns Westward

Here we are, O Islam of the honourable.
We are here in defence of all that is sacred.
Here we are.
Let us create for your glory, stairs made of our skulls.
Here we are, Here we are, Here we are.

Prayer of Abu Yasser al-Nashmy, an Arab mujahid in Bosnia.

The events of 1993 demonstrated quite unequivocally that the Arab-Afghans thrived in an atmosphere of chaos and civil disorder. The breakdown in relations with the Croats had created exactly such a situation during the tragic summer of 1993. The prevalent atmosphere of hatred and cruel vengeance allowed the thuggish foreigners to mix in well with local society. But the friction between the *mujahideen* and local Bosnian Muslim authorities underscored that there were still critical ideological, political, and strategic differences between the two loosely allied forces. In the end, the Bosnians were much less concerned with *jihad* than fighting for a just peace. As the tide of the war shifted, it became increasingly apparent that no such peace would be possible without first patching up the various grievances between the Muslims and the Croats.

Western political leaders played prominent roles in putting pressure on the two sides to forgive and forget. American officials privately demanded that Croatian President Franco Tudjman rein in Bosnian Croat militants who were pursuing the disastrous civil war with the Muslims. They also insisted that Tudjman withdraw an estimated 5,000 regular Croatian combat troops dispatched to aid their ethnic brethren in Bosnia. Moreover, in February 1994, the UN Security Council took the landmark step of threatening official economic sanctions on Croatia if it did not withdraw its troop deployment.[1] Also on the table was a tantalizing economic aid package that Tudjman and the Croatians craved. Clearly, persisting in the civil war with the Muslims would have nothing but ill consequences for those involved.

A sudden rash of terror attacks on Westerners in the Zenica region heightened Western concern with mending fences between the Bosnian Croats and the Muslims. In October 1993, after completing a preliminary investigation, UN sources blamed foreign *mujahideen* forces for the unexplained murder of a Danish humanitarian driver. That conclusion caused significant consternation among UN officials, who subsequently halted all relief agency convoys for four weeks.[2] It certainly was a dramatic turn of events when not only local civilians, but even international aid workers were now the deliberate targets of violence. Then, on 27 January 1994, three Britons – Simon King, David Court, and Paul Goodall – working for their government's Overseas Development Administration (ODA), were travelling through Zenica at night in a UN-marked Land Rover. The men, following the main road through the town center, were heading for a nearby hotel. Earlier in the evening, they had encountered a grey Volkswagen Golf on the outskirts of Zenica – it was an unusual occurrence to see an unmarked civilian vehicle, given the extreme gasoline shortages and the obvious danger of driving by moonlight in a warzone.

Suddenly, in the darkness, the suspicious Golf had returned and actively pursued the Land Rover. Within moments, the car sped alongside the British vehicle and forced it to the side of the road. Five Arabic-speaking 'bearded gunmen' in combat fatigues quickly alighted from the Golf and aimed their pistols and Kalashnikov rifles at the hapless Land Rover. King, Court, and Goodall immediately surrendered, assuming their unknown attackers were only interested in stealing the Rover. However, it soon became clear that there were larger forces at work. There is some dispute over what exactly was said during the car ride. Several media reports indicated that one of the gun-toting strangers 'spoke to the Britons in broken English, saying they would not be harmed, but were being taken as hostages to get the release of their "brothers."'[3] However, one aid official claimed the carjackers in fact told the three men: 'We are kidnapping you because of the oppression of our Moslem brothers by the West.'[4] In either case, the men drove the three relief workers outside of Zenica, and took them at gunpoint to a nearby riverbank. Then, survivor Simon King explained, 'they made us stop while they waited for their leader.'[5]

If kidnapping was indeed the original motive for the ambush, something went dreadfully wrong at this point. Instead of holding the Westerners hostage, their assailants confiscated their coats and wallets, and forced them to lie on the ground. Within 20 minutes, another unidentified car arrived with two more gunmen. After a 'short discussion,' one of the men suddenly turned and shot Paul Goodall twice at short range in the back of his head.[6] Jan Lowe, a British pathologist, later testified before a hearing on the matter that one of the shots had been fired 6 to 8 inches from Goodall's head. The angle of the bullet wounds were 'typical of an execution-style murder'; moreover, Lowe suggested that a final third bullet from a 9 mm automatic pistol was fired when Goodall was already dead.[7] A coroner involved in the UK inquest of Goodall's death commented that the Briton's fate was 'most horrid and unnecessary,' and even admitted feeling 'deep and burning anger' at what he had seen: 'It is hard to grasp how any human beings can behave in such a fashion to fellow human beings, but it happens . . . I hope those who were responsible for that man's death can be found and brought to justice.'[8]

Simon King recalled witnessing the death of his friend: 'I heard a shot and quickly looked up and saw Paul shot . . . I jumped for the river.' As King and Court attempted to flee, they were showered with a hail of gunfire. Both men were hit and seriously injured; King was shot twice and Court took a round in his chest. Nevertheless, the wounded Britons fought for their lives, charging across a minefield and diving headlong into the swiftly-moving river. King narrated: 'I felt a round hit my arm . . . It was so cold I lost all feeling. I swam under water for as long as I could. We were helping each other and were encouraging ourselves to keep going. At the time I didn't realise I had got a leg wound as well. I know I'm very lucky to be alive.'[9]

The incident caused wide reverberations throughout the aid worker community and the British media. Jim Stuart, another British volunteer aid worker active in the Zenica area, told journalists, 'I am very shocked. This appears quite calculated and callous . . . It is one thing to run the risk of sniper fire but to be taken off the street and executed is a completely new ball game.'[10] Ron Redmond, the UNHCR spokesman in Sarajevo, denounced the Goodall's murder as 'cold-blooded and brutal and quite different to what has happened before. It is very worrying.'[11] Larry Hollingworth, the head of the UNHCR delegation in Zenica, went even further: 'It's a terrorist act. It's obvious that murder was the intention and it's frightening.' Hollingworth warned that new instructions had been issued by his office to Western aid workers to avoid isolated villages, to travel in groups, and to only travel at night while accompanied by military escort. 'I don't know who wants to stop us but that is the line some groups are taking,' Hollingworth continued. 'There are various elements here who are not under government control.'[12] British Prime Minister John Major even added his own thoughts, stating that he was 'profoundly shocked and distressed' by the attack.[13]

However, this would not be the end of the tale of Paul Goodall's murder. The incident was yet a further strain on relations between the Bosnian government and the Arab *mujahideen* deemed responsible. Now, with the Western aid lifeline to central Bosnia in possible jeopardy as a result, local officials sprang into action and took an unusual (and short-lived) interest in the investigation of Goodall's murder. A police checkpoint near the crime scene had incidentally noticed the Golf as it passed by and marked its licence number. The owner, Abdul Hadi al-Qahtani (also known as Abdul Hadi al-Gahtani), was arrested two days later in the Golf while accompanied by two other foreign men. Al-Qahtani was a Saudi member of the foreign *mujahideen* in his early thirties who, at the time of his arrest, was carrying an identification card issued by the Zenica office of the Saudi High Commission for Relief.[14] When Italian police later raided Anwar Shaaban's headquarters at the Islamic Cultural Institute in Milan, they likewise discovered twenty blank employee identification cards for the Saudi High Commission for Relief in Bosnia.[15] Al-Qahtani was apparently only one of many foreign fighters in the former

Yugoslavia masquerading as relief workers for the well-known Saudi charitable organization.

Dzemaludin Mutapcic, the deputy prosecutor of Zenica, announced to reporters that al-Qahtani had come to Bosnia 'to fight in the way of God, to save Bosnia's Muslims.' [16] The Saudi prisoner told Bosnian authorities that he was a theology teacher from Riyadh, and denied involvement in Goodall's murder.[17] But, when shown a photograph of al-Qahtani, both King and Court positively identified him as the *mujahid* who had spoken to them in English while they were being held at gunpoint. [18] To their further puzzlement and dismay, UK officials learned that the Saudi murder suspect was also in possession of a British passport in the name of 'A. Jordan,' a 31-year-old Briton who went missing in the Zenica area in late 1993.[19] Despite maintaining his innocence, al-Qahtani refused to otherwise cooperate. According to Mutapcic, 'He does not want to say anything, he keeps silent. That's his defence.' The two other men detained in the Golf vehicle, both carrying false Pakistani documentation, were a 19-year-old Jordanian and a 21-year-old Yemeni. Both were later released for lack of evidence, after neither Court nor King could positively identify them.[20] The case was still very complicated, and Bosnian police admitted that there was much they did not know about the alleged perpetrators. Asim Fazlic, the chief of police in Zenica, commented: 'One of the strangest elements is that we still do not know the exact identity of [those] . . . we hold in Zenica. They are very uncooperative and so far still insist, in spite of their car, uniform and weapons, that they are humanitarian aid workers helping privately funded organisations.'[21]

There was also, of course, still the unresolved matter of the stolen British Land Rover. Within only two days, police officials received an intelligence tip that several suspects were travelling in the same vehicle from central Bosnia toward the Butmir airport south of Sarajevo.[22] The Bosnian Ministry of Interior believed that this was part of a desperate attempt by the wanted men to flee a manhunt by local authorities. Bosnian military police located and chased the stolen jeep, which made a quick stop en route while its *mujahideen* occupants seized two civilian hostages, ironically choosing an Iranian national and another unidentified Muslim man as victims. As the Land Rover attempted to race up Mount. Igman, it approached a pre-constructed police checkpoint. According to Bosnian radio, the police issued several warnings to the approaching car to stop. Instead of halting, the Rover raced forward and attempted to ram through the roadblock, while its occupants fired automatic weapons at Bosnian military personnel. By the end of the deadly shootout, all three Arab guerrillas and their Iranian hostage were killed, and one Bosnian policeman was badly wounded.[23] The three dead *mujahideen* were identified as Ahmed al-Abdela, Saad Maboul Ali, and Abu Muaz al-Muhajir. The men carried identification cards for a 'second Middle Eastern relief agency in Sarajevo,' a passport issued in Great Britain, and a forged Pakistani passport with a Croatian entry and transit visa.[24] Moreover, police said ballistics tests showed that, at the time of their death, al-Abdela, Ali, and al-Muhajir had been in possession of the same pistol used to kill aid worker Paul Goodall.[25]

Though the investigation did not last long, it did temporarily refocus international attention on the presence of the foreign *mujahideen* in central Bosnia. In an interview at the time, Bosnian defence minister Hamdo Hadzihasanovic estimated that 'several hundred' foreign *mujahideen* fighters 'generally Arabs or from central Asia' were based in Bosnia to provide military aid to the Muslim government. But, Hadzihasanovic had no illusions as to the nature of the freelance Islamic guerrillas, especially those accused of involvement in the Goodall murder: 'We treat them as criminals and we already have proof that we are dealing with terrorists . . . The latest incident in Zenica, the killing of the UN staff member, confirms this.' The defence minister also added that those arrested during the investigation had been in the possession of British, Danish, and French passports. 'Probably there are some Muslims as well as European nationals among them,' he suggested.[26]

United Nations sources generally agreed with Hadzihasanovic's assessment of the situation. One acknowledged that 'there are quite a few' foreign *mujahideen* in the Zenica region. 'The Bosnians are trying to sort out their army now and the 3rd Corps (based) in Zenica are trying very hard to bring them into line.'[27] Other sources indicated that at least between 200 and 300 Islamic mercenaries were based in the area of Zenica alone. Other aid workers recounted a litany of bizarre and violent confrontations with the mysterious foreign fighters. Francisco Guevarra, a French nurse with Medecins du Monde in Zenica, told a French journalist: 'We had to move out of a house where he had planned to stay because of threats from one of the mujahedeen who came and told us to get out because we were too close to one of their bases. The local people are scared of them and we avoid them as much as possible.'[28] A week later, an anonymous threat was broadcast by radio announcing that more UN refugee agency workers would be targeted for assassination. That threat, later determined to have been transmitted on a radio stolen from Paul Goodall's Rover, was apparently never carried out.[29]

Despite the vocal bravado, following the shootout on Mount Igman, the Bosnian government soon allowed the investigation of Abdul Hadi al-Qahtani and his role in the foreign *mujahideen* to grind to a total halt. For unknown reasons, police officials never questioned anyone at the foreign Islamic relief organizations implicated in the probe. Likewise, their offices were never searched. Alija Izetbegovic's government discounted any direct link between the Arab guerrilla battalion and Goodall's murder, and insisted that al-Qahtani was a rogue element following his own personal agenda. Six weeks after the arrest of the Saudi theology teacher, the police were still attempting to keep his identity secret, even from the UN. Meanwhile, the same Bosnian officials who had initially championed the aggressive investigation of al-Qahtani suddenly stonewalled at the notion of re-opening the case. Referring to the bloody gun battle on Mount Igman, Asim Fazlic, the police chief in Zenica, contended: 'The killer has been killed and two associates too. And as far as I'm concerned the case is closed.'[30]

However, there were other more reasonable explanations for why the Bosnians were so eager to put the Goodall case behind them, and permit the *mujahideen* to continue operating unfettered. Aid workers theorized that the Bosnian government under Izetbegovic was afraid of the repercussions of putting al-Qahtani on trial for murder. First, such a court case would further highlight the presence of foreign Muslim units outside the direct control of the Bosnian military. Moreover, the trial might uncover damaging evidence of complicity by the *mujahideen* in a number of terror attacks and savage human rights violations. Not only would such revelations damage Bosnian Muslim relationships with the United States and Western Europe, but moreover, they would almost certainly be used by the Serbs to downplay reports of their own horrific atrocities and massacres.

Finally and perhaps most importantly, the Bosnians may have also feared that by convicting al-Qahtani, an employee of the Saudi High Commission for Relief, they would alienate their allies among the Islamic countries in the Middle East, particularly Saudi Arabia. Izetbegovic and his advisors were cozying up to the Saudis, hoping that the wealthy petro-dollar regime would help finance post-war reconstruction in the Balkans. According to Sakib Sokolovic, a prominent local doctor familiar with Islamic aid organizations in Sarajevo, estimated that these groups, mostly based in Saudi Arabia and Kuwait, had contributed at least $62 million in 1994 alone to Bosnia.[31] Thus, the Bosnians considered their amicable relations with the Saudis quite lucrative, and were reluctant to endanger the critical financial support that came with it. Captain David Chown, a British liaison officer with the Bosnian army based in Vitez, provided credence to this theory: 'What I am always told is that the [Bosnian] army has to tolerate the mujahedeen because of the money coming in from fundamentalist countries.'[32] Even Zijad Imamovic, director of the Zenica mayor's office, acknowledged of the Arab-Afghans that 'there has been some economic impact from having them here.'[33] As a result, as one senior Western aid official acridly noted: 'No one wants to know about this case . . . Not the Bosnian government, not the UN, not even the British. The British have a peace plan and they want to be on good terms with the Bosnians.'[34]

Even so, local Bosnian authorities were still torn between cracking down on the *mujahideen* and simply overlooking their criminal behaviour. Bosnian military commanders in the region were apparently in favor of dramatically 'purging' the ranks of the Arab guerrillas in order to bring them into line. Those that would not follow the lead of the BiH army leadership would either be arrested or expelled. However, this idea was quickly shot down by the central government in Sarajevo, which was desperate to avoid a confrontation with their erstwhile fundamentalist allies. In the end, not only was no purge authorized but, quite to the contrary, the *mujahideen* were once again permitted to operate on their own mandate and outside official Bosnian government policy. A silent confrontation developed between local law enforcement in Zenica on one side, and Bosnian fundamentalists and collaborators on the other. Westernized, secular state prosecutors in Zenica insisted that al-Qahtani should be put on trial like any other criminal. They were suspicious of stiff resistance to such a trial by the Zenica town council, which had taken over by hardline Bosnian Muslims.[35]

As the weeks passed, there was less and less indication that the Bosnians had any intention of prosecuting al-Qahtani. Then, in mid-March, a Sarajevo Judge issued orders to the Zenica jail to release the Saudi into police custody. The judge later explained that the release was instigated following orders of the city prosecutor who evidently had asked the judge for an opportunity to question al-Qahtani to determine if he was associated with the three Arab suspects shot to death in Goodall's Land Rover on Mount Igman. This was immediately odd, because the three men were already dead, and there was no indication of any other possible suspects on trial in Sarajevo. The judge's order was issued directly to the Zenica police, and local prosecutors in Zenica were not told that the alleged murderer was being released.[36] The judicial decision was legal and enforceable because it was issued under the presumption that al-Qahtani was considered a witness in a separate criminal trial being held in Sarajevo. However, the idea that the Saudi would be rendered to authorities in Sarajevo was bizarre. After more extensive research, British reporters were unable to uncover any record of any such trial in Sarajevo at the time. Furthermore, the capital remained under a tight Serb siege, and the only access to the city from central Bosnia was through a lone, hazardous military tunnel passing under the Butmir airport.[37] This was hardly a safe or protected route for routine prisoner transfers.

Predictably, 10 days later, police officials quietly informed the justice department in Zenica that al-Qahtani had 'mysteriously' escaped their custody and vanished from sight. This was an extremely perplexing development for the local prosecutors, who did not even know that he had been initially released, and yet still had the responsibility of explaining the disappearance to both wary British envoys and the doubtful Western media. Hasagic Mensur, the chief judicial investigator in Zenica, defended the role of his office in the matter and maintained that he had personally asked the police, to no avail, for more information. Unfortunately, as he added, 'we are still waiting for a reply.' The judge denied any knowledge of al-Qahtani's escape, or of what had happened to the missing prisoner.[38]

The British government took a strangely relaxed approach towards the bungled investigation of Paul Goodall's murder. Until early April, over 2 months after the crime happened, no representative from the British Overseas Development Administration or the UN ever visited the local prosecutor's office in Zenica. There were some reports that the ODA had only learned of al-Qahtani's true identity and his subsequent escape through published articles in mainstream British news-papers. Finally, on 8 April, with al-Qahtani having already been missing from police custody for almost a month, the ODA dispatched a representative to discuss the case with the prosecutor's office. The British Foreign Office nevertheless insisted, 'We are doing all we can to ensure that the Bosnian authorities carry out a proper investigation into the killing of Paul Goodall.'[39] But even Foreign Secretary Douglas Hurd admitted that the investigation was confusing and haphazard. 'There's a lot of obscurity and murk, murkiness, about this episode but we are trying to bring light to bear on it.'[40]

The family of Paul Goodall was more realistic and not nearly as confident that al-Qahtani would ever be recaptured. Goodall's father-in-law, Michael Palmer, demanded that the truth be revealed, but also acknowledged that, in all likelihood, the wanted Saudi would never face prosecution:

> We would like the murderers brought to justice, but there's no justice out there . . . There's no law and order. We're not surprised at anything that happens there . . . It all seems very convenient. We would have wanted to see the killers brought to justice, but I don't think there's any chance of that. We'll never know the full story.[41]

In the end, Palmer's predictions turned out to be exactly correct. The case was never pursued by Bosnian, British, or UN investigators, and at least several of those deemed responsible for the 'profoundly shocking' and 'distressing' death of Paul Goodall remain at large. Abdul Hadi al-Qahtani's ultimate fate is still unknown.

On 11 March, echoes of the Goodall case were felt in additional unconfirmed Serb news reports indicating that possibly another British humanitarian convoy driver had been targeted and assassinated by foreign troops in Bosnia. According to a Yugoslav Telegraph Service report, sources in Banja Luka indicated that Abu Musa al-Yemeni, a *mujahideen* fighter based in Zenica, had killed the Briton on 8 March 'without any reason simply because he was drunk and could not control himself.' The YTA alleged that no public fuss was made of the murder because local Bosnian authorities were 'trying to cover [it] up . . . The fact that the murder took place in [Muslim-held] Zenica is a particular problem.'[42]

Thus, for good reason, the United States and its NATO allies were dramatically increasing the diplomatic pressure in late 1993 and early 1994 on Croatian and Muslim factions to put their quarrels in the past and team up militarily against the more menacing Serb threat. Undoubtedly, one hope among Western diplomats was that such a coalition alliance would make foreign 'mercenaries' in Bosnia obsolete and would encourage the clearly reluctant Bosnian Muslim authorities to expel the *mujahideen*. According to one United States 'senior official,' 'What we have in mind is that the central government of [Bosnia] would be weak, but the Muslim-Croat part would be stronger. The links to Croatia on the outside could be stronger than those to the Serbs within the country of Bosnia. You'd end up with an asymmetrical federation in Bosnia.'[43] Naturally, given the horrific events that had transpired in 1993, the negotiations between the Muslims and the Catholics were tense and complex.

After several months of behind-the-scenes bargaining, on 23 February 1994, a truce known as the 'Washington Accord' was finally agreed upon by Rasim Delic and Ante Roso, the commanders of the Bosnian Muslim and Croat militaries, respectively. The initial agreement, signed at a UN base in Zagreb, was presided over by General Jean Cot, UN commander in former Yugoslavia, and Lieutenant General Sir Michael Rose, commander of UN forces in Bosnia. After the historic completion of the accord, Ante Roso attempted to distance himself from the failures at previous peace talks and explained that these were 'new times, new dialogues.' On his part, Rasim Delic voiced his hope that this new truce would 'show us the way to a political agreement.' In addition to ending hostilities, the two sides also agreed to allow UN peacekeepers in 'sensitive areas,' to hand over or withdraw frontline artillery, and to open routes for international aid convoys and peacekeeping troops.[44]

By this time, the Arab-Afghans were already having major problems in their tenuous relationship with the local community. The Washington Accord, which transformed their presence in central Bosnia a relative anachronism, only added to their troubles. Even in Zenica, the stronghold of the *mujahideen*, Arab-Afghans were forced to shave their wispy beards and conceal their *shahadaa* bandanas as they assumed a much lower profile. In spite of vigorous efforts to 'Islamicize' the nominally Muslim Bosnian populace, the locals could not be convinced to abandon pork, alcohol, or public displays of affection. Many Bosnian women persistently refused to wear hijab or follow the other mandates for female behaviour prescribed by extreme fundamentalist Islam. Even the foreigners themselves admitted serious setbacks in the recruitment of local Muslims. A young Arab *mujahid* pleaded: 'The way of Allah will take time here; we've got to be patient.' But, in the hotbeds of *jihad* power, the fundamentalist wave had already peaked and was quickly receding. A spokesman for the town of Zenica attempted to explain what had happened: 'Those who came here from the East came ill-[in]formed about the Bosnian Muslims, who are both easterners and westerners. Their plan to impose their way of seeing the religion and teach us how to pray has failed. They tried to plant trees here, palm trees, which can't grow in Bosnia.'[45]

A Bosnian imam in the town who had resisted the call of the militant Islamists enthusiastically testified to the failure of their cause. According to him, 'There are fewer and fewer of them every day.' Another similarly unpersuaded local imam noted: 'When people in a boat are caught in a storm, they turn to God. When the sea becomes calm again and they touch land, they forget him.'[46] In the hour of crisis, the Muslim fanatics had stepped forward with money and weapons when no one else would. With the sudden change in tempo of the Bosnian war, the bizarre and artificial Islamist phenomenon slowly began to fade into the shadows.

Simultaneously, as Bosnian society resisted and rejected the fanatical ideology of the Arab-Afghans, under the Washington Accord, the Croats now had a freer hand to police the foreign fighters. In the aftermath of the renewed alliance between the Bosnians and the Croats, Croatian authorities arrested a number of notorious Muslim militants and forced others into hiding. The *mujahideen* were infuriated with the Washington Accord, which they naturally angrily viewed as a complete betrayal. They bitterly resisted attempts by Croatian and even Muslim authorities to rein them in, even as their local adherents wavered in their commitment to a pure Islamic state. Stjepan Radic, a Franciscan brother in the region, commented: 'The Croats are still having problems with the mojaheddin, to whom the Croat-Muslim agreement is unacceptable. But the Croatians can feel the change in the air. Islamic fundamentalism didn't stand chance here, except for a very brief period. The Muslims here are Europeans.'[47] Finally, in 1994, Husaamudeen al-Masri, the veteran Egyptian *mujahideen* commander and close friend of Wahiudeen and Moataz Billah, was killed under unexplained circumstances. Billah was now the last remnant of the original group of Egyptian Arab-Afghan veterans who had initiated the development of the foreign battalion in Bosnia alongside Shaykh Abu Abdel Aziz Barbaros and Anwar Shaaban.[48]

Nevertheless, the Arab *mujahideen* were known for nothing if not their stubborn persistence against incredible odds. Despite the terms of the Washington Accord and growing irritations with the local Bosnians, the foreign fighters continued to spread their network and bring in replacement soldiers from Arab-Afghan training camps in the Sudan, Yemen, and Afghanistan. On 4 May 1994, a new rising member of the Arab-Afghan movement arrived in Bosnia: Abu Muaz al-Kuwaiti (also known as Adil al-Ghanim). The al-Ghanim family is part of a cluster of merchant families in Kuwait that dominate the private sector and are closely linked to the government. Abu Muaz, no exception among his clan, was a 31-year-old former Olympic athlete and the privileged son of a Kuwaiti governor. Following his appearance at the Olympics, he left Kuwait during the mid-1980s and joined the militant Arab *jihadis* who gathered in Afghanistan. He spent six years training and fighting among the *mujahideen*, leaving only periodically to return to Kuwait and 'raise money and awareness about the Jihaad in Afghanistan. He would stand up after the prayers in the Kuwaiti mosques and deliver speeches to the congregation reminding them of their duty to assist their brothers in Afghanistan.'[49] During the Afghan *jihad*, Abu Muaz gained valuable experience in both military matters and in the movement's organizational hierarchy. According to his brother, Abu Muaz had even 'worked with' the local Kuwaiti resistance movement during the six-month Iraqi occupation beginning in August 1990.[50]

His arrival in Bosnia coincided with a time when the Arab fighters there were in desperate need of leadership in the absence of Wahiudeen al-Masri and in the aftermath of the Washington Accord. Shortly after his arrival, Abu Muaz was quickly promoted to be a senior commander of the *mujahideen* in Bosnia. One Arab militant close to Abu Muaz recalled:

> A very rich man from Kuwait but he still knew the obligation of Jihad . . . This brother used to speak very fast but when he spoke he used to give us Islamic lessons and news of what was going in Bosnia. And when he would speak, he would make you feel so good. Even if it was the worst news that he was giving you, it would make you feel so happy to hear it. Because of his good manners and his organisational skills, the brothers chose him to be [a] Commander of the Foreign Mujahideen section.[51]

Dr Abul-Harith relinquished his position as *Amir* of the foreign *mujahideen* during the summer of 1994 to the fiery young Algerian, Abu el-Ma`ali.[52] In the wake of Abu el-Ma`ali's ascent to power, incidentally or not, several noteworthy clashes occurred between Croats and *mujahideen* fighters. On 1 September, the leader of the Third Corps of the Bosnian army met with civilian representatives from nearly 800 Croatians living in the Zenica region. The meeting had been arranged to quell growing protests from locals about the bizarre and frightening behaviour of the Arab-Afghans, who would typically throw violent temper tantrums during relatively minor confrontations with Western aid workers and Croat civilians. At that time, a compromise agreement was drawn up for the total withdrawal of Arab soldiers from the predominantly Croat village of Podbrezje, the location of Abu Ma`ali's primary Zenica-area headquarters. Despite the accord, no move was taken by the Bosnian army to forcibly eject the *mujahideen* from Podbrezje or restrict their activities there.[53] On 3 September, Croatian HVO troops attempted to themselves intervene and stop a group of foreign militants from travelling from Travnik south towards Mostar and central Croatia. Two *jihadis*, a Malaysian and an Iranian, were killed during the fierce resulting battle.[54]

The friction continued unabated despite further efforts by Bosnian army officials to mediate through the winter of 1994–5. 'Zeljko,' a Croat neighbor of the *mujahideen* base in Podbrezje, was willing to talk to journalists but was too afraid to give his last name. Pointing to the Vatrostalno Factory building nearby, he explained:

> Either the mujahedeen in that house leave, or we will have to leave. On Dec. 23, we were told to turn off the lights on our Christmas trees and they have been harassing us daily ever since . . . They come with local Muslim extremists to our houses and inquire if the house is for sale. They ask whether we will be leaving soon. They shout insults at us in the street. But we are determined to stay.[55]

Another local Croatian farmer, Jazo Milanovic, was not nearly as optimistic: 'They walk in and take what they want and the one time I protested to them they fired a burst over my head. The bullet holes are still in the wall. We will all be forced out soon.'[56] Most reporters who tried to approach the Podbrezje base were quickly sent packing by grim-looking guerrillas who were more than willing to take aim at Western reporters with their rifle muzzles.

In October 1994, one British journalist managed to visit the *Kateebat al-Mujahideen* headquarters in Podbrezje and certainly saw no evidence indicating that the Arabs were considering abandoning Bosnia or even the Podbrezje camp, for that matter. Anthony Loyd, in the London *Times*, described what he witnessed at the Vatrostalno building: 'A black Islamic flag hung in the courtyard. In front of a row of wearied four-wheel-drive vehicles, the fighters gathered in groups. There were Arabs, Caucasians and Africans. Most of them were bearded, some with shaven heads, all in well-worn combat dress and heavily armed hawk-eyed, lean and unforgiving.'[57]

A Tunisian recruit at the camp told Loyd:

> We are coming here to die, not to leave. That is why we shall win . . . The West says we are terrorists, but look what it did in Africa, in Algeria; nobody tells them that they are Fascists and terrorists . . . To become a member of the Mujahidin is something very serious, a sacrifice. You cannot return to your home once the government there knows what you are. Instead, we must follow the eternal path of jihad.[58]

Moreover, when interviewed personally, Abu el-Ma`ali angrily denied widespread media allegations that his units had committed gross atrocities or presented a threat to peace and stability in the region.

The foreign guerrillas continued to cooperate very fluidly with the local branches of sympathetic Islamic charitable organizations, in spite of the unwanted outside focus resulting from the Goodall affair. After all, as one *mujahideen* middleman admitted, 'Jihad is not just about fighting . . . It is also about food, money, and the media.' [59] Anthony Loyd, again reporting from Zenica, interviewed several Bosnians who had received support from programs run by the Kuwaiti Revival of Islamic Heritage Society (Jamiat al-Ahya al-Tirath). 'Azera,' the widow of a fallen BiH Muslim soldier, told Loyd that she received a monthly pension from 'Islam Sans Frontieres,' in exchange for which she was expected to send her son for a daily hour of fundamentalist indoctrination to the Kuwaiti Society's office in Zenica. The lessons, based on the foundation of Arabic and Qur`anic studies, taught a violent and confrontational brand of Islam.[60]

Among the textbooks at the school was a treatise titled *Attitudes that we have to Change*. This work, published by the Revival of Islamic Heritage Society, was written by Abu Imad al-Masri (also known as Imad el-Misri, Husayn al-Aramawi,

Jamal al-Husayni, Abu Ahmad al-Masri), an up-and-coming Egyptian *mujahideen* commander based at the headquarters in Zenica. Since even the early days of the Arab battalion in the fall of 1992, Abu Imad had been well known for delivering regular lessons and lectures about Islam. His book distributed by the Kuwaitis was a condemnation of the '*kuffar*' [infidels] and their various attempts at self-governance. Socialism and democracy alike were attacked as the 'enemies of Allah.' In *Attitudes that we have to Change*, Abu Imad also promoted Taliban-style ideas about video and audio recordings of music and human figures: their possession alone would certainly lead to a hellish fate. Azera acknowledged the cyclical tragedy of Bosnian families like hers. 'It is sad that they use our children to spread Islam, children who have already lost their fathers. But I do not have any other income and I have to agree to this. It means that we are being paid for believing.'[61]

Some of the Islamic charitable workers showed remarkably little pity for the indigent people they had been sent to help. It seemed that those missionaries were much more imbued with missionary, rather than humanitarian ideals. A Palestinian representative of the Revival of Islamic Heritage Society in Zenica explained: 'The Muslims here have turned their back on their faith . . . God and the Koran tell Muslims "who abandons my orders resists me this one will be punished." So these people are being punished by the war until they return to the real way.' The Kuwaiti fundamentalist group financed the establishment of the Balkan Islamic Center in Zenica in the summer of 1993. The center became an important local institute for the teaching of holy war, and a recruitment center for the *mujahideen* brigade. One 'student' of the center, 15-year-old Elzedin Berbic, offered an insightful description of the center's activities: 'We learn, we talk, we pray together, we are shown films about the Islamic jihad . . . The films are different, some in Bosnian, some in Arabic, but they are all about jihad. The war was started to destroy the Muslim people, so now it must be a jihad.'[62]

More ominous signs emerged in this period that seemed to confirm the greater danger that the fanatical mercenaries based in Bosnia posed to the rest of the world. On 9 October 1994, Radio Mauritania reported that several Islamic fundamentalists had confessed under interrogation by local authorities to forming a 'jihad group in preparing for guerrilla war and in taking part in military training organized in a neighbouring country.' The men were led by an Iraqi Kurd and 'another soldier who came from [had fought in] Afghanistan and Bosnia-Hercegovina.' The unidentified veteran of the Bosnian war, of Moroccan origin, was believed to be principally responsible for supervising the military training of the would-be *jihadis*.[63]

In November 1994, Italian authorities were deeply dismayed when they learned of a new assassination plot organized by elements of the Egyptian terrorist groups Al-Jihad and Al-Gama`at Al-Islamiyya. The conspiracy aimed to target Egyptian President Hosni Mubarak during a three-day diplomatic trip to Rome, who promptly changed his schedule to avoid the visit.[64] As a result, the Italian police stepped up their counterterrorism efforts, and particularly their focus on Shaaban's Islamic Cultural Institute. On 26 June 26 1995, in a mission codenamed 'Operation Sphinx,' Italian police arrested 11 suspected members of Al-Gama`at Al-Islamiyya (including ten Egyptians and one Palestinian) and carried out formal searches of seventy-two addresses across northern Italy, including Milan. The detainees were charged with criminal conspiracy, robbery, extortion, falsifying documents, and illegal possession of firearms. The police had recorded a phone conversation in which one suspect openly stated: 'We are not carrying out terrorism in Italy but in the mother country.' One of those that Italian counterterrorism authorities were particularly seeking to arrest, Shaykh Anwar Shaaban himself, was nowhere to be found. Evidently, having been tipped off to the intentions of the Italian government, Shaaban had escaped and found asylum at his *mujahideen* military stronghold in Zenica.[65]

Shaaban's exodus to Zenica marked a critical period of development for the Arab-Afghan *mujahideen* in southern Europe. Once again, the contrasts between the romantic idealism of the fundamentalist clerics and the fanatic practices of the Arab-Afghans shone clear. Despite all the Arab-Afghan propaganda decrying the suffering of the Bosnian Muslims, just as in Afghanistan, their participation in the war was ultimately channelled toward a different purpose. The movement was transforming its operations to focus beyond the narrow confines of the Balkans – and, thus, was confronting the 'infidel' regimes head on. Central Bosnia was more than a mere frontline for Al-Qaida – by the start of 1995, it was a strategic foothold for Usama Bin Laden and his fanatical allies to infiltrate Europe and the Western world.

Notes

1. Schmidt, William E. 'Croats and Muslims Reach Truce to End the Other Bosnia Conflict.' *The New York Times*, 24 February 1994, section A, p. 1.
2. Beelman, Maud S. '"Mujahedeen" Volunteers Cause Problems for Bosnia.' *Associated Press*, 21 February 1994.
3. Stephen, Chris. 'Shots First then the Questions,' *Guardian* (London), 16 June 1994, p. T4.
4. Shawcross, William. 'Lunacy of life in Bosnia.' *Evening Standard* (London), 3 February 1994, p. 18.
5. Williams, David. 'How They Executed a Caring Man.' *Daily Mail* (London), 29 January 1994, pp. 1 and 6.

6. Stephen, Chris. Op. cit.
7. 'Aid Worker "was executed."' *Guardian* (London), 5 February 1994, p. 9.
8. Wilkinson, Paul. 'Anger at Bosnia death.' *The Times* (London), 30 July 1994.
9. Stephen, Chris. Op. cit.
10. Williams, David. Op. cit.
11. Williams, David. Op. cit.
12. Moutot, Michel. 'Briton's murder prompts security alert for aid workers.' *Agence France Presse*. 1 February 1994.
13. Loyd, Anthony. 'Gulf veteran killed in aid convoy attack.' *The Times* (London), 29 January 1994.
14. Higgins, Andrew, Robert Block and Glenn Simpson. 'Assault on Charities is Risky Front for US' *The Wall Street Journal*, 16 October 2001.
15. Italian Division of General Investigations and Special Operations (DIGOS) Anti-Terrorism Report. 'Searches at the Islamic Cultural Center, Viale Jenner 50, Milano, 6/26/1995.' Dated 15 September 1997.
16. Stephen, Chris. 'No Justice over Murdered British Aid Worker as Suspect Languishes Behind Prison Bars.' *Guardian* (London), 23 March 1994, p. 1.
17. Stephen, Chris. 'Shots First then the Questions.' Op. cit.
18. Stephen, Chris. 'No Justice over Murdered British Aid Worker as Suspect Languishes Behind Prison Bars.' Op. cit.
19. Stephen, Chris. 'Shots First then the Questions.' Op. cit.
20. Stephen, Chris. 'No Justice over Murdered British Aid Worker as Suspect Languishes Behind Prison Bars.' Op. cit.
21. Loyd, Anthony. 'Three held for Goodall murder.' *The Times* (London), 2 February 1994.
22. Sudetic, Chuck. 'Bosnians Say Police Killed 3 Men Sought in Death of a Briton.' *The New York Times*, 1 February 1994, section A, p. 9.
23. Radio Bosnia-Hercegovina. Sarajevo, Bosnia. Broadcast in Serbo-Croat. 31 January 1994, 19.00 GMT.
24. Stephen, Chris. 'Shots First then the Questions.' Op. cit. See also: Radio Bosnia-Hercegovina. Sarajevo, Bosnia. Broadcast in Serbo-Croat. 31 January 1994, 19.00 GMT.
25. Stephen, Chris. 'No Justice over Murdered British Aid Worker as Suspect Languishes Behind Prison Bars.' Op. cit.
26. 'Mujahideen "Terrorists" blamed for Briton's Murder.' Press Association. 1 February 1994.
27. Heinrich, Mark, (1994). 'Bosnians shoot murder suspects dead.' *Herald* (Glasgow), 1 February, p. 1.
28. Moutot, Michel. 'Briton's murder prompts security alert for aid workers.' *Agence France Presse*, 1 February 1994.
29. Beelman, Maud S. Op. cit.

30. Stephen, Chris. 'No Justice over Murdered British Aid Worker as Suspect Languishes Behind Prison Bars.' Op. cit.
31. Rohde, David. 'Islamic Money Helps Muslims in Bosnia, but Not Enough to Win.' *The Christian Science Monitor*, 26 January 1995, p. 1.
32. Cohen, Roger. 'Foreign Islamic Militants Strain Bosnian Alliance.' *The New York Times*, 18 February 1995, section 1, p. 3.
33. Fesperman, Dan. 'Zenica resists Islamic fundamentalism.' *The Baltimore Sun*, 6 August 1995, p. 4A.
34. Stephen, Chris. 'No Justice over Murdered British Aid Worker as Suspect Languishes Behind Prison Bars.' Op. cit.
35. Stephen, Chris. 'Shots First then the Questions.' Op. cit.
36. Stephen, Chris. 'Shots First then the Questions.' Op. cit.
37. Stephen, Chris and Adam Holloway. 'Aid worker's suspected killer escapes.' *Guardian* (London), 2 April 1994, p. 1.
38. Stephen, Chris. 'Shots First then the Questions.' Op. cit.
39. Stephen, Chris. 'Shots First then the Questions.' Op. cit.
40. Mulligan, Peter. 'Britain Presses Bosnia over Murdered Aid Worker.' Press Association. 2 February 1994.
41. Colley, Teilo. 'Escape reports outrage Murdered Briton's Family.' Press Association. 2 April 1994.
42. Yugoslav Telegraph Service. Broadcast in Serbo-Croat in Belgrade. 11 March 1994, 10.06 GMT.
43. Cohen, Roger. 'Washington Might Recognize a Bosnian Serb State.' *The New York Times*, 13 March 1994, p. A10.
44. Vukic, Snjezana. 'Bosnian Government, Croat Forces Agree on Cease-Fire.' Associated Press. 23 February 1994.
45. Naudet, Jean-Baptiste. 'Fundamentalists fail to create Islamic state in Bosnia.' *Manchester Guardian Weekly*, 3 April 1994, p. 11.
46. Ibid.
47. Ibid.
48. 'Under the Shades of Swords.' Audiocassette sequel to 'In the Hearts of Green Birds.' November 1997. Azzam Recordings: London.
49. 'Abu Mu'aadh al-Kuwaitee,' http://www.azzam.com.
50. 'Kuwaiti Fighter Killed in Bosnia.' Associated Press. 23 July 1995.
51. 'Abu Mu'aadh al-Kuwaitee,' http://www.azzam.com.
52. 'Under the Shades of Swords.' Op. cit.
53. 'Croat-Muslim tension in Zenica area over "al-Mujahid" unit.' Croatian Radio. Broadcast in Croatian in Zagreb, 20 September 1994; 13.00 GMT.
54. Yugoslav Telegraph Service. Broadcast in English language, 3 September 1994; 19.14 GMT.

55. Cohen, Roger. 'Foreign Islamic Militants Strain Bosnian Alliance.' *The New York Times*, 18 February 1995, section 1, p. 3.

56. Hedges, Chris. 'Foreign Islamic Fighters in Bosnia Pose a Potential Threat for G.I.s.' *The New York Times*, 3 December 1995, section 1, p. 1.

57. Loyd, Anthony. 'Disciples of holy war answer call to fight and die.' *The Times* (London), 21 October 1994.

58. Ibid.

59. Loyd, Anthony. 'Islamic radicals offer pensions in return for jihad.' *The Times* (London), 22 October 1994.

60. Ibid.

61. Ibid.

62. Ibid.

63. 'Members of "extremist jihad group" arrested; confessions broadcast.' Radio Mauritania (Nouakchott). Arabic-language broadcast, 9 October 1994, 22.00 GMT.

64. Rodan, Steve. 'Mubarak on a powder keg.' *The Jerusalem Post*, 30 June 1995, p. 11.

65. Willan, Philip. 'Italians arrest suspected Islamic militants.' *United Press International*, 26 June 1995.

−7−

The Final Campaign

Allah has bought from the believers their lives and their belongings and given them Paradise as a reward. In their struggle in the way of Allah, they are being fought against and they fight back. This is a fulfillment of the promise made in the Torah, the Gospel, and the Qur`an. And Allah will fulfill his promise and grant them a great victory.

'The Balkan War' – video

By late 1994, the *mujahideen* had persevered in their efforts at waging war in Bosnia for almost three years, despite much strife and controversy. In 1995, the foreign guerrillas would finally manage to win significant battlefield victories independently and have a telling impact on the overall progress of the Bosnian civil war. The *mujahideen* leadership carefully plotted to take advantage of new prevailing political conditions and prepared to make a dramatic public resurgence. The Arabs would leave behind the bitterness of the Croat-Muslim Washington Accord for the moment, and try to re-capture the populist zeal that had been such a key asset during the lean months of 1992 and 1993 by concentrating their energies on the hated Serb enemy. Indeed, between May and September of 1995, three major combat offensives took place involving sizeable numbers of foreign *jihadis*: 'Operation Black Lion,' 'Operation Miracle,' and 'Operation Badr.' These confrontations would eventually come to define the legacy of the foreign fighters in the Balkans.

The re-unification of the Bosnian Croat and Muslim factions, though detestable to the foreign *mujahideen*, had helped turn the course of the war. For the first time since 1992, the Bosnians were finally making real progress in gruelling combat with Serb military forces. Faced with a united enemy and the threat of NATO airstrikes, the Serbs had little choice but to attempt to hold on to as much territory as possible before a peace agreement was signed. Naturally, the dispute between Croat and Bosnian Muslim forces continued to fester over the supposed September 1994 agreement by the Bosnian army to voluntarily close the Arab-Afghan training camp in Podbrezje. In the beginning of February, public pressure from Croatian civilians against the *mujahideen* presence in Podbrezje resulted in a conciliatory visit by Ejup Ganic, the Muslim vice-president of Bosnia-Herzegovina.[1] United Nations military intelligence sources indicated that Ganic had served as the 'envoy' between Izetbegovic's regime in Sarajevo and the leadership of the Kateebat al-Mujahideen.[2] Yet, Ganic publicly supported the complaints of the Croats. He responded sympathetically: 'We meet Muslim fanatics who want to fight, we tell them, "You are the kiss of death." We don't need them, there are plenty of us. We need arms.'[3]

Though Ganic listened patiently to what the protesters had to say and assurances were again given, still nothing was done by the Bosnians to reign in the Arab-Afghan fighters. Spahija Kozlic, a Bosnian army spokesman for the Zenica-based III Corps, attempted to justify the deafening silence of the Bosnian government on the issue of the troublesome foreign fighters in Zenica: 'These people came here to help us. They are doing their job in a normal way . . . We do not know if they will move. Mr. Ganic heard the Croatian side of the story. But we have had no problems with the mujahedeen.' Jadranko Prlic, the Defence Minister of the Muslim-Croatian federation, was much less cavalier about the situation. 'We can no longer accept these mujahedeen terrorizing a Croatian neighborhood,' he insisted. 'Progress on the federation depends on a resolution of this problem.'[4] On 11 March, a collection of local political groups (including the Croatian Democratic Union of Zenica, the Croatian Peasants' Party of Zenica and Doboj Canton, the Croat Civic Party of Bosnia-Hercegovina, the Zenica branch of the Croat cultural society Napredak, and the Zenica branch of the Croatian Culture Club) issued a joint media statement emphasizing that 'promises given by top military and state officials . . . finally be fulfilled regarding the removal of the Al-Mujahid unit from Podbrijezje in Zenica.'[5]

With hindsight, it was abundantly clear why the *mujahideen* were still being protected by their estranged Bosnian allies: the Bosnian army desperately needed their advice and expertise for major upcoming military projects. Bulletins issued by the Arab headquarters in Zenica (led by Abu el-Ma`ali) in February 1995 stated that this was 'a busy month for Mujahideen,' with 'several groups, each made up of 3 or 4 brothers' visiting key Muslim-held cities and towns, including Sarajevo, Tuzla, Zavidovic, Breza, Travnik and Novni-Travnik. These representatives conducted negotiations and indoctrination sessions with both civilians and 'Bosnian army units.' Moreover, a number of fresh *mujahideen* recruits had just arrived (mostly from Yemen) and were diligently training for immediate combat roles. The *jihadi* reports also lashed out at the Croats, accusing them of 'spreading rumors and intimidating Mujahideen units . . . Croats have been trying for the longest time to expell [sic] Mujahideen from Bosnia, so that they can freely control the Muslim land to their advantage.'[6]

A month later, a subsequent bulletin from the Zenica stronghold reported that the Arab *jihadis* had already begun 'reorganizing frontline trenches and distribution of forward lookouts on a large area, in order to be prepared for the upcoming period in anticipation of a renewed wave of Serb-Croat arrack [sic].' New 'highly professional Muslim trainers with long experience' were allegedly specially imported to the Al-Farooq camp to enhance the education and abilities of the foreign battalion. Little mention was made of any actual combat operations; the *mujahideen* did claim to have launched a retaliatory attack on the Serbs in the 'Flaschish mountains killing 26 Serbs, however they had to withdraw later.' Additionally, Serb paramilitary forces had apparently fired several rockets and mortar shells at *mujahideen* targets in Zenica and Travnik, perhaps in nervous anticipation of an expected Muslim offensive.[7]

As was suggested by the bulletin, the *mujahideen* were indeed preparing for a series of significant operations in conjunction with the Bosnian Muslim army. In the aftermath of the Washington Accord with the Croats, the Izetbegovic government in Sarajevo was understandably eager to mobilize its full military capability and aggressively push the Serbs out of Muslim-claimed territory. Several of these operations, by virtue of the participation of illegal foreign combatants, however, took on an ominous and less-than-admirable character. In May 1995, the Bosnian military conceived a new plan for the 'liberation' of the town of Vozuca, near Zavidovici. Since the height of the Muslim-Croat war in 1993, the Serbs had been blockading Zavidovici from the surrounding mountains, blasting the riverside town with an estimated 3,000 to 4,000 howitzer and mortar rounds.[8] A victory at Vozuca, though daunting, would open the main highway between Zenica and the besieged Muslim enclave of Tuzla. The Bosnian government also hoped to use Vozuca to house some 15,000 Muslim refugees fleeing from Srebrenica and Zepa.[9]

In a bold move northward through central Bosnia, the army was directed to eliminate the defences at Mount Ozren and relieve frontline towns and defensive units in the Podrinje region. Bosnian commanders assembled the equivalent of four brigades of armor and artillery for the task.[10] The overall strategical plan, known as 'Hurricane '95,' would rely heavily on the advanced combat skills of foreign *mujahideen* forces during a sustained campaign that lasted more than four months.[11] Enes Saletovic, a communications technician with the Bosnian army, recalled, 'Our commander said: "Can you take this hill, and when?" They said, "We will take it when Allah says so."'[12] In anticipation of their role, the Arab-Afghan leadership in Travnik and Zenica decided to establish a temporary frontline base camp for foreign fighters in Zavidovici.

At first, the Bosnians harboured serious reservations about using Arab-Afghan forces as part of their offensive. The uneasy confrontations between local Muslim authorities and the incorrigible *mujahideen* were not easily forgotten; nor was the latter's unrelenting opposition to the Washington Accord generally well received. A Bosnian army representative admitted, '[t]hey are superb fighters . . . But you can't argue with them. It's best to have nothing to do with them.'[13] Unfortunately, under the tense circumstances during the spring of 1995, as a weapon of last resort, the *mujahideen* would have to be forgiven and let loose from their cages. French army Major Herve Gourmelon noted that, in general, the militant foreign fighters were 'held in reserve and never given defensive tasks. Their presence indicates imminent conflict . . . If a moujahedeen unit is there, we know by experience that we shall have problems.'[14] A gunsmith in Zavidovici who worked for the *mujahideen*, spoke of the continuing tensions: 'Some people claimed that [the Arab fighters] were not willing to attack until a page from Q[u]ran showed up in the sky. When I asked them whether that was possible, they laughed: "That is not true. We attack when the military conditions are right, when emir orders us to attack and when Alija [Izetbegovic] orders attack."'[15]

The *mujahideen* were taking the final steps in late May necessary to jump into action. They codenamed their upcoming military operation *al-Faath al-Mubeen*, or 'The Clear Victory' (also known as Operation 'Black Lion').[16] Just prior to the battle, Abu Muaz al-Kuwaiti rallied the guerrilla ranks with an inspiring motivational speech and prayer. Abu Muaz told the fighters assembled before him:

> . . . we ask Allah (Glorified and Most High), with all His beautiful Names and all His highest Attributes, to grant us a clear conquest and help us with a clear victory, as He is All-Powerful over that. And I also ask Allah (Glorified and Most High) to accept the martyrs from amongst us, if there are any martyrs . . . As for why we came to Bosnia-Hercegovina, we did not come here except for Jihad in the Way of Allah (Glorified and Most High), and to assist our Mujahideen brothers.[17]

During the speech, Abu Muaz ridiculed news reports that trivialized the impact of the *mujahideen* brigade on the overall progress of the war. He joked to his audience: 'If I am killed in the battle (if Allah accepts me from the Shuhadaa) then take my picture from the left, from the right and from the top, to show the people that this is an Arab, not a Bosnian!'[18]

The commander of Operation 'Black Lion' was Abu Abdullah al-Liby.[19] Abu Abdullah had gained his first military experience as a tank driver in the Libyan army. In 1992, he travelled from Libya to Bosnia and soon joined the foreign battalion on frontline combat duty. His formal training made him a welcome addition amongst the *mujahideen*. According to Al-Qaida sources, Abu Abdullah was a quiet *jihadi* who gained the respect of his peers through action not words; '[h]e was amongst those brothers of whom Allah Most High says ". . . harsh towards the infidels and kind towards believers."' Abu Abdullah was personally responsible for a dangerous reconnaissance mission behind enemy lines to assess Serb military positions on three mountains neighboring the town of Podsijelovo.[20] The peaks, offering essential control of the surrounding valleys, were of key strategic value to both the Muslims and the Serbs. The town was also a critical hub of Serbian communications lines towards Vozuci.

For several months during the winter of 1995, Abu Abdullah carefully mapped out the three kilometres of mountainside. As part of this responsibility, he was used to 'going in the night, going in the day in all times of weather going by himself, switching off his radio, sometimes even so close to the Serb bunkers that they would throw rubbish on him without even knowing that he was there. So this brother, he knew those three kilometers like the back of his hand.'[21] During World War II, this distinctive locale had been nicknamed the 'Gate of Moscow.' Following 1992, after regular Muslim army units tried and failed several times to seize the area, Bosnian military experts eventually concluded that the Posijelovo area was so well defended that it could only be overrun with the substantial use of close air support.[22] Not known to shy away from a challenge, the *mujahideen* mobilized their resources and sought to prove the conservative Bosnian estimates wrong.

After much preparation, the landmark operation commenced at dawn on Saturday 27 May. The progress made by the *jihadis* was fast and impressive. Afterwards, Abu el-Ma`ali wrote of what happened during the battle in the first and second official communiqués issued by the *Kateebat al-Mujahideen*:

> And after the Battalions of believers advanced and took over the peaks of the 'Gate of Moscow,' the Serb Crusade became crazed and tried to collect its fleeing units and recalled its reservists, and started its cowardly habit of [targeting] civilian areas [with] heavy artillery bombardment. But Allah was encircling them from behind. And facilitated for them His brave soldiers who started raining the Serb enemy with concentrated guided shells, on which they read the Name of Allah, and they asked Allah to carry the shells to its targets.[23]

Evidently, the battlefield intelligence that Abu Abdullah al-Liby had so carefully collected had been marshalled to direct devastating pinpoint artillery strikes on the heart of Serb defences. The triumph came at a cost: five Bosnian recruits and fourteen foreign Islamists were killed during the battle. Abu el-Ma`ali was quick to justify the human price of *al-Faath al-Mubeen*: 'The way of Jihad must have its pure blood which Allah picks and chooses to be a fuel for those who are left . . . We think of them as Martyrs.'[24]

One of the casualties among the Arabs was Abu Abdullah al-Liby himself, slain shortly after the battle by an enemy sniper while in the company another Yemeni *mujahid*. Thus, in the annals of Al-Qaida, the 'Clear Victory' became famous by another name: *al-Layth al-Aswad*, or Operation 'Black Lion,' in honour of the departed Abu Abdullah.[25] Other fatalities during the battle included Abu Zayd al-Qatari, a 17-year-old young Muslim from Qatar who reportedly shot and killed several Serb soldiers before being cut down himself; Muhammed Badawi, another popular *mujahideen* recruit originally from Egypt, injured first in the torso and then shot in the head; and Abdullah Shaybaani, a 19-year-old who was fatally wounded while attempting to cross the battlefield with an Arab volunteer comrade, Abu Muslim al-Yemeni.[26]

Nonetheless, by all accounts, in Podsijelovo, the *mujahideen* had scored a respectable success. According to many eyewitnesses, in less than one hour, they were able to seize control of all three peaks and silence Serbian artillery positions. Soldiers from the Bosnian army claimed that the *mujahideen* had overwhelmed Serb trenches, killing sixty, and disabling three Serb battalions.[27] The radios in the frontline base camp began to crackle with reports of victory from enthusiastic unit commanders. They had even captured additional weapons and ammunition to further bolster their future combat capabilities.[28]

As for the unfortunate Serb prisoners, according to Abu el-Ma`ali, 'they were interrogated, and gave valuable information, and then they received the punishment that they deserve.'[29] But videotapes circulating in Bosnia and allegedly representing the 'interrogation' of Serb prisoners offer a much more horrific notion of what Abu el-Ma`ali may have had in mind. Prisoners were held like animals and starved for days, slowly being tortured to death. In several cases, Serb detainees were given knives and ordered to kill each other, or face death themselves. The frightened men would eventually attack one another:

> [o]nce they fell from wounds, Mujahedeen would decapitate them, with cleavers or chain saws, and those who were still alive were forced to kiss severed heads that were later nailed to the tree trunks. Prisoners were hung upside down by ropes, they were nailed, or the Mujahdeen [sic] tied bricks to their testes and penises and pushed them into barrels where they slowly drowned pulled down by the weight of the bricks.

Videos of these bloodcurdling executions were allegedly so easy to obtain that one could even find them in the video store of the Zavidovici municipal 'Culture Hall.'[30] A Bosnian army soldier who served alongside the foreign *mujahideen* confirmed to journalists: '[t]hey like to kill. Whenever they could kill with their knives, they would do so.'[31]

The military victory during Operation Black Lion near Vozuci was followed by a wave of eager encouragement from fundamentalist Muslim leaders who sought to rally the Islamic world behind the new Bosnian army campaign. In mid-July, Srebrenica and Zepa, two supposedly UN-protected Muslim 'safe areas,' were nevertheless allowed to be overrun by Serb paramilitary forces. As many as 30,000 innocent Muslim refugees fled advancing Serb troops in Srebrenica alone, and many others were massacred or detained as prisoners. The nightmare of Srebrenica remains one of the most horrific chapters of the Bosnian civil war. In a sad twist of irony, a UN safe zone had quickly transformed into the locale for arguably the worst case of genocide in Europe since World War II.

News of these events caused a wave of anger and outrage to surge throughout the Middle East, directed not only at the Serbs, but moreover, at the waffling UN, Europe, and the United States. A zealous cleric in Abu Dhabi, UAE, castigated:

'[w]e should support our brothers in Bosnia. They are being butchered like sheep. Jihad is a must now for every Muslim.'[32] On 21 July, Shaykh Abdulaziz bin Baz, the grand mufti of the Kingdom of Saudi Arabia, concurred in a statement to his followers: 'Islam underscores the importance of Jihad and cooperation and in particular when a Muslim is threatened by an enemy.' As a result, he continued: 'Oh Muslims[,] don't hesitate in supporting your brothers in Bosnia-Herzegovina with all possible means including weapons, financial assistance and prayers to the Almighty Allah . . . As enemies have mobilized their potential to fight Muslims in Bosnia-Herzegovina, it has become an inevitable matter for the Muslims through-out the world to assist their brothers.'[33]

Precisely at this moment in mid-July, the Arab *mujahideen* in Bosnia launched a second major sweeping assault codenamed the 'Dignity Battle' or 'Operation Miracle.' This operation was led by the respected commander Abu Muaz al-Kuwaiti, and aimed to capture Mount Ozren, another critical strategic landmark.[34] Preparation for this battle can be traced back to as early as April 1995: at the beginning of that month, Serb patrols reported discovering a covert reconnaissance team of twenty-two foreign *mujahideen* sent to commit sabotage and terror attacks against the Serbs, evidently in a bid to 'soften' the area before all-out hostilities broke out. The fate of those twenty-two men is unclear; however, Serb military police confiscated 'many documents' they had left behind in haste, including passports, other identification, and 'battle conduct reports.' According to those documents, the group included Algerians, Tunisians, Egyptians, Yemenis, Saudis, and even a citizen of Azerbaijan.[35]

No amount of subterfuge or preparation could change the fundamental challenge of Operation Miracle: the geography of the combat zone. This was another hazardous mission that required an uphill offensive through a dense forest that would nevertheless still be fearsome enough to dislodge the Serbs from their bunkers and entrenchments. On 21 July, Abu Muaz al-Kuwaiti led several attack groups of *mujahideen* against those tenacious defensive positions. Shaykh Anwar Shaaban himself addressed a gathering of the Arab fighters just prior to the commencement of hostilities in 'Operation Miracle':

> I congratulate you with the permission of Allah (SWT) on a near victory and on a conquest from Allah (SWT). And we ask Allah to make us from amongst those who hurt our enemies time after time. We love martyrdom in the way of Allah. Its time is when Allah wishes. But, we ask our Lord (SWT), that he makes us from those who damage his enemies and from those who make his enemies taste punishment upon punishment.[36]

A special unit, led by Abu Umar al-Harbi, a Saudi in his early twenties from Medina, was tasked with capturing three Serb bunkers 'in the most dangerous terrain on the battlefield.' Abu Umar al-Harbi had first arrived in Bosnia in 1993 and reportedly never again left the frontline. He remained steadfastly cloistered at the camps or the combat zones, harbouring an utter distaste for modern civilization. Abu Umar had been particularly moved by the tragic stories of massacres involving the Muslim residents of Srebrenica in 1995. He was visibly upset when he learned of what had happened there, and his burning anger was reflected by fearless determination in combat. The first Serb bunker in was in a clearing at the top of a large open minefield. There were no hope of encirclement or shielded points where *mujahideen* units could seek temporary refuge as they advanced on the bunkers; rather, 'there was only one avenue of approach to this bunker, and that was head on, from the front.' The attack plan was brutish and simple: an Arab guerrilla would suddenly unleash a barrage of RPG (rocket-propelled grenade) rounds aimed at the bunker from the far side of the field. Then, the special attack group would rush forward across the minefield and suicidally storm the damaged bunker. This was exactly the sort of bloody, one-man-against-all desperado mission that native Bosnian troops were usually sensible enough to avoid.[37]

However, minutes before the advance could go forward, the Serbs opened fire on *mujahideen* positions across the field, in possible anticipation of the impending raid. At this point, most of the Arab guerrillas were very reluctant to go ahead with what appeared to mean certain death. Before they could talk him out of it, Abu Umar decided to unilaterally undertake the mission, with or without the support of his hesitant comrades. According to witness accounts, he sprang from hiding and sprinted across the minefield shouting *Allahu Akhbar*! Though his men did eventually follow him, this would be a fatal adventure for Abu Umar. He was shot in the head before he could penetrate any of the menacing Serb bunkers.[38]

During Operation Miracle, another enterprising Arab-Afghan would take on his own independent special assignment. Al-Battar al-Yemeni, 'The Cutting Edge,' was a well-travelled Arab-Afghan veteran fighter originally from Yemen. During the early 1980s, al-Battar was reportedly trained as a tank driver in the former communist army of Yemen. As part of his instruction, al-Battar was dispatched by his Moscow-backed government to receive specialized 'revolutionary' combat training in Cuba, where he had learned 'the ins-and-outs of tanks until he knew nearly every thing about them.' But, when al-Battar returned to Yemen, he experienced a reawakening in his Islamic faith and became disillusioned with the atheist regime that he was fighting for.[39] He left his homeland and fought doggedly with the Arab-Afghan *mujahideen* against his former Soviet allies in central Asia until the conquest of Kabul in 1992. He rejoined his fundamentalist peers several months later in Tajikistan, where he aided extremist guerrillas allied to Al-Qaida battle the Russian-backed post-communist regime.

Al-Battar eventually turned his attention to the new *jihad* attracting Arab-Afghan fighters to the heart of the Balkans. When he first arrived in Bosnia, he enlisted with a foreign reconnaissance unit and attempted to pass on his learned expertise in tanks to other *jihadis*: 'He taught the brothers how to lie under a moving tank, in order to build their confidence whilst dealing with the Serb tanks on foot. His ultimate dream was to take a tank in the fighting as booty (ghaneema) and use it against the enemy. He wanted to be the first one to capture a tank for the Mujahideen.'[40]

In this battle, the venerated al-Battar was placed in charge of 'Peak No. 702.'[41] He was quickly injured, but temporarily bandaged his wounded hand so that he could remain at the frontlines. However, at this point, several Arab *mujahideen* frantically began calling al-Battar over the radio: a disabled, but evidently functional Serb tank had been captured, but it sat in a vulnerable position to enemy fire. The Serbs were naturally desperate to prevent their equipment from being stolen and eventually were simply attempting to destroy the abandoned vehicle. Al-Battar answered the call and raced forward to commandeer the tank and move it safely back to the Arab frontline base camp. Despite his wounds, according to *mujahideen* reports, he insisted on returning to the top of Mount Ozren and the frontline of Operation Miracle. Four hours later, in a failed attempt to rescue a wounded Arab fighter in an empty Serb bunker, al-Battar was killed when his position was hit by a mortar shell. In death, the legendary tale of al-Battar was perhaps even more useful to the Bosnian *mujahideen* than in life. His 'martyrdom' had provided a powerful lesson in determination, skill, and sacrifice, three of the primary motivational ideals that Abu el-Ma`ali and the other Arab-Afghan commanders sought to instill in their radical troops.[42]

Another of the men responsible for the confiscation of the tank also was slain during Operation Miracle: Abu Muslim al-Imaraati, a 'Field Commander' of the foreign *mujahideen*. Abu Muslim, from the United Arab Emirates along the Arabian Gulf, was a young father and a committed fundamentalist. He first learned of the *jihad* ongoing in Bosnia soon after his wife became pregnant. Before his son was born, Abu Muslim left his home to join the growing numbers of foreign Islamic fighters in the region. The fanatical combat experience he gained there hardened him from a family man into an eager soldier who was 'extremely fierce in his fighting and his courage.' The *mujahideen* traded debatably accurate stories of Abu Muslim going out on long reconnaissance missions by himself and returning with 'plastic bags full of mines' that he himself had independently searched for, disarmed, and collected. But this young man had a more meaningful personal life beyond the limited confines of *jihad* and sought to return home and see his son for the first time. Abu Muslim had been among the group of Arab guerrillas who initially seized the tank commandeered by al-Battar al-Yemeni. After they relinquished control to al-Battar, Abu Muslim continued to advance past the frontline and was killed soon after in unexplained circumstances. *Mujahideen* sources said of him, '[h]e did not see his son in this world, but [God-willing], Allah will reunite him with his family in Paradise.'[43]

Local news sources reported that '[t]he Serbian forces sustained human and material losses in this battle.' In total, there were allegedly sixteen foreign *muja-hideen* killed during Operation 'Miracle.'[44] Among this number, there were also at least a few European Muslim recruits. One of these individuals was Abu Musa al-Almaani, a German of Turkish background who served as the cameraman of the foreign *mujahideen* in Bosnia. Though he was born to Turkish parents, he was raised from an early age in an adopted German family as a non-Muslim. Until his slipshod teenage years, Abu Musa fit in perfectly with his new lifestyle. He was a decent student, well-behaved, and his light-coloured skin allowed him to blend easily into European society.[45]

Around the age of fifteen, like many teenagers, Abu Musa became more rebel-lious, got in trouble at school, and, as he developed a sense of self-awareness, began to realize that his background was distinctly different than that of his German classmates. The friction between him and his adopted parents was soon too much to bear; his German family finally admitted to him that he was not their natural-born son. Of course, this discovery played havoc with Abu Muslim's sense of identity. A friend of his among the *mujahideen* recalled what Abu Muslim had told him of the realization: 'it reverberated in my mind and I went back and I asked my mum what does this mean and she refused to tell me, and after much persua-sion she told me the whole story. She was still in touch with my Turkish parents, my real parents and I went to see them and began to live with them.'

Only a few years after that traumatic life-change, at the age of twenty-one, Abu Musa decided to travel to Bosnia and join the Arab-Afghan fighters based in Zenica and Travnik.[46] It is hardly farfetched to suggest that there was a link between Abu Musa's tumultuous personal experience with his family and his involvement in radical Islamic activities. Perhaps after being a social misfit for so long, he hoped that such behaviour would, at a minimum, legitimize him in the eyes of his extremist compatriots. Indeed, much like American Taliban John Walker Lindh, Abu Musa seems to have been motivated – above all else – by a desperate need to belong to something bigger than himself and to be finally accepted as an equal by his peers.

At the time, his superiors in Zenica and Travnik were deliberately recruiting European Muslims with advanced technical skills and experience that had not been available to militant exiles languishing for years in Afghanistan. Abu Musa, talented in shooting and editing video, was assigned to be the official cameraman of the *mujahideen* battalion; in one hand he held a camera, and in the other, an AK-47. He dreamed that his unprecedented combat footage of the Arab-Afghans in action would galvanize other impressionable young Westerners with a penchant for Islam to support and join the *jihad*, as he himself had. Abu Musa apparently also had a fascination with the idea of martyrdom in the name of his newly adopted faith. According to Al-Qaida sources, he took an oath with three other *mujahideen* of Turkish origin before Operation Miracle 'to fight to the death. They were true to Allah, so Allah was true to them.'[47]

Salman al-Farsi, a Tunisian *mujahideen* recruit, was yet another casualty of Operation Miracle. Al-Farsi was a formidable soldier and an imposing sight; he was a large, powerful man who kept a fearsome broadsword strapped to his back with an unusual chest rig and had a black bandanna tied around his forehead. Training videos produced by the Arab-Afghan battalion in Bosnia depict al-Farsi repelling expertly off buildings in full combat fatigues. Al-Qaida sources commented that 'he loved to train . . . so that he could be as strong in fighting as he could and do as much damage to Allah's enemies as possible.' After his death, a compatriot implausibly claimed that al-Farsi's dead body smelled not of rotting flesh, but of sweet perfume. The unnamed guerrilla explained: 'It was beautiful and made us feel relaxed and comforted. [God-willing], this is a good sign for Salman that he is Shaheed [a Martyr], and it is a sign for the brothers who smelt this perfume, that this is the right path and to have patience on this path.'[48] Certainly, if nothing else, these men had become experts in turning the outcome of any battle, no matter how high the cost, into an upbeat and encouraging sign of divine intervention and guidance.

However, the *mujahideen* could hardly conceal their depression at the passing of the venerated commander of Operation Miracle, Abu Muaz al-Kuwaiti. Abu Muaz had reportedly survived the initial hostilities, only to be shot in the leg soon after the battle was over by a lingering Serb sniper. As he had mockingly requested in his motivational speech prior to Operation Black Lion, the Arab-Afghans were careful to take documentary video of his corpse to prove that '(i) that this was a Foreign non-Bosnian fighter and (ii) it is true that some martyrs are actually found with smiles on their faces, after they have been killed.' Several days after his death, in a session chaired by speaker Ahmad al-Sa`adun, a group of parliamentarians in the Kuwaiti National Assembly demanded that 'public utilities' be named in honour of Abu Muaz (Adil al-Ghanim) and also Shaykh Kulaib al-Mutairi, the representative of the Society for the Revival of Islamic Heritage who had been released in the infamous April 1993 prisoner exchange only to die in 1995 when his car reportedly hit a land mine. According to one of the legislators in favor of the proposition, Abu Muaz and al-Mutairi 'must be immortalized because they have expressed Kuwait's principled stance on Islamic issues.'[49] The *mujahideen* themselves could not have asked for a more sweeping public endorsement.

The unfortunate Serbs who were captured during Operation Miracle met a hellish fate. One soldier amongst a group of twelve Serbs taken prisoner on 21 July recounted how he was held in a *mujahideen* camp in Gostovici for 24 terrifying days:

I was captured by a group of 12 mujaheddins including a Bosnia Muslim who served as interpreter . . . One of the mujaheddins ordered me to kneel down, took out his butcher knife with semi-circular blade and small handle which he held hanging around his neck, on his chest. He wanted to cut my had [sic] off, but the Muslim interpreter intervened, telling him something in Arabic . . . They put a knife under our necks, as if they were going to cut our throats. Then they brought a cardboard box in which there were two cut off human heads with blood still dripping . . . One day, they brought us out in the camp area for all the mujaheddins to see us. In my assessment, there were one thousand of them. They lined us up in such a way that we were surrounded by them, and they were singing and shouting something in Arabic. One of them had a knife in his hands and was persistently trying to come close and cut our throats, but two others prevented him. He was foaming with rage.[50]

In Gostovici, the bleeding and bruised men were placed in a half-completed, roofless house flooded with water. Another Serb prisoner recalled: 'As soon as we arrived, the mujaheddins tied us with a hose, into which they let air under pressure, to make it expand and press our legs. This cause terrible pains and Gojko Vujièiæ swore [to] God, so one mujaheddin took him aside and cut his head off. I did not see what he used for the cutting, but I know that he brought the head into the room and forced all of us to kiss it. Then the mujaheddin hung the head on a nail in the wall.'[51]

The Arab-Afghan leadership was too preoccupied to mourn for long the death of Abu Muaz al-Kuwaiti. There were increasing signs that, at the insistence and urging of radical clerics, hundreds of new Muslim volunteers were being organized abroad to join the Kateebat al-Mujahideen. The foreign fighters, egged on both by the results of 'Black Lion' and 'Miracle' and the flattering exhortations of militant religious figures, were taking a central role in planning and executing the 'grand finale' of the Bosnian army's summer military campaign codenamed 'Hurricane '95': the Muslim re-conquest of Vozuca.

To help guarantee victory, the Bosnian army (under the lead of Colonel Refik Lendo, commander of Operative Group 'Bosna' in Zepce and Zavidovici) mobilized some of its most elite and feared assets, including the notorious 'Black Swans' unit and the Kateebat al-Mujahideen. At the request of the Bosnian government, Arab-Afghan units streamed out of the towns of Zenica and Travnik, and assembled at frontline basecamps in Zavidovici. Launching from Zavidovici, the *mujahideen* aimed to capture the strategic Banja Luka mountains, in their most ambitious project yet: Operation 'Badr.' The foreign guerrillas, this time led by the legendary Moataz Billah, were specifically tasked with the capture of Mount Poceljevo and Mount Paljenik. At 1,943 m, the highest peak in the Vlasic mountains north of Travnik, the location and size of Paljenik made it naturally a key strategic chokepoint in the area. Moreover, there was an important RTV transmitter and receiver installed on its peak.[52] The Arab *jihadis* tasked with its conquest, who claimed to now number over 10,000, fortified their resolve by retelling emboldening legends of how Paljenik was somehow considered 'sacred' by the Serbs because it was here that local partisans had successfully resisted Nazi armies in

World War II. The Bosnians had themselves been trying to capture Mount Paljenik for three years, with little to show for their efforts.[53]

On 10 September 1995, at 6:00am directly following morning Fajr prayers, the *mujahideen* forces under Moataz Billah set out towards their objectives. By several accounts, in a matter of minutes, the militants were able to seize both peaks despite heavy rain and wind.[54] An intelligence office who witnessed the attack was impressed by the performance of the *mujahideen*: 'About 300 of them got up and started running towards the Serb line, screaming "Allahu akbar" . . . It was unbelievable. You could see them get shot and get up and run again . . . like animals. The Serbs withdrew.'[55] Indeed, Serb troops fled Vozuca, and during the battle, Abu Thabit al-Muhajir and Moataz Billah, the commanders of the foreign units, entered the vacant town as a triumphant victors. After two days of continuing operations, the Arab-Afghan guerrillas slowly returned to their frontline base camps. The Serbs took heavy casualties, and lost several tanks and other heavy weapons to the collective force of Arabs and Bosnians. Serb prisoners faced indescribable treatment at the hands of the foreigners; the lucky ones were approached by Anwar Shaaban after the battle, who demanded that they convert to Islam. According to the militants, several accepted that offer.

Operation Badr had far-reaching effects; with Vozuca in hand, the Arab-Afghans soon moved forward and capture the town of Maglaj. Maglaj had a certain special significance for the *mujahideen*, because it had first been built by the Muslim Ottoman Empire.[56] For a group of men who had dedicated their lives to the re-establishment of the *khalifah* ('Muslim empire') lost by the Ottomans, the symbolism was glaring and self-apparent. On 17 September, the fighters broke the heavy-handed Serb grip on Maglaj, causing the Serbs to suffer heavy casualties and consequently to order a general retreat in the surrounding area.[57] Indeed, military operations continued even near Mount Paljenik through at least 13 September. According to a communiqué issued by Abu el-Ma`ali, 'Mujahideen have taken many more mountains and new strategic positions. Several Serb-held villages were over-run, all grace be to Allah, many enemy soldiers were killed and 60 were taken prisoners . . . The soldiers of Allah are still continuing their deployment throughout Serb-held areas, and are now spreading in forests and mountain peaks.'[58]

Approximately thirty *mujahideen*, overwhelmingly of foreign origin, were killed during Operation Badr, including commander Moataz Billah, commander Abu Thabit al-Muhajir, Abu Mujahid al-Brittani, Abu Maryam al-Busni, Abu al-Yusr al-Masri, Abu al-Munthir al-Yemeni, Abu Talha al-Sharqi, Ibn Luqman al-Djazairi, Abdallah al-Tunisi, Al-Sa'Sa' al-Jiddawi, Abu Qutaibah al-Jiddawi, Abu Alsa al-Jiddawi, Abu Rida al-Tunisi, Seif al-Rahman al-Yemeni, Abu Asim al-Yemeni, Abul Harith al-Masri, Abu Asa'd al-San'ani, Abu Ra'ed al-Djazairi, Abu Udayy al-Masri, and Ibn al-Akwa' al-Yemeni.[59]

Moataz Billah, the most senior military commander of the *mujahideen* throughout much of 1994 and the summer operations of 1995, had remained as the last living member of the original group of three legendary Egyptian Arab-Afghans to arrive in Bosnia in 1992. For Operation Badr, the Arab-Afghans would draw upon Muataz's 'special forces' expertise, and he was centrally responsible for planning the offensive. But shortly after the resounding triumph at Paljenik (when the operation was already considered over), Moataz was unexpectedly killed by a mortar bomb. This was truly a blow to the capabilities of Abu el-Ma`ali and the Kateebat al-Mujahideen: Moataz 'had carried the responsibilities of the Jihad in Bosnia from the very beginning to the very end and then Allah gave him the treasure that he sought.' They mourned his death and vigilantly prayed that he would join Wahiudeen al-Masri and Hussamudeen al-Masri in Paradise 'to keep them companions of each other on the stones of paradise facing each other in happiness.'[60]

During Operation Badr, the late Moataz had appointed another Egyptian Arab-Afghan to be his frontline military chief: Abu Thabit al-Muhajir. In his early thirties, Abu Thabit was a veteran soldier of the Egyptian army. After receiving much formal training in Egypt, he then decided to join the Arab *mujahideen* in Afghanistan, where he fought for more than six years. During that time, he also played a key role in training new recruits at Al-Qaida-sponsored terrorist camps along the Pakistani-Afghani border region. Arriving in Bosnia early in 1992 during the opening phases of the civil war, Abu Thabit secured himself an important position in the leadership hierarchy of the foreign battalion, often serving as *Amir* of front line combat operations. With his training and combat experience, he was a deadly asset on the battlefield. His comrades declared that he was 'so tough and so brave that when he fought, he would not even duck from the bullets, that is how fearless he was.' But, during Operation Badr, he would pay the consequences for that reckless abandon. Within the opening minutes of the confrontation, Abu Thabit was shot several times, until ultimately taken down by a fatal bullet to the chest.[61] Once again, though the *mujahideen* had managed to defeat the Serbs, the victory was bittersweet, even pyrrhic, as a result of the corresponding loss of critical leadership personnel.

Another repeating phenomenon was the significant presence of European Muslims from Western countries who fought with the foreign battalion during Operation 'Badr,' including Abu Mujahid al-Brittani, who lost his life early in the battle on 10 September. Abu Mujahid was a recent British university graduate who had finished his studies in 1993, when the Islamic community in the United Kingdom was still in an uproar over the war crimes being committed by the Serbs in Bosnia. He first came to the Balkans in 1993 as a humanitarian aid worker purportedly transporting food and medicine to the embattled Muslims in central Bosnia. Abu Mujahid was using his position as charity employee as a cover for other, more nefarious activities: 'Over the next two years Abu Mujahid hurried back and forth between Bosnia and Britain carrying valuable supplies to the brothers there. Between trips he travelled the length of Britain reaching its smaller parts in his efforts to raise money for the cause and increase the awareness among Muslims there.' According to the *mujahideen*, Abu Mujahid first fought in real combat during the glorious summer campaign organized by men like Moataz Billah and Abu Muaz al-Kuwaiti. Abu Mujahid returned to Bosnia in August 1995 and enlisted in a *jihad* training camp soon after his arrival. For all his anti-Western vigour, he nonetheless proudly wore a G-Shock watch and American army boots. According to his teachers, he 'excelled' at shooting and throwing grenades and he insisted that he would remain in Bosnia:

'until either we get victory or I am martyred' . . . One thing which was strange about him was that he always used to say, thinking back, I remember, maybe three, four, five times a day, he would say to me that 'Inshallah ["God-willing"] I am going to be martyred. Inshallah, this time in Bosnia, I am going to be martyred.'[62]

Following the initial assault on 10 September, Abu Mujahid, who had been given a prestigious assignment in one of the frontline units, disappeared in the fog of war. When his fellow guerrillas returned to their base camp, they realized that Abu Mujahid was oddly absent. At first, they hoped that he had merely stayed behind on Mount Paljenik to help guard the new territorial acquisition. However, when a week went by with no news from Abu Mujahid, Abu Hammam al-Najdi, the Saudi commander of the *mujahideen* frontline camp, ordered a search party to be sent out to recover him. They traversed the battleground and reached the empty Serb bunkers. Nearby, they found a body with a green scarf similar to that of Abu Mujahid's. One of the men in the search party recalled:

At that point, the thought that went through my mind was that the brother had been there, left behind when I was there in Bosnia and he intended to stay there longer than me. But only Allah knew what could he have done for him to die in such a beautiful way? And the thought that's still in our minds, Inshaallah, may Allah accept it from him, and may the people who loved him in this life, Inshaallah join him in the next.

Abu Mujahid's body was brought back down from the mountain and then taken in a van to the frontline base camp. Abu Hammam would only allow British *mujahideen* to go inside the van to see the remains of their departed fellow compatriot.[63]

By 15 September 1995, the significant involvement of Arab-Afghan fighters in the long and brutal Bosnian war came to a close with the dying embers of Operation Badr. From May to September, in 'Black Lion,' 'Miracle,' and 'Badr,' the *mujahideen* had proved a point that they had desperately insisted on throughout the conflict: they could be a militarily effective unit in battle if properly organized and integrated with sustained local army offensives. Their suicidal style of warfare was inefficient and bloody, but remarkably effective in its precise application. Indeed, following the summer campaign, even Western media reports were admitting that Arab-Afghan units were typically more useful and courageous in combat than their Bosnian indigenous counterparts.

However, these legendary battles also convinced many key policymakers that the membership of the foreign battalion in the Balkans presented a clear and unambiguous security threat to the citizens of Western Europe and the United States. The last summer of the war was perhaps the zenith of the power and influence of the foreign *mujahideen* active in Bosnia. Even though the Bosnian war was almost over, the tactical network of Al-Qaida nonetheless grew steadily during the as Balkan training camps produced hundreds of new North African and European *mujahideen* volunteers. Impressionable young men were being openly recruited and indoctrinated by some of Al-Qaida's elite inner circle – on European soil. As combat opportunities slowly faded in the Balkans, the enthusiastic new generation *mujahideen* would have to test their deadly skills on another battlefield. One could see this as either a major symptom of, or alternatively, a central cause for the upswing in militant Sunni Islamic terrorism in Europe beginning in the mid-1990s.

As such, this destabilizing situation was bound to have its ill consequences for Bosnia's regional neighbors. On 1 July, the French paper *La Tribune* carried an intriguing news report on a group of five Arab-Afghan veterans based in Bosnia and led by a then-28-year-old Algerian *mujahideen* commander.[64] The Algerian commander had formerly been in charge of the Zagreb office of Human Concern International (HCI), another purported international charitable organization that has been directly linked to the Egyptian Islamic Jihad, Al-Gama`at Al-Islamiyya, Al-Qaida, and Usama Bin Laden. Ahmad Said Khadr (also known as Abu Abdurrahman al-Kanadi), HCI's regional director in Pakistan, was a longtime financier and coordinator for the Arab-Afghan movement since the mid-1980s. Khadr's adopted homeland of Canada formally accused HCI in June 1999 of supporting international Islamic terrorism.[65] United States intelligence concurred with this assessment and added that HCI was additionally known to have firm contacts within Al-Gama`at Al-Islamiyya.[66] Human Concern International's operations in Bosnia served as a tactical hub for North African terrorists spread across the Mediterranean basin. Another well-informed article published in *Le Figaro* indicated that 'vast amounts of money' destined for the Algerian Armed Islamic Group (GIA) were transferred through the HCI office in Zagreb.[67]

According to the first *La Tribune* piece, the group of Algerian mujahideen were dispatched from Bosnia destined for France. There, they planned to form a terrorist cell and carry out a campaign of violence 'to punish the French government.' The paper also named several more moderate French Islamic leaders as intended targets of the cell, including the prominent Imam of a Paris mosque and co-founder of the Algerian Islamic Salvation Front (FIS), Shaykh Abdelbaki Sahraoui. After carrying out these attacks in France, the terrorists would travel across Western Europe in a killing spree aimed at silencing other Algerian dissidents in exile (labelled as 'traitors' for their resistance to the cruel dictates of the GIA).[68]

Mysteriously, just as the report had eerily predicted, on 11 July, Shaykh Sahraoui was murdered in a crime linked by French authorities to two suspected GIA activists. While alive, Sahraoui prominently urged his followers to respect the territorial integrity of France and keep the Algerian civil war confined to the other side of the Mediterranean. He consistently worked towards a peaceful and diplomatic understanding between the Algerian Islamist movement and the French government.[69] Thus, he was also the perfect target to spark a campaign of violence by Algerian fundamentalist terror cells.

Then, on 25 July 1995, a bomb explosion tore apart the inside of a commuter train in Paris at the RER St Michel station, killing ten and injuring 116. Fears ran high, as the station was heavily frequented by Western tourists visiting the nearby Notre Dame cathedral. An anonymous phone call to a radio station claimed responsibility for the bombing on behalf of the GIA General Command. The bomb was simple gas canisters attached to a detonator and a timer and packed with screws to create shrapnel.[70] This type of device was remarkably similar to one presented in a lesson from a Arab *mujahideen* military guide published in Pakistan.[71] French counter-terrorism magistrate Judge Jean-Louis Bruguière later testified in US court:

> There was something particular regarding the ignition system, you know, there to ignite the mixture. They were using small light bulbs that were coming from cars and with sandpaper they would rub the top part of the bulb so far that the filaments would appear and as those filaments heated up, why the circuit was closed. These filaments became incandescent. Then they would serve as detonators. And this system worked very well.[72]

The search for potential suspects in connection with the metro bombing led investigators to a suspected GIA member, hiding in Stockholm, Sweden. The Algerian was mistakenly identified by a Parisian gendarme as one of two men who exited the commuter train seconds before the explosion. The gendarme had noticed the two engaging in suspicious behaviour as they passed a fake leather bag back and forth between them. During the forensic examination of the crime scene, a piece of that bag was discovered stuck to bomb debris. Though Swedish authorities later cleared him of involvement in the metro bombing, they continued to hold the Algerian suspect in Stockholm in detention as French officials maintained that he was tied to GIA terrorism.[73]

The original *La Tribune* report had named the Stockholm detainee as a former employee of the Bosnian HCI office in Zagreb. According to the CIA, the HCI office in Stockholm was under scrutiny for primary involvement in a covert Bosnian arms smuggling operation.[74] The widely read French paper *Le Monde* confirmed that national police suspected that the Zagreb branch of HCI had acted as a possible 'staging point' for the GIA cell responsible for the 25 July bombing.[75] A French intelligence report in late July aptly concluded that, while 'it would be going too far to assert that a "Green International" exists at the present time,' there was a definite security threat in Western Europe posed by Arab (particularly North African) *mujahideen* terrorist sleeper cells trained in Bosnia.[76]

Echoing these sentiments, on 17 August, the GIA took responsibility for yet another bombing of a Paris metro station, this time at Place de l'Etoile. Then, only 9 days later, police discovered a new crude gas canister bomb attached to a rail line near Lyon used by the high-speed TGV bullet train. Fortunately, the bomb had evidently failed to explode, averting a potentially serious tragedy and a frightening blow to the security of the French national transportation system. Police managed to lift a set of fingerprints off the tape that was used to secure the detonator to the canisters. Those prints matched Khaled Kelkal, a French citizen of Algerian descent who had allegedly received instruction in Al-Qaida-affiliated terrorist training camps near the mountainous Pakistani-Afghan border.[77] Heavily involved with the international Arab-Afghan network, Kelkal was 'believed to run an "information bureau" at a secret address and to be in constant contact with an organization called Human Concern International,' suspected by French authorities of secretly 'financ[ing] terrorist and guerrilla operations.'[78] Thus, HCI's European activities, particularly in the former Yugoslavia, connected Kelkal to other conspirators involved in the string of Paris bombing attacks attributed to the GIA.

Kelkal quickly became the most wanted man in France, as police initiated an intensive, nationwide search for him. By chance, a German academic had randomly interviewed him several years earlier during a study of France's ethnic divisions. Kelkal, reflecting many of the same concerns as his North African immigrant peers, spoke enthusiastically of his militant faith and told the interviewer:

> I'm neither Arab nor French. I'm Muslim . . . When I walk into a mosque, I'm at ease. They shake your hand, they treat you like an old friend. No suspicion, no prejudices . . . When I see another Muslim in the street, he smiles, and we stop and talk. We recognize each other as brothers, even if we never met before.[79]

Several weeks later, authorities finally picked up his trail when they intercepted a car carrying supplies to him in the mountainous, wooded suburbs of Lyon. Police arrested several suspected accomplices in the car, including his close friend, Karim Koussa. Knowledgable intelligence sources later alleged that Koussa was not only a graduate of Arab-run military camps in Afghanistan but, moreover, that he had taken a 'more intensive' supplementary course in Pakistan where he was taught how to build advanced car-bombs.[80] French officials told reporters that Koussa had been intimately involved in the various GIA terror plots that had unfolded during the summer. According to French Interior Minister Jean-Louis Debre, 'I can tell you that Karim Koussa is one of the accomplices in the attack on Imam Sahraoui.'[81] Kelkal reacted to the arrests by retreating further into the mountains, living much like a hardened guerrilla combatant from Bosnia, Afghanistan, or Algeria and deftly eluding the massive dragnet clamping down on the region. Finally, he was located and killed during a dramatic final shootout with French police. In his possession, investigators discovered two shotguns, one of which was determined by forensic specialists to have been the very weapon used in the 11 July murder of Imam Abdelbaki Sahraoui.[82]

Though French authorities seem to have been reluctant to draw any definitive ties between the GIA terror cells in Europe and the Arab-Afghan leadership in Bosnia and Afghanistan, many observers were in agreement that, at a minimum, Khaled Kelkal and others held responsible were disciples of the 'Afghano-Bosniaque brotherhood.'[83] One Western intelligence source anonymously admitted to an Associated Press reporter that a disturbingly significant number of conspirators deemed responsible for the GIA terror campaign 'came through Bosnia, and probably had training and some combat experience [t]here.'[84] Other media reports indicated that a number of the suspects had freely discussed with investigators how they 'were trained in Afghanistan or Bosnia-Herzegovina.'[85]

French investigators centrally focused on the international *mujahideen* phenomenon warned of serious regional security threats stemming from 'young Algerians who, after leaving the country, went to Pakistan, Yemen, Lebanon, or Bosnia, to train or to fight.'[86] French intelligence estimated that more than 1,000 foreign fighters, mainly from North Africa and the Arabian peninsula, had trained and fought with Arab-Afghan forces during the Yugoslav civil war. Sources in Paris alleged that these fanatical volunteers were entering Bosnia 'posing as members of Muslim aid agencies. These non-governmental organizations, often headed by former "Arab Afghans", provided backup for military operations by foreign mojahedin in Bosnia.'[87]

Prior to the summer of 1995, many observers had been satisfied with treating Afghano-Bosniak terrorist activities in Europe as aberrations – a series of coincidental, but unrelated events carried out by nominally interlinked Islamic dissident factions. Yet, after the reverberations of the Kelkal-Koussa case, the realization quickly spread that there was perhaps a greater conspiracy at work. French Interior Minister Jean-Louis Debre added that '[a]lthough these groups have a certain freedom of action, they have close links to and obey those who give the orders who are the pivots of a campaign of destabilization.'[88] Indeed, though at times these men seemed to be energized by their own independent motives and priorities, they were nevertheless still operating within the aegis of general overarching commands given to them by senior members of Al-Gama`at Al-Islamiyya, the GIA, and Al-Qaida.

Notes

1. Cohen, Roger. 'Foreign Islamic Militants Strain Bosnian Alliance.' *The New York Times*, 18 February 1995, section 1, p. 3.
2. Brown, Adrian. 'Islamic warriors become liability.' Agence France Presse. 30 November 1995.
3. Squitieri, Tom. 'In Bosnia, a "volunteer" war.' USA Today, 19 June 1995, p. 8A.
4. Cohen, Roger. 'Foreign Islamic Militants Strain Bosnian Alliance.' *The New York Times*, 18 February 1995, section 1, p. 3.
5. Radio Bosnia-Hercegovina. Broadcast in Serbo-Croat in Sarajevo. 11 March 1995, 18.00 GMT.
6. 'Theater of Operation: Muslim Bozowa.' *Islam Report*. Newsletter of the American Islamic Group (AIG). 16 February 1995.
7. Ibid. 20 March 1995.
8. Dahlburg, John-Thor. '"Holy Warriors" Brought Bosnians Ferocity and Zeal.' *The Los Angeles Times*, 6 August 1996, p. A11.
9. Rogosic, Zeljko. 'Vast investigation in Bosnia Herzegovina.' *Nacional* (Bosnia), Issue 306, 27 September 2001.
10. Clark, Mark Edmond. 'US Army Doctrinal Influence on the War in Bosnia.' *Military Review*, November–December 1999, p. 24.
11. Rogosic, Zeljko. Op. cit.
12. Dahlburg, John-Thor. Op. cit.
13. Dahlburg, John-Thor. Op. cit.
14. Dahlburg, John-Thor. Op. cit.
15. Andjelic, Suzana. '"Uragan '95" and Mujahedeen.' *Slobodna Bosna* (Sarajevo), 13 September 2001.
16. 'The Jihad in Bosnia: Operation Black Lion.' Cassette tape obtained from http://www.maktabah.com.
17. 'Abu Mu'aadh al-Kuwaitee.' http://www.azzam.com.
18. 'In the Hearts of Green Birds.' Audiocassette transliterated by Salman Dhia Al Deen.

19. Ibid.
20. Ibid.
21. Ibid.
22. Rogosic, Zeljko. Op. cit.
23. 'Battle of the Manifest Victory – The Lion-Bravery of Bosnia. Communique No. 1 (29 May 1995).' Op. cit.
24. Ibid.
25. 'The Jihad in Bosnia: Operation Black Lion.' Op. cit.
26. 'In the Hearts of Green Birds.' Op. cit.
27. Dahlburg, John-Thor. Op. cit.
28. 'Battle of the Manifest Victory – The Lion-Bravery of Bosnia. Communique No. 1 (29 May 1995).' Op. cit.
29. 'Battle of the Manifest Victory – The Lion-Bravery of Bosnia. Communique No. 1 (29 May 1995).' Op. cit.
30. Andjelic, Suzana. Op. cit.
31. Dahlburg, John-Thor. Op. cit.
32. Mardini, Ahmad. 'Muslim Clergy Calls for "Holy War" in Bosnia.' Inter Press Service. 27 July 1995.
33. 'Bin Baz calls on Muslims to aid Bosnians.' *Riyadh Daily*, 21 July 1995.
34. 'Under the Shades of Swords.' Audiocassette sequel to 'In the Hearts of Green Birds.' November 1997. Azzam Recordings: London, UK.
35. Annex III: Letter dated July 14, 1995, from the Permanent Mission of the Federal Republic of Yugoslavia (Serbia and Montenegro) to the United Nations Office at Geneva addressed to the Assistant Secretary-General for Human Rights. 'Right of Peoples to Self-Determination: Use of mercenaries as a means of violating human rights and impeding the exercise of the right of peoples to self-determination.' United Nations General Assembly. Fiftieth session; Item 106 of the provisional agenda. 29 August 1995.
36. 'Under the Shades of Swords.' Op. cit.
37. 'Abu Umar al-Harbi.' http://www.azzam.com.
38. Ibid.
39. 'Al-Battaar al-Yemeni.' http://www.azzam.com.
40. 'Biography of a Martyr.' *Islam Report* (American Islamic Group (AIG)), 25 September 1995.
41. Ibid.
42. 'Al-Battaar al-Yemeni.' Op. cit.
43. 'Abu Muslim al-Imaraati,' http://www.azzam.com.
44. 'Sixteen Arab troops killed in Bosnian fighting: official report.' Agence France Presse. 22 July 1995.
45. 'Abu Musa Al-Almaani,' http://www.azzam.com.'
46. Ibid.

47. Ibid.
48. 'Salman al-Farsi,' http://www.azzam.com.
49. Kuwait News Agency (KUNA). Broadcast in Arabic language, 25 July 1995, 16.21 GMT.
50. Testimony of Witness 260/97/10. 'Mujaheddin Prisoner Camps in the Municipality of Zavidoviæi,' Committee for Collecting Data on Crimes Committed Against Humanity and International Law, Federal Republic of Yugoslavia, Belgrade, Yugoslavia. January 1998.
51. Ibid.
52. Andjelic, Suzana. Op. cit.
53. 'Under the Shades of Swords.' Op. cit.
54. 'The Battle of "Badr al-Bosna" – Conquest of Vosica.' Armije Republike BH 3, Korpus; Odred 'El-Mudzahidin': Communique No. 1. *Islam Report* (American Islamic Group (AIG)), 13 September 1995.
55. Hamzic, Edin and Nick Fielding. 'Balkan zealots plotted suicide attacks.' *Sunday Times* (London), 28 October 2001.
56. 'The Jihad in Bosnia: Operation BADR.' Cassette tape obtained from http://www.maktabah.com.
57. 'The Battle of Badr Al-Bosna (Freeing of Maglaj).' Armije Republike BH 3, Korpus; Odred 'El-Mudzahidin': Communique No. 4. *Islam Report* (American Islamic Group (AIG)), 23 September 1995.
58. 'The Battle of "Badr al-Bosna" – Conquest of Vosica.' Op. cit.
59. 'Under the Shades of Swords.' Op. cit.
60. 'Under the Shades of Swords.' Op. cit.
61. 'Abu Thabit Al-Muhajir.' http://www.azzam.com.
62. 'Under the Shades of Swords.' Op. cit.
63. 'Under the Shades of Swords.' Op. cit.
64. 'Algeria – July 25 – Militants Suspected in Paris Blast.' *APS Diplomat Recorder*, No. 4, Vol. 43, 29 July 1995.
65. June 17, 1999. 'ININ: Human Concern International Accused by Canadian Government of Sponsoring Terrorism. You could be next.' Newsgroup posting on Islamic News and Information Network, January 1996, p. 13. http://www.inin.net.
66. CIA Report on 'International Islamic NGOs' and links to terrorism. See also: Affidavit by Senior Special Agent David Kane (Bureau of Immigration and Customs Enforcement, Department of Homeland Security). United States of America v. Soliman S. Biheiri. United States District Court for the Eastern District of Virginia, Alexandria Division. Case #: 03-365-A. 14 August 2003, p. 2.
67. Bouilhet, Alexandre and Thierry Oberiez. 'The Providential London Fog.' *Le Figaro* (Paris), 3 November 1995, p. 26.

68. 'Algeria – July 25 – Militants Suspected in Paris Blast.' Op. cit.
69. 'Political Backdrop to Paris Attacks.' *Indigo Publications Intelligence Newsletter*, No. 274, 26 October 1995.
70. 'Reporter's Transcript of Proceedings.' United States of America v. Ahmed Ressam, aka Benni Noris. United States District Court for the Western District of Washington. Case #: CR 99-666-JCC. Dated 2 April 2001, p. 28.
71. 'Political Backdrop to Paris Attacks.' Op. cit.
72. 'Reporter's Transcript of Proceedings.' Op. cit.
73. 'Paris bomb suspect says has alibi in Sweden-report.' Reuters. 23 April 1995.
74. CIA Report on 'International Islamic NGOs' and links to terrorism. Op. cit., p. 13. See also: Affidavit by Senior Special Agent David Kane (Bureau of Immigration and Customs Enforcement, Department of Homeland Security). Op. cit., p. 2.
75. 'Paris bomb suspect says has alibi in Sweden-report.' Op. cit.
76. Inciyan, Erich. 'France uncovers Islamist networks.' *Manchester Guardian Weekly*, 21 July 1996, p. 17.
77. Drozdiak, William. 'France's "Unwanted"; Alienated Arab Youths Turning to Violence.' *The Washington Post*, 14 November 1995, p. A14.
78. 'Paris Bombings "Were Ordered from London."' *The Daily Telegraph*, 4 November 1995.
79. Viorst, Milton. 'The Muslims of France.' *Foreign Affairs* (Council on Foreign Relations), September/October 1996, p. 78.
80. 'Political Backdrop to Paris Attacks.' Op. cit.
81. Simons, Marlise. 'Dead Bomb Suspect's Ties Still a Mystery in France.' *The New York Times*, 1 October 1995, section 1, p. 6.
82. Smith, Alex Duval. 'Dead Suspect is Linked to Most French Terror Attacks.' *Guardian* (London), 2 October 1995, p. 9.
83. Valle, Alexandre del. 'La Bosnie : un Etat islamiste pro-américain en plein coeur du monde orthodoxe.' 5 April 2000, http://www.geo-islam.org.
84. Latal, Srecko. 'Mujahedeen Fighters Threaten British Peacekeepers.' The Associated Press. 28 October 1995.
85. Nundy, Julian. 'France Trial (L-Only).' Voice of America. 24 November 1997.
86. Milleu, Gilles. 'Complex, Flexible Organization.' *Liberation* (Paris), 3 November 1995, p. 2.
87. Inciyan, Erich. 'France uncovers Islamist networks.' *Manchester Guardian Weekly*, 21 July 1996, p. 17.
88. 'France to maintain anti-terrorist guard.' Agence France Presse. 16 November 1995.

–8–

A Post-Dayton Wave of Terror

To those champions who avowed the truth day and night . . . And wrote with their blood and sufferings these phrases . . . The confrontation that we are calling for with the apostate regimes does not know Socratic debates, Platonic ideals, nor Aristotelian diplomacy. But it knows the dialogue of bullets, the ideals of assassination, bombing, and destruction, and the diplomacy of the cannon and machine-gun . . . Islamic governments have never and will never be established through peaceful solutions and cooperative councils. They are established as they [always] have been by pen and gun, by word and bullet, by tongue and teeth.

From an Al-Qaida training manual exhibited during the trial of conspirators from the 1998 east Africa embassy bombings

It would be undoubtedly simplistic to assume that the United States, the UK, and France were the only responsible international bodies concerned with the presence of menacing Islamic militants entrenched in the heart of south-eastern Europe. A number of Arab governments, even several with mixed diplomatic relations with the West, were apprehensive of their proximity to the ambitious *jihadi* corps in Bosnia. During the 1980s, it had seemed an attractive policy move for Egypt, Saudi Arabia, Algeria, and others to encourage their Islamist zealots to seek exile in Afghanistan. At the time, short-sighted local regimes decided that Afghanistan, in the heart of Central Asia, was thousands of miles and 'a world away' from the turmoil and politics of the Middle East. Isolated there, the utopian approach reasoned, the fundamentalist movement would be so cut off from current events and its indigenous supporters that it would quickly wither and die. By 1992, as Arab militants continued to organize violent dissident activity in central Asia despite the rise and fall of the Soviet-backed regimes there, this imaginative logic was recognized as an unabashed failure. The mostly undemocratic governments of north Africa, under siege by radical Islam, were particularly concerned at this time with the threat posed by Al-Qaida and the Arab-Afghans.

On 26 July 1995, a day after the devastating GIA bombing of the St Michel metro station in Paris, the Egyptian ruling elite was shocked when it unearthed yet another elaborate assassination attempt against Hosni Mubarak to take place during a visit to Addis Ababa, Ethiopia for an African diplomatic summit.[1] The attack was eventually linked to elements of Al-Gama`at Al-Islamiyya and a 37-year-old (in

1995) senior Egyptian Al-Qaida military commander known as Mustafa Hamza (Abu Hazim al-Masri). Abu Hazim was highly placed in the Arab-Afghan hierarchy; moreover, he was an intimate confidant and longstanding partner of Abu Talal al-Qasimy, the infamous patron of the foreign *mujahideen* in Bosnia and the primary international spokesperson of Al-Gama`at.[2] Abu Hazim, 'who used to travel a lot,' played an important role in Al-Qaida's international efforts to aid the Bosnian *mujahideen*. In a military court, Sabri Ibrahim al-'Attar, a confessed Egyptian *jihadi*, testified that when he decided to join the struggle in Bosnia, he immediately sought counsel with Abu Hazim for advice how to proceed.[3]

Working together, Abu Talal and Abu Hazim had struggled for almost 20 years to consolidate Egyptian *jihadis* into a unified military and ideological force to eliminate the pro-Western secular regime in Egypt. Al-Qasimy was already a wanted man with a death sentence on his head for organizing several murders and assassination attempts on army, police, and government officials, in addition to a number of peaceable intellectuals opposed to the reign of fundamentalist Islam.[4] But now he had gone too far, and the Egyptian government prepared to even the score. In retaliation, it initiated an aggressive policy of uprooting militant dissident activity both domestically (by arresting hundreds of suspects and conducting mass trials) and internationally (by increasing surveillance of Islamist security threats abroad and taking pre-emptive counterinsurgency action to protect national interests).[5]

For the suspicious governments of north Africa, the mistakes made in the past by tacitly supporting the growth of the Arab-Afghan corps in Afghanistan could never again be repeated, certainly not in Bosnia. The Balkans were right at their doorstep and far too close for comfort. It would be all too easy for Muslim radicals gathering and coordinating in south-eastern Europe to turn around and focus their energies on the adjacent 'apostate regimes' of the southern Mediterranean. A forceful move targeting Abu Talal al-Qasimy would remove a key link in the international Islamic terror network, and would perhaps produce actionable information on the identity and location of Mubarak's other failed assassins.

The added scrutiny from international 'security organs' did not, at first, deter al-Qasimy from continuing his work in the Balkans. According to his wife, Amani Farouk, on 12 September, Abu Talal was on his way back to Bosnia, this time in the interest of writing a book on the Arab battalion in Zenica. Evidently he had first arrived in Croatia on 11 September under a false identity, and then proceeded inland the next day. En route to Zenica and the headquarters of the *mujahideen*, Abu Talal mysteriously vanished without a trace. For 2 weeks, he remained missing and his disappearance was the subject of much rumor and discussion in radical Islamic circles.

Then, Egyptian officials announced to journalists at *Al-Ahram*, the largest national government-owned paper, that the erstwhile cleric had been 'taken into custody' by Croatian authorities in Zagreb. Arab intelligence used the incident as an opportunity to take a swipe at naïve European governments that had provided asylum or shelter to men like al-Qasimy. One Egyptian government official wisely warned:

> His arrest proves what we have always said, which is that these terror groups are operating on a worldwide scale, using places like Afghanistan and Bosnia to form their fighters who come back to the Middle East . . . European countries like Denmark, Sweden, Switzerland, England and others, which give sanctuary to these terrorists, should now understand it will come back to haunt them where they live.[6]

The detention of Abu Talal al-Qasimy was a complex but deftly handled snatch-and-grab operation coordinated by Egyptian and Croatian intelligence services and allegedly overseen by the CIA. Not surprisingly, the Egyptians had been closely tailing al-Qasimy ever since the failed assassination bid on Mubarak in Addis Ababa on 26 June. Evidently they tracked him on his way to the Balkans and tipped off Croatian security about his imminent arrival. The Croatians held Abu Talal for several days while agents of several international intelligence and law enforcement bodies interrogated him. The United States Federal Bureau of Investigation was reportedly among the interested parties; FBI specialists 'wanted to link him to sheikh Omar Abdel Rahman and others behind the (1993) attack on the World Trade Center' in New York.[7] At the Islamic Cultural Institute in Milan, Italian investigators found a letter from Abu Talal al-Qasimy to militant Afghan warlord Gulbuddin Hekmatyar, urging him to welcome and offer shelter to Shaykh Omar Abdel Rahman. Another subsequent letter was also discovered at the ICI from the board of Al-Murabeton (including Ayman al-Zawahiri and Abu Talal al-Qasimy) thanking Hekmatyar for agreeing to host the blind shaykh.[8]

The Croatians claimed that after only six days of detention, Abu Talal al-Qasimy was 'released,' expelled, and banned from returning to the country for one year. But, in reality, al-Qasimy never saw the light of day; rather, through one means or another, the Croatians effectively rendered him to Egypt to face trial and a near-certain death sentence. According to knowledgeable intelligence sources, this had been accomplished by first transferring Abu Talal to temporary confinement on an American military vessel in the Adriatic, very similar to the way that high-value captured Al-Qaida and Taliban targets were treated during the United States' war in Afghanistan in 2001–2.[9] The operation had been a success, but it was not nearly as quiet or covert as those responsible had hoped it would be. In London, the Arab paper *Al-Hayat* cited representatives of Al-Gama`at Al-Islamiyya who condemned the arrest and warned that Croatia's latest hostilities against the Arab *mujahideen* would put it along with Mubarak's regime in Egypt 'in direct line for revenge by Islamic groups.'[10]

Certainly, a good portion of this anger was also directed against another party deemed responsible for the ongoing problems of the foreign *mujahideen*: the United States. The Arab fighters were already infuriated that United States and European diplomats were using the Bosnian victories at Vozuca and elsewhere (battles paid for with the blood, sweat, and tears of the *mujahideen*) as leverage to intimidate the Serbs into a general ceasefire. The radical Islamists had certainly not intended their terrible sacrifices during Operations Black Lion, Miracle, or Badr to be the harbingers of peace or the implements of negotiation by Western policy-makers. Rather, quite simply, they had hoped to spark a renewed offensive by the Bosnian army aimed at prolonging the war with the Serbs. They saw United States air strikes on Serb targets and NATO promises of finally lifting the arms embargo against the Muslims as blatant attempts to arrogantly expropriate the hard-earned efforts of the *jihadis* in order to achieve diplomatic agreements absolutely anti-thetical to their interests. On 22 September, in a communiqué from Zenica, Abu el-Ma`ali adamantly demanded of his 'enemies' in the United States, French, and British governments:

> [W]hy were you surprised to see the victory of Muslims? The reason is well-known; the US which controls this ailing world along with the Jews and Christians . . . hated to see the Muwahideen (Worshippers of one God, Muslims) becoming victorious over the worshippers of the cross, the Orthodox, and they wanted to use this for their own advantage . . . We know that we will have a day in which to fight the Jews, and the Almighty will grant us victory, and also we know that the best soldiers will fight the Christians and all of these are promises and rejoices from the Messenger of Allah . . . We assure our brothers that we are firm on their path until we meet in Paradise InshaAllah [God-willing].[11]

Several days later, Abu el-Ma`ali followed this declaration with an appeal directly to the international supporters and sympathizers of the Bosnian Arab-Afghan movement to 'RISE UP IN SUPPORT OF YOUR BROTHERS, and remove the obstacles from around you. We send you our greetings . . . despite the plots of the enemies and the un-believers in an evil attempt to suppress these successes and conquests in order to claim it for themselves.' The *Amir* of the *mujahideen* further noted that '[t]hese attempts are led by the US and the Crusade West, so be aware of the plots of the enemies of Allah and their hate of Islam and Muslims, and Allah is well aware of what they do.'[12]

The first real Arab-Afghan response to Abu Talal al-Qasimy's arrest came on 20 October, when a massive explosion shook the quiet Croatian port town of Rijeka just before noon.[13] At 11.22 a.m., a suicide bomber detonated 70 kg of TNT hidden in a Fiat Mirafiori parked outside the Primorje-Gorani county police headquarters.[14] The mysterious suicide bomber was killed, two bystanders were seriously wounded, and twenty-seven other people received lighter injuries. The bomb was powerful enough to destroy the police headquarters and damage several nearby buildings, including a Zagreb Bank branch and a primary school.[15] In the blast debris, Croatian police found fragments of the bomber's Canadian passport (a document issued by Ottawa's Embassy in Kuwait), identifying him as 31-year-old John Fawzan. Fawzan had previously been investigated by Italian counterterrorism officials for his connections to the Islamic Cultural Institute in Milan, controlled by senior *Amir* of the Bosnian Arab-Afghan *mujahideen*, Anwar Shaaban.[16] According to the CIA, the suicide bomber, 'a member of Al-Gama`at [al-Islamiyya],' was also known to be an employee of the notorious Third World Relief Agency (TWRA).[17] At a press conference hastily organized by the authorities, the Croatian Interior Minister, Ivan Jarnjak, stated that the bombing was regarded as a 'serious terror attack.'[18]

A day later, Western news agencies in Cairo received an anonymous faxed communiqué allegedly from representatives of Al-Gama`at Al-Islamiyya. The fax took responsibility for the Rijeka bombing, an act committed in order 'to prove that the case of Sheik Talaat Fouad Qassem . . . will not pass but will bring cascades of blood bleeding from Croatian interests inside and outside . . . You Croats will be mistaken if you think that this matter will go peacefully.'[19] In the document, Al-Gama`at spoke in very frank terms and firmly demanded that the Croatian government 'release Sheikh Qassimi and apologize formally through the media . . . Close the gates of hell which you have opened upon yourselves . . . otherwise you will be starting a war the end of which only Allah (God) knows.' The apocalyptic warning was taken seriously enough to cause Egyptian President Mubarak to cancel a planned appearance at the United Nations in New York for fears of a repeated assassination attempt in the wake of both the new communiqué and the failed Addis Ababa plot during the past summer.[20]

American intelligence indicated that Shaykh Anwaar Shaaban himself was personally responsible for overseeing the terrorist operation in Rijeka. The bombing was meant to be a mere prelude to a new strategy employed by the *mujahideen*. As the long Balkan war began winding down, Shaaban 'and other mujahedin leaders had begun planning to attack NATO forces which would be sent to Bosnia.'[21] Interviewed in the fall of 1995 in the 'Call to Jihad' newsletter bulletin of the *mujahideen* battalion, Abu el-Ma`ali seemed to be particularly satisfied by the results of the Rijeka bombing. French investigators believed that the October terror attack 'demonstrated that Abu el-Maali was closely related to [Al-Gama`at], both ideologically and in practice.'[22]

For several years afterwards, Croatian authorities sought other suspects believed responsible for arranging the Rijeka bombing. Witnesses, including a police guard in the headquarters parking lot, described a suspicious Mercedes driven by an Arab man that sped away from the scene just before the blast. After looking at mugshots, those witnesses were able to positively identify a wanted 36-year-old Egyptian militant loyal to Al-Gama`at Al-Islamiyya named Hassan al-Sharif Mahmud Saad. Saad, who had lived in Cologno Monzese (a suburb of Milan), was a prominent figure at the Islamic Cultural Institute. He even sat on the board of trustees of Anwar Shaaban's own Italian charitable organization 'Il Paradiso.' In Italy, Saad was known to own a Fiat 131 Mirafiori with Bergamo plates, the very same vehicle later used in the Rijeka attack. As early as 1993, he was travelling back and forth between Bosnia and Italy using a Yemeni passport under the name Abdullah Essindar. But everyone at the ICI mosque was aware that something was different in June 1995, when Hassan Saad packed his family and belongings in the Fiat and left permanently for Bosnia. His friends at the ICI said he had gone away to join the Kateebat al-Mujahideen led by Anwar Shaaban.[23] Four months later, in Rijeka, Al Sharif would use John Fawzan and his own trusty Fiat as cannon-fodder in a terrifying demonstration of resolve to the Croatians and anyone else who dared to defy Al-Gama`at Al-Islamiyya.

Finally, Hassan Saad was identified and captured by Bosnian police in July 2001. BiH interior minister Muhamed Besic told journalists: 'We established that a person is involved in the planting of the car-bomb in Rijeka, but due to other crimes that Egypt wants him for, he will be extradited to that country.' Another Egyptian citizen arrested alongside Saad was also due to be extradited to Cairo as per a specific request from Mubarak's government.[24] This individual was later identified as Abu Imad al-Masri (also known as Imad el-Misri), the very same author responsible for the *jihad* textbooks at the Zenica youth center sponsored by the Kuwaiti Revival of Islamic Heritage Society.[25] By the time of his capture, some sources estimated that Abu Imad had become Usama Bin Laden's top representative in Bosnia. His capture was no doubt regarded as a major victory by Egyptian intelligence services against radical Islamic dissidents based in Europe.

Meanwhile, reflecting the chaotic and tense atmosphere created in the fall of 1995 by the arrest of al-Qasimy and the resulting Al-Gama`at bombing in Croatia, it was only a matter of time before a confrontational and deadly grudge match would resurface between the enraged *mujahideen* and Western peacekeepers active in the Bosnia. Paranoid about alleged 'Crusader conspiracies' against them, the Islamic militants were in the mood to strike out at their various real and imaginary infidel enemies. According to one British relief worker, the Arabs 'were looking for a fight, and it happened that a Brit killed one.'[26]

This was exactly the scene that unfolded on 5 October, when a British UN soldier was involved in an altercation with Elvedin Hodzic, a veteran of the Bosnian army and a local volunteer in the Arab-run *mujahideen* brigade.[27] During a patrol guarding an armored personnel carrier on the road between Gornji Vakuf and Bugojno, in the small town of Rudina, the British soldier was suddenly approached by Hodzic, who was allegedly energetically shouting anti-British and anti-UN slogans.[28] Hodzic pulled out a gun, aimed it at the Briton's head, and cocked the pistol. Acting in what he believed to be in legitimate self defence, the British soldier preemptively shot Hodzic once. When the wounded Bosnian radical continued to threaten him, the soldier shot him again, fatally.[29] Unaware of Hodzic's precise relationship with the foreign battalion, neither British nor UN officials initially realized the wide-ranging implications of what had happened in Rudina.

Local Bosnian authorities eventually accepted the justification offered in a British UN report, but word spread in the area that 'family and friends wanted blood for blood.'[30] According to them, Hodzic was innocently pushing a wheelbarrow of potatoes across a field and was shot needlessly when he approached the UN representative merely to speak with him.[31] As a result, rumors were rampant of frightening threats made by the Arab *mujahideen* to murder four British soldiers in revenge for the killing of Hodzic.[32] On 10 October, suspected foreign Muslim combatants fired automatic weapons and an RPG at a UN armored observer vehicle on the road between Bugojno and Novni Travnik, gutting the car but causing no serious injuries. Ironically, the observers inside were predominantly peacekeepers on assignment from other Muslim states.[33] On 22 October, a Norwegian aid convoy was briefly held hostage by Arab militants near Tuzla. Two humanitarian workers were blindfolded, abducted, and threatened with execution. However, when the *jihadis* realized that the convoy staff were Norwegian and not British, they abruptly released them. One of the gunmen was identified as speaking Arabic and was suspected of having participated with the Kateebat al-Mujahideen in the major battles of the summer of 1995.[34]

On 24 October, UK Defence Secretary Michael Portillo confirmed in a meeting of the House of Commons that, out of security concerns stemming from the foreign Muslim extremists, British peacekeepers were no longer being fully deployed in their designated capacity. Portillo lamented that 'a situation that has arisen in central Bosnia where Mujahedin appear to be operating with some sort of vendetta against British troops and for the time being the UN has withdrawn British troops from certain convoy escort duties in central Bosnia . . . That is on the recommendation of the UN for their own protection.'[35] Kris Janowski, a spokesman for the United Nations High Commissioner for Refugees (UNHCR) in Sarajevo, gloomily added: '[t]hey seem to have been looking for Britons. They may be carrying a grudge. It is alarming.'[36] Another UN spokesperson, Chris Gunness, warned that the international peacekeeping body would 'hold the Bosnian government responsible for threats or action against British personnel.'

The Bosnians should not have needed much more encouragement. Ever since frontline combat had ended in September, 'battle-weary' Arab-Afghan units were left stranded in the Balkans, causing problems with local authorities everywhere they went. As Captain Colin Armstrong-Bell, a British military spokesperson, explained it: 'The problem is that they were on the front line, but there is no front line anymore.' The foreign battalion, '800 guys with nothing to do,' was obsolete and now a powderkeg waiting to explode.[37] In the long term, it posed a threat to both international troops based in the region and also innocent native civilians. The Bosnians were furious that the *mujahideen* were interfering with desperately needed international humanitarian aid convoys, and evidently issued a number of stern warnings to the foreigners to stop their destabilizing behaviour.[38]

Yet still the Bosnian government was either unwilling or unable to take firm action to restrict the training or recruitment activity of Abu el-Ma`ali's battalion in Zenica. In a public statement, the Bosnian military charged that negative media coverage of the *mujahideen* was a deliberate 'effort to hide the truth and conceal how serious an act the murder is of [Elvedin Hodzic] who had still not recovered from wounds suffered during the liberation of Vozuca on Mt. Ozren.' Though they were quick to roundly condemn 'any illegal acts' committed by Muslim combatants, Bosnian Muslim officials also adamantly insisted that the 'El Mujahidin unit is one of the most disciplined units in the Republic of Bosnia-Hercegovina and its soldiers are now carrying out their regular military duties after brilliant victories on Mt. Ozren.'[39] Nevertheless, several weeks later, local Zenica civil authorities commissioned their own independent statement on the negative effect 'certain foreigners' were having on 'efforts to establish peace, security and equality for all the citizens of our town.'[40]

On 27 October, a small convoy of two British Army Land Rovers, a UN military Observer's Jeep, and two Bosnian government army vehicles, was on Mount Bliz near Zavidovici, monitoring the tenuous ceasefire. Among the convoy's passengers was the commander of the Bosnian army's 35th division and a patrol of five British Royal Regiment of Fusiliers soldiers serving as UN peacekeepers.[41] While on patrol in the area, the Britons had encountered three foreign *mujahideen* who demanded to know what they were doing. When the blue-helmeted soldiers returned from the mountain to their vehicles, according to Lt Col. Chris Vernon, they found themselves surrounded by fifteen hostile-looking Arab *jihadis* 'with another 15 taking up firing positions along the route through the nearest town . . . They were threatened effectively: "We are going to kill you."'[42] The Bosnian army division commander quickly jumped forward and, after some tense minutes and frenetic discussions, managed to dissuade the reluctant guerrillas from killing anyone. As the convoy quickly assembled to leave, the irate *mujahideen* ran alongside banging and rocking the vehicles, while making motions and shouting that they intended to slit the five Britons' throats.[43]

This drew an uncomfortable amount of international media and political attention to central Bosnia. The homes of British aid workers in three towns in central Bosnia were vandalized with painted warnings by militant Muslims promising vengeance. British licence plates and government markings were quietly removed from trucks and other vehicles operating in the region. One head of a British charitable group active in Bosnia commented, '[t]here is considerable concern that they will carry out a revenge attack . . . Aid organisations are pulling their people out and it is a very serious situation.'[44] Even Paul Goodall's former employer, the British Overseas Development Administration (ODA), temporarily suspended its operations for security reasons. Senior UN military and diplomatic leaders in Bosnia, mindful that they would be blamed for any preventable act of terror that might spill British blood, stepped up their covert and public pressure on the Bosnian government to take pre-emptive action and ensure the safety of British peacekeepers. Chris Vernon pronounced to journalists, '[w]e understand that the Bosnian military authorities do have some difficulty in getting these guys in line.'[45] However, '[w]e have made it clear to the Bosnian military authorities here in Sarajevo that we are not happy about this at all. They say it is difficult to control this element, and we say that isn't a good enough excuse.' Vernon went as far as to say that he had already taken precautionary measures to arrange unspecified military means of protecting Western soldiers from revenge attacks by a group of approximately 1,000 Islamic extremists 'comprised mostly of Afghans' based in Zenica.[46] Later statements by Vernon referred to a 'rapid reaction force' comprised of French and British troops who were poised and ready to take action against the foreign battalion.

The tough talk from the UN was swiftly met with a new terrorist threat in response from the *mujahideen* to simply target 'blue berets' from all European countries.[47] A UN peacekeeper from New Zealand was abducted in Zenica for several hours, but later released unharmed. His captors sternly warned him that the *mujahideen* 'view all Europeans in the same light as they do the British, and that the only European and US interest in Bosnia was a financial one.'[48] The next victims of the erratic rampage by the foreign militants were two more UN soldiers from New Zealand attempting to organize rugby matches in Bosnia. As they travelled near Zenica, they were taken into custody and held in an unspecified building for almost two hours, suffering 'mild verbal abuse.' Once they were satisfactorily identified as New Zealanders, they were freed and given back their weapons.[49] A British aid official in Zenica agreed that the situation was tense enough that '[y]ou definitely think long and hard before getting into your car and driving somewhere.'[50] The Bosnian military forced the *mujahideen* out of Zenica proper, but they clearly remained in force in the suburbs, including at their headquarters in Podbrezje. This hardly added to the safety of humanitarian aid convoys who had little choice but to travel through areas frequented by the zealous guerrillas. In a patently symbolic act of vandalism, the memorial stone on the road south of Zenica to slain ODA driver Paul Goodall was smashed by an unidentified perpetrator.[51]

Once again, the violence of the foreign *mujahideen* in Bosnia was 'answered' by allied Muslim militants elsewhere. On the morning of November 13, 1995, a car bomb exploded in Riyadh, Saudi Arabia at a U.S. training center for the Saudi National Guard. United States Colonel Albert Bleakley had just left the building and was about to get inside his Chevy Yukon. Suddenly, there was a flash and a blast wave shredded the cars parked nearby. Bleakley 'felt a splash of heat' on his face, 'as if he had shoved his head into an oven.' The Yukon was torn to bits by shrapnel so dramatically that Bleakley at first believed the bomb had actually been inside his own car.[52] Seven people were killed, including five United States citizens, and thirty-seven other Americans were injured. Several months later, Saudi officials under the lead of Interior Minister Prince Nayif, announced the arrest and confessions of four suspects in that terror attack: Abdulaziz bin Fahd Nasser al-Mutham, Riyad Suleiman Ishak al-Hajiri, Muslih Ali Ayed al-Shamrani, and Khalid Ahmed Ibrahim al-Saeed.[53]

Al-Mutham, al-Hajiri, and al-Shamrani were all admitted Arab-Afghan veterans who, while in Afghanistan, had 'met groups from so many nationalities who had extremist ideas about the rulers, governments and ulema.' In their confessions, all three also spoke of receiving faxed communiqués from Usama Bin Laden 'as well as bulletins of the Islamic groups in Egypt and Algeria.' Al-Shamrani, an apparent leader of the conspiracy, had first trained in a 3-month course at the Al-Farooq military camp run by Al-Qaida. He was also a veteran of the *jihad* in Bosnia, where he had fought with the Kateebat al-Mujahideen for approximately four months. Almost immediately upon his return to Saudi Arabia from Bosnia, al-Shamrani formed and activated a terror cell with other Arab-Afghan veterans and began planning a campaign of assassinations and bombings against the Saudi regime and Western targets. This activity soon culminated in the dramatic November explosion in Riyadh.[54] Shortly thereafter, the Saudis hastily beheaded all four men, before United States, Italian, or French investigators could question any of them and determine if they had acted as part of a larger conspiracy.

Indeed, the unsettling events occurring in Bosnia and the Middle East were causing repercussions that reached as far as Washington DC. As peace negotiations progressed between the various Bosnian factions, it appeared increasingly that a final accord was in the works that would bring almost 60,000 NATO troops into the region starting in December 1995 as peacekeepers. At the Pentagon, generals and analysts nervously watched the developing 'war' between European UN soldiers and the unpredictable Arab militants. Under the proposed Dayton peace accords, American troops would take control of 'Sector North,' an area stretching from Zenica to Tuzla. This meant that US soldiers would be responsible for policing a large region controlled by the *mujahideen*.[55] Domestic political support for United States military involvement in Bosnia could only be sustained with a surgical, bloodless operation with no signs of local resistance. Interviewed at the time, Lt Col. Chris Vernon cautioned that the antipathy of the *mujahideen* was 'mainly toward the British. It is difficult to say whether it will extend to the Americans.'[56]

The fears of United States policymakers were certainly not assuaged when Abu el-Ma`ali, interviewed in a Croatian newspaper on 17 November, predicted that the confrontation with the British in central Bosnia would only grow worse. He scoffed at the United States sponsored diplomatic efforts, and swore, '[i]f the peace talks hit a snag, we'll very soon advance into (Serb-held) Doboj. This is our direction . . . Bosnia is the country conquered by Islam. For us, there is no difference between the Serbs and the Croats.'[57] In mid-November, between twenty and twenty-five Saudi and north African terrorist leaders reportedly met in Bulgaria at an Islamic center controlled by Ayman al-Zawahiri to discuss the appropriate response to the arrest of Abu Talal al-Qasimy and the impending deployment of NATO troops in central Bosnia. As a preliminary indication of what they intended, they dispatched a gunman to open fire outside the Egyptian embassy in the Bulgarian capital Sofia on 20 November.[58]

Two days earlier, the first American blood would be spilled by the Arab *mujahideen* in Bosnia. Late on 18 November, the body of William Jefferson, a 43-year-old UN aid worker and native of Camden NJ, was found near Banovici. He had been shot twice in the head, apparently execution style. United Nations investigators strongly suspected that he was mistakenly killed by foreign guerrillas who thought he was British.[59] The Bosnian government subsequently assured UN officials that it had captured and killed the three Islamic soldiers deemed responsible for the murder.[60]

Then, on 2 December, a CBS news crew led by well-known American journalist, Bob Simon, ran into problems a few miles outside of Maglaj. Simon spoke of what happened in a news broadcast later that day:

> Bosnia is a country of roadblocks . . . Every few miles you come across a checkpoint, you show your credentials, have a little chat and move on . . . we passed a big house on the side of the road and I saw some guys hanging around with beards and Kalashnikovs, and they were clearly not from here. They were clearly Mujahedeen. And 100 yards further on there was a checkpoint, but they didn't wave us on. Instead, they ordered us out of our van at gunpoint. They loaded their weapons and cocked their weapons and . . . clicked off the safeties . . . [our interpreter] overheard one of the [guerrillas] saying to another, 'I think you should kill them right away.' And the reply was, 'Yeah, but there are 60,000 more coming. What do we do with all of them?' . . . They were clearly the Mujahedeen, which I'd always taken to be something of a phantom force here. I'd heard a lot about them, but I'd never really believed they existed as an organized force. Well, they do.[61]

After half an hour, the news crew was abruptly released after having its film confiscated. But Simon was clearly shaken by the surreal and frightening episode. In his report, he gravely concluded, '[t]he problem is that [the *mujahideen*] are, indeed, professional terrorists. That's what they do best. And the Americans are their enemy, as are the British and the French, and they might just decide to take some action.'[62]

The worst fears of conservative United States political and military pundits seemed to be coming true. United States officials were now referring to the *mujahideen* as 'hard-core terrorists' and 'very brave fighters . . . They have taken large casualties. They have taken on some important operations and are willing to take some tough action.'[63] Though the terms of the Dayton Accord mandated the expulsion of all foreign fighters from Bosnia within 30 days of the NATO deployment, United States defence officials were not optimistic that this would happen. Just in case, NATO peacekeeping troops were backed up with a fearsome array of weaponry, including state-of-the-art 60-ton American Abrams and British Challenger tanks. One defence analyst explained: '[t]here are certain elements of the Bosnian government who don't want to separate themselves from these particular elements . . . They will find a way of hiding these elements.'[64] A senior UN official concurred: 'The problem is that the local authorities have no control over the mujahedeen. The mujahedeen are protected by the Bosnian Government. They operate with total impunity. We do not know who controls them, perhaps no one.'[65]

Near Zenica, the Arab fighters arrogantly denied that they were going underground and solemnly vowed: 'The American tanks do not frighten us . . . We came here to die in the service of Islam. This is our duty. No infidel force will tell us how to live or what to do. This is a Muslim country, which must be defended by Muslims. We are 400 men here, and we all pray we will one day be martyrs.' Another guerrilla in combat fatigues, speaking with an Arabian Gulf accent, claimed '[t]he American soldiers will be just like the U.N. soldiers . . . They will corrupt the Muslims here, bring in drugs and prostitution. They will destroy all the work we have done to bring the Bosnians back to true Islam. The Americans are wrong if they think we will stand by and watch them do this.'[66]

However, in the *mujahideen* camp in Zenica, Abu el-Ma`ali and his supporters could not deny that these were 'troubled times.' Despite valiant efforts on their part to disrupt the process, the Bosnian government was decidedly giving in to international pressure and cooperating in finalizing the Dayton Accords. This was regarded by the Arab militants as a major defeat because, as Al-Qaida sources noted in reflection, 'the most hated thing for the *mujahid* is the peace of the enemy.'[67] Moreover, if the much-cursed Dayton Accords were signed (as they were on 21 November), for the first time, the membership of the foreign battalion would be forced to either truly go underground in Bosnia or leave the country altogether.

After two months of low-intensity conflict with the British and UN forces in central Bosnia, the *mujahideen* leadership anticipated the obvious: that such confrontations would only increase in frequency and severity with the arrival of massive numbers of United States troops. One British Muslim guerrilla close to the venerated Dr. Abul-Harith al-Liby (former *Amir* of Kateebat al-Mujahideen) recounted the discussions taking place at the Vatrostalno factory building outside of Zenica:

[W]hen the Americans came to Bosnia . . . the situation had developed in such a way that it seemed as if we were going to have to fight the Americans. And Abul-Harith, he turned to me and he said, 'We will become an example for these Bosnians. We will fight for our belief and the lost land. Please Allah, will give us victory and we will defeat [the Americans] or they will kill us. But we will not flee, and we will be an example for the Bosnians.[68]

True to his word, Abul-Harith was 'instrumental' in 'preparing the mujahideen medical supply line should they need to fight the Americans.'[69]

Mindful of these threats, the Clinton administration started placing enormous pressure on the Bosnians to reign in the Islamic extremists prior to the arrival of any NATO troops. United States diplomats began issuing warnings of their own, cautioning the Bosnians that they would receive no American weapons as promised if they did not comply with the terms of the Dayton Accord vis-à-vis the treatment of foreign combatants. On 2 December, Chief United States peace negotiator in Bosnia, Richard Holbrooke, confidently told a White House press briefing: 'The mujahedeen must leave . . . It's a huge issue. If Bosnia does not get rid of the mujahedeen within the 30-day period [after a peace treaty is signed next month], we have plenty of carrots.' This statement came only one week before the arrival of the first 700 United States soldiers in Bosnia.[70] In order to try and resolve the dispute, the Bosnian government immediately dispatched BiH Vice President Ejup Ganic to discuss the situation further with Abu el-Ma`ali.

But from Holbrooke's words, it was clear that the American administration still had failed to recognize the critical difference between limited local activity by suspected agents of Iran and, by contrast, the primary regional threat emanating from the Sunni militants loyal to Usama Bin Laden. Holbrooke again made references to exaggerated allegations regarding Iranian involvement in training Bosnian troops. Several days later, State Department spokesperson Nicholas Burns confessed that United States intelligence was finding it 'hard to distinguish' between radical Shiite elements in the Balkans loyal to Iran and the Saudi-sponsored *jihadi* disciples of Afghanistan.[71]

On 3 December, General John Shalikashvili, the chairman of the American Joint Chiefs of Staff, repeated the charges laid out by Holbrooke the day before regarding the *mujahideen* and then noted that 'President Izetbegovic has agreed . . . they (Bosnian government officials) assure us that they will make sure these forces leave.' If, however, United States troops would come under enemy fire while on duty in Bosnia: '[w]e have given them rules of engagement to deal with these kinds of forces like the mujahedeen should they threaten us. But I don't think that's going to be the case. They know very well that we are coming in with a very, very strong force with very robust rules of engagement.'[72] Secretary of Defence William Perry chimed in and agreed that '[w]e consider this a serious issue.'[73] Perry added, 'We have no reason to doubt that they're going to be able to fulfill that requirement.'[74]

Nevertheless, on 7 December 1995, Richard Holbrooke was dispatched on an urgent diplomatic trip to Bosnia. According to State Department spokesman Nicholas Burns, Holbrooke met with President Izetbegovic in Sarajevo to stress 'the absolutely critical need' for the Bosnian government to remove any vestiges of between 700 and 3,000 'Iranian' or 'Afghan' veteran fighters remaining in the region.[75] Burns explained, 'We believe they do represent, possibly in the future, a threat to the American and other forces there, and we want that threat removed . . . We don't believe that their presence there is at all helpful and we won't tolerate it.'[76] Several days later, another senior United States official stated for the record that if NATO troops were 'in any way impeded in its action by Mujahedeen, they will deal with them quite forcefully.'[77] The White House also suggested that a failure by the Bosnians to live up to their promises could result in the loss of $200 million in American foreign aid, crucial to rebuilding the devastated local economy.[78]

After an hour-long meeting with Holbrooke in Sarajevo, Izetbegovic acknowledged the grave American security concerns, and assured the uneasy envoy that the *mujahideen* would leave by mid-January at the latest.[79] This was partly a simple issue of public relations: the Bosnians were greatly dismayed at the negative media coverage they had received on the troublesome issue of foreign combatants. But less than 3 days later after his discussion with Holbrooke, Izetbegovic turned up in Zenica to preside over a Bosnian army military parade challenging the NATO-led peace effort. Approximately 10,000 Bosnian troops and several allied 'elite units' (including foreign *mujahideen*) marched in front of Izetbegovic and his commanders shouting *Allahu Akhbar!* and 'American tanks will not scare us!' A spokesman for the BiH army present in Zenica explained: 'This is our demonstration of power. We must prove we have the power for further fighting if it's needed; if Dayton doesn't work.'[80]

The fundamentalist fighters, for all their faults, had formed and trained a critical frontline unit of the Bosnian military. Thus, until the Bosnians could be certain that the war with the Serbs and Croats would not restart, the *jihad* battalion would not be sacrificed at the behest of fickle American foreign policy prerogatives. Brigadier General Sakib Mahmulijin, the commander of the Bosnian Third Corps based in Zenica, echoed that ambiguous and guarded outlook: 'We will do whatever the peace agreement calls for. It is not a problem for our forces,' Mahmulijin insisted. When asked what would happen if the Arab militants resisted demobilization, Mahmulijin darkly warned: 'We will do whatever our president decides.' Yet, like Izetbegovic and others, he again added strong words of praise for the foreign *mujahideen* battalion who 'helped us very much. They were together with us in the fight against fascism.'[81]

Nicholas Burns categorically insisted in State Department briefings that it was illogical to expect the United States 'just to forget about this issue and assume that everything was in place.' Hence, by the account of Burns, America was ready to enforce a stiff no-tolerance policy on the issue of lingering foreign combatants in Bosnia. In reality, this was not at all the case. Cutting off aid money to the Muslim government over the issue of the *mujahideen* was a farcical threat. It could never be considered a credible option for the Clinton administration, whose overriding priority at this stage was simply to maintain and safeguard the delicate peace established in the Dayton Accords. Therefore, despite the fierce media bluster, many prominent United States policymakers were not nearly as confident that the Bosnians would put serious pressure on the Arab fighters to leave. Rather than placing more weight on Izetbegovic and his advisors to kick them out, they instead focused on merely dealing with the *mujahideen* as an unavoidable reality on the ground.

The Dayton Accords had specifically mandated that the Bosnian government expel soldiers who were not of 'local origin.' In order to evade this provision, Izetbegovic's regime simply issued thousands of BiH passports, birth certificates, and other official paperwork to various members of the foreign battalion. According to one former United States State Department official, the *mujahideen* 'would get boxes of blank passports and just print them up themselves.' Another military official added, 'for the right amount of money, you can get a Bosnian passport even though it's the first time you've stepped foot into Bosnia.'[82] On this issue, Nicholas Burns responded to American reporters that if illegal combatants were found to be 'indeed really foreigners, then they should not be given the right to stay and fight under a different – in a different uniform.'

In fact, armed with valid local documentation, the lingering groups of *mujahideen* were able to operate more or less openly without any significant interference from the UN, United States, or NATO.[83] Many of the most dangerous ones (including Abu el-Ma`ali) were protected by religious and political hardliners at the most senior levels of the Bosnian government, and thus were able to easily 'melt into' mainstream Bosnian society. As the first UN commander in Sarajevo, Retired Canadian Major General Lewis MacKenzie, explained: 'it's not a matter of getting rid of them . . . it's a matter of coping with them.'[84] Everyone knew what no one wanted to say: Dayton or no Dayton, the *mujahideen* threat was not going away. 'We know how it has been here,' confessed a senior Bosnian police official in Zenica, 'and we don't have any reason to believe it will change just because of an agreement in Dayton or a ceremony in Paris.'[85]

While these diplomatic niceties were being exchanged in Western capitals, the Arab-Afghan *mujahideen* already had concrete tactical plans of their own in place. According to various accounts, on the day of 12 December, several fighters had parked a nondescript delivery van in the lot of *mujahideen* headquarters in the Vatrostalno factory in Podbrezje. A Bosnian police investigation later concluded that these radicals were in the final stages of 'trying to rig a car bomb' when they ran into an unknown technical error, and it prematurely exploded.[86] The massive and unexpected detonation killed as many as four *mujahideen* bombmakers and injured several other foreigners in the area. One wounded *mujahid* recounted:

> You could feel the explosion . . . like a shining light . . . as I was on the floor, I remember seeing the face of Abul-Harith [al-Liby] as he ran to me. And he took me and put me on the stretcher . . . And the building that he wanted to open, it was locked. And Abul-Harith he didn't look for the key, he just knocked the door down and took me inside.[87]

All evidence indicates that this weapon was to be used in a second revenge terror attack by Al-Gama`at Al-Islamiyya. As the October bombing in Rijeka had been in direct response to the arrest of Abu Talal al-Qasimy, some sources claim that this one in December would be a violent challenge to the coinciding 1 October 1995 conviction in United States federal court of Al-Gama`at's spiritual leader Shaykh Omar Abdel Rahman, charged with thirteen counts of seditious conspiracy for leading plots to assassinate Egyptian President Mubarak and to bomb New York City landmarks. In pamphlets sent to security authorities and posted for public display in at least two southern Egyptian provinces two days after Shaykh Omar's conviction, Al-Gama`at Al-Islamiyya issued a dire and very serious threat: 'We warn you (Americans) with the use of all means of violence.'[88] At the time, Shaykh Omar's son Abdallah scoffed at the notion that an American jury would find his father guilty: 'We are not surprised because the United States is the enemy of Islam.'[89] A year later in 1996, American intelligence acknowledged several reports from a 'foreign government service' that 'an Algerian national' (affiliated with the Al-Kifah Refugee Centre) and another senior Algerian 'commander of the mujahedin' were, in the late fall of 1995, 'preparing for an unspecified terrorist attack in Europe if Shaykh Umar Abdal-Rahman . . . were convicted.'[90] The latter Algerian suspect was almost certainly a reference to the venerated Abu el-Ma`ali.[91]

Curiously, there may have been a significance to the nationalities of those designated to carry out these suicide bombings on behalf of *Al-Gama`at*. As the October bombing had used a Canadian citizen as a detonator, this December kamikaze attack also involved another young disillusioned Muslim who had grown up in the West. In this case, as reported by both Al-Qaida and Bosnian authorities, the deceased would-be terrorist was an 18-year-old British honours student from southwest London known as Sayyad al-Falastini. Sayyad was born in the United Kingdom but spent most of his early youth in the Kingdom of Saudi Arabia. When he returned to London at age 12, he soon became involved in the radical Islamic fundamentalist movement there that was recruiting young volunteers for *jihad* in Bosnia. At age 16, he first sought unsuccessfully to join the *mujahideen* battalion in the Balkans after hearing an inspiring Friday *khutba* (religious sermon) from an Arab veteran of Bosnia.[92]

However, after being elected president of the Islamic society at his college, Sayyad started to methodically plan and save his money in a fund that would finance his dreamed *jihad* adventure. According to Al-Qaida, Sayyad possessed this instinct because he was of Palestinian descent, and therefore, there was 'a background of realizing the importance of Jihad in his family.' During the summer of 1995, he left London and travelled to a Bosnian *mujahideen* training camp. After spending some time there 'where he learned many things,' Sayyad was deployed to the *jihadi* frontline base camp near Zavidovici. In the period leading up to September, he was assigned on three-day missions to stand guard in Muslim bunkers on forbidding Mount Ozren. Then, between 10–13 September, he fought in the second line of the principle *mujahideen* attacking group during Operation Badr.[93]

When combat hostilities gradually came to a halt after 'Badr,' many foreign volunteers began filtering out of Bosnia and returning home, including a number of British recruits. But Sayyad was not ready to leave; his first taste of battle had exhilarated him and changed his life. Among the foreign guerrillas, despite his young age, he was well liked and highly esteemed for his proficiency in English, Arabic, and Bosnian. He did not want the war to end, grumbling (like many of the Arabs) that the peace accords had been negotiated only 'in order to halt the victories of the Mujahideen in Bosnia . . . For three years the world had sat back and allowed the slaughter of the Muslims to continue. But now as soon as the Muslims began to fight back and win, they ended the war.' Even in light of the Dayton agreement, Sayyad stubbornly refused to leave, and he recommitted himself to keeping the Islamic *jihad* alive in Bosnia. In the first few days of December, as the terms of Dayton were about to become a reality, Sayyad was torn by despair as he saw his beloved combat tour coming to an inexorable end. He angrily demanded of his fellow *mujahideen*: 'Why are we all lost? Look at the [infidels]. Are they thinking of us and then they are laughing because they have their own state. But look at us, the Muslims, we do not even have a state yet but we continue to laugh!'[94]

At this point, Sayyad started to act peculiarly, as if he was readying himself for a 'martyrdom' operation. He would pray all night long and continuously recite verses from the Qu`ran. Previously, he had telephoned his mother to ask her to send some money for him to visit home. Suddenly, on 10 December, he called her and told her not to wire the cash as 'he would not be needing it.' There is good reason to believe that Sayyad may have been knowingly preparing mentally and religiously for an imminent role as a suicide bomber. In any event, on 12 December, something in his plan went terribly wrong. While Sayyad stood beside the van, it prematurely detonated, shaking the entire neighborhood and thoroughly frightening nearby Croatian civilians.[95] By the 'official' count of Al-Qaida, Sayyad became the sixth British Islamic volunteer soldier killed in Bosnia only two days shy of his nineteenth birthday. He was buried next to the grave of Moataz Billah in a ceremony attended 'by over three hundred of the cream of the foreign Muja-hideen fighters in Bosnia.'[96] The Arab battalion later eulogized him:

> Sayyad was a brother who made Jihad his wealth and his life giving every penny of his wealth for the pleasure of Allah and eventually giving every drop of his blood for him. We ask Allah (SWT) to accept Sayyad as a martyr, to make him an example for the millions of youth in the West who have chosen this life in preference with the hereafter.[97]

According to a Pentagon spokesman, there was yet another Westerner among the foreign *mujahideen* in central Bosnia suspected of stalking US troops in preparation for a possible terrorist attack: Isa Abdullah Ali, a former groundskeeper at Howard University in Washington DC.[98] Ali was an eccentric and enigmatic figure who had thoroughly tested the patience of the Pentagon and the US State Department. Ali had received his initial military education serving as a US Marine in Vietnam, yet turned down a different path in the early 1980s. A former co-worker of Ali's at a bar in Washington DC offered an equally curious portrait:

> He certainly looked the part of the doorframe heavy, showing up for work in biker leathers or military fatigues. A pair of goggles strapped around his balding head gave him the air of somebody who was always combat-ready; through the thick lenses, his small brown eyes looked like floating saucers. A mole on his right cheek came into focus whenever he leaned forward, either to make a point or to shift his weight off a bullet fragment still lodged in his left thigh, a souvenir from his final gunfight in West Beirut. Isa told me his Creator had put him on Earth to defend innocent Muslim civilians.[99]

By the closing months of the Bosnian war in 1995, Isa Abdullah Ali seemed less concerned with the atrocities committed by the Serbs than with scheming to disrupt the US-led peace process in the Balkans.[100] Isa Abdullah Ali quickly aroused the suspicions of United States and NATO troops across the region soon after the signing of the Dayton Accords. A number of sentinels and junior officers distrib-uted at various checkpoints in northern Bosnia reported that they had seen him several times during January and February, near a United States base adjacent to the northern Bosnian town of Orasje. Other sightings placed Ali not far off in the Lasava river valley. According to the American soldiers, he was travelling around in a 'beat-up' Humvee and deliberately harassing them. One sargeant at a NATO checkpoint said that Ali had driven right up to the base near Orasje before conceal-ing a booby-trapped device under a glove on the ground, and then driving off again. As he had previously been cited for falsely posing as an authorized military member, American officials worried that with 'the proper uniform and equipment, he could easily disguise himself as a US soldier.'[101] At the Pentagon, spokesman Lt. Col. Arnie Owens would only say that Ali was 'regarded as a potential security threat to American personnel.'[102] He was the perfect operative to scout potential

American targets in Bosnia and to evade NATO security cordons setup to deter terror attacks.

Blissfully ignorant of the violent events transpiring in central Bosnia in December, United States policymakers were looking entirely in the wrong direction. A day after the stunning misfire explosion in Zenica, United States Secretary of State Warren Christopher announced in a press conference that he had received convincing evidence showing that 'Iranian fighters' in Bosnia were voluntarily 'either departing or are planning to depart.'[103] Pentagon spokesman Kenneth Bacon confidently asserted to reporters, 'they're leaving.'[104] This news may very well have been true; indeed, various intelligence reports over the past few years have concluded that most, if any, Iranian agents aiding the Bosnian army meekly left the country in 1995 or soon afterwards as per the terms of the Dayton accord. A number of the foreign *mujahideen* also disappeared, now that the war against the Serbs and Croats appeared to be finally over. In mid-December, the Croatian embassy in Sarajevo confirmed that sizeable groups of radical Islamic fighters had recently passed through Croatia on their way out of Bosnia.[105]

Anwar Shaaban and Abu el-Ma`ali had decided to ironically profit from the U.S. interest in expelling the *mujahideen* from Bosnia. Hundreds of veteran fighters, accused of brutal wartime atrocities and expertly trained in urban warfare, were readily granted political asylum in a collection of European countries, Australia, and Canada. Canada, particularly, was favored among North African ex-fighters because of its lax immigration laws and Quebec's eager preference for francophone speakers. It was a devious tactic that allowed Al-Qaida to infiltrate key Western democracies with highly skilled and motivated terrorist sleeper cells. A French report written by the highly esteemed French counterterrorism magistrate Jean-Louis Bruguière later concluded that the 'exfiltration' of significant numbers of veteran fighters from Bosnia was beneficial for Al-Qaida in the sense that it enabled the *mujahideen* 'to be useful again in spreading the Jihad across other lands.' In fact, 'among the veterans of the 'Moudjahiddin Battalion' of Zenica, many would go on to carry out terrorist acts following the end of the Bosnian conflict.'[106]

Others travelled to receive more training and experience in other still active *jihad* lands like Chechnya and Afghanistan. Sources in Egypt told Arab reporters that 'some members' of Al-Gama`at Al-Islamiyya and Al-Jihad were heading directly to fight Russian troops in Chechnya after leaving the battlefields of Bosnia under the terms of the Dayton Accords. According to *Al-Hayat*, these militant Egyptian *jihadis* 'preferred to go to Chechnya, instead of heading for European states to seek political asylum, especially in view of Egyptian efforts to persuade European states not to receive them.'[107]

However, many of the hardcore Arab-Afghan elite (who presented the most serious security threat to Europe and the United States) were giving no signs that they planned to seek a new refuge. The botched car bombing that killed Sayyad al-Falastini was certainly compelling evidence that the leaders of the Kateebat al-Mujahideen were entrenched and intended to stay just where they were. On 13 December, Dr Abul-Harith al-Liby debriefed a group of British volunteers in Bjala-Bucha about to return home to the United Kingdom. Evidently, Abul-Harith was ordering them not to forget their obligation to the *jihad* and to keep in regular contact with their guerrilla commanders in Zenica.[108]

Even if the White House did not understand the significance of what the *mujahideen* were preparing for in December 1995, the Croats must nonetheless have been deeply concerned to learn about the failed car bombing in Podbrezje, especially since they were the second most logical target. Perhaps this is what precipitated one of the most serious confrontations of the war between the Croats and the Arab *mujahideen* in Bosnia less than 48 hours later on 14 December. On that day, according to Al-Qaida sources, Shaykh Anwar Shaaban gave a lecture to the battalion after morning prayers. He discussed the evolving situation in the Balkans and 'how the world's powers were trying to suppress the right of Islam from Bosnia with the Dayton Peace Accords. He exalted the brothers to have patience and use this time to better themselves.' Beside him stood some of the cream of the Arab-Afghan elite in Europe: Dr Abul-Harith al-Liby, Abu Hammam al-Najdi (Amir of the 'Lion's Den' frontline base camp in Zavidovici), Abu Ziyaad al-Najdi (a senior military commander of the *mujahideen* and a old friend of Abu Hammam's), and likely also Abu el-Ma`ali, who was now second only to Anwar Shaaban in the *mujahideen* pecking order. Representatives of the foreign battalion claimed that, given the presence of these 'key commanders' in central Bosnia, 'the entire world felt threatened after the success of the peace deal.'[109]

Abu Hammam al-Najdi, a 24-year-old university graduate from Saudi Arabia, was not only responsible for running the Lion's Den base, but was also an accomplished English speaker. He was educated and clearly intelligent, and was quite proficient at coordinating the Arab combat command center. Abu Hammam had first arrived in Bosnia in 1994 with his compatriot and friend Abu Ziyaad al-Najdi.[110] Abu Ziyaad, another talented Saudi *jihadi* military commander, was reputed for his focus on martyrdom as a requirement for the establishment of an Islamic state. He was once quoted as reasoning that 'Allah takes martyrs from the Mujahideen at a time He sees fit, whilst others he leaves to battle His enemies. If all the Mujahideen were to be taken as martyrs, who would fight the enemies of Allah? If, on the other hand, none of the Mujahideen were to be martyred, how would they get the reward for their actions?'[111]

Following the morning lecture on 14 December, Shaaban, Dr. Abul-Harith, Abu Hammam, and Abu Ziyaad got inside a Land Cruiser driven by a *mujahideen* chauffeur, Abu Hamza al-Djazairi. The commanders intended to travel from Zenica to the frontline near Zavidovici. Oddly, when they telephoned for a Bosnian army escort and explained the circumstances (as was usual in these situations), the Bosnian officer casually advised them that they needed no escort and would be permitted to travel freely. Given that the peace agreement seemed to be holding, they took no additional soldiers for protection and were armed only with several automatic weapons. Abu Hamza was at the wheel, with Anwar Shaaban and Abu Ziyaad in the front seat next to him; in the back sat Abul-Harith and Abu Hammam.[112]

Along the road to Zavidovici, the Land Cruiser was able to pass the first Croatian HVO checkpoint without incident. However, according to Al-Qaida sources, at the second checkpoint at the entrance to Zepce, they were stopped by Croat soldiers for several minutes. While they were being inexplicably held, they watched a large Croat army truck pass by them and continue along the road to Zavidovici. Finally, by the late afternoon, the commanders in the Land Cruiser were allowed to continue onward through Croatian-held territory and reached the third checkpoint on the outskirts of Zepce.[113]

At approximately this point, Shaaban and the other *mujahideen* realized that they had run into serious trouble. The army truck they had seen earlier was parked next to the checkpoint. Croatian soldiers stepped forward and ordered the Arabs to get out of their vehicle. Shaaban worriedly radioed his last words to Abu el-Ma`ali in Zenica: 'They have stopped us.' What happened next is a matter of some dispute. The Arabs allege that the canvas was drawn back off the army truck to reveal a PK machine gun emplacement manned by several Croatian soldiers. The Croats unleashed their deadly weapon, instantly killing the legendary Anwar Shaaban, Dr Abul-Harith al-Liby, and Abu Hamza al-Djazairi. Abu Hammam and Abu Ziyaad fled from the car and, though wounded, vigorously fired back until they were both killed.[114]

United Nations and Croatian sources told a somewhat different tale. According to UN spokesman Major Lindsay Rumgay: 'A vehicle with three or four Muja-hedeen drove through an HVO (Bosnian Croat) checkpoint quite close to Zepce about midday. The HVO got into another vehicle and pursued them to a junction where a firefight followed with both sides firing small calibre weapons.' At least one Bosnian Croat policeman who had given chase to the Land Cruiser was killed in the gunfire.[115] When the Croats searched the bodies of the Shaaban and his entourage, they found employee identification cards for the Third World Relief Agency (TWRA), the same Sudanese front company that both Bin Laden and the Saudis used to funnel money and weapons to militant Islamic movements in Bosnia.[116]

Shaaban's body was eventually returned to the *mujahideen*, and the men from the Land Cruiser were all buried together. Al-Qaida sadly eulogized his death:

Out of the thousands of scholars preaching in the world today, Sheik Anwar was among the few who took their knowledge to the frontline and used it where it was most effective . . . Sheik Anwar played his role in leading the Muslim ummah against its enemies speaking the truth wherever he was until he paid for it with his life. He had carried the Mujahideen regiment in Bosnia on his shoulders throughout the three years of the war . . . And finally we say to the enemies behind the assassination of Sheik Anwar that for every Mujahid scholar that you remove, a hundred more youth will be ready to replace him.[117]

A joint investigation carried out by Croat and Bosnian investigative officials eventually concluded without contention that, despite the claims of the *mujahideen* battalion, Shaaban's Land Cruiser did not have the requisite government permission to travel from their sanctuary in Podbrejze to the Tesanj region. In a high-level meeting, the Croatian HVO commander in Vitez, Drago Dragcevic, and BiH Army Third Corps General Sakib Mahmuljin both lent their support to the report of the investigators and sharply criticized the *mujahideen* for instigating hatred and causing renewed civil conflict in Bosnia.[118] In a brief summit to discuss the progress of the implementation of the Dayton Accords (and on the very day of Shaaban's untimely death), Izetbegovic roundly assured Clinton that his forces 'were moving forward now with dismantling the foreign military forces.'[119] Simultaneously, Al-Gama`at Al-Islamiyya responded to Anwar Shaaban's murder with a promise to unleash 'the full force of revenge' on its enemies.[120]

The United States government remained positive, at least for the cameras, that all the foreign *mujahideen* were leaving. But Defense Secretary Perry nonetheless admitted that several prominent members of the Clinton administration were 'concerned that some of them will decide that instead of leaving they will try to blend into the landscape . . . We don't see that happening yet, but we will watch for it very carefully.'[121] In fact, that is precisely what was transpiring, even as Perry spoke those fateful words. Muhamed Filipovic, Bosnia's ambassador to the UK, decried the situation in the Croatian media, confessing that although some of the foreign guerrilla's were indeed departing, 'many of them refuse to cooperate . . . I deem it very difficult that they will leave voluntarily.'[122]

The American 'Frankenstein' scenario was coming true in Bosnia just as it had in Afghanistan: the Arab fighters would not leave their training camps and had surrounded themselves with enough sympathetic and powerful locals to defy the will of America. NATO was now active and engaged in Bosnia; but, even with 60,000 troops on the ground, the United States military was paralysed by greater foreign policy concerns. For President Bill Clinton and his staff, the Arab *mujahideen* were not enough of a priority at the time to start a feud with the Izetbegovic government. Thus, even when it was apparent that a good number of the fighters intended to remain at their posts, there was great reluctance to unilaterally use military force to remove them. No one wanted to admit it, but this Clinton administration 'priority' was destined to be pigeon-holed. When asked why his soldiers were taking no action to reign in the remaining *mujahideen*, a NATO officer cautioned: 'We will have to wait and see . . . Moving them is the responsibility of the Bosnian Muslim army.'[123]

The Egyptian Islamists, stewing with rage over the death of Anwar Shaaban, were still out for Croat blood. The display of Christian religious symbols celebrating the first peaceful Christmas in at least 4 years for Bosnia could not have helped the situation. In the early hours of Christmas day, according to a spokesman for the Bosnian Croat army, an unknown number of foreign *mujahideen* ambushed a Croat HVO vehicle near Zepce returning from Catholic midnight mass services. The guerrillas sprayed automatic weapons fire at the vehicle, killing two soldiers and wounding one.[124] No confirmation was offered by Croatian sources in Zagreb, NATO, or UN peacekeepers.

Meanwhile, at about this time, the public received one of the first real written responses of the *mujahideen* to the tumultuous events of December and the principles of the Dayton Accord. It was issued as a communiqué titled 'Beware of Erroneous Handling of Mujahedin Issue' by a previously unknown group calling itself the 'Islamic Committee for the Defense of the Persecuted (ICDP) . . . a body comprised of prominent leaders of Arab religious groups that are in close contact with the Arab mujahedin in Bosnia.' The document accused the Croats, the US, and NATO of leading a 'hostile' coalition campaign against Islam in Bosnia. It noted the assassination of Anwar Shaaban and his aides, and cited this as justification for an unwavering war of terror against the enemies of the 'true Muslims.' It further warned:

> If some of them [US/NATO forces] try to use the big stick and the language of threats, intimidation, and treachery with the mujahedin, the Arab proverb says: They have brought it upon themselves . . . Here is the weapon of martyrdom and death for the sake of Allah's cause being highly valued once again: the lethal weapon that is worrying the United States.[125]

Officially, the foreign battalion in Bosnia was disbanded in early 1996 and converted into a training unit for Bosnian Muslim recruits in the new national army. As far as the authorities were concerned, Abu el-Ma`ali had stepped aside, demilitarized, and handed over control of the battalion headquarters in Podbrezje to a younger Palestinian militant.[126] In reality, Abu el-Ma`ali was still playing a central role at the Podbrezje headquarters and in the general activities of the remaining Arab *mujahideen*. Throughout the winter of 1995–6, the Vatrostalno Factory building in Zenica remained abuzz with *mujahideen* activity. American Special Forces patrolling the area were repeatedly denied access by the Turkish UN soldiers surrounding and guarding the huge factory compound.[127] The Turkish battalion was deliberately based in Zenica in order to ease tensions and prevent violence by providing a buffer between local radical Islamists, neighboring Croat civilians and UN forces.[128] But even they had confrontations with the unpredictable religious fanatics: 'Our main problem is with the fundamentalists, who do not like us because Turkey is a secular state,' explained Levent Rudar, a spokesman for the soldiers.[129]

Rather than winding down their wartime operations, many Islamic charitable groups active in Bosnia were organizing a renewed campaign to aid the stranded foreign *mujahideen* in their remaining enclaves. Arabic-language flyers distributed in the United States in January 1996 (bearing a full-page advertisement for the Illinois-based Global Relief Foundation (GRF), also known as Fondation au Secours Mondiale), gloated that lingering *mujahideen* units were 'a nightmare for the American troops in Bosnia' and argued that their continued presence was absolutely necessary to enable local Bosnians 'to stay true to their Islamic values and open their mind to Jihad and the love of martyrdom for Allah.' Moreover, according to the flyer, '[t]he mujahideen have a school which trains hundreds of mujahideen every month . . . those fighters win all their battles because of their love of martyrdom for Allah.'[130] Even though the peace agreement in the Balkans had held firm for several months, GRF and the other Muslim evangelical charities were hard at work to keep the *jihad* ongoing in the region. Correspondingly, on 14 December 2001, the United States Treasury Department froze GRF's assets on the alleged grounds that it had served for many years as an Al-Qaida financial conduit throughout southeastern Europe.[131]

Abu el-Ma`ali and his comrades forced underground in Bosnia were encouraged by a defiant sermon issued by Shaykh Omar Abdel Rahman from prison in the United States in mid-January 1996. The blind shaykh made the following accusations:

> America worked tirelessly to weaken Muslims in Bosnia . . . Such action made America a partner to the Serbs in killing hundreds of thousands of Muslims, and in raping women and annihilating children. If Germany is supporting the Croats, and Russia is strengthening the Serbs, we see that everyone, led by America, have united to isolate and weaken Muslims, and the whole plan is for destroying Muslims in the Balkans. Behold, the whole world, listen! Islam cannot be stopped with violence, with warfare, with spending millions of dollars, with lies, deception, corruption, and with fabricated trials like this one . . . The US, with its power and influence, must not bruise itself in stopping these Islamic forces, and whatever they do towards that end will only harm them, and they will bring upon themselves bankruptcy and destruction if they try to stop Islam.[132]

On 31 January 1996, NATO spokesman Lieutenant-Colonel Mark Rayner announced to a formal media briefing that the last 'remaining foreign forces' loyal to the *mujahideen* were escorted to the Croatian border by civil police and had left Bosnia.[133] Yet within two weeks of these vague assurances, French NATO soldiers backed up with heavy weapons and armed helicopters raided a ski chalet about six miles south of Fojnica, west of Sarajevo.[134] According to NATO spokesmen and other sources, the chalet had served as an Iranian-run terrorist training school for Bosnian intelligence operatives and foreign *mujahideen*. When the French soldiers took control of the compound, they detained eleven people, including three alleged Iranian intelligence officers and two other foreign nationals, believed to be of Pakistani or 'Afghan' origin.[135] Alongside these men, the French found a selection of sniper rifles, submachine guns, RPGs, grenades, detonators, blasting caps, and other even more disturbing devices.

NATO commander Admiral Leighton Smith insisted: 'It's an abomination. We have clearly terrorist training activities: These weapons here, in particular, with this plastic child's toy with plastic explosives and a detonator inserted in it.' Even worse, according to Smith: 'It has direct association with people in the government.' Bosnian officials defensively contended that these were, in fact, innocent 'anti-terrorist' training centers for Bosnian Interior Ministry units.[136] This, of course, did not explain the detailed models and diagrams found that were made in obvious preparation for terror operations, or the folder labelled 'the special operations project to kidnap the Serbian officer or liaison at the PTT [telecommunications] engineering building.' The folder contained frightening details of an elaborate abduction plot and more than thirty photographs and sketches of the building, also used as a NATO regional headquarters.[137]

At the State Department, Nicholas Burns was back again, responding with ominous tones on the issue of the *mujahideen*, but presenting no real consequences to the Bosnian government for noncompliance. 'We have received extremely disturbing reports this morning that some Bosnian government officials may have been involved in the activities of this facility . . . We expect full cooperation.' For the record, Burns reiterated, '[t]he United States has pressed and will continue to press the Bosnian government to effect the withdrawal of all foreign fighters immediately.'[138] A few days later, the State Department spokesman would even charge that '[w]e know they know where these [mujahideen] are.'[139] In a media interview, Izetbegovic seemed to be every bit as shocked as the Clinton administration, admitting that the Fojnica base uncovered by NATO was 'our big mistake and in violation of what we had signed.'[140] As the head of Bosnia's main intelligence organ, Bakir Alispahic was held responsible for the camp abomination and demoted by Izetbegovic under heavy American pressure.[141]

A month later, despite these renewed promises, NATO forces raided another suspected *mujahideen* camp run by the Bosnian army's Fourth Muslim Brigade north of Mostar in the town of Radesina. One source close to the investigation explained: 'The operation is on-going, it's the same thing as before and it is near

Mostar.' After photographing the men in the compound and seizing an unimpressive weapons cache, the French troops left for lack of finding anything sufficiently 'alarming.'[142] Yet again, the United States State Department appealed to the Bosnian government to remove any remaining foreign *mujahideen*, or face losing American military assistance.

Still, the *mujahideen* showed no sign of leaving, and were making no great secret of their presence. In Bocinja Donja, Abu el-Ma`ali, along with about 100 other veteran guerrillas, had faded into Bosnian society and had taken over a number of abandoned Serb and Croat houses with the explicit permission of the Bosnian government. They dominated local politics and religion, and forced their neighbors to adhere to strict Islamic *Shariah* law. At the time, a sign on the road into town warned passers-by to 'Fear Allah,' which was wise advice for the uninitiated. Unlike the mostly secular society of mainstream Bosnia, men in Bocinja Donja were required to wear beards and women donned long black veils, while smoking and drinking alcohol was absolutely forbidden.

In the years following the signing of the Dayton Accord, a number of incidents underscored the serious extremist threat lurking in Bocinja, not only to the West but to Bosnia itself. Two Serbs who wandered too close to the village were beaten and tortured by three local Muslim men, who were subsequently given suspended sentences by a sympathetic judge. When several United States military officers tried to take a tour of Bocinja in January 1999, they were accosted by angry residents and quickly departed for personal safety reasons. A British general who arrived in Bocinja for an inspection visit was attacked by anti-Western villagers, one of whom tried to forcibly pull open the door vehicle and made slashing motions across his throat. The general admitted: 'It was a very threatening atmosphere . . . They do not like [peacekeeping] troops patrolling there.' A Norwegian commander of NATO, who had attempted to intervene to save the life of an ethnic Serb in the area, suddenly found himself threatened: 'We were approached by two residents, both of foreign origin, who physically tried to attack the Serb and pushed me away . . . We decided immediately to return to our armored vehicle, where a third foreigner flashed a knife. It was quite tense.'[143]

Abu Sulaiman al-Makki, the veteran Saudi Arab-Afghan fighter who was permanently handicapped early in the war in 1992, was living as part of the same growing ex-guerrilla residential community in the town of Bocinja Donja. He also established an Islamic 'relief organization' in the Tuzla area, providing charitable and religious assistance to local Bosnians and also the community of foreign veterans of the Kateebat al-Mujahideen. Abu Sulaiman publicly stated in the local media that cells of foreign *mujahideen* remained deployed in Tuzla, Zenica, Sarajevo, Konjic, and Bihac. In Bihac, one of the *jihad* havens named by Abu Sulaiman, an American reporter interviewed 'Ali,' a Saudi citizen 'interested in the situation' who had been in Bosnia for over a year. At first, the young Arab had tried to pass himself off as a Turkish exchange student, but eventually admitted the truth of his identity, smiling and adding 'All of us have our secrets.' 'Ali' was one of many foreign *mujahideen* who were in the process of establishing permanent residence in Bosnia through marrying Bosnian women or by bringing their families to Bosnia.[144] 'Abu Salim,' a local Algerian commander in Zenica, likewise warned: 'We did not come here just to leave as soon as the Americans arrive. We are living in the time when Islam will prevail. Bosnia is a Muslim country and we will defend it.'[145]

The Mayor of Bihac Adnan Alagic insisted that these men would not be expelled so long as they only desired citizenship and would 'respect the law . . . The West does not understand the situation if they are afraid of a few hundred Middle Eastern men . . . What about the 8,000 Muslims slaughtered in Srebrenica?' For four long years, the United States and Western Europe had refused to provide military aid to the embattled Bosnians. Even as international television viewers watched the genocide of Muslim civilians in Srebrenica and elsewhere, no 'civilized' democratic government stepped forward to defend the innocents and stop the violence. At that time, the only ally the Bosnians had were the uncontrollable *mujahideen*. This was a blood debt: Izetbegovic and many of the hardline Muslim leaders from the war won out over Bosnian moderates, and the Arabs who had sacrificed their lives for Islam in the Balkans would not be handed over to their enemies. Abu Hamza al-Masri likewise admitted that Abu el-Ma`ali 'depended on Alija Izetbegovic . . . to protect him.'[146] Certainly, the easiest loophole to avoid the terms of the Dayton Agreement was through intermarriage and the organized settlement of former foreign *mujahideen* into civilian society. Once issued passports, these naturalized 'Bosniaks' melded into the local population beyond the view of NATO troops. Major Ralph Coleman, a NATO spokesman, acknowledged to the media: 'We are aware that some have married into communities and have decided to settle down.'[147]

Meanwhile, in March 1996, Alija Izetbegovic fired off an angry response to a joint written appeal from United States Senators Bob Dole and Joseph Lieberman. He correctly denied the significant presence of Iranian military personnel in Bosnia, but also acknowledged that between fifty and sixty former members of the Kateebat al-Mujahideen had been debriefed and were now considered civilians. They had subsequently been resettled in two villages, including the town of Bocinja. Izetbegovic pleaded in his letter that it was 'incompatible with the moral principles of our people to expel the people who fought on our side and have no place to go because they cannot return to their [own] countries.'[148] This explanation was given no credence, either in Washington circles or by NATO commanders on the ground. United States Naval Captain Mark Van Dyke stated conclusively: 'They are here in violation of the peace accord. We have long passed the deadline to remove those foreign forces. They need to be expelled immediately. They have been involved in training. It needs to stop.'[149]

Ultimately, American and European demands for the Bosnians to cast out their former Arab-Afghan allies went substantially unfulfilled until even after 11 September 2001. By then it was already too late – generations of new foreign *mujahideen* were given safe haven, training, financing, and ideological inspiration by supposedly demobilized Al-Qaida fighters hiding in Bosnia. The frontline against the Serbs was closed with the signing of the Dayton Accords, allowing the *mujahideen* leadership to distribute the human seeds of *jihad* cultivated in Bosnia across the major centers of Western civilization. The arrest of Abu Talal al-Qasimy and the assassinations of Anwar Shaaban and Dr. Abul-Harith al-Liby had only fuelled the flames of hatred in the hearts of these men as they plotted new acts of violence and mayhem. Starting in 1996, with a transnational terrorist underground in place across Europe, many of those plans moved from the preparatory to the operational phase.

Notes

1. Jansen, Michael. '16 die, 60 injured in bomb attack on Egyptian embassy.' *The Irish Times*, 20 November 1995, p. 13.
2. Sharaf-al-Din, Khalid. 'Fundamentalists' Leaders Formed Bogus Organizations To Confuse the Security Organs.' *Al-Sharq al-Awsat*, 7 March 1999, p. 6. By 1999 both Swiss and Egyptian authorities concluded that Abu Hazim had 'ordered directly or indirectly' the infamous November 1997 terrorist attack in Luxor, Egypt, which killed 58 European tourists. Egyptian officials added that, following the attack, Abu Hazim fled his temporary residence in the Sudan for the safety of Bin Laden's camps in Afghanistan. See also: Hauser, Christine. 'Bin Laden "behind Luxor strike."' *Middle East Times*, 23 May 1999.
3. Sharaf-al-Din, Khalid. 'Fundamentalists' Leaders Formed Bogus Organizations To Confuse the Security Organs.' *Al-Sharq al-Awsat*, 7 March 1999, p. 6.
4. Ibrahim, Youssef, M. 'Muslim militant leader arrested on way to Bosnia, Egypt reports.' *The Houston Chronicle*, 24 September 1995, section A, p. 31.
5. Jansen, Michael. '16 die, 60 injured in bomb attack on Egyptian embassy.' *The Irish Times*, 20 November 1995, p. 13.
6. Ibrahim, Youssef, M. Op. cit.
7. 'Egyptian Islamists Hit Back.' *Indigo Publications Intelligence Newsletter*, 23 November 1995, No. 276.
8. Italian Division of General Investigations and Special Operations (DIGOS) Anti-Terrorism Report. 'Searches at the Islamic Cultural Center, Viale Jenner 50, Milano, 6/26/1995.' Dated 15 September 1997.

9. 'Egyptian Islamists Hit Back.' Op. cit.

10. Ibrahim, Youssef, M. Op. cit.

11. 'Importat[sic] Communique to Muslims.' Armije Republike BH 3, Korpus; Odred 'El-Mudzahidin': Unidentified communiqué issued by Abu el-Ma`ali, dated 22 September 1995. *Islam Report*, The American Islamic Group (AIG). 23 September 1995.

12. 'Congratulations [sic] to the Muslim World.' Armije Republike BH 3, Korpus; Odred 'El-Mudzahidin': Unidentified communiqué issued by Abu el-Ma`ali. *Islam Report*. The American Islamic Group (AIG). 25 September 1995.

13. Croatian Radio. Broadcast in Serbo-Croat language in Zagreb. 20 October 1995, 16.00 GMT.

14. Gatti, Fabrizio. '1995: From Milan a car bomb leaves for Fiume.' *Corriere della Sera* (Italy), 11 November 2001.

15. Croatian Radio. Broadcast in Serbo-Croat language in Zagreb. 20 October 1995, 16.00 GMT.

16. Gatti, Fabrizio. '1995: From Milan a car bomb leaves for Fiume.' *Corriere della Sera* (Italy), 11 November 2001.

17. January 1996 CIA Report on 'International Islamic NGOs' and links to terrorism, p. 13. See also: Affidavit by Senior Special Agent David Kane (Bureau of Immigration and Customs Enforcement, Department of Homeland Security). *United States of America v. Soliman S. Biheiri*. United States District Court for the Eastern District of Virginia, Alexandria Division. Case #: 03-365-A. 14 August 2003, p. 2.

18. 'Car-bomb rocks Croatian city.' *Independent* (London), 21 October 1995, p. 13.

19. 'Egyptian Radical Group Claims Bombing in Croatia.' The Associated Press, 21 October 1995.

20. 'Jamaa claims Croatia bombing, Mubarak cancels New York trip.' Deutsche Presse-Agentur. 21 October 1995.

21. January 1996 CIA Report on 'International Islamic NGOs' and links to terrorism, p. 13. See also: Affidavit by Senior Special Agent David Kane (Bureau of Immigration and Customs Enforcement, Department of Homeland Security). Op. cit.

22. Jean-Louis Bruguiere and Jean-Francois Ricard. 'Requisitoire Definitifaux aux Fins de Non-Lieu. De Non-Lieu partiel. De Requalification. De Renvoi devant le Tribunal Correctionnel, de mantien sous Controle Judiciaiare et de maintien en Detention.' Cour D'Appel de Paris; Tribunal de Grande Instance de Paris. No. Parquet: P96 253 3901.2, p. 160.

23. Gatti, Fabrizio. Op. cit.

24. HINA News Agency. Broadcast in English language in Zagreb. 28 September 2001, 13.32 GMT.

25. Gatti, Fabrizio. Op. cit.
26. Peterson, Scott. 'Bosnia's Holy Warriors: Sinister, or Just Bored?' *The Christian Science Monitor*, 7 December 1995, p. 1.
27. Brown, Adrian. 'Islamic warriors become liability.' Agence France Presse. 30 November 1995.
28. 'Islamic "Vendetta" Targets British Troops.' *Guardian* (London), 25 October 1995, p. 13.
29. Peterson, Scott. Op. cit.
30. Peterson, Scott. Op. cit.
31. 'Bosnian Mujahedeen Will Welcome, Not Threaten, US Soldiers.' The Associated Press. 4 December 1995.
32. Borger, Julian. 'Vengeful Islamic Guerillas Threaten British Troops Bound for Bosnia.' *Guardian* (London), 28 November 1995, p. 2.
33. Latal, Srecko. 'Mujahedeen Fighters Threaten British Peacekeepers.' The Associated Press. 28 October 1995.
34. 'Islamic 'Vendetta' Targets British Troops.' Op. cit.
35. Cracknell, David. 'Portillo confirms Islamic threat to Bosnia troops.' Press Association, 24 October 1995.
36. 'Islamic 'Vendetta.' Op. cit.
37. Peterson, Scott. Op. cit.
38. Bellamy, Christopher. 'Mujahedin threats "disturb" UN in Bosnia.' *Independent* (London), 26 October 1995, p. 14.
39. Radio Bosnia-Hercegovina. Broadcast in Serbo-Croat language in Sarajevo. 4 November 1995, 18.00 GMT.
40. Borger, Julian. Op. cit.
41. Ravina, Pazit. 'Britons targeted in Bosnia.' *Sunday Times*, 29 October 1995.
42. Latal, Srecko. 'Mujahedeen Fighters Threaten British Peacekeepers.' The Associated Press. 28 October 1995.
43. Ravina, Pazit. Op. cit.
44. Williams, David. 'Fleeing for their lives; British aid workers quit Bosnia as Islamic guerrillas threaten death.' *Daily Mail* (London), 2 November 1995, p. 14.
45. Smith, Tony. 'UN Warns Islamic Fighters After They Detain Peacekeeper.' Associated Press. 2 November 1995.
46. Simon, Chris. 'UN expands convoy movement in Bosnia.' United Press International. 30 October 1995.
47. 'Mujahedin group threatens European "blue berets."' Deutsche Presse-Agentur. 2 November 1995.
48. Smith, Tony. Op. cit.
49. Bell, Cathie. 'Soldiers seized on rugby mission .' *The Dominion* (Wellington), 4 November 1995, p. 1.

50. Borger, Julian. Op. cit.
51. Borger, Julian. Op. cit.
52. Dennehy, Kevin. 'Cape man relives close call with terrorist bombing while in Saudi Arabia.' *Cape Cod Times*, 25 October 2001.
53. 'Culprit in Riyadh bombing arrested; Prince Naif lauds General Investigations.' *Riyadh Daily*, 23 April 1996.
54. Ibid.
55. Priest, Dana. 'Foreign Muslims Fighting in Bosnia Considered "Threat" to US Troops.' *The Washington Post*, 30 November 1995, p. A33.
56. 'Bosnian Mujahedeen Will Welcome, Not Threaten, U.S. Soldiers.' *The Associated Press*, 4 December 1995.
57. The Associated Press. 17 November 1995.
58. Bodansky, Yossef. *Some Call It Peace: Waiting For War In the Balkans.* International Media Corporation: London, 1996, part I.
59. Hedges, Chris. 'Foreign Islamic Fighters in Bosnia Pose a Potential Threat for GIs.' *The New York Times*, 3 December 1995, section 1, p. 1.
60. Priest, Dana. Op. cit.
61. 'Possible Threat the Mujahideen Pose in Bosnia.' Report by Bob Simon. CBS Evening News. 2 December 1995.
62. Ibid.
63. Priest, Dana. Op. cit.
64. Priest, Dana. Op. cit.
65. Hedges, Chris. Op. cit.
66. Hedges, Chris. Op. cit.
67. 'Under the Shades of Swords.' Audiocassette sequel to 'In the Hearts of Green Birds.' November 1997. Azzam Recordings: London.
68. 'Under the Shades of Swords.' Op. cit.
69. 'Under the Shades of Swords.' Op. cit.
70. Nelson, Lars-Erik and William Goldschlag. 'Bosnia told to kick out Foreign Extremists.' *Daily News* (New York), 2 December 1995, p. 2.
71. State Department Regular Press Briefing. 7 December 1995. Provided by Federal News Service.
72. 'Mujahedeen to leave Bosnia: Shalikashvili.' Agence France Presse. 3 December 1995.
73. 'Secretary of Defense William Perry addressed the risks that are facing U.S. troops when they reach Bosnia.' Report by John McWethy. ABC World News Tonight. 4 December 1995.
74. Wright, Robin. 'Iranian presence in Bosnia worries US officials.' *The Los Angeles Times*, 5 December 1995, section A, p. 1.
75. State Department Regular Press Briefing. 12 December 1995. Provided by Federal News Service.

76. Diamond, John. 'International News.' The Associated Press. 7 December 1995.
77. 'Christopher warns Bosnians on Moslem activists.' Agence France Presse. 13 December 1995.
78. Schweid, Barry. 'Christopher Rules Out Role for Iran in Arming Bosnia.' The Associated Press. 13 December 1995.
79. Lewthwaite, Gilbert A. and Mark Matthews. 'US wary of Bosnia's Islamic allies; Important fighters don't support peace, may be tough to evict.' *The Baltimore Sun*, 9 December 1995, p. 1A.
80. Bodansky, Yossef. Op. cit.
81. Sisk, Richard. 'Islamic Fighters Vow to Exit.' *Daily News* (New York), 10 December 1995, p. 18.
82. Pyes, Craig with Josh Meyers and William Rempel. 'Bosnia Seen as Hospitable Base and Sanctuary for Terrorists.' *Los Angeles Times*, 7 October 2001.
83. State Department Regular Press Briefing. 7 December 1995. Provided by Federal News Service.
84. 'Retired Major General Lewis MacKenzie, Former UN Commander in Sarajevo, discusses the situation in Bosnia.' CBS This Morning with Paula Zahn. 4 December 1995.
85. O'Connor, Mike. '5 Islamic Soldiers Die in Shootout With Croats.' *The New York Times*, 16 December 1995, p. 6.
86. O'Connor, Mike. Ibid.
87. 'Under the Shades of Swords.' Op. cit.
88. Nasrawi, Salah. 'Islamic Group Warns Americans Over Conviction of Sheik.' The Associated Press. 3 October 1995.
89. Ghalwash, Mae. 'Sons of Omar Abdel-Rahman.' The Associated Press. 2 October 1995.
90. January 1998 CIA Report on 'International Islamic NGOs' and links to terrorism, p. 10.
91. The Algerian Al-Kifah employee mentioned in the report is most likely a reference to a Fateh Kamel, a senior assistant to Abu el-Ma`ali in Bosnia and a known international terrorist. For more on Fateh Kamel, see Chapter 9: Blowback – The North African Sleeper Cell Network.
92. 'Under the Shades of Swords.' Op. cit.
93. 'Under the Shades of Swords.' Op. cit.
94. 'Under the Shades of Swords.' Op. cit.
95. 'Under the Shades of Swords.' Op. cit.
96. 'Under the Shades of Swords.' Op. cit.
97. 'Under the Shades of Swords.' Op. cit.
98. 'Issa Abdullah Ali (Bosnia).' *Indigo Publications Intelligence Newsletter*, No. 282, 22 February 1996.

99. Tracey, Patrick. 'Taking a Powder.' *City Paper* (Washington DC), 29 June 2001.

100. 'Issa Abdullah Ali (Bosnia).' Op. cit.

101. Rice-Oxley, Mark. 'Islamic maverick toying with US forces in Bosnia: soldiers.' Agence France Presse. 10 February 1996.

102. 'NATO forces warned of US extremist in Bosnia.' *The New York Times*, 23 January 1996.

103. Schweid, Barry. Op. cit.

104. 'Mujahedin leaving Bosnia, US says.' Deutsche Presse-Agentur. 14 December 1995.

105. Cerkez, Aida. 'Local Officials, U.N. Report Islamic Fighters Trickling Out.' The Associated Press. 15 December 1995.

106. Jean-Louis Bruguiere and Jean-Francois Ricard. Op. cit.

107. Salah, Muhammad. 'Egypt: members of Islamic Group, Jihad organization headed for Chechnya.' *Al-Hayat* (London), 29 March 1996.

108. 'Under the Shades of Swords.' Op. cit.

109. 'Under the Shades of Swords.' Op. cit.

110. 'Under the Shades of Swords.' Op. cit.

111. 'Khattab Martyred but the Jihad Continues.' http://www.azzam.com. 2 May 2002.

112. 'Under the Shades of Swords.' Op. cit.

113. 'Under the Shades of Swords.' Op. cit.

114. 'Under the Shades of Swords.' Op. cit.

115. 'One dead as Mujahedeen clash with Bosnian Croats.' Agence France Presse. 14 December 1995.

116. Pomfret, John. 'Bosnian Officials Involved in Arms Trade Tied to Radical States.' *The Washington Post*, 22 September 1996, p. A26.

117. 'Under the Shades of Swords.' Op. cit.

118. 'Five mujahidin killed in clash with Bosnian Croats in central Bosnia.' Croatian TV satellite broadcast in Serbo-Croat language in Zagreb, 14 December 1995, 18.30 GMT.

119. 'Izetbegovic promises to disband Moslem volunteer units in Bosnia.' Agence France Presse. 14 December 1995.

120. 'Bosnia at risk from cruel war of revenge.' *The Evening Standard* (London), 19 December 1995, p. 16.

121. Gertz, Bill. 'Mujahideen appear to be pulling out, as accord requires; Wary GIs to monitor exit, Perry says.' *The Washington Times*, 21 December 1995, p. A11.

122. Hranjski, Hrvoje. 'International news.' Associated Press. 20 December 1995.

123. Bellamy, Christopher. 'Nato ready to keep the peace with an iron fist.' *The Independent* (London), 24 December 1995, p. 9.

124. Agence France Presse. 28 December 1995.
125. Bodansky, Yossef. Op. cit.
126. Bodansky, Yossef. Op. cit.
127. Bodansky, Yossef. Op. cit.
128. 'NATO to dispatch further flights to Tuzla: spokesman.' Agence France Presse. 22 December 1995.
129. Cohen, Roger. 'Foreign Islamic Militants Strain Bosnian Alliance.' *The New York Times*, 18 February 1995, section 1, p. 3.
130. *Al-Thilal.* Published by the Central Information News Agency Network and the Global Relief Foundation. January 1996.
131. Office of Foreign Assets Control (OFAC) Bulletins. Subject: Benevolence International Foundation, Inc. and Global Relief Foundation, Inc.' 14 December 2001.
132. Bodansky, Yossef. Op. cit.
133. 'Last of Islamic Mojahedin Troops Bow out.' *Guardian* (London), 1 February 1996, p. 10.
134. Spolar, Christine. 'NATO Finds Arms Cache Near Sarajevo; Islamic Volunteers Apparently Detained.' *The Washington Post*, 16 February 1996, p. A24.
135. Op. cit.
136. 'NATO Raid on Training Camp Uncovers Flagrant Violations of Dayton Accord.' Report by Bob Simon. CBS Evening News. 16 February 1996.
137. Bodansky, Yossef. Op. cit.
138. 'Washington asks for explanations of Bosnian training camp.' Agence France Presse. 16 February 1996.
139. 'US repeats calls for mujahedin to leave Bosnia.' Deutsche Presse-Agentur. 26 March 1996.
140. 'Iranian training camp was 'big mistake': Izetbegovic.' Agence France Presse. 30 March 1996.
141. Martin, Harriet. 'Europe: Bosnia yields to US over ties with Iran.' *The Financial Times* (London), 4 April 1996, p. 2.
142. 'New 'Mujahideen' camp raided in Bosnia: NATO source.' Agence France Presse. 21 March 1996.
143. Smith, Jeffrey. 'A Bosnian Village's Terrorist Ties; Links to U.S. Bomb Plot Arouse Concerns about Enclave of Islamic Guerillas.' *The Washington Post*, 11 March 2000, p. A1.
144. Smucker, Philip. 'Foreign "holy warriors" in Bosnia remain for fellow Muslims' sake.' *The Washington Times*, 17 February 1996, p. A8.
145. Bodansky, Yossef. Op. cit.
146. Interview with Shaykh Abu Hamza al-Masri at the Finsbury Park Mosque, 28 June 2002.
147. Smucker, Philip. Op. cit.

148. 'Mujaheddin Presence; President says some mujaheddin veterans remain but no Iranian military.' Radio Bosnia-Hercegovina in Serbo-Croat language, in Sarajevo. 25 March 1996, 18.00 GMT.

149. 'Mujahedeen still in Bosnia and they must go: IFOR.' Agence France Presse. 26 March 1996.

Blowback – The North African
Sleeper Cell Network

[The Jews and Christians] are the ones that are fighting every Muslim resurrection in the whole world, they act to spread prostitution, usury, and other kinds of corruption all over the land. Oh, Muslims everywhere! Cut the transportation of their countries, tear it apart, destroy their economy, burn their companies, eliminate their interests, sink their ships, shoot down their planes, kill them on the sea, air, or land. Kill them when you find them, take them and encircle them, paralyze their every post. Kill those infidels . . . Allah will torment by your hands those who wish to kill you; Allah will put shame upon them, he will blow wind in the chests of the believers and show the anger of their hearts.

Shaykh Omar Abdel Rahman, writing from an American prison cell.

The 1993 World Trade Center attack and the Paris metro bombings had proved the particular strength of the Al-Qaida-linked North African *mujahideen* organizations such as Al-Gama`at Al-Islamiyya and the GIA. The Egyptian and Algerian Islamic militants gained a distinct reputation among their comrades for employing fanatic methods and fielding a relatively impressive international sleeper cell network. During the Bosnian civil war, an unusually large number of foreign Muslim fighters claimed an affiliation with these Maghribi groups, including *jihad* training camp managers, frontline unit commanders, elite bodyguards, and volunteers for suicide missions. Conversely, in Afghanistan, Usama Bin Laden surrounded himself with predominantly Egyptian advisors and appointed them to senior positions in Al-Qaida – even to head its prestigious military committee. In February 1998, Bin Laden publicly formalized his partnership with Al-Gama`at and Al-Jihad during the inauguration of the World Islamic Front Against Jews and Crusaders. The Egyptian extremists eagerly signed on to Bin Laden's edict advocating the murder of American civilians as an individual religious duty for every Muslim.

For the radical north African *mujahideen* fighters educated and headquartered in the Balkans, the campaign of terror targeting France, the UK, Italy, and the United States had already been initiated years earlier. Perhaps the final warning of this campaign surfaced in early May 1996 when an Egyptian veteran of the

Bosnian war, known as Salim al-Korshani, issued a direct threat on behalf of Al-Gama`at Al-Islamiyya in Croatian newspapers. Al-Korshani had settled down after the Bosnian war ended, married a Bosnian woman, and was legally living as a Bosnian citizen. However, he was also identifying himself as the commander of the 'Bosnian Islamic Jihad,' the regional military branch of Al-Gama`at Al-Islamiyya, comprised primarily of Arab-Afghan veteran commanders and fanatical European Muslim adherents. Al-Korshani stressed that European 'Bosniak' veterans were being specifically trained to return to their homelands and infiltrate Western society. He threatened:

> Very soon the world will hear their message. They are trained for kidnapping, murder and suicide missions . . . We'll attack the invader [UN peacekeepers] and their allies [NATO troops] until we liberate our country [Bosnia]. [We] will do the same things that [our] brothers in Lebanon and Palestine do. What is happening in Bosnia-Herzegovina today, reminds me of Kuwait. Americans came to liberate, but stayed on. NATO . . . want[s] to form bases in Bosnia. We won't allow that. With our brother Bosniaks, we'll attack them everywhere . . . My message to Croatia is to release Abu Talal [al-Qasimy] or give us information on him before it is too late. Time will show this is not an idle threat.[1]

The Arab-Afghan wave of terror directed from central Bosnia starting in 1996 bore the distinct characteristics of traditional Al-Qaida operations, including through the use of Islamic charitable front groups. In this case, the notorious Al-Kifah Refugee Center office in Zagreb served as the initial rendezvous point for many of the eventual conspirators. As previously discussed, the Al-Kifah office in Zagreb was run a collection of unusual employees, mostly of Algerian origin – including a hardened Arab-Afghan veteran named Fateh Kamel (also known as 'Mustapha the Terrorist,' 'El Fateh'). Kamel, who had lived in Canada since 1988, was a sadistic genius with a dangerous propensity for violence. He was born on 14 March 1960, in El Harrach, Algeria, and spent a good part of his life in a quarter of the capital Algiers.[2] His slick, polished exterior boasted a professionalism that was matched only by his pure coldbloodedness.

At the twilight of the Afghan anti-communist *jihad*, between 1990–1, Kamel was trained in the Hindu Kush at Arab-Afghan military camps financed and managed by Usama Bin Laden. This was a key organizing period for Usama Bin Laden, and a significant number of those trained at the 'terror university' at this time later became prominent figures in the senior hierarchy of Al-Qaida. French intelligence determined that Kamel and his associates had 'multiple links' with 'diverse Islamic terrorist organizations around the world, and particularly in Bosnia, in Pakistan, in Germany, and in London.'[3] Kamel was not permanently based in the Balkans, but rather would travel frequently across the world in order to traffick in illegal passports and other documents, and to overall maintain the widespread terrorist network loyal to Anwar Shaaban of Al-Gama`at Al-Islamiyya and Abu el-Ma`ali of the Algerian Armed Islamic Group. Between 1994 and 1997, Fateh Kamel moved constantly between (at least) Milan, Montreal, Paris, Hamburg, Frankfurt, Zagreb, Bosnia, Copenhagen, Austria, Slovenia, Freibourg (Germany), Morocco, Ancone (Italy), Istanbul, Belgium, and Amsterdam.[4]

Kamel first came to the attention of Italian authorities while encouraging attendees at Anwar Shaaban's Islamic Cultural Institute in Milan to join the *mujahideen* in Bosnia. By 1995, according to French intelligence, Kateebat al-Mujahideen in Bosnia was headed politically by Anwar Shaaban, seconded militarily by Abu el-Ma`ali, and in the third position was Fateh Kamel, in charge of the battalion's 'logistical matters' (a role that consisted mostly of coordinating the transfer of weapons, new recruits, and false documents to and from the Arab headquarters in Zenica).[5] Investigators reviewing the phone records of lines serving the ICI between 1994 and 1995 found evidence of regular contacts between the triumvirate of Abu el-Ma`ali, Anwar Shaaban, and Fateh Kamel.[6]

Kamel was recorded on one occasion by Italian intelligence, discussing potential terror attacks and bragging to his henchmen, 'I do not fear death . . . because the jihad is the jihad, and to kill is easy for me.'[7] He hated the very society he lived in and cynically mocked Western attitudes towards Muslims: 'And you know, the people [here] imagine a Muslim on the back of a camel, four wives behind him and the bombs that explode . . . terrorists, terrorists, terrorists.'[8] In another communications intercept in 1996, just after the end of the Bosnian war, Kamel confided in his terrorist partners: 'I prefer to die than go to jail. I almost lost my wife. I am 36 years old with a son four and a half months old. My wife is playing with him and me, I am here. I am almost a soldier.'[9]

The evidence in Kamel's address book alone seems to confirm his role as a key liaison and coordinator between assorted European sleeper cell terrorist networks and senior Al-Qaida commanders based in Bosnia and Afghanistan. Among other numbers, Fateh Kamel had several contacts for senior Algerian terrorist leaders in the United Kingdom affiliated with both the GIA and its perceived splinter successor group,[10] the Algerian Salafist Group for Da'wa ['the Islamic Call'] and Combat (GSPC).[11]

Fateh Kamel drew particularly close to loose network of units of North African immigrants and European converts to Islam who had come to aid the *mujahideen* during the early stages of the Bosnian war. For all intense and purposes, he became their handler, giving assistance and issuing orders on behalf of Anwar Shaaban and Abu el-Ma`ali, the two most senior European Al-Qaida leaders still active in Bosnia in the wake of Abu Talal al-Qasimy's untimely abduction. Over a nine-month period in 1996, Kamel suddenly began activating a number of his 'Bosniak' terror units implanted in Europe at the apparent behest of Abu el-Ma`ali and other senior representatives of the GIA and Al-Gama`at Al-Islamiyya, instructing them to prepare for new *jihad* operations to take place inside France and Italy.

Between 6 and 10 August 1996, Fateh Kamel stayed at the Milan apartment of two GIA supporters, including Rachid Fettar, who had close ties to the master-minds of the 1995 Paris metro bombing spree. Fettar was well-placed in the GIA leadership hierarchy, considered the 'heir' to the European extremist network established by Safé Bourada, the deputy-in-command of the Algerian terror cell deemed responsible for the metro bombings.[12] Thus, Kamel's visit to Fettar and his companion Youcef Tanout came with a definite purpose: to direct a terror cell in the construction and deployment of more crude gas-canister bombs like those used during the Paris metro campaign. Kamel respected Rachid Fettar as an equal and complained to him that Tanout and the others were too reluctant to produce the explosives without elaborate and time-consuming covert pro-cedures. 'I insisted as much as I could, but there was nothing I could do. In France, we can make [the bombs], even if their destination is France. You know very well that in France, I have no problems; I return and I leave when I want, clandestinely.'[13]

In a discussion with the more amateurish Youcef Tanout, Kamel coldly asked, 'What are you afraid of? That everything will explode in your house? Tell me at least if Mahmoud has gotten the gas canister.' Tanout meekly related to Kamel how one of his fellow cell members had sought the shelter and anonymity of a nearby deep forest in order to fabricate the required bombs. He admitted to Kamel, 'I feel no shame in telling you that I am extremely afraid.' Evidently, Tanout's hesitant concerns were well founded; on 7 November 1996, both himself and Fettar were arrested and their Milan apartment was searched by experienced Italian counter-terrorism investigators. They discovered two 400 g gas canisters, five remote-control transmitters, thirty-eight metallic cylinders, and other bomb-making materials.[14] Though this Milan cell never managed to carry out a major terrorist act, it provided ominous clues as to what was to develop in Italy and nearby France over the coming months.

The second 'Bosniak' terror cell allegedly activated by Fateh Kamel met with arguably more success. This unit was based in the Roubaix-Lille region of north-eastern France, and was led by two native Frenchmen who had fought with the foreign *mujahideen* in Bosnia: Lionel Dumont (also known as Abu Hamza) and Christophe Caze (also known as Abu Waleed). According to French judicial officials, Abu el-Ma`ali 'exerted a lot of influence' on both Dumont and Caze 'which led them to commit . . . violent actions under the cover of Islam.'[15]

Dumont grew up in a family with a Christian background, and studied history in hopes of becoming a journalist. In 1992, he suddenly dropped out of his French university to volunteer for mandatory French army service, resulting in a stint as a UN peacekeeper in Somalia. There, he was a firsthand witness to the collapse of the international humanitarian effort and the United States military debacle in Mogadishu. He brooded in a local church bulletin: 'The sight of such poverty strangles me.' He was shaken by what he had seen in Africa, and was unsuccessful in finding any employment at home when he returned to France.

The prolonged experience in East Africa had also radically changed Dumont. He became a convert to fundamentalist Islam, who refused to consume alcohol or pork and insisted that his friends call him 'Abu Hamza.' His sister attempted to explain the cryptic personality of Dumont: 'He is a sincere person . . . Anyone who hasn't been in a war can't imagine what derailed him.'[16] Determined to act as an 'armed humanitarian' on behalf of Islam, Dumont travelled to Bosnia and, at the end of 1993, volunteered as a aid convoy driver for the Al-Kifah Refugee Center in Zagreb, known to be affiliated at that time with a group of 'militant Algerians.'[17]

Dumont bonded closely with one of the men he met there: Christophe Caze, a French medical student who was likewise an extremist convert to Islam. Caze had first gone to Bosnia to offer his services to the *mujahideen* near the end of 1992.[18] In Zenica, he worked in the local hospital where other Arab fundamentalist volunteers gathered. It was the same hospital where Fateh Kamel later spent time recuperating from a battlefield wound to his foot.[19] By most accounts, Caze also participated in military actions and was trained in advanced guerrilla warfare skills at the battalion's headquarters at the Vatrostalno building. His combat experiences pushed him further along the path of radical Islam and its calls for the shedding of blood.[20] During this time, Caze fell under the influence of two Islamist religio-political ideologues who have formed an integral part of the overseas Al-Qaida terrorist network: Abu el-Ma`ali and Shaykh Abu Hamza al-Masri (also known as Mustafa Kamel, 'Le Manchot').[21]

Abu Hamza al-Masri is an exiled fundamentalist dissident originally from Alexandria, Egypt now living in London. From the UK, he operates an organization known as the 'Supporters of Shariah' (SOS), (also known as Ansar al-Shareeah), which admitted on its former Web site to supporting 'the Mujahideen . . . in, Afghanistan, Bosnia, Kashmir, etc.,' including recruiting and aiding 'front line soldiers.'[22] During the mid-1990s, Abu Hamza maintained a close relationship with the GIA terrorist network in Europe, and helped them by coordinating fundraising efforts and publishing their *Al-Ansaar Newsletter*.[23] Until recently, Abu Hamza was also the firebrand cleric at the unassuming but notorious Finsbury Park Mosque in northeast London. He estimated to me that '1,200 people usually come every week [to the mosque]. If it's too difficult or raining sometimes 900 people. On the festivals we have 6,000 people.'[24]

A walk through the mosque seemed to confirm his assessment. On a given Friday, hundreds of young men, including many European and American converts, climb the building's stairwells to meet and absorb the wisdom of their eccentric leader. This is a subject of some amusement to the bearded cleric; when asked if visitors from the United States often come and visit him, he chuckled and responded: 'Oh absolutely. But most of them are journalists. They all come, journalists. [Also] American converts, many American converts from the army converted to Islam, many.'[25] In the immediate wake of the 11 September suicide hijackings, Abu Hamza offered a sermon titled 'The World Trade Series: The Believers vs. the [Infidelity] of America.'[26] To a rapt audience, he thundered: 'Terrorism is a tool for everybody to get his way. And it has also been a tool for Islam . . . It is a tool, it is a weapon. Allah said, to terrorize the enemies of Allah and your enemies, it is a weapon, and it is a very effective weapon. And if you leave this weapon, then Allah's destruction and wrath will be upon you.'[27] He also has called Usama Bin Laden a 'victim from the American policies' and a 'good-hearted person.'[28]

European intelligence agencies have correspondingly concluded that Abu Hamza is an integral recruiter and financier of the north African sleeper cell network and a major figure in the overall European 'foreign legion' of Al-Qaida. Abu Hamza's own son and godson, were convicted in 1999 in a Yemeni court for taking part in an attempted bombing conspiracy against 'un-Islamic' targets in that country.[29] Also that year, the militant cleric was profiled in a British documentary by reporter Deborah Davies. One of his sermons cited in the documentary was a call for Muslims to 'get training' in order to 'get the [infidel] and crush his head in your arms, so you can wring his throat, so you can whip his intestines out. That's why you are doing training . . . to rip the people to pieces. Forget wasting a bullet on them . . . cut them in half!'[30]

In the same video, Abu Hamza is shown at a conference explaining a diagram for the 'Muslim Anti-Aircraft Net,' a design for a floating net laced with mines intended to randomly entrap and destroy civilian passenger aircraft in Great Britain and the United States.[30] In a later press release about the conference, SOS representatives explained that the anti-aircraft grid was

> designed by our Brothers in Afghanistan. These nets will increase the hazard and risk to flying, and are a response to the destructive inventions of the infidel West . . . These nets, if mass produced, can cost less than £10, and are undetected by radar. They can be launched from any point, and move to anywhere in the world. We urge all brothers and sisters to also begin thinking of designs and techniques such as these, because the time for talking has long since passed.[32]

The eccentric Abu Hamza received his nickname 'Le Manchot' from injuries that have left him, among other things, with no hands and an austere metal hook in their place. Although the bearded cleric does not like discussing how those wounds occurred, French intelligence concluded that they were the result of his handling explosives in Afghanistan.

Despite his quite noticeable infirmities, Abu Hamza also spent time in Bosnia with the Arab *mujahideen* brigade, where he indoctrinated young students of *jihad* including Christophe Caze. Abu Hamza admits helping the Arab-Afghan network in Europe 'rebuild the [*mujahideen*] battalion' in Bosnia and in collecting 'their donations and this and that. I was trying to redraw the things for them.'[33] Caze was entirely devoted to Abu Hamza, who he considered to be a 'great figure' in modern Islam. Unfortunately, Caze's relationship with Abu Hamza was not appreciated by everyone. According to Lionel Dumont, Christopher Caze was also very close to Abu el-Ma'ali, and the latter grew jealous of Abu Hamza's popularity.[34] Eventually, the Algerian considered the Finsbury Park cleric to be enough of an unwanted competitor 'to the point of inviting him to leave the "Moujahiddin Battalion" after only a few months.'[35]

Nevertheless, even after Abu Hamza's abrupt departure for London, Caze remained in contact with him and considered him as his personal 'religious guide.'[36] And though the London-based Imam was no doubt insulted by the petty behavior of Abu el-Ma'ali, he does not appear to have held a grudge. He does not speak of the incident publicly, only commenting that, despite his interest in helping the *mujahideen*, he 'couldn't actually stay for long' in Bosnia.[37] Indeed, Abu Hamza continued to encourage Caze's participation in terror plots allegedly conceived by Abu el-Ma'ali, even by issuing supporting *fatwahs*. Interviewed by French investigators in London, Abu Hamza admitted his relationship with Caze, including meetings with him on the eve of two trips made by the latter to Bosnia in 1995 and 1996.[38] Under the constant influence of Abu Hamza and Abu el-Ma'ali, Dumont and Caze were introduced to a life of blood sacrifice and were 'plunged into violence.'[39]

Christophe Caze came home to France a changed man when his tour of duty with the *mujahideen* ended in the early months of 1993. He would incessantly speak of his combat experiences and try to convince his friends to leave their 'worldly' lives and join the 'heroic' *jihad* in Bosnia.[40] Caze's return to Western society had clearly not been a step towards resuming his mundane past life as a medical student. Rather, as a result of his training in Bosnia, he was now dead-set on a path to construct a network of like-minded Muslim militants in his locality (Roubaix) in immediate preparation for military operations aimed at 'infidel' targets in France.

The planning for those operations began as early as the summer of 1995. In June, less than two months prior to the string of GIA metro bombings, Lionel Dumont contacted Abderahman Cheffah, a sympathetic Muslim fundamentalist, to warn him of his imminent arrival in Paris. Dumont told Cheffah that the purpose of his visit was to establish local 'contacts' in the Paris area. Cheffah told investigators that in his mind, there was never any question that, if men like Dumont or Caze with known GIA connections were being brought in, definite plans had already been finalized for terrorist 'actions' on French territory.[41] It is unclear what, if any, role Dumont may have played in the first GIA terror campaign during the summer of 1995. Nevertheless, following his Paris visit, Dumont returned to Zenica to confer with his superiors among the *mujahideen.*

One day after the Dayton Accords were signed, Dumont again left Bosnia bound for France. He and Caze, now reunited, quickly began to formulate a plan to commit a series of violent armed robberies in France. The plot would succeed in inspiring terror among the French and any financial proceeds would be further donated to help support the GIA in Algeria. To obtain the necessary heavy weapons, Dumont and Caze relied on the hidden stockpiles in Bosnia presided over by Abu el-Ma`ali. The latter was 'protected' by Bosnian President Izetbegovic and was able to amass a fearsome armory even after the signing of the Dayton Accords, including most notably 'a vast panoply of Strella [shoulder-launched, surface-to-air] missiles.'[42] Modern Western warplanes were easily able to evade the antiquated Soviet-built SA-7 Strella, but slower moving aircraft (like helicopters and commercial jetliners) were still vulnerable prey for the device. Caze and Dumont knew that with their close relationship to Abu el-Ma`ali, it would be easy to smuggle a powerful arsenal back to France with them.[43]

Though officials in Washington DC were claiming that the *mujahideen* were all leaving Bosnia, Caze and Dumont prepared to re-enter the Balkans to acquire the necessary 'equipment' for their planned rampage. Once in Bosnia, the two would amass a formidable collection of AK-47s, pistols, grenades, RPGs, and more. These men were preparing themselves for much more than a mere life of crime – they were mobilizing to take part in a larger suicidal holy war. Intriguingly, just as Caze and Dumont were assembling to travel to Zenica, Fateh Kamel was busy organizing the parallel transfer of new *jihad* recruits from Europe to Bosnia, in concert with Anwar Shaaban and Abu el-Ma`ali.[44]

The two errant Frenchmen returned home from their arms-trafficking trip in December 1995, shortly after the death of Anwar Shaaban. In Roubaix, a quiet town in northeastern France, Caze began aggressively recruiting among his friends for volunteers to help in the 'struggle.' With his plan in mind, Caze desperately urged them to help him '"prolong" the Jihad on French territory.'[45] These generalizations encapsulated a more specific strategy to commit a 'particularly violent' crime spree, possessing no 'qualms whatsoever about shooting' innocent bystanders.[46] Simultaneously, between December and January, Caze spoke with Abu el-Ma`ali numerous times at the telephone number of the *mujahideen* 'General Command' in Zenica.[47]

Within a month, the 'Roubaix Group,' more resembling a gang of thugs than a terrorist cell, had formed under the cell leadership of Lionel Dumont. Their hideout at 59 Rue Henri Carette was a dreary two-story house located in the Alma ghetto of central Roubaix, nicknamed 'the Casbah.'[48] The neighborhood was plagued by drugs and crime, and was widely considered to be a 'no-go area' for police.[49] Thus, it was undeniably ideal for the purposes of the Roubaix gang. In a meeting with

Mouloud Boughelane (also known as Carlo Mazzoni) and other loyal recruits, Dumont asked members of the cell if they were 'ready to participate in armed actions on French territory.' The men dutifully responded that they were ready to assist as necessary.[50]

Between January and March, the Roubaix Gang lived up to its, albeit, limited vision and was the prime suspect in at least six holdups of vehicles carrying cash deposits from supermarkets along the French-Belgian border and a botched attack with an RPG on a Brinks armored car. Police were at first baffled, because the trucks carrying the supermarket money were considered low-value targets, especially given the amount of firepower involved. The modus operandi of these criminals was quite distinct and they seemed to be more interested in creating chaos and taking innocent life than actually stealing anything valuable.[51] In one incident, Caze and his men shot and killed a French Muslim who did not hand over the keys to his prized Mercedes-Benz fast enough. In total, for all their hard work, the gang only netted about $10,000 total – not a very impressive take for a risky career robbing armored cars.[52]

The Roubaix conspirators, including Dumont and Caze, unwisely travelled openly around in their vehicles, flaunting their freedom, even as they knew police were eyeing them suspiciously. Indeed, at some point in mid-March, the cell became aware that a number of its members were under direct surveillance by local French police, who considered them the prime suspects in the chain of robberies. Infuriated that the authorities would even dare to pursue them (much like the attitude of the *mujahideen* towards British peacekeepers in Bosnia), the Dumont gang swore that they would punish the meddling of the infidels. On 29 March, a small blast went off in a white Peugeot 205 parked outside police headquarters in the nearby city of Lille, 10 miles southwest of Roubaix. Inside the car, authorities found three 28 pound gas canisters (eerily similar to the devices used by the GIA the summer previous) that had failed to explode when their detonator, a smaller explosive with a simple remote transmitter, was successfully ignited.[53] What really worried the French government was that, two days later, French President Jacques Chirac was scheduled to open a major G-7 international diplomatic summit less than 200 m away from the ill-fated Peugeot.

Police quickly suspected the inhabitants of 59 Henri Carette, especially after two suspected members of the Roubaix gang (identified as the owners of the car) were witnessed driving it in the Lille area on the day of the bombing.[54] The men chose to deliver the weapon themselves and made remarkably little effort to conceal their tracks, especially in light of their supposed 'elite military training' in Bosnia. Police called the failed car bombing a 'provocation' – this was a deliberate challenge to authorities from an egotistical crew of dangerous hoodlums.[55] It was almost as if Dumont and Caze were daring the police to try and fight it out with them; 'They acted out of pure hatred of cops,' stated judicial policeman Bernard Gravet in the *Voix du Nord* newspaper.[56]

If this was indeed a dare, than it was graciously accepted by the French police, who did not take being targeted lightly. The *mujahideen* hideout was already under scrutiny stemming from the robberies, and now police carefully surrounded the house with snipers and GIGN counter-terrorist commandos. The fanatics inside opened fire first, unloading the heart of their in-house armory of between six and eight AK-47 assault rifles, hand grenades, boxes of ammunition, and other equipment.[57] The firefight became so fierce that French officials were forced to evacuate the entire neighborhood. The GIGN commandos eventually attempted to storm the house amid a hail of gunfire, wounding two policemen.[58] Either as a deliberate act of arson by the suicidal terrorists or simply as the result of the sheer number of bullets and grenades flying through the walls, the sagging house finally burst into flames. The roof and the upper floor of the structure caved in and collapsed on top of its stubbornly resisting occupants.[59] Investigators found three very badly charred bodies inside: two Moroccans, Rachid Souindi and Said el-Laihar; and an Algerian, Teli bel Hachem.[60] They also came across an impressive collection of Islamic fundamentalist magazines, including several tied to radical Algerian terrorist groups, in the remains of the house.[61]

Simultaneously, in the suburbs of Lille, police attempted to separately arrest Omar Zemmiri and Christophe Caze by constructing a roadblock. The two opened fire on authorities and forced their way through the barricade in a stolen car. Caze aimed to flee France, and took the E17 motorway towards the Belgian border. Police closed in and finally intercepted the vehicle on the E17 bridge between Mouscron, France and Kortrijk (Courtrai), Belgium. Motorists fled in panic as Caze and Zemmiri fiercely battled with their pursuers and bullets whizzed across the bridge.[62] Caze was unceremoniously killed in the crossfire, but Zemmiri managed to escape the highway melée. He fled across the Belgian border on foot, entering a posh suburban area of Kortrijk.[63] Zemmiri broke into the house of a local dentist and held his wife and her housecleaner hostage. Belgian police surrounded the house with gendarmes and snipers, determined to avoid any further security breaches.[64] Elite special units burst into the home after a seven hour siege and disarmed Zemmiri before any further violence could occur.[65] More magazines, weapons and grenades, were found in the car alongside the limp body of Christophe Caze.[66]

It did not take long for police to discover that the Roubaix Group had strong connections to the GIA and Al-Gama`at Al-Islamiyya, as particularly evidenced by the involvement of foreign *mujahideen* veterans from the Bosnian war. In Caze's electronic address book, investigators found extensive contact information for both Abu el-Ma`ali and Fateh Kamel.[67] The address book also contained telephone numbers for another alleged member of the Roubaix Group, master document forger Zohair Choulah – a commander of the Bosnian *mujahideen* and key associate of Fateh Kamel deemed 'officially unwelcome' in France since 1995. Choulah's alias 'Abdul Barr' was printed in Caze's organizer along with a corresponding Sarajevo number linked to alleged members of Al-Gama`at Al-Islamiyya.[68]

State investigators led primarily by Judge Jean-Louis Bruguière were already familiar with the name of Caze's fugitive accomplice Omar Zemmiri. On 25 January 1996, Hocine Senoussaoui (also known as Hassine Ben Snoussi), a Tunisian-born resident of Bosnia, was detained in Zagreb airport *en route* to Rome after being caught attempting to use a fraudulent French passport in the name of Zemmiri. Previously, Senoussaoui had been observed by Italian intelligence as a frequent visitor to the Islamic Cultural Institute in Milan and was considered 'close to the GIA and the [Egyptian] Gama`at Islamiyya.' Senoussaoui was also reputedly working at the Al-Kifah Refugee Center in Zagreb alongside Fateh Kamel.[69] In Senoussaoui's address book, investigators predictably discovered several contact numbers for Abu el-Ma`ali's 'communications centre' in Zenica.[70] A high-ranking French police official admitted that they were studying the Afghano-Bosniak phenomenon very closely: 'It was enough here that one person served in Bosnia. This sort of thing will repeat itself.'[71]

Two central figures in the Roubaix Gang, Lionel Dumont and Mouloud Boughelane, were still on the run from police. From Paris, they fled to the Italian province of Bologna. Falsified passports with Dumont and Boughelane's photos were later found at the offices of a terror suspect in Bologna.[72] With intelligence and law enforcement agencies still on their heels, the two soon made their way across the Adriatic Sea and 'disappeared' into newly-established *mujahideen* settlements in central Bosnia. Dumont assumed the name 'Abu Hamza' and married a local 17-year-old Bosnian Muslim girl. In this environment, he was well protected and absolutely indistinguishable from his nearby surroundings.[73]

The shameless Dumont-Boughelane duo once again resumed their petty thievery under the cover of *jihad*. In central Bosnia, they teamed up with several other veterans of the foreign *mujahideen* brigade including Biniam Zefferini (also known as Abu Badr, Abdullah Badr), originally from Djibouti. Like Christophe Caze, Zefferini was very close to Shaykh Abu Hamza al-Masri and had stayed with him for an extended period in London in early 1996. When Zefferini mentioned to the cleric that he was planning on returning to Bosnia, Abu Hamza gave him 'many hundreds of pounds Sterling' to give to Christophe Caze. Abu Hamza also asked Zefferini to procure in Bosnia a number of pistols with silencers, which he was instructed to bring back with him during a future visit to London.[74]

Only a few months after their arrival in Bosnia, the re-formed Dumont *mujahideen* gang was already planning new Roubaix-style military operations, this time inside Bosnia. On 15 February 1997, Lionel Dumont, Mouloud Boughelane, and Biniam Zefferini attempted to holdup the 'Autotech' gas station in Raspotocje, near

Zenica.[75] The operation went haywire, and the trigger-happy militants shot and killed a Bosnian policeman, Rusmir Dizdar, who happened by chance on to the robbery.[76] In the midst of the shootout, Boughelane was arrested, but Dumont and Zefferini were able to escape. Bosnian law-enforcement authorities issued arrest warrants and offered a reward of 1,000 German marks for information on the whereabouts of the two Islamic militants.[77] After long interrogation on the subject of his involvement in Islamic terror gangs in France and Bosnia, Boughelane named Abu el-Ma`ali as the overall *Amir* of the Roubaix Group.[78]

While the Bosnians were reticent about forcibly removing the *mujahideen*, this was not the sort of thing they would let pass easily. On 9 March, acting on tips from neighbors and intent upon finding Dumont and Zefferini, elite police units surrounded and burst into an apartment in the Zenica suburb of Mokusnice. The two gang members again chose to battle it out with police, who promptly resorted to tear gas in order to flush them out. A spokesman for the Bosnian Interior Ministry noted: 'They didn't want to surrender, one of them tried to escape.'[79] This time, Zefferini was killed, yet still somehow Dumont survived and was arrested. Two pistols, suspected to have been involved in the 'Autotech' robbery, were found in the apartment, as well as black ski-masks.[80] Bosnian authorities told reporters that Dumont was being held to face possible charges over the bungled holdup and also a series of related 'serious terrorist attacks . . . All this points to the existence of an infiltrated and organized terrorist group charged with destabilizing central Bosnia and achieving other objectives.'[81] The Assistant District Attorney in Zenica, Idriz Katkic, agreed with that assessment: 'We expect a large and complicated case. We have indications that Dumont and [Boughelane] committed a few more crimes, in which one person was killed.'[82]

In July, Dumont and Boughelane were put on trial for masterminding several holdups of service stations and a warehouse in the Zenica area occurring between 19 October 1996 and 15 February 1997 that resulted in the death of at least two people. The other murder happened during a November ambush on a warehouse, in which a night watchman was killed. According to prosecutors in the case, Dumont told police interrogators that he turned to a life of crime at the end of the Bosnian war because 'I need money to live.'[83] Despite their impressive record as members of the *mujahideen*, a fact specially noted by the court in its verdict, they nonetheless received the maximum sentence of 20 years in prison.[84]

But Dumont was not quite finished yet: on 26 May 1999, he and his cellmate, Dzihan Edin, were able to make a daring evening escape from prison by cutting through the bars of a kitchen window.[85] Days later, Edin was recaptured in Sarajevo and confessed that Dumont had fled to Bosnian Serb-controlled territory immediately after their joint escape.[86] French counterterrorism investigators were particularly suspicious about Dumont's escape from the poorly guarded Sarajevo jail. It seemed all too convenient that it had occurred just as they were pushing for

Dumont's extradition to face charges in France stemming from his involvement in the Roubaix gang. Perhaps, the Bosnian government was embarrassed at the prospect of what Dumont might testify to in a French court; namely, that although the overwhelming majority of Bosnian Muslims rejected the fanatical Islamic fundamentalist dogma, senior-level members of the Bosnian government continued to provide covert protection to the Arab *mujahideen*, even after they had committed cold-blooded crimes against innocent Bosnian Muslims themselves.

With the Roubaix cell in tatters by mid-summer 1996, Fateh Kamel was back at work and having long discussions with Abu el-Ma`ali. Telephone calls were made directly or indirectly by Fateh Kamel to Abu el-Ma`ali at the *mujahideen* headquarters in Zenica on 1 July 1996; 8 July 1996; 10 July 1996; 14 July 1996; and 15 July 1996. Kamel also contacted Abu el-Ma`ali at his personal residence in Zenica on 11 July 1996; 12 July 1996; 13 July 1996; 16 July 1996; 17 July 1996; 5 September 1996; and 15 September 1996.[87] In August, the only period of time where there was an absence of calls, Kamel made a sudden key organizational trip across Europe, with significant stops in Germany, Italy, and Bosnia (where he held a personal face-to-face meeting with Abu el-Ma`ali).[88]

At about this time, Mohammed Kaddari (also known as Tahar Jalal), presenting himself as a close friend of Abu el-Ma`ali, had contacted the Islamic Cultural Institute in Milan from a refugee camp in Holland, where they were processing his demand for political asylum. Following a discussion between Fateh Kamel and Abu el-Ma`ali, the former was entrusted to visit and provide aid to the stranded Kaddari in the Netherlands. Approximately a year later, on 12 May 1997, Mohammed Kaddari was stopped in Sydney, Australia, carrying a valid but falsified Italian passport, belonging to a group of 6,000 passports stolen in Naples in 1996. His address book contained the Montreal telephone number for Karim Said Atmani, a veteran of the Zenica *mujahideen* brigade who was also an assistant to Fateh Kamel in Canada and Bosnia. Following the arrest of Dumont and Boughelane in Bosnia, both Roubaix-cell militants were found carrying passports later proven to belong to the same 1996 lot stolen from Naples.[89]

The robberies committed by Dumont and Boughelane in Bosnia at the warehouse and gas station during the winter of 1996–7 had occurred amidst a rash of similar unexplained thefts, murders, and explosions throughout central Bosnia and neighboring Croatia. In one bizarre episode, Michael Fahey Calvin, an American military instructor working on behalf of a US-based mercenary group for the Bosnian government, was attacked in a suburb of Zenica on 20 October 1997. A month earlier, on 18 September a Volkswagen Golf, packed with 80 kg of mixed explosives (including anti-tank mines) strapped to a timer, exploded in the western district of Mostar, Croatia. The attack, which took place in the vicinity of the central police building, caused extensive damage and injured about fifty people, twenty-three seriously.[90]

Within months, Bosnian investigators issued arrest warrants for nineteen men wanted in connection with the Mostar bombing and several other incidents in the Zenica area. The list of suspects included the infamous Saudi-Bosniak veteran commander Abu Sulaiman al-Makki, accused of having provided secret refuge and safety to the fugitives; Karray Kamel bin Ali (also known as Abu Hamza, 'Omar the Tunisian'), a thirty-something North African *mujahideen* veteran; Ahmed Zuhair (also known as Abu Handala, Abu Hanzala), a Saudi fighter during the Bosnian war who had been granted local citizenship; Saber Lahmar, an Algerian Arabic-language teacher in his mid-thirties working with the Saudi High Commission for Relief; Ali Ahmed Ali Hamad (also known as Ali Hamed Ubeid, Abu Ubaidah al-Bahraini), a former worker at the Saudi High Commission who had been tasked with 'the distribution . . . of books;' Nabil Ali al-Hil (also known as 'Abu Yemen,' Saleh Nedal); Omar Khalil (also known as Abu Abdullah); Ali Said Baawara (also known as Abu Hudhaifa); and a number of local Bosnian volunteers.[91] After making a number of detentions and searches, in a public statement, the BiH federal prosecutor's office announced the confiscation of

> 24 rifles, 10 pistols, 30 hand bombs, four hand grenade launchers, three hand rocket launchers, three machine-guns, 15 grenades, five hand grenades, 95 antitank mines (PT-6, PT-1, PT-3 and PT-4), one container with a rocket for rocket launcher, more than seven thousand pieces of ammunition of various calibres, 100 metres of slow-burning fuse with initial caps and much more.

Two sets of men among the nineteen were also considered suspects in an abortive robbery of the battered Franciscan monastery in Guca Gora and of wiring explosives in an attempt to blow up the Catholic church in the village of Puticevo. According to the federal prosecutor's office: 'Before carrying out their terrorist acts, the suspects observed the targets of their attacks for days, which indicates that they are an organized group which prepared and committed classic terrorist acts.'[92]

One of the men sought by Bosnian authorities, Karray Kamel bin Ali, was a former member of an Arab *jihad* unit based in the traumatized town of Guca Gora. French intelligence uncovered clear evidence that Karray Kamel was in frequent close communication with Fateh Kamel and his military *Amir*, Abu el-Ma`ali.[93] Karray first received Bosnian citizenship in 1994, and was quickly shielded after the war by the Bosnian government, even after he committed crimes against native locals. A former Bosnian *mujahid* later put on trial for aiding Karray Kamel, insisted that the local police knew where he was, and that they were simply not eager to find him. 'He was in Kokici and he lived without hiding. Everybody knew he was up there. Since he has been in Bosnia since 1992 a large number of people knew him. He was in Kokici near Jajce, Travnik, Zenica and near Zavidovici and I'd like to see that proof of this is presented . . . The neighbors knew and the majority of the refugees there knew too.'[94]

After an extensive investigation, Bosnian authorities determined that Karray was responsible for the 1997 murder of Hisham Diab (also known as Abdul Walid), a supposed Shi'ite religious activist, in front of the Balkan Islamic Centre in Zenica, with nine bullets fired from an automatic rifle.[95] Lionel Dumont and Mouloud Boughelane both later told investigators that Diab was assassinated by Karray Kamel Bin Ali on the specific orders of Abu el-Ma`ali at the Zenica *mujahideen* command center.[96] Thus ended any lingering speculation that the Arab-Afghan militants in Bosnia were adherents of a revolutionary Shi`ite ideology imported from Iran. Karray Kamel fled to Germany, where in June 1999, he was embroiled in an aggressive shootout with a group of German police officers in Frankfurt.[97] He was eventually caught only a few weeks later on 11 August 1999, hiding in Cologne.[98]

Ahmed Zuhair, originally from Jeddah, Saudi Arabia, had come to Bosnia from the Sudan and allegedly fought amongst the foreign *mujahideen*.[99] Ironically, he was also a recent release from a Bosnian prison where he had been held since January 1996 on charges of possessing three illegal machine-guns.[100] Yet, inexplicably, he was pardoned on 27 May 1997, by an unidentified senior representative of the Bosnian government. Among other acts, Police suspected Zuhair of prime involvement along with Ahmed Faiz al-Shemberi in the cruel murder of American aid worker William Jefferson in November 1995.[101] He was additionally named by the Bosnians as the mastermind behind the October 1997 car bombing in Mostar attributed to Al-Gama`at Al-Islamiyya. According to subsequent Bosnian news reports, Zuhair was finally arrested by Western authorities in late August 2002 while thousands of miles away in Pakistan, and was thereupon immediately transferred to the American Al-Qaida prisoner holding facility in Guantanamo Bay, Cuba.[102]

Saber Lahmar, one of the suspects affiliated with the Saudi High Commission, first arrived in Bosnia on 17 March 1993. Lahmar was a known member of the GIA, and had fled prosecution in Algeria. He later married a Bosnian woman, and his father-in-law curiously turned out to be a past employee at the US embassy in Sarajevo. Following the comprehensive Bosnian police investigation in 1997, Lahmar was caught and sentenced to prison for armed robbery and home invasion, but was soon pardoned in 2000 in a general amnesty.[103] He was again apprehended in late October 2001, when caught among a group of eleven Islamic militants plotting to fly small aircraft from the tiny airport at Visoko in central Bosnia and suicide crash them into two NATO military bases in Tuzla and Bratunac. Emina Susic, his wife, admitted he kept many things to himself, but defended her husband, insisting he was not capable of terrorist acts: 'He is a quiet man . . . He is actually very shy.'[104]

Within months of the exposé of the Karray Kamel gang in 1998, new events were already under way in the troubled Balkan peninsula. United States and

Egyptian intelligence, among others, were closely following several groups of radical Islamic dissidents operating in Bosnia, particularly Egyptian adherents of Al-Gama`at al-Islamiyya and Al-Jihad. One of the men being tracked, Sabri Ibrahim al-'Attar, narrated his fate in his subsequent trial:

> I stayed [in Bosnia] for almost another year during which I took part in the jihad with the Arab brothers under the command of a Muslim mujahid who had US citizenship but of Arab origin. But after the signing of the Dayton peace agreement, we the Arabs felt that our stay in Bosnia was not desirable anymore . . . we were compelled to flee to Kosovo. On the way there, I was arrested with others by the Serb intelligence services and I believe CIA agents. We could not check the identity of those who arrested us. All I remember was that they were very harsh and treated us inhumanely. We were held for about a month until I was handed over with others to the Egyptian authorities.[105]

These men, known as the 'Albanian Returnees,' caused a huge stir when they were rendered over to Egypt, and subsequently brought before one of the largest north African mass trials of Islamic militants during the 1990s. The involvement of the United States in the extraction of the extremist Egyptians was not taken lightly by their particular Amir, Ayman al-Zawahiri. Several of Al-Jihad's most prominent commanders were arrested in Albania and deported to Egypt, including Ahmad Salamah Mabruk, Zawahiri's 'right-hand man.'[106] Neither had Zawahiri forgiven or forgotten the disappearance of Abu Talal al-Qasimy under similar circumstances, and so, he prepared to wreak revenge on America. On 23 February 1998, Usama Bin Laden had issued a joint statement with Ayman al-Zawahiri and other allied radical Islamic leaders in the name of the 'World Islamic Front Against Jews and Crusaders' (Figure 9). Bin Laden called 'on every Muslim who believes in God and wishes to be rewarded to comply with God's order to kill the Americans and plunder their money wherever and whenever they find it. We also call on Muslim ulema, leaders, youths, and soldiers to launch the raid on Satan's US troops and the devil's supporters allying with them.'[107]

The first apparent response to Zawahiri and Bin Laden's call to *jihad* came on 7 August 1998, when two United States embassies in east Africa were suicide-bombed almost simultaneously by Al-Qaida cells deemed loyal to Zawahiri's Egyptian Al-Jihad faction. A day earlier, the 'Information Office of the Jihad Group in Egypt' had issued a statement through *Al-Hayat* accusing the American government of masterminding the arrest of the 'Albanian returnees' for 'declaring jihad against the United States and Israel and their trade, and cooperation with the mujahidin in Kosovo outside US influence.' The statement added: 'We are interested in briefly telling the Americans that their message has been received and that the response, which we hope they will read carefully, is being [prepared] . . . in the language that they understand.'[108]

Figure 9. Usama Bin Laden, flanked by Egyptians Ayman al-Zawahiri (on left) and Abu Hafs al-Masri (on right), declares the formation of an international terrorist front against 'Jews and Crusaders' at a press conference held in February 1998.

Italian investigators later claimed to find direct links between the Al-Qaida plotters responsible for the August 1998 embassy bombings and Anwar Shaaban's former headquarters at the Islamic Cultural Institute in Milan.[109] One of those links was Abu Hajer al-Iraqi (Mamdouh Mahmud Salim), a veteran face in Al-Qaida and one of the lead conspirators indicted by the United States Justice Department in connection with the August attacks (Figure 10). Intriguingly, only weeks before putting the finishing touches on the twin bombings in East Africa, Abu Hajer had slipped into Bosnia for an important three-day-long 'business meeting.' His visa, issued by the Bosnian consulate in Turkey, was sponsored by a Bosnian corporation known as the Ljiljan Commerce Group, an entity controlled by Enaam Arnaout and the Saudi-based Benevolence International Foundation (BIF). On 5 May 1998, a letter was sent to the Metalurg Hotel signed by Arnaout requesting a residence for 'one of the directors of the organization BIF in Bosnia.' As promised, hotel receipts indicate that Abu Hajer did stay at the Metalurg several days later from 7 May to 10 May, with Arnaout's Ljiljan account picking up the tab.[110] The purpose of his sudden and curiously-timed visit to Bosnia has yet to be fully revealed.

Simultaneously, the United States Central Intelligence Agency was becoming more vocal about its concerns stemming from the presence of Abu el-Ma`ali and his advisors in Bosnia. At an undisclosed point during 1998, the CIA allegedly uncovered a new plot masterminded by the young, battle-worn Algerian to

Figure 10. Mamdouh Mahmud Salim, a senior Al-Qaida leader who visited Bosnia shortly prior to the 1998 US Embassy bombings in East Africa.

smuggle large quantities of C-4 plastic explosives and blasting caps to an 'Egyptian terrorist group' for the purpose of attacking United States military bases in Germany. Fortunately, the CIA was able to intercept the explosives shipment before it could reach the Egyptians, and the terrorist plan was foiled.[111] However, even with these unmistakable clues, the United States administration still took no action to secure the arrest or punishment of the infamous Abu el-Ma`ali in Zenica; the best the White House was willing to push for was the total expulsion of foreign combatants, something the Bosnians had been required to do since February 1996, and yet had still failed to accomplish.

Fateh Kamel, for his part, was mysteriously absent from both the Middle East and Europe at this time. In the lingering wake of the March 1996 Roubaix debacle, French intelligence tracked Kamel as he returned to Canada and started recruiting a new group of young, willing, north African terrorist accomplices, many of whom were tied (like Kamel) to the Bosnian war. Judge Jean-Louis Bruguière, who witnessed the development of Kamel's network in Canada, argues that Kamel's sudden interest in north America heralded a dangerous new era for Abu el-Ma`ali and his disciples: 'the structure of the organization and the targets had changed. The targets weren't just in France or Europe [anymore].'[112] Unbeknownst to most Americans, Al-Qaida and its international terrorist foreign legion were now taking determined aim at the homeland of their most powerful and hated enemy: the United States.

In Montreal, Fateh Kamel worked closely with another Bosnian *mujahideen* veteran living illegally in Canada: Karim Said Atmani (also known as 'Abu Hisham'), born in Morocco in 1966. He was widely reputed to have 'considerable jihad experience in Algeria . . . he was a leader, and he was a veteran of fighting in Algeria during the 1990s.'[113] One United States official has since called Atmani a 'crazy warrior with a nose so broken and twisted that he could sniff around corners.'[114] In particular, Atmani had previously served as part of an infamous GIA terror cell – known as the Mansour Meliani Commando Group – responsible for the 26 August 1992 bombing of the Algiers International Airport, killing nine and wounding 123.[115]

Afterwards, for roughly five years between 1994 and 1999, Atmani worked as Fateh Kamel's 'right hand' man amongst the Bosnian *mujahideen*.[116] Atmani's links with the Arab fighters based in the Balkans were long and substantial; in particular, like Fateh Kamel, Atmani reportedly had a close personal relationship with Abu el-Ma`ali. Throughout 1994 and 1995, Atmani was officially tasked with organizing the transfer of foreign guerrillas to Bosnia from staging points in Milan and elsewhere in Europe. Italian police found corresponding evidence at the Islamic Cultural Institute of frequent calls from Atmani to Abu el-Ma`ali in Zenica during the mid-1990s.[117] Atmani was more than just a foot soldier; he was a fairly well known figure among the Bosnian *mujahideen*. On 26 June 1995, during Operation Sphinx, the Italians searched the office of Shaykh Anwar Shaaban in Milan and found, under Shaaban's personal writing pad, a fraudulent passport with the photo of Karim Said Atmani.[118]

Atmani, though perhaps only a mid-level operative in the loosely organized international *jihad* network, has a fearsome reputation in the counterterrorism community. However, despite his undeniable years of terrorist 'expertise,' Atmani was not a terribly original thinker. Once in Canada, true to form, he began scheming 'the armed robbery of the bureau of exchange in Montreal' and a GIA Meliani Group-signature 'terrorist attack on a US airport.'[119]

In Canada, Fateh Kamel and Atmani befriended a mixed group of other young, unemployed, and restless north African immigrants, including recent arrival Ahmed Ressam.[120] Ressam was a native of Algeria, where it did not take long for him to get in trouble with local authorities. Fed on stories of the 1962 independence war by his parents, the unemployed Ressam grew bored with his comparatively meaningless existence and quickly became 'fascinated by [television] shows about "unsolved" conspiracies like the Kennedy assassination.'[121] In the early days of the Algerian civil war, Ressam fled his homeland after he was accused by Algerian authorities of arms-trafficking for Islamic fundamentalists in north Africa. He travelled first to France, and then to Montreal in 1994. Atmani, Labsi, Boumezbeur, and Ressam together moved into a small apartment in an unimpressive brown-brick building called Place de la Malicorne, in the working-class district of Anjou, east Montreal. Ressam had come to Montreal for nightclubs and Armani suits, not *jihad* and Usama Bin Laden. However, unable to find employment, he turned to petty crime as a means to finance his desired lifestyle in the West.

By January 1995, Ressam had become an adept thief, stealing the Armani clothes he so coveted. In June, a Canadian judge found him guilty of shoplifting, fined him $100, and ordered him to leave Canada by 23 July 1995. Ressam did not let his court conviction stand in the way of his new criminal profession, learning simple scams, credit card fraud, and false documentation. His deportation order was never executed by Canadian Immigration officials, and Ressam never left. He developed his skills enough to gain the attention of a wealthy and influential member of the Montreal Muslim community who was working closely with Ressam's roommates: Afghano-Bosniak guerrilla Fateh Kamel. At the time, Kamel was using his storefront business as a cover for his growing role as an international terrorist mastermind. He employed the promising Ressam as an invaluable source of passports, credit cards, petty theft, and the other necessary functional tools of terrorist activity.[122] Once again, as French Judge Jean-Louis Bruguière would later testify in United States court, Fateh Kamel had become the leader of yet another 'conspiratorial cell,' this time based out of Montreal.[123]

Kamel, Atmani, and the others at Place de la Malicorne drew Ahmed Ressam deep into their world of radical Islam. The men discussed the GIA terror attacks in France and agreed 'that it would be a good thing to carry out another operation in France in the future . . . [we] were in agreement with those bombings.'[124] They brought Ressam into the mosque to listen to the wisdom of Abderraouf Hannachi, an older Tunisian-born man who originally came from a rural family in Tunisia and immigrated to Canada in 1994 'to make a life for himself, like other Tunisians.' Hannachi had few successes at finding employment with little education or formal experience. But, Hannachi was always regular about his daily visits to the local As-Sunnah An-Nabawiya Mosque in Montreal, where he was considered a respected and influential personality.[125]

Since its inception, the As-Sunnah mosque has developed into a major community landmark that attracts as many as 1,500 faithful each Friday. Throughout the 1990s, its bookstore sold many books and videos on *jihad* and the *mujahideen*, including one tape featuring the first *Amir* of the Bosnian *mujahideen*, the Saudi veteran Shaykh Abu Abdel Aziz Barbaros. The Shaykh pleaded with viewers in broken English, 'Come to Afghanistan . . . Only pay the fare for tickets. I am not asking you to get rid of your vacation or retire from your job or get rid of your business. I suggest that you come with vacation for training, and next year, second vacation, you come for jihad. If you are real believers, Allah is expecting you to do an extra job.'[126]

In 1997, allegations also emerged from within the local Muslim community that 'certain very influential members' and 'certain leaders' at Masjid As-Sunnah An-Nabawiya and Masjid as-Salaam (another mosque frequented by Ahmed Ressam and his friends) had 'helped and protected' an effort to raise 'hundreds of thousands of dollars' since 1992 to aid militant Islamic terrorist groups in Algeria. Working together to collect *jihad* donations from North American Muslims, they allegedly gathered more than $100,000 in 1997 alone.[127] Despite the very public rumors, no legal action was taken against the mosque or its supervisors by Canadian authorities.

At the As-Sunnah mosque, Abderraouf Hannachi railed against Western culture as a regrettable disease and expressed his burning hatred of the United States. He also spoke proudly of how he had been trained by Al-Qaida experts at the Khalden camp in eastern Afghanistan, and how this life was only meaningful if offered as sacrifice for the next. The Malicorne gang all worshipped Hannachi and Fateh Kamel, who were highly respected as men of status in the local Muslim community. Atmani, Ressam, and the others dreamed of achieving similar glory in the name of Islam, and began planning their own *jihad* fantasy. In the trial of one of his co-conspirators, Ressam testified that he became firmly convinced to join the *mujahideen* after several of his friends returned to Montreal in 1997 from Al-Qaida camps in Afghanistan. According to Ressam, 'My friends came back and talked to me about the training that they have received, the learning that they have gotten, and about jihad, and I got – they encourage me – so I got interested.' He further explained that he had approached Hannachi, 'a friend who was [formerly] in Afghanistan,' to arrange the details of his own planned journey to join Al-Qaida.[128]

Several members of the Malicorne gang quietly left Montreal in March 1998 on a quest to seek military training in Afghanistan. Ressam flew to Karachi, Pakistan, where Abderraouf Hannachi had arranged contacts for him with notorious Afghano-Bosniak terrorist training camp manager Abu Zubaydah.[129] In court, Ressam explained Abu Zubaydah's role in the Al-Qaida network: '[h]e is the person that is charge of the camps. He receives young men from all countries. He accepts you or rejects you. And he takes care of the expenses of the camps. He makes arrangements for you when you travel coming in or leaving.'[130] At the time, the cold-blooded terror ringleader Zubaydah and a host of senior Al-Qaida aides around the world were planning to send two loyal sleeper cells, one based in Jordan and one in Montreal, to launch devastating attacks on American targets on the eve of the millennium.

Unbeknown to Ressam, one of the central leaders of the parallel Jordanian cell, Palestinian-American Khalil al-Deek (like Karim Said Atmani in Montreal) was also an Arab veteran of the Bosnian war, affiliated with the *mujahideen* battalion. Deek was later charged by Jordanian authorities with having played a role in arranging the travel between Afghanistan and Jordan for those involved in the Jordan plot. Deek was very familiar in Bosnia, where he had arrived in 1994 with 'Convoy of Mercy,' a 'relief' agency based in the UK.[131] For the record, Khalil al-Deek officially denies entering combat. But Bosnian passport and residency records do indicate that al-Deek was living in the largely *mujahideen*-controlled area around the Muslim village of Bocinja Donja, likewise home to Abu el-Ma`ali.[132]

In Karachi, Abu Zubaydah gave Ahmed Ressam a new identity, Afghan clothes, an authorized letter of transit to a guesthouse in Jalalabad. Shortly thereafter, Ressam was moved on to the nearby Khalden training camp.[133] The camp had about 100 men in total, divided into cells of between six and fourteen recruits each. The cells were taught to exist and operate independently of any central command structure. At the Khalden camp, Ressam took part in military training conducted by two members of the Jordanian Millenium terror cell identified as 'Khaled' and 'Mughirah.'[134] According to Ressam, at Khalden, they learned 'how to blow up the infrastructure of a country . . . Electric plants, gas plants, airports, railroads, large corporations . . . Hotels where conferences are held.'[135] While in Afghanistan, Ressam also participated in gruesome chemical weapons experiments on dogs and learned 'how to mix poisons with other substances, put them together and smear them on doorknobs . . . designed to be used against intelligence officers and other VIPs.'[136]

At 'theoretical sessions,' members of the cells studied and discussed strategy behind past terror operations, including Hizballah's war against the United States in Beirut and the failed 1995 assassination plot on Hosni Mubarak in Addis Ababa. Every Friday at Khalden, they would all meet and discuss ways to establish terror support networks on the ground in Algeria, Europe, and North America. Al-Qaida religious and military officials, such as Shaykh Omar Abdel Rahman's son Asadallah, would lecture to the cells about important targets and the priorities of the *jihad* movement. Ressam later testified in court: 'we were speaking about America as an enemy of Islam.'[137] In particular, he recalled a *fatwah* distributed widely in the Afghan camps 'issued by Sheikh Omar Abdel Rahman with his picture on it . . . It said it was a fatwah by Omar Abdel Rahman from prison. It says fight Americans and hit their interest everywhere.'[138] A copy of this very same *fatwah* was reproduced and distributed on a short-lived Arabic-language Web site created by fellow Millenium terror conspirator Khalil al-Deek.[139]

Ressam met several individuals at the Khalden camp involved in a 60-man Al-Qaida cell, predominantly comprised of Tunisian *mujahideen* veterans from

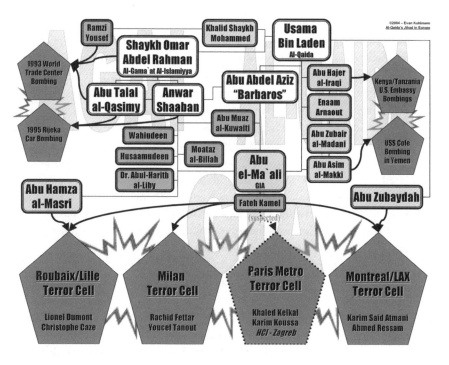

Figure 11. The Afghano-Bosniak network.

Bosnia. The cell was spread across Germany and Italy, and was headed by an unnamed *Amir* living in Yemen. Ressam indicated that a number of other experienced *mujahideen* commanders were working with the cell, including three quite infamous Afghano-Bosniaks: Abu Sulaiman al-Makki, Abu Ishaq al-Makki, and Abu Zubair al-Haili.[140] It is possible that the 'unnamed *Amir*' in Yemen mentioned by Ressam is none other than the three Saudis' old crippled Bosniak comrade, Abu Asim al-Makki (also known as Muhammad Hamdi al-Ahdal) (Figure 11).

For his part, Karim Said Atmani never forgot his strong past links to the *mujahideen* communities of central Bosnia. In a later search of the dingy cell headquarters at Place de la Malicorne, police found a Canadian government form for refugee status in the name of Said Atmani, containing a blank paper with the letterhead of 'The Embassy of the Republic of Bosnia and Herzegovina in Malaysia.' The paper had traces of a telephone number in Zenica.[141] Atmani had temporarily left Canada in April 1998, just after the departure of Ressam and his Afghanistan-bound comrades.

On 14 October 1998, while Ahmed Ressam was making final preparations to return to North America, Canadian authorities apprehended Atmani at Niagara Falls, when he tried to cross into Canadian territory from the United States with two other Algerians. He was travelling on a fraudulent Canadian passport that had apparently already allowed him to breach immigration controls in the United States; he was also found in the possession of stacks of stolen credit cards taken from unwitting British and Asian tourists. In the arrest warrant against him, Canadian authorities noted that Atmani had used seven different aliases and was a 'person known to be a violent Islamic extremist.' But rather than being imprisoned or otherwise punished, following his detention at Niagara Falls, Said Atmani was instead promptly expelled back to Bosnia on 18 October 1998.[142] Atmani's release from Canadian custody came even though French intelligence had repeatedly expressed a strong interest in Atmani for his connections to the Roubaix Gang and other GIA terror attacks in France. French authorities also allege that Canadian intelligence officials rejected their initial efforts to investigate Atmani's commander, Fateh Kamel, scoffing at the reports of militant activity and referring to the master terrorist as 'just a businessman.'[143]

French counterterrorism experts now believe that Atmani was attempting to enter Canada in order to play a central role in the Millennium bombing conspiracy with Ahmed Ressam. In late 1998, Ressam met with several other cell members and Al-Qaida representatives in Afghanistan. They agreed to return to Canada in three carefully programed phases. Atmani, mostly likely back in central Bosnia during the summer of 1998, was scheduled to arrive in Montreal in the third and final phase. Upon the successful return of all the cell members, Atmani, Ressam, and the others were planning to commit a series of Roubaix-style operations (mainly bank robberies) in order to finance a major terrorist strike against the United States; specifically, a massive bomb explosion at Los Angeles International Airport coinciding with the start of the new millennium. The choice was made because 'an airport is sensitive politically and economically.'[144] Ressam later admitted in court the chilling details of his plan:

> I will go to the city of Los Angeles. I will surveil the airport. I will survey the airports until I find one – a good one, and then I will bring a cart that is used for luggage. I will put the cart in a place that is not suspicious and then I will observe the reaction of security, how long it took them to observe it . . . this was for rehearsal only.

Upon the execution of the actual plot, 'I will first try to put the explosives in one suitcase and if there was not enough room in one suitcase, then I would use another suitcase.'[145]

But with Atmani's expulsion, the cell was starting to fall apart. Ressam had made it safely back to Montreal, but minus one of his most experienced *jihad* partners. He tried contacting Atmani in Bosnia, but the latter now refused to come back to Canada to carry out an operation. Atmani was clearly a known figure in European and North American counterterrorism circles, and it was too risky for him to once again attempt to illicitly enter Canada or the United States.[146] With or without Atmani, Ressam was prepared to go ahead with the mission assigned to him by Abu Zubaydah. He was given $3,500 to help subsidize the cost of the terror attack by another known north African veteran of the 'jihad in Bosnia' residing in Canada.[147] Other members of the cell already positioned inside the United States were reassured by their handlers based in Montreal that Ressam 'used to be in Afghanistan and Bosnia' and that 'the fire is on.'[148] They referred to Ressam's imminent arrival as 'a great blessing'; one conspirator later admitted that he knew exactly what this meant: '[t]his guy was coming for some violent act.'[149]

On 14 December 1999, Ressam was stopped by United States border patrol agents at the Port Angeles crossing near Vancouver. In his car, investigators found the precursors to terror: 100 lbs of explosives and simple timing devices. Ressam made a bold effort to escape, reminiscent of the slippery Lionel Dumont; one customs agent recalled:

> I was looking right at him, had my weapon pointed in his direction . . . He quickly darted into traffic, bounced off a car, continued to run hard. And that was what really triggered me, caused me to get very nervous, when he came up to a passenger vehicle and tried to commandeer it or open the car door. I thought, 'This guy really wants to get away, and he's dangerous.'[150]

Perhaps in anticipation of the upcoming millennium attack, Fateh Kamel had abruptly left his home in Canada in the spring of 1999, after giving the profits from the sale of his businesses to Mokhtar Haouari, another key member of the Malicorne terror cell and an intimate accomplice of Ahmed Ressam. Kamel was clearly leaving Montreal for good. He first travelled to Germany, then to Syria, and on to Jordan, where he was finally detained by the famed Jordanian intelligence service Al-Mukhabarat.[151] In Kamel's address book, they found a Bosnian telephone number in Teslic where one could be connected directly to Abu el-Ma`ali.[152] Within days, on 16 May 1999, Jordan extradited the infamous Islamic terrorist Kamel to France to face a host of criminal charges.[153] At almost precisely this time, Al-Mukhabarat was reported to have alerted the United States Central Intelligence Agency to 'at least three plots' it had uncovered by suspected Arab *mujahideen* veterans based in Bosnia to attack American targets in Europe.[154] Bosnian local press indicated that Abu el-Ma`ali had fled United States pressure in the Balkans for his arrest and instead found alleged temporary asylum in the Netherlands.[155] No longer could the Afghano-Bosniak terrorist threat be denied, even by the most sceptical minds in the United States government.

Notes

1. 'Has a New Wave of Terror been Created?' *Vjesnik* (Zagreb), 16 May 1996.
2. Jean-Louis Bruguiere and Jean-Francois Ricard. 'Requisitoire Definitif aux Fins de Non-Lieu. De Non-Lieu partiel. De Requalification. De Renvoi devant le Tribunal Correctionnel, de mantien sous Controle Judiciaiare et de maintien en Detention.' Cour D'Appel de Paris; Tribunal de Grande Instance de Paris. No. Parquet: P96 253 3901.2, p. 7.
3. Ibid., p. 126.
4. Ibid., p. 148.
5. Ibid., p. 99.
6. Ibid., p. 100.
7. Pyes, Craig and Josh Meyer et al. 'Bosnia Seen as Hospitable Base and Sanctuary for Terrorists.' *The Los Angeles Times*, 7 October 2001, p. A1.
8. Jean-Louis Bruguiere and Jean-Francois Ricard. Op. cit., p. 104.
9. 'Mustapha the Terrorist.' *National Post* (Canada), 24 February 2001.
10. According to testimony before an Algerian tribunal from Mohamed Berrached, a captured leader of the GSPC, Usama Bin Laden himself contacted certain GIA leaders via satellite telephone in the summer of 1998, and urged them to set up a new armed faction known as the GSPC in order to present a 'better image of the Jihad' against the secular government in Algiers. See: 'Bin Laden held to be behind an armed Algerian Islamic movement.' Agence France Press. 15 February 1999.
11. Jean-Louis Bruguiere and Jean-Francois Ricard. Op. cit., p. 146.
12. 'Bombing trial opens in Paris.' CNN Online. 24 November 1997. See also: Jean-Louis Bruguiere and Jean-Francois Ricard. Op. cit., p. 105.
13. Jean-Louis Bruguiere and Jean-Francois Ricard. Op. cit., p. 103.
14. Jean-Louis Bruguiere and Jean-Francois Ricard. Op. cit., p. 105.
15. Pyes, Craig and Josh Meyer et al. Op. cit.
16. Marlowe, Lara. 'Errant Frenchman became wanted criminal after adopting Bosnian case as mujahid.' *The Irish Times*, 18 July 1997, p. 8.
17. Vermaat, Emerson. 'Bin Laden's Terror Networks in Europe.' A Mackenzie Institute Occasional Paper. Mackenzie Institute. Toronto, Canada, 26 May 2002.
18. Jean-Louis Bruguiere and Jean-Francois Ricard. Op. cit., p. 157.
19. Jean-Louis Bruguiere and Jean-Francois Ricard. Op. cit., p. 165.
20. Jean-Louis Bruguiere and Jean-Francois Ricard. Op. cit., p. 157.
21. Jean-Louis Bruguiere and Jean-Francois Ricard. Op. cit., p. 158.
22. http://www.ummah.net/sos
23. Jean-Louis Bruguiere and Jean-Francois Ricard. Op. cit., p. 159.
24. Interview with Shaykh Abu Hamza al-Masri at the Finsbury Park Mosque, 28 June 2002.

25. Ibid.

26. 'World Trade Series – "The Believers vs. the Kufr of America."' Friday Khutba given by Abu Hamza Al-Masri at the Finsbury Park Mosque.

27. Ibid.

28. Interview with Shaykh Abu Hamza al-Masri at the Finsbury Park Mosque, 28 June 2002.

29. Carroll, Rory. 'Terrorists or Tourists?' *Guardian*, 26 June 1999.

30. Davies, Deborah. 'Kill or be Killed.' *Dispatches*. Channel 4 UK, 1999.

31. Ibid.

32. Supporters of Shariah (SOS) Newsletter, Vol. 2, Issue 2, March/April 1999.

33. Interview with Shaykh Abu Hamza al-Masri at the Finsbury Park Mosque, 28 June 2002.

34. Jean-Louis Bruguiere and Jean-Francois Ricard. Op. cit., p. 159.

35. Jean-Louis Bruguiere and Jean-Francois Ricard. Op. cit., p. 159.

36. Jean-Louis Bruguiere and Jean-Francois Ricard. Op. cit., p. 158.

37. Interview with Shaykh Abu Hamza al-Masri at the Finsbury Park Mosque, 28 June 2002.

38. Jean-Louis Bruguiere and Jean-Francois Ricard. Op. cit., p. 159.

39. Pyes, Craig and Josh Meyer et al. Op. cit.

40. Jean-Louis Bruguiere and Jean-Francois Ricard. Op. cit., p. 157.

41. Jean-Louis Bruguiere and Jean-Francois Ricard. Op. cit., p. 74.

42. Jean-Louis Bruguiere and Jean-Francois Ricard. Op. cit., p. 159.

43. Jean-Louis Bruguiere and Jean-Francois Ricard. Op. cit., p. 159.

44. Jean-Louis Bruguiere and Jean-Francois Ricard. Op. cit., p. 166.

45. Jean-Louis Bruguiere and Jean-Francois Ricard. Op. cit., p. 157.

46. *United States of America v. Ahmed Ressam, aka Benni Noris*. United States District Court for the Western District of Washington. Case #: CR 99-666-JCC. Dated 2 April 2001, p. 9–10.

47. Jean-Louis Bruguiere and Jean-Francois Ricard. Op. cit., p. 166.

48. 'Hostage drama after five killed in police raids.' Agence France Presse. 29 March 1996.

49. Dejevsky, Mary. 'Islamic terror link to French siege.' *Independent* (London), 2 April 1996, p. 10.

50. Jean-Louis Bruguiere and Jean-Francois Ricard. Op. cit., p. 75.

51. Dahlburg, John-Thor. '"Holy Warriors" Brought Bosnians Ferocity and Zeal.' *The Los Angeles Times*, 6 August 1996, p. A11.

52. Pyes, Craig. 'Arrest at U.S. Border Reverberates in France.' *The New York Times*, 22 December 1999, p. A1.

53. DeCroix, Christophe. 'Four Suspects Killed in Shootout After Car Bomb Found.' *The Associated Press*, 29 March 1996.

54. 'Belgian police overpower gunman, free hostages.' Deutsche Presse-Agentur. 29 March 1996.
55. 'French fugitive takes Belgian hostages.' United Press International. 29 March 1996.
56. Glass, Pierre-Yves. 'Bandits or Terrorists? Violent Ghetto Gang Seemed a Bit of Both.' *The Associated Press*. April 1, 1996.
57. 'French fugitive takes Belgian hostages.' United Press International. 29 March 1996.
58. 'Belgian police overpower gunman, free hostages.' Op. cit.
59. 'Belgian police overpower gunman, free hostages.' Op. cit.
60. 'Hostage drama after five killed in police raids.' Agence France Presse, 29 March 1996.
61. Dejevsky, Mary. 'Islamic terror link to French siege.' *The Independent* (London), 2 April 1996, p. 10.
62. 'Hostage drama after five killed in police raids.' Op. cit.
63. 'Police arrest gunman, hostages released in Belgium.' Agence France Presse. 29 March 1996.
64. 'Hostage drama after five killed in police raids.' Op. cit.
65. 'Belgian police overpower gunman, free hostages.' Op. cit.
66. Dejevsky, Mary. Op. cit.
67. *United States of America v. Ahmed Ressam, aka Benni Noris*. Op. cit. p. 9–10.
68. Jean-Louis Bruguiere and Jean-Francois Ricard. Op. cit., p. 109.
69. Jean-Louis Bruguiere and Jean-Francois Ricard. Op. cit., p. 106.
70. Jean-Louis Bruguiere and Jean-Francois Ricard. Op. cit., p. 107.
71. Dahlburg, John-Thor. Op. cit.
72. Jean-Louis Bruguiere and Jean-Francois Ricard. Op. cit., p. 92.
73. Tanjug News Agency. 7 July 1997.
74. Jean-Louis Bruguiere and Jean-Francois Ricard. Op. cit., p. 158.
75. Jean-Louis Bruguiere and Jean-Francois Ricard. Op. cit., p. 79.
76. TWRA News Agency. 23 February 1997.
77. 'Two foreigners sought for killing Bosnian policeman.' Agence France Presse. 24 February 1997.
78. Jean-Louis Bruguiere and Jean-Francois Ricard. Op. cit., p. 159.
79. 'Bosnian police kill Italian murder suspect.' Agence France Presse. 9 March 1997.
80. 'Biniam Killed, Dumont Arrested, Fetic Wounded.' TWRA Press Agency. 9 March 1997.
81. Reuters. 9 March 1997.
82. Liberation (Sarajevo). 14 March 1997.
83. Groult, Sylvie. 'Two Frenchmen go on trial in Bosnia for fatal holdups.' Agence France Presse. 7 July 1997.

84. 'Frenchmen sentenced to 20 years in prison for holdups in Bosnia.' Agence France Presse. 16 July 1997.

85. International Police Task Force-Operations and Information Unit. United Nations Mission in Bosnia and Herzegovina; Mission Headquarters-Sarajevo. Daily activity log covering period between 27 May 1999, 07.00 hrs; and 28 May 1999, 07.00 hrs.

86. 'French convict to be extradited to France.' Agence France Presse. 1 June 1999.

87. Jean-Louis Bruguiere and Jean-Francois Ricard. Op. cit., p. 147.

88. Jean-Louis Bruguiere and Jean-Francois Ricard. Op. cit., p. 147.

89. Jean-Louis Bruguiere and Jean-Francois Ricard. Op. cit., p. 100–1.

90. 'Spate of Attacks Against Bosnian Croats goes Unnoticed.' Communiqué issued by the Croatian Mission to the United Nations, 22 September 1997.

91. Karic, Eldin. 'Trial to Jihad Warriors Soon.' AIM (Alternative Information Network) Press. http://www.aimpress.org. December 28, 1997. See also: Hedges, Stephen J. 'Extremism lingers after Balkan wars.' *The Chicago Tribune*, 25 November 2001. See also: 'Abu Hamza has wings.' *Dani* (Sarajevo), 24 April 1998. See also: Toholj, Miroslav [former Minister of Information of the Serb Republic]. 'Mujaheddins in Bosnia and Herzegovina.' http://www.karadzic.org/rat/svedok_mudzahedini_e.html.

92. Karic, Eldin. Op. cit.

93. Hecimovic, Esad. 'Zenica police caught the two leaders of the Roubaix Group.' *Lily* (Sarajevo), 19 March 1997.

94. 'Abu Hamza has wings.' Op. cit.

95. 'Abu Hamza has wings.' Op. cit.

96. Jean-Louis Bruguiere and Jean-Francois Ricard. Op. cit., p. 160.

97. Jean-Louis Bruguiere and Jean-Francois Ricard. Op. cit., p. 160.

98. Jean-Louis Bruguiere and Jean-Francois Ricard. Op. cit., p. 122.

99. Rogosic, Zeljko. 'Vast investigation in Bosnia Herzegovina.' *Nacional* (Bosnia), Issue 306, 27 September 2001.

100. Hranjski, Hrvoje. 'International News.' The Associated Press. 21 February 1996.

101. Karic, Eldin. Op. cit.

102. SRNA News Agency. Broadcast in Serbo-Croat language in Bijeljina. 28 August 2002, 8.20 GMT.

103. 'Six Algerian terror suspects in US custody.' Reuters. 18 January 2002.

104. Hedges, Stephen J. 'Extremism lingers after Balkan wars.' *The Chicago Tribune*, 25 November 2001.

105. Sharaf-al-Din, Khalid. 'Fundamentalists' Leaders Formed Bogus Organizations To Confuse the Security Organs.' *Al-Sharq al-Awsat* (London), 7 March 1999, p. 6.

106. 'Al-Sharq Al-Awsat Publishes Extracts from Al-Jihad Leader Al- Zawahiri's New Book.' *Al-Sharq al-Awsat* (London), 2 December 2001, p. 6.

107. 'World Islamic Front Statement Urging Jihad Against Jews and Crusaders.' Joint press statement by Shaykh Usamah Bin Laden, Ayman al-Zawahiri, Abu Yasir Rifa`i Ahmad Taha, Shaykh Mir Hamzah, and Fazlul Rahman, 23 February 1998.

108. 'Islamic Jihad vows Revenge.' *Al-Hayat* (London), 6 August 1998.

109. Ryan, Kelly. 'From Milan to Madrid to Montreal: the world-wide web of terror.' Canadian Broadcasting Company (CBC). Originally aired: 14 December 2001.

110. 'Government's Evidentiary Proffer Supporting the Admissibility of Co-Conspirator Statements.' *United States of America v. Enaam M. Arnaout.* United States District Court Northern District of Illinois, Eastern Division. Case #: 02 CR 892. 31 January 2003, pp. 69–70.

111. Pyes, Craig with Josh Meyers and William Rempel. 'Bosnia Seen as Hospitable Base and Sanctuary for Terrorists.' *Los Angeles Times*, 7 October 2001.

112. Berton, Hal et al. 'The Terrorist Within; Chapter 5: "The Terrorist Tracker."' *The Seattle Times*, 23 June–7 July 2002.

113. Cross-examination of Ahmed Ressam. *United States v. Mokhtar Haouari.* United States District Court Southern District of New York. Case: 00CR15. 27 June–6 July 2001, p. 653.

114. Pyes, Craig with Josh Meyers and William Rempel. Op. cit.

115. Cross-examination of Ahmed Ressam. Op. cit., p. 651. See also: Algiers Television. Arabic-language broadcast: 31 August 1993, 19.00 GMT.

116. Jean-Louis Bruguiere and Jean-Francois Ricard. Op. cit., p. 225.

117. Jean-Louis Bruguiere and Jean-Francois Ricard. Op. cit., p. 139.

118. Jean-Louis Bruguiere and Jean-Francois Ricard. Op. cit., p. 140.

119. Cross-examination of Ahmed Ressam. Op. cit., p. 649.

120. Berton, Hal et al. Op. cit.

121. Johnson, Scott. 'Tale of the Wayward Son.' *Newsweek*, 8 May 2000, p. 39.

122. Berton, Hal et al. Op. cit.

123. *United States of America v. Ahmed Ressam, aka Benni Noris.* Op. cit., pp. 9–10.

124. Direct Examination of Ahmed Ressam. *United States v. Mokhtar Haouari.* United States District Court Southern District of New York. Case: 00CR15. 27 June–6 July 2001, pp. 589–90, 704.

125. Marsden, William and Nicolas Van Praet. 'Mystery surrounds "Raouf": Montrealer seen as key link between local terror cells, bin Laden camps.' *Montreal Gazette*, 16 February 2002, p. B1.

126. Berton, Hal et al. Op. cit.

127. Ali Ben Mohammed (Ali@mohammed.com). 'Subject: Vol de l'argent du Djihad.' Newsgroups: soc.culture.algeria, soc.culture.maghreb. 15 February 1997.
128. Direct Examination of Ahmed Ressam. Op. cit., pp. 545–6.
129. Marsden, William and Nicolas Van Praet. Op. cit.
130. Direct Examination of Ahmed Ressam. Op. cit., p. 547.
131. Dellios, Hugh. *The Chicago Tribune*, 5 March 2000, p. 1.
132. Smith, Jeffrey. 'A Bosnian Village's Terrorist Ties; Links to U.S. Bomb Plot Arouse Concerns about Enclave of Islamic Guerillas.' *The Washington Post*, 11 March 2000, p. A1.
133. Marsden, William and Nicolas Van Praet. Op. cit.
134. Italian Division of General Investigations and Special Operations (DIGOS) Intelligence Report on Ahmed Ressam. Dated 24 July 2001.
135. Dickey, Christopher. 'Training for Terror: From credit-card fraud to the art of disguise, how bin Laden schools his recruits in mayhem.' *Newsweek*, 24 September 2002.
136. Cross-examination of Ahmed Ressam. Op. cit., p. 626.
137. Cross-examination of Ahmed Ressam. Op. cit., p. 622.
138. Direct Examination of Ahmed Ressam. Op. cit., p. 552.
139. *Al-Minhaj*, p. 27. http://www.badr.com. Dated: 1997.
140. Italian Division of General Investigations and Special Operations (DIGOS) Intelligence Report on Ahmed Ressam. Dated 24 July 2001.
141. Jean-Louis Bruguiere and Jean-Francois Ricard. Op. cit., p. 125.
142. Jean-Louis Bruguiere and Jean-Francois Ricard. Op. cit., p. 139.
143. Pyes, Craig with Josh Meyers and William Rempel. Op. cit.
144. Direct Examination of Ahmed Ressam. Op. cit., p. 572.
145. Direct Examination of Ahmed Ressam. Op. cit., pp. 573–4.
146. Italian Division of General Investigations and Special Operations (DIGOS) Intelligence Report on Ahmed Ressam. Dated 24 July 2001.
147. Cross-examination of Ahmed Ressam. Op. cit., pp. 655, 662.
148. Direct Examination of Abdelghani Meskini. *United States v. Mokhtar Haouari*. United States District Court Southern District of New York. Case: 00CR15. 27 June–6 July 2001, pp. 323–36.
149. Ibid., p. 337
150. McKenna, Terence. 'Trail of a Terrorist' – Program #2004. Canadian Broadcasting Company (CBC). 25 October 2001.
151. Trueheart, Charles and Anne Swardson. 'French Link Algerian to Islamic Radicals; Man Jailed in Seattle Lived With Member of Group That Carried Out Robberies.' *The Washington Post*, 23 December 1999, p. A8.
152. Jean-Louis Bruguiere and Jean-Francois Ricard. Op. cit., p. 145.
153. Jean-Louis Bruguiere and Jean-Francois Ricard. Op. cit., p. 144.

154. Goldberg, Jeffrey. 'Learning How To Be King.' *The New York Times Magazine*, 6 February 2000, p. 42.

155. Habul, Emir. 'Reactions in South East Europe to the attacks on 11 September.' *AIM (Alternative Information Network) Press.* http://www.aimpress.org. 22 October 2001.

–10–

Post-9/11 Implications for Bosnia

O' Alija [Izetbegovic], O' honored! You drive America crazy!

Line from Arabic poetry sung by the foreign *mujahideen* in Bosnia.

We are Muslim but we are different to these people. We're Europeans. I love to drink and I like seeing women in mini-skirts. It's too late for me to be a real Muslim and that goes for 90 per cent of the people here. Everybody in Bosnia likes to drink and sing.[864]

Officer from the 17th Krajina Brigade, BiH Army.

Four years after the final deadline for all foreign *mujahideen* to leave Bosnia as per the terms of the United States-negotiated Dayton Accord, the United States government finally took punitive measures against the Bosnian government for failing to live up to its promises. After the discovery of numerous terrorist plots linked to both Abu el-Ma`ali and Al-Qaida, the American military aid program to Bosnia was suddenly suspended without further explanation. When that achieved no progress, the Clinton administration allegedly went a step further and threatened to cut all United States economic aid to Bosnia. Alija Izetbegovic, in his last days as the President of Bosnia-Herzegovina, once again agreed to submit to United States pressure and deport Abu el-Ma`ali. And, yet, once again, within a year, the Algerian terrorist commander had returned to Bosnia and was reported to be fluidly moving in and out of the Balkans without interference by local authorities.[1] The carrot-and-stick approach suggested by numerous State Department representatives in the winter of 1995 had officially failed.

The investigation that followed the millennium plot would turn up information about terrorist cells in Bosnia that stunned the White House. In late 2000, the Clinton administration was presented with a classified United States State Department report on the Bosniak issue; it warned of a problem of such size and scope that it 'shocked everyone.' The report specifically dealt with the known terrorist operatives hiding in the Balkans, including Karim Said Atmani. President Clinton ordered diplomatic representatives to revisit Alija Izetbegovic and personally convey the heightened American concern and the dire need to remove remaining members of the foreign *mujahideen*. This group of elite envoys even included

Secretary of State Madeleine Albright herself; according to one former State Department official:

> It wasn't just one meeting, it was 10 to 12, with orders directly from the White House . . . The point we kept making to Izetbegovic was that if the day comes we find out that these people are connected to some terrible terrorist incident, that's the day the entire U.S.-Bosnia relationship will change from friends to adversaries.[2]

The renewed and more public pressure on the Bosnians achieved some limited victories. On 6 April 2001, Karim Said Atmani was convicted in absentia in a Paris court on charges relating to his involvement with the Roubaix gang and other GIA terrorist networks in France. On the same day, in a United States federal court in Los Angeles, Ahmed Ressam was found guilty of conspiring to commit terrorist attacks during millennium celebrations in the United States. Between April and July, the Bosnians consented to conduct limited arrests of the most prominent militants hiding in the region, namely the convicted terrorist Atmani, Abu Imad al-Masri, and Hassan Al Sharif Mahmud Saad (the mastermind behind the October 1995 car bombing in Rijeka).[3] There seems little doubt that the names of these three men featured prominently in the original classified State Department report on the Bosnia issue. Atmani was promptly extradited to France, where on 25 October 2001, he was sentenced to five years in prison for distributing false identification documents to an international terrorist recruitment and support network.[4]

For the Bosnian government, the real turning point in their relationship with the United States vis-à-vis the issue of the *mujahideen* came on 11 September 2001, when the vast majority of Bosnians, like much of the rest of the world, were horrified to learn about the devastation in New York and Washington caused by radical Islamic militants loyal to Usama Bin Laden. In Bosnia, the shock of the attacks finally brought the government in Sarajevo in line with the policy of the United States with regards to the issue of international terrorism. The Bosnian foreign minister Zlatko Lagumdzija has since argued that, on 11 September 'the world . . . split into a modern civilization and one of barbarism and terrorism . . . Bosnia-Herzegovina has chosen to ally itself with the civilized world. It has decided to be part of the solution, not part of the problem . . . For our own sake . . . we chose sides.'[5]

The first apparent political casualty of the Bosnian change of heart vis-à-vis the *mujahideen* was former President Alija Izetbegovic. Izetbegovic was mired in a firestorm of controversy as many Bosnians began to probe the extent of his relationship with the Arab-Afghan *mujahideen*. Izetbegovic desperately lashed out in the media, condemning terrorism as an abstract concept, yet still arguing that 'the mojahedin and terrorists are not the same thing.'[6] While admitting the presence of 'fewer than 100' former foreign *mujahideen* left in Bosnia, he insisted, 'None of them is suspected of any terrorist action in Bosnia-Hercegovina, nor has Sfor NATO-led Stabilization Force had any problems with the former mojahedin in the past six years.'[7] This, despite unmistakable court evidence and verdicts handed down in Izetbegovic's own judicial system proving otherwise. The former President also denied that Al-Qaida operatives were knowingly given passports and safe haven in the Balkans: 'I think it is a disgusting lie. By whom had they been given them? . . .I also think that there are no Bin-Ladin's associates in Bosnia-Hercegovina.'[8] Despite desperate attempts to conceal his duplicity in his dealings with Muslim militants, Izetbegovic's days as a respected political leader were permanently over. A month after the terrorist attacks in New York and Washington, he officially stepped down as head of Bosnia's most powerful Muslim nationalist party, citing personal health reasons.

Izetbegovic's controversial departure did not serve to end Bosnia's brush with Usama Bin Laden and the Arab-Afghans. By late September 2001, Bosnian news reports were leaking news that groups of individuals belonging to suspected terrorist organizations had recently slipped through border controls and were hiding in local towns. Then, a Sarajevo newspaper published damning information it claimed had come from the files of Bosnia's Muslim intelligence agency AID, showing that one of the chiefs of the Third World Relief Agency and the Bosnian Interior Ministry's State Border Service was directed by former President Izetbegovic in May 1996 (three months after the final Dayton deadline to remove all foreign fighters) to provide official Bosnian documentation to at least forty former foreign members of Kateebat al-Mujahideen.[873] Nevertheless, Bosnian authorities vigorously asserted that, with the departure of Izetbegovic, there was no lingering support for the Arab-Afghans in the Balkans. Bosnian Foreign Ministry spokesman Amer Kapetanovic explained: 'Both [the American and Bosnian governments] cooperate to a maximum degree in that domain because nobody wants Bosnia to be associated with the countries which support terrorists.'[10]

To underscore that point, the Bosnian government freely cooperated with United States authorities on a number of high-profile and successful terror raids in local areas. A NATO officer explained what was to unfold in an article later published in a United States military newspaper: 'These raids were small . . . Two to three guys on surveillance, a few SUVs drive up, a few guys go in quietly, bag 'em, tag 'em, and drag 'em out to SUVs and then on to the detention facility.' As described, on 25 September, at 3:30 a.m., six United States special forces Green Berets travelling in four rented SUVs stopped outside the Hotel Hollywood in a suburb of Sarajevo. The soldiers smashed open the front door of the hotel with weapons drawn, and seized two Middle-Eastern men sleeping inside: Hamed Abdel Rahim al-Jamal, a Jordanian, and Al-Halim Hassam Khafagi, an Egyptian. Both were deported to their respective homelands about 10 days later.

Nine hours later, the same six United States commandos repeated their raids at the local headquarters of the Saudi High Commission for Relief in Ilidza. Despite its close links to the government of the Saudi Arabia, the High Commission was still allowed to be raided 'because it seemed to be a meeting point and a central location for some of the guys [SFOR intelligence agents] were trailing or monitoring,' according to one NATO source. Aided by supporting Italian carabinieri stationed with the military police, the Americans arrested two more suspects and seized a number of intriguing documents. The NATO officer added: 'That's when we discovered the extent that NGOs are used as a cover for some suspicious activities.' Representatives of the American government reportedly confronted the Saudi ambassador in Sarajevo with the damning evidence, who was 'surprised, and [he] promised to look into it.' The United States subsequently asked the Bosnian government to officially shut down the local operations of four Islamic charities, including the Saudi High Commission.[11]

Encouraged by the results, SFOR counter-terrorism operations continued on 27 September with a raid of the Visoko airfield, northwest of Sarajevo. This action was quite significant; it consisted of at least two to three M2 Bradley armored fighting vehicles, thirty to forty Humvee jeeps, and eight to ten armed combat helicopters. According to United States military officials, their intelligence had indicated that Visoko airport served as a hub for 'organizations that supported transnational terrorist organizations.' One of their chief concerns was the prospect of crop-dusting aircraft being retrofitted for germ warfare.

In fact, a few days later, their fears that Visoko was hiding an anti-Western terror plot proved to be well founded. Between 17 and 21 October, Bosnian authorities detained at least eleven Islamic militants linked to the international north African sleeper cell network who were plotting a crude aerial attack on two American military bases in Bosnia: Eagle Base and Camp Connor. An unnamed NATO source was quoted in the *Wall Street Journal* as stating that the terrorists were suspected of planning to collect a small armada of light planes and helicopters from Visoko airfield, and suicide-crash them into the foreign military installations. The information had come from an intelligence intercept on 16 October in Sarajevo on a conversation discussing United States bombing in Afghanistan and 'what the response should be' in Europe. After a discussion of hitting a collection of American and British targets in the region, the callers ended with a definite, 'Tomorrow, we will start.' The apparent ringleader of the group of primarily Algerians and Egyptians was a 41-year-old Algerian named Bensayah Belkacem, (also known as Majed). American intelligence had become familiar with Belkacem through monitoring of the satellite telephones of a number of his terrorist cohorts in Afghanistan. Police who raided Belkacem's various local residences found Algerian and Yemeni identity papers, blank passports, and, according to Bosnian Interior Minister Muhammad Besic, the telephone numbers of senior Al-Qaida terrorist recruiters and Bosnian war veterans Abu Zubaydah and Abu el-Ma`ali.[12] A closer look at his cell phone records revealed that Belkacem had also called locations in Afghanistan at least seventy times in the month following September 11.

One of the other eleven suspects arrested included the recently pardoned Saber Lahmar, a known GIA terrorist who had already been imprisoned for his role in terrorist acts in Bosnia. On 19 October, a local Bosnian news magazine reported that a telephone number ascribed to Abu el-Ma`ali was found among Lahmar's belongings at the time of his arrest.[13] Lahmar was also a known employee of the Saudi High Commission for Relief.[14] The involvement of the charities in the plot, especially as parallel investigations of BIF and other organizations in the United States picked up pace, was no longer ignored. The Saudi High Commission came under obvious scrutiny, and its role became exposed in preying on the poor and destitute and using its vast weapon of wealth to aggressively propagate strict Wahhabi Islam. In July 2001, the High Commission publicly disclosed that over nine years, it had collected $600 million for its programs in Bosnia.[15] It has yet to offer a credible explanation for where the lionshare of that money went.

United States officials, aided by novel enthusiasm on behalf of the Bosnian government to crack down on their former Arab allies, were finally starting to uncover the truth about the staggering recruitment and financial arms of the loosely assembled Arab-Afghan movement, despite being hidden by a humanitarian face. Saber Lahmar's arrest was particularly embarrassing for the Bosnian government, as he had already been in their custody for his past acknowledged role in the local north African sleeper cell terrorist network. His pardon from jail in 2000 seems to have been a grave error by the Bosnian government; indeed, it nearly cost the lives of potentially hundreds of United States and British peacekeepers in the Balkans.[16] The discovery of the Visoko airport terror conspiracy caused a minor-furor both in the Bosnian press, and also in Western capitals still reeling from the shock of the devastating 11 September suicide hijackings. European governments were particularly concerned about the notion that a new similar airborne plot was being hatched so close to home. Almost immediately, the United States and UK temporarily closed their embassies and consulates in the region until a renewed strategic assessment could be completed about potential terrorist threats lurking in Bosnia. On 17 October, BiH Foreign Minister Lagumdzija was immediately dispatched to Belgium for high-level talks with German Chancellor Gerhard Schroeder.

After six years of incredible ignorance, investigators from across the world were finally seeing the role of Bosnia as a major center for terrorist recruitment and fundraising, especially for individuals working on behalf of Al-Qaida. Bosnian intelligence and police officials admitted that they were tracing several hundred documents taken from recently-detained terrorist suspects and were also directly monitoring at least seventeen other foreigners possibly linked to terrorism. Deputy Bosnian Interior Minister Tomislav Limov explained to the media: 'We do not have enough evidence yet to arrest these people . . . but we can control their movements and activities, and prevent any possible action by them.'[17] Limov also admitted that the Bosnian government (under the control of Alija Izetbegovic and his cronies) had issued a total of 750 passports to Balkan residents of Arab origin, including 120 that were known to have been issued during a particularly critical period in the mid-1990s in the midst the Bosnian war. Since the Dayton Accords in 1995–6, according to Limov, an additional 1,000 Bosnian passports were issued by Izetbegovic to newly settled foreign residents, 200 of whom were reportedly people of 'Arabic background.'[18]

Several months later, in January 2002, despite decisive injunctions by the Bosnian Supreme Court, the Bosnian government deported the North African terror suspects led by Belkacem and immediately transferred them (with American assistance) to the holding facility at 'Camp X-Ray' in Guantanamo Bay, Cuba. Whatever sympathetic political capital that Al-Qaida imagined that it had harvested among the Bosnian Muslim people was discounted when less than 300 people showed up in Sarajevo to protest the unambiguously extralegal deportations of Belkacem and his friends. As regional expert Stephen Schwartz has written, in a city of 400,000 that is overwhelmingly Muslim, this sort of dissident turnout was laughable, bridging on pathetic.[19] The lionshare of the Bosnian people – Croat, Muslim, and Serb alike – had long since tired of the antics of the Arab *mujahideen* and felt powerful revulsion at the horror of the September 11 terror attacks.

However, the job of intelligence agencies and counter-terrorism law investigators was far from finished in Bosnia. An SFOR officer familiar with the recent operations commented: 'We shook the bushes really hard . . . We disrupted them, but it's gonna be a long haul.[20] Western officials, for the first time, were quick to credit the Bosnian government for their definite shift in the treatment of Al-Qaida and the *mujahideen*. A NATO officer concurred: 'Our biggest victory was getting the government of Bosnia-Herzegovina involved and active . . . They are on board. They don't want terrorists [in Bosnia] either.'[21] NATO Secretary-General Lord Robertson took an unusual opportunity to add his own musings. 'We . . . welcome and have been impressed by the actions of the government authorities in Bosnia-Herzegovina,' he announced in a public statement. But, he warned, '[t]he threat . . . has not gone. These networks have been disrupted, not eliminated. Investigations are continuing. Our work is therefore not finished.'[22]

Bosnian officials were finally in agreement that terrorism had found an unwitting shelter in their homeland. They stressed their cooperation with the American government and acknowledged the threat posed by Islamic militants and other groups using turmoil in the Balkans as an excuse for violence. BiH Federal Minister of Internal Affairs, Muhamed Besic, told a Sarajevo press conference unequivocally: 'Terrorism represents a threat to all of Bosnia-Hercegovina's interests, its nations and citizens and in that struggle Bosnia-Hercegovina has to cooperate closely with neighboring countries and the international community.'[23] Officials such as Besic and Bosnian Foreign Minister Lagumdzija also repeatedly emphasized the differences between the modern, 'civilized' European Islam of the Balkans and the brutal fundamentalist Islam of Afghanistan, Saudi Arabia, and Usama Bin Laden. Lagumdzija insisted to reporters that, despite the discovery of Al-Qaida sleeper cells in Bosnia, 'I do not believe Bosnia is living on the other side of the line, on the dark side of the world where terrorism rules.'[24]

Lagumdzija was remarkably straightforward and quite accurate as to the individual socio-political factors responsible for helping to foster the threat of Islamic terrorism in the region: a civil conflict pitting neighbors of various ethnicities against each other, a devastated economy, weak government institutions, and the flourishing of organized crime.[25] An International Crisis Group (ICG) report on Al-Qaida's presence in the Balkans came up with the same exact findings, and concluded these factors 'combine to produce an environment where international terrorist networks can hide personnel and money.'[26] During the 1990s, Al-Qaida and the Arab-Afghans were able to thrive in regions like Bosnia by feeding on the suffering and misery of those left out of the post-Cold War peace dividend. In almost every Muslim zone of conflict that has imploded over the past fifteen years, Al-Qaida has used populist dogma clothed in vague and fanciful notions of religious and Islamic history to recruit war-scarred, shell-shocked volunteers who have lost all sense of individual identity and self-worth. Bosnia, like many of the other nations victimized by roving bands of Arab-Afghan Islamic militants, was embroiled for several years in a catastrophic war that has permanently changed the political, cultural, and religious face of its people. The failure of the United States and Europe to intervene before 1995 to stop that genocidal war was a regrettable foreign policy error that inadvertently opened the door in Bosnia to anti-Western Islamic fanatics.

Even after the end of the bloody and futile war, lingering intra-ethnic suspicious and widescale doubts as to the longevity of the Dayton Accord stifled a post-war explosion of much-needed economic growth. Alija Izetbegovic's stubborn efforts to remain loyal to Abu el-Ma`ali and his merry men had definite consequences for the Bosnian people, at least financially speaking. Though Izetbegovic may have garnered some additional support from supporters of radical Islam in Saudi Arabia and the Gulf, these funds were clearly offset by hesitant and skittish Western and European economic reinvestment in the Balkans. Even during the early days of the Ottoman Empire, Bosnia has always profited from its strategic position as a major confluence point for the various civilizations of Europe and the Middle East, and particularly as a facilitator of key Western trade routes. By frightening away European and American businessmen with tolerance for anti-Western extremism and Islamic militancy, Izetbegovic endangered not only the delicate terms of

Dayton, but moreover, centuries-old patterns of international trade and business in south-eastern Europe.

Luckily for his downtrodden people, the longtime Bosnian president failed in this unfortunate mission. Even former members of Izetbegovic's pride and joy – the seventh Muslim Army Brigade – dismissed his support of the Arab *mujahideen* with heavy scepticism. In 1993, one such soldier, calling himself 'Mustafa,' told a British reporter through long cigarette drags: 'Many people from foreign countries come here. They want to make us strict Muslims, with no alcohol, and harems.' However, as Mustafa noted with humorous indignation, 'We like drink and we don't need harems. I can get any girl I want anyway.'[27] With regards to the scandalous behaviour of Izetbegovic, Foreign Minister Lagumdzija noted the crucial (if slow-in-coming) changes and reforms that had taken with regards to both Bosnian domestic and foreign politics. 'A year ago the authorities were part of the terrorism problem, today they are an integral part of the solution,' offered Lagumdzija. 'Our priorities are the struggle against corruption and crime, and the strengthening of state institutions.'[28]

Even Al-Qaida representatives will, to this day, admit that their experiment in Bosnia did not go exactly to plan. When asked if Bosnia would become the 'next Afghanistan' any time soon, militant London cleric and Afghano-Bosniak veteran Abu Hamza al-Masri responded hesitantly: 'I think Bosnia has very soft people and at the moment they are just confused. They like Islam, they love Islam, but they are confused by the efforts from Saudi Arabia and the war against Islam from the West. They are still disoriented.'[29]

Abu Hamza's disappointment is underscored by the fact that, overwhelmingly, veteran Arab-Afghan terrorist recruiters met a dead end when they sought to enlist post-war sleeper cells from amongst groups of indigenous Bosnians. Regional expert Stephen Schwartz argues in his latest book that Bosnian guerrillas failed to follow their Arab *mujahideen* mentors to new battle grounds in Chechnya or Central Asia (as had happened in Afghanistan and elsewhere) simply because the hardline philosophy of Al-Qaida and that of their Wahhabi sponsors in Saudi Arabia did not conform to unique aspects of Bosnian culture and society. At most, the piecemeal collection of native Bosnians who supported or joined the *mujahideen* were beckoned into a short-lived alliance of pure convenience. Few entertained any serious notions of continuing with *jihad* once their homes were liberated from the penetrating grasp of the Serb military. In the end as a result, no matter what their propaganda, as Schwartz writes, 'the scruffy mujahidin enlisted by Abdullah Azzam and Bin Laden found the streets of Sarajevo inhospitable.'[30] French counterterrorism magistrate Judge Bruguière largely concurs with this assessment and writes of the massive rejection of the 'Salafist Jihadists' by the Bosnian people, Muslim admittedly, but not fundamentalist.[31]

The result was, when push came to shove, neither the Bosnian Muslim government nor its people stood up to defend the Arab radicals as the Taliban did in Afghanistan. Instead, in the wake of 11 September, the indigenous Bosnians changed paths dramatically and became a key ally in the war against terror. This has caused a partial (if temporary) collapse in the Afghano-Bosniak network, and many headaches for the leadership of Al-Qaida forces in the region. On 12 February 2002, BIF executive Enaam Arnaout worriedly contacted his brother 'Dr Hisham' to discuss how 'they' had taken Al Hajj Boudella (a former instructor at the Al-Sadda terrorist camp in Afghanistan and longtime director of BIF's office in Bosnia) 'in a special plane . . . [t]o Cuba.' Arnaout, convinced of his own inevitable fate, explained to Hisham how he would attempt to shoulder the blame and exonerate BIF's Saudi founders. He sombrely reflected: 'It means, we, I mean, there is death that we will be swallowing. Meaning, the razor will fall on us, but we do not know how.'[32] Less than a month later, the razor did fall; Bosnian police raided BIF's regional headquarters in Sarajevo and detained its manager, Munib Zahiragic, a former Muslim intelligence officer affiliated with the Bosnian Foreign Ministry. Zahiragic reportedly turned over nearly 100 top-secret documents about suspected fundamentalist terrorists operating in Bosnia.[33]

Frantically, Enaam Arnaout, about to be arrested himself in the United States, contacted Zahiragic in jail to discover the extent of the damage. The latter admitted on the phone, '[T]hey took things . . . I had documents from, from, intelligence, where I worked before, and I had various documents, from the, from the, from the, what is it called, from the job.' Arnaout, not realizing how much Zahiragic had already betrayed, ordered the Bosnian spy, 'not to give information about the others . . . Meaning we now, I don't know a thing about you . . . I don't know your life . . . [W]hat do you know about me, you don't know a thing about me.'[34] Even without the evidence gathered from Zahiragic, having failed to anticipate a wiretap on his phone, Arnaout gave the U.S. Justice Department all it needed to finally indict him for his critical role in Al-Qaida, including its operations in Bosnia-Herzegovina. In this respect, the Bosnians proved to be much more unreliable as partners in *jihad* than comparable local guerrilla movements in Chechnya, Kashmir, and Afghanistan. Arnaout has since pled guilty to defrauding BIF donors and illicitly funnelling aid to armed militant groups in Chechnya and Bosnia, though continues to contest federal charges that he actively aided Usama Bin Laden and Al-Qaida.

Nonetheless, there remains the question of whether even the Bosnian Muslims would have ultimately endured against the Croat-Serb onslaught without the erstwhile help of the albeit troublesome foreign *mujahideen*. Even some prominent Western policymakers have conceded that the contribution of the Arab-Afghans to the Bosnian conflict may be more significant than has been acknowledged in the past. Richard Holbrooke, the former chief American peace negotiator in the

Balkans, has gone as far as to say that Bosnia's Muslims likely 'wouldn't have survived' without foreign assistance from the Arab-Afghans and other assorted members of the foreign *mujahideen* corps. While the UN threw its hands in the air and refused to intervene to stop massacres of innocent civilians, the Arab-Afghans were already well trained to commit brutal revenge attacks designed to strike fear in the hearts of the 'enemies of Islam.' They took their divine mission, as first dictated by the powerful philosophy of Shaykh Abdullah Azzam, with a fanatic intent, much more so than the Bosnian government could have ever dreamed. As a result, as Richard Holbrooke also points out, the alliance with the Arab militants orchestrated by Alija Izetbegovic was undoubtedly 'a pact with the devil' from which Bosnia has yet to fully recover.[35]

This is the true danger of allowing tricky ethno-religious regional conflicts in the developing world to fester and spiral while the Western world looks on indifferently. Though it may seem after the 1993 debacle in Mogadishu that there is a heavy price to be paid for military and diplomatic intervention in these various 'regional' crises, the lesson of 11 September is that no one can escape the violence that breeds in them. When we leave smaller, embattled peoples to the whims of purely diabolical men – be it Slobodan Milosevic or Usama Bin Laden – we permit the gravest of injustices. In the end, the bravery and goodwill of the Bosnian people may have been the most crucial factor responsible for the ultimate failure of the Arab-Afghan experiment in Bosnia. Despite terrible war and starvation, the Bosnians desperately clung to their individual identity and held out against Salafi and Wahhabi brainwashing. The Balkans certainly proved a very educational experience and a useful stepping stone for Al-Qaida's entrance into Europe, but it could only be a short-term base of operations for the terrorist group. In time, as the Bosnian people reclaimed their pre-war existences and their unique Euro-Asian heritage, the Islamic missionary radicals from the Middle East would naturally be seen as clownish and out-of-touch. Since the end of the Bosnian war, this is exactly what has apparently transpired.

Notes

1. Pyes, Craig with Josh Meyers and William Rempel. 'Bosnia Seen as Hospitable Base and Sanctuary for Terrorists.' *Los Angeles Times*, 7 October 2001.
2. Ibid.
3. Sanderson, Ward. 'Bosnian police arrest four men, including one suspected of terrorist ties.' *Stars and Stripes*, 27 July 2001.

4. Von Derschau, Verena. '2 Sentenced for Islamic Network Roles.' The Associated Press. 25 October 2001.

5. Schwartz, Steven. *The Two Faces of Islam*. Doubleday: New York, 2003, p. 191.

6. 'Former Bosnian president says mojahedin and terrorists not synonymous.' HINA News Agency. Broadcast in English in Zagreb. 9 October 2001, 13.34 GMT.

7. 'Muslim leader denies there are Bin-Ladin's supporters in Bosnia.' SRNA News Agency. Broadcast in Serbo-Croat language in Bijeljina. 9 October 2001, 07.18 GMT.

8. Ibid.

9. 'Ten suspected terrorists reportedly enter Bosnia, whereabouts unknown – weekly.' SRNA News Agency. Broadcast in Serbo-Croat language in Bijeljina. 27 September 2001, 19.42 GMT.

10. Altier, Jean-Pierre. 'Bosnia denies links to Islamic terrorists.' Agence France Presse. 29 September 2001.

11. Naylor, Sean D. 'Routing Out Terrorism in Bosnia.' *Army Times*, 10 December 2001, p. 12.

12. McGrory, Daniel. 'Bin Laden aide arrested in Bosnia.' *The Times* (London), 11 October 2001.

13. Habul, Emir. 'Reactions in South East Europe to the attacks on 11 September.' AIM (Alternative Information Network) Press. http://www.aimpress.org. 22 October 2001.

14. Purvis, Andrew. 'Targeting "Eagle Base."' *Time*, 5 November 2001, p. 36.

15. Schwartz, Steven. Op. cit., pp. 189–90.

16. Rubin, Daniel. 'NATO: Terrorist attacks against U.S. installations in Bosnia averted.' Knight Ridder News Agency. 25 October 2001.

17. 'Algerians arrested in Bosnia had links with Al-Qaeda: police.' Agence France Presse. 29 October 2001.

18. 'Limov says 19 arrested in wake of Sept 11 suicide attacks.' ONASA News Agency. 29 October 2001.

19. Schwartz, Steven. Op. cit., p. 190.

20. Naylor, Sean D. Op. cit., p. 12.

21. Naylor, Sean D. Op. cit., p. 12.

22. Ulbrich, Jeffrrey. 'NATO Secretary-General says at least one suspect in Bosnia linked to bin Laden.' The Associated Press. 26 October 2001.

23. 'Bosnian Federation government voices concern about internal terrorist threat.' SRNA News Agency. Broadcast in Serbo-Croat language in Bijeljina. 8 October 2001, 16.30 GMT.

24. Jahn, George. 'Police arrest terrorist suspect after tracing phone call to bin Laden.' The Associated Press. 8 October 2001.

25. 'Bosnian FM admits risk of terrorism at home.' Agence France Presse. 30 October 2001.
26. Cerkez-Robinson, Aida. 'New report urges West to keep close tabs on Islamic groups across the Balkans.' The Associated Press. 12 November 2001.
27. Eagar, Charlotte. 'Muj more fun if you're a Cool Dude in Bosnia.' *Observer*, 7 November 1993, p. 19.
28. 'Bosnian FM admits risk of terrorism at home.' Op. cit.
29. Interview with Shaykh Abu Hamza al-Masri at the Finsbury Park Mosque, 28 June 2002.
30. Schwartz, Steven. Op. cit., p. 175.
31. Jean-Louis Bruguiere and Jean-Francois Ricard. 'Requisitoire Definitifaux aux Fins de Non-Lieu. De Non-Lieu partiel. De Requalification. De Renvoi devant le Tribunal Correctionnel, de mantien sous Controle Judiciaiare et de maintien en Detention.' Cour D'Appel de Paris; Tribunal de Grande Instance de Paris. No. Parquet: P96 253 3901.2, p. 170.
32. 'Government's Evidentiary Proffer Supporting the Admissibility of Co-Conspirator Statements.' *United States of America v. Enaam M. Arnaout.* United States District Court Northern District of Illinois, Eastern Division. Case #: 02 CR 892. 31 January 2003, p. 74. See also: Government's Response to Defendant's Position Paper as to Sentencing Factors.' *United States of America v. Enaam M. Arnaout.* United States District Court Northern District of Illinois Eastern Division. Case #: 02 CR 892, p. 38.
33. Whitmore, Brian. 'Bosnian Charities Tied to Terror.' *The Boston Globe*, 2 July 2002, p. 1.
34. 'Government's Evidentiary Proffer Supporting the Admissibility of Co-Conspirator Statements.' *United States of America v. Enaam M. Arnaout.* United States District Court Northern District of Illinois, Eastern Division. Case #: 02 CR 892, 31 January 2003, p. 103.
35. Pyes, Craig and Josh Meyer et al. Op. cit.

Epilogue: Lessons of the 'Afghano-Bosniaks'

There is much room for debate over the enduring legacy of the Arab *mujahideen* in south-eastern Europe. One can say conclusively that the attempt to create a local fundamentalist state in Bosnia (parallel to the development of the Taliban in Afghanistan) failed utterly. Muslim hardliners and their sympathizers within Bosnian government and society have largely been sidelined or removed. Even at his most radical, Alija Izetbegovic was far from a Mullah Omar or even a Radovan Karadic. Rather, Izetbegovic is more comparable to the various personalities who have dominated Chechen nationalist politics since 1992, such as Dzokhar Dudayev. While they are far from committed fundamentalists themselves, men like Izetbegovic are weak enough both ideologically and militarily to cooperate with Muslim radicals, led primarily by Al-Qaida, out of desperation. This phenomenon is not entirely illogical, and some blame must fall on Western governments for failing to provide alternatives to embattled but generally popular Third World governments like the nascent regime in Sarajevo in 1992. This is true especially when the United States government itself has recognized the sovereign right of those legitimate governments to defend themselves, yet paradoxically simultaneously prevents them from acquiring weapons in order to exercise that fundamental right.

While this may serve as a mitigating factor, it does not explain why Alija Izetbegovic continued to support and defend the Arab *mujahideen*, even after he had been presented with irrefutable evidence that Abu el-Ma`ali and his followers presented a direct threat not only to the United States and Europe, but rather, to Bosnian Muslims themselves (the Dumont robberies in Zenica, the Croatian car bombings, and so forth). The longstanding effects of Izetbegovic's cooperation perhaps have yet to be felt. In November 2001, United States soldiers discovered a collection of documents and weapons hidden by Al-Qaida in the basement of a 'mansion' in the recently-liberated city of Kabul, Afghanistan. Among those papers was a bomb-making guide written in the Bosnian language by several Balkan recruits working for Usama Bin Laden. The guide was stunningly complete, featuring diagrams, mathematical equations, and chemical formulas. On one page, under the title *Explosivija za Oklahomu*, the author listed the appropriate molecular recipes for TNT, ammonium nitrate, and nitroglycerine. Evidently, these men had carefully studied the April 1995 terrorist attack in Oklahoma City, and were ready to emulate the example put forth by right-wing militants Timothy McVeigh and

Terry Nichols. American troops also found twenty-two Milan anti-tank missiles nearby, as well as intricate instructions on how to demolish skyscrapers.[1]

Despite these chilling discoveries, the Islamic extremists never stood a chance in Bosnia of recruiting more than a piecemeal group of local volunteers. A functional alliance between the foreigners and indigenous Bosnians was never a reality because the two groups were working towards vastly different objectives. As Stephen Schwartz has since written: 'While the frustrated middle class youth of the Saudi kingdom sought martyrdom as an alternative to uselessness and boredom, the Bosnian Muslims, whose forebears were lions of the faith, refused to die. Here were the two faces of Islam in their most compelling images: the true *jihad* of the Bosnians versus the false '*jihad*' of Saudi vagabonds.'[2] For the Bosnians, this was a war for survival, plain and simple. It was wildly far fetched for Anwar Shaaban to believe that thousands of Balkan Muslim youth would join the 'caravan of martyrs' as had happened in Afghanistan and Kashmir. The relaxed and scholarly European Islam developed in Bosnia was absolutely opposed to the harsh tenets of Wahhabism and Salafism that the Arab-Afghans desperately sought to export elsewhere. The clash between local Islam and foreign fundamentalist Islam was critical: many local Muslim leaders especially resented the haughty attitude of the Saudis, who sought to teach their 'backward' brothers about 'real' Islam. The irony, of course, was that Bosnian Muslims had practised their own rich faith and religious traditions since the time of the Ottomans, long before the Saudi-Wahhabi Kingdom was even a speck on the horizon of history. In contrast to the valiant Bosnians, the Arab militants were a barely legitimate entity and, moreover, often served as a hostile transitory phenomenon that was erasing true Islam and replacing it instead with a contradictory and hateful collection of tribal dogma and xenophobic propaganda. Thus, the importance of Bosnia cannot be ascribed to the success of the Arab-Afghans in local recruitment or in the establishment of an Islamic state.

For Al-Qaida, the real value of Bosnia was as a step in the ladder towards Western Europe. It was a place, with proximity to London, Riyadh, and Cairo, where terrorist recruits could train, coalesce into cells, and seek shelter from prosecution by foreign law enforcement. Especially for North African militant groups like the Algerian GIA, Bosnia was the best uncontrolled warzone where they could set up nearby overseas operations. According to one unnamed former State Department official, '[t]hey come to Bosnia to chill out, because so many other places are too hot for them.'[3] Bosnia was also ideal for some of the economic projects of Al-Qaida, particularly revolving around the Islamic charitable organizations mostly based from and heavily funded by the Kingdom of Saudi Arabia. With the veil of secrecy that has been brought down on these matters, one wonders if we will ever learn the truth about where the hundreds of millions of dollars that groups like the Saudi High Commission and Benevolence International Foundation collected went. Nonetheless, let it be no surprise to anyone that the Al-Qaida network in Europe remains quite well funded to this day.

Bosnia's key role was in drawing together the various components of an amorphous group of disaffected, unemployed European-North African youths who were susceptible to the same stories of *jihad* and martyrdom that had lured so many Saudis and Kuwaitis to Afghanistan in the 1980s. Amazingly, it took many years for global intelligence agencies, particularly in Europe, to recognize the new emerging threat from North African Islamic exiles and sleeper cells. An anonymous Spanish security official admitted to *Time* magazine reporters, 'In Europe we were too preoccupied with our own terrorist problems – E.T.A. in Spain, the I.R.A. in the U.K., the Corsicans in France and so on – and we devoted our resources to these threats . . . Even after the attacks on the U.S. embassies in Kenya and Tanzania, the Islamic threat seemed distant.' According to the Spaniard, 'Everything changed after Sept. 11. Before then we looked on bin Laden as someone from another planet, like a Martian.'[4]

Bosnia provided the ultimate meeting ground for the mostly Saudi, Egyptian, and Yemeni lieutenants of Usama Bin Laden and the North African *jihad* foot-soldiers (a good number of whom were European citizens). Bosnia was the link that tied the European and Canadian terrorist networks of men like Fateh Kamel and Khaled Kelkal to the senior *mujahideen* leadership in Sudan and Afghanistan. Though these men were adherents of the Algerian GIA, they were receiving their marching orders directly from the Al-Qaida terrorist masterminds at Bin Laden's side like Abu Zubaydah. It was almost as if Bin Laden had 'contracted out' a terror campaign to a generic GIA sleeper cell. Even some Saudis themselves, such as journalist Jamal Kashogji, had predicted that 'allowing [Islamic militants] to go to Bosnia and get military training there will make them good prospects for something else later on.'[5] Stefano Dambruouso, a prosecutor in Milan investigating local Al-Qaida links, now admits: 'The real problem in Europe before 1998 was Algerian nationals, who were involved in mostly single episodes that weren't coordinated . . . After that, bin Laden began to connect and coordinate all these cells that already existed, rendering the phenomenon much more radicalized and potent.'[6] In other words, the spark met the powder keg when the intricate network of would-be international terrorists in Europe and Canada constructed by Anwar Shaaban, Abu Talal al-Qasimy, Abu el-Ma`ali and others met the financial and political influence of the Saudi exile Usama Bin Laden.

None of the mighty martyrs of Bosnia would fade so easily into history. At least two of the nineteen September 11 suicide hijackers – Nawaf al-Hazmi and Khalid al-Mihdar – fought in Bosnia with the foreign *mujahideen* battalion in 1995.[7] Abdelaziz al-Muqrin (also known as Abu Hajer) – top Al-Qaida terrorist in Saudi Arabia and formerly the Kingdom's most wanted man – claimed to have trained at militant camps in Bosnia, witnessing the martyrdom of eight Arab *mujahideen* fighters in combat there.[8] Indeed, in a statement released in May 2002, senior Kuwaiti *Al-Qaida* spokesman Sulaiman Abu Ghaith took great lengths to praise the early achievements of Shaykh Abdullah Azzam and the leaders of the Arab *mujahideen* in Bosnia, including 'the friend of Anwar Sha`aban, Moataz [Billah], Husaamudeen, Wahiudeen, [and] Abu Muaz al-Kuwaiti . . . [they] stayed firm in the Path of Allah because he who devotes himself to Allah does not ask back for it. He who flies high above his enemies will not give the enemy the chance to gloat over his grief.'[9]

Thus, for the Arab-Afghans, Bosnia remains both a legend and a sob-story; a propaganda tale, and an open wound requiring cruel vengeance. It was offered by Al-Qaida recruiters to desperate Middle Eastern youth in many European capitals as a mythical escape from the drudgery of their own urban jungle prisons. Yet even some of the smartest and most promising members of the European Muslim community were sucked into this bizarre netherworld. Abu Ibrahim, a 21-year-old London representative of Azzam Publications (an Al-Qaida propaganda center in Britain), took a break during *jihad* training in Bosnia to be interviewed. He revealed an interesting insight into the mindset of these indoctrinated warriors:

> When you come here, people they think, 'when you go into Bosnia you are sitting around and there are shells coming down and they are firing everywhere around you.' They don't know that we sit here and we have kebab. They don't know that we have ice cream and we have cake here. They don't know that we can telephone or fax anywhere in the world. They don't know that this is a nice holiday for us where you meet some of the best people you have ever met in your life. People from all over the world, people from Brazil, from Japan, from China, from the Middle East, from America, North, South, Canada, Australia, all over the world you meet people.[10]

Given the recent arrests of new North African sleeper cells in the UK, Spain, and Canada tied to Al-Qaida, it certainly does not seem like the old Afghano-Bosniak network has been crushed by the United States-led international campaign against terror. Though many of its most prominent faces, Anwar Shaaban, Abu Zubaydah, Fateh Kamel, Abu Talal al-Qasimy, and others have since been arrested or killed, some of its most enduring legacies continue to live on. The weapons and combat skills endowed by men like the venerated Arab-Afghan Moataz Billah commander in Bosnia in 1993 are now being re-educated to new generations of *jihadi* volunteers. Abu el-Ma`ali continues to evade the intelligence apparatus' of multiple countries, including the United States, Canada, France, Italy, and the UK He is far from alone: on a regular basis, groups of Bosniak-veterans are discovered across Europe and elsewhere plotting new acts of mayhem and destruction.

And so, the story finally returns to the *shuhadaa* ['martyrs'] themselves who fought and spilled their blood in the killing fields of wartime Bosnia. As the accounts in this work should reveal, there was no one single factor bringing these particular volunteers together. Their backgrounds varied wildly from Olympic athletes and spoiled Gulf princes, to petty thieves and thuggish twits. Yet, together, they jointly sacrificed their lives for a greater religio-political cause that was willing to stop at nothing to achieve victory. They abandoned a civilized existence in the modern world, choosing instead to join a crusade of global combat and terror. Essentially, measured up to the generic Al-Qaida playbook, they had performed fantastically. In the words of Abu Uthman al-Kuwaiti, another senior Afghano-Bosniak veteran:

> They were the brothers who attained what we hope for: martyrdom in the path of Allah. They searched for martyrdom everywhere and Allah chose them to join the Caravan of Martyrs in the Land of Bosnia. They answered Allah's call of Jihad. In this world, people have wishes. Those who long for something will attain it. They are the ones who stayed and they gained martyrdom in the Path of Allah. Those brothers, they were united. But they had not been united on nationalism, neither were they united on socialism, nor were they united by a common tongue. But they were joined together by *tawheed* [religious unity] and their obedience and devotion to Allah. It can truly be said that these brothers of ours are the cream of society. By Allah, we have not seen men such as these before! A poet once said: 'Let the tears flow from our eyes and let us remember the promises. We have lost a friendship which we will not find again in this world.' Abu Husaam and Kulaib and even the young boy Khubayb, fought in battle like lions. Their target being the worshippers of the Cross (the Christian fundamentalists). They responded to the call, 'Come to Jihad!'[11]

So long as the story of the Martyrs of Bosnia continues to be retold by the radical clerics and through the wide collection of recordings and propaganda films made by Al-Qaida supporters, there is little doubt that the Bosniak veterans, and their brothers left slain on the battlefield, will continue to inspire newfound Islamic fanatics across the world. But, perhaps in the wake of the tragic lessons learned on 11 September 2001, the regrettable mistakes made by United States and European policymakers during the Bosnian war vis-à-vis the Arab *mujahideen* will be carefully avoided in the coming future.

Notes

1. Fielding, Nick. 'Secrets of Al-Qaida: Network studied Oklahoma-style bomb.' *Sunday Times* (London), 18 November 2001.

2. Schwartz, Steven. *The Two Faces of Islam*, Doubleday: New York, 2003, p. 175.

3. Pyes, Craig and Josh Meyer et al. 'Bosnia Seen as Hospitable Base and Sanctuary for Terrorists.' *The Los Angeles Times*, 7 October 2001, p. A1.

4. 'Hate Club.' *Time*, 5 November 2001, p. 26.

5. Ford, Peter. 'Islamic Conference Yields Cautious Words, No Action.' *The Christian Science Monitor*, 4 December 1992, p. 6.

6. 'Hate Club.' *Time*, 5 November 2001, p. 26.

7. 'Report of the Joint Inquiry into the Terrorist Attacks of September 11, 2001.' House Permanent Select Committee on Intelligence/Senate Select Committee on Intelligence. Senate Report No. 107-351/House Report No. 107-792. 107th Congress, 2nd Session; December 2002, p. 131.

8. http://www.aal3ah.net. 1 June 2004.

9. Abu Ghaith, Sulaiman. 'A message from Abu-Ghaith to the Mujahideen fee kuli makaan.' http://www.jehad.net. 23 May 2002.

10. Video interview clip of Abu Ibrahim al-Brittanee; 21-years old, Golders Green, London.

11. 'The Martyrs of Bosnia: Part I.' Videotape. Azzam Publications: London, 2000.

Index

Index